Fionn mac Cumhaill

Irish Studies

Irish Studies

Irish Studies presents a wide range of books interpreting important aspects of Irish life and culture to scholarly and general audiences. The richness and complexity of the Irish experience, past and present, deserves broad understanding and careful analysis. For this reason an important purpose of the series is to offer a forum to scholars interested in Ireland, its history, and culture. Irish literature is a special concern in the series, but works from the perspectives of the fine arts, history, and the social sciences are also welcome, as are studies which take multidisciplinary approaches.

Irish Studies is a continuing project of Syracuse University Press and is under the general editorship of Richard Fallis, associate professor of English at Syracuse University.

IRISH STUDIES, EDITED BY RICHARD FALLIS

Fionn mac Cumhaill
Celtic Myth in English Literature

JAMES MacKILLOP

SYRACUSE UNIVERSITY PRESS 1986

The paper used in this publication meets the minimum requirements of American
National Standard for Information Sciences-Permanence of Paper for Printed Library
Materials, ANSI Z39.48–1984. ∞

Library of Congress Cataloging-in-Publication Data

MacKillop, James.
  Fionn mac Cumhaill: Celtic myth in English literature.

  (Irish studies)
  Bibliography: p. 197.
  Includes index.
  1. English literature—History and criticism.
  2. Finn MacCumhaill, 3rd cent.—Legends—History and
  criticism.   3. Mythology, Celtic, in literature.
  4. Celts in literature.   5. Ireland in literature.
  6. Heroes in literature.   7. English literature—Irish
  authors—History and criticism.   I. Title.   II. Series:
  Irish studies (Syracuse University Press)

  PR408.F55M23 1985   820'.9351   85–22116
  ISBN 0–8156–2344–5
  ISBN 0–8156–2353–4 (pbk.)

For
Colin MacKillop
Margaret Ann Gillis MacKillop (1902–1985)

Theid Dìchioll air Thoiseach

JAMES MACKILLOP is Professor of English at Onondaga Community College, Syracuse. Professor MacKillop has been a Visiting Fellow in the Department of Celtic Languages and Literatures at Harvard University. He is a film and drama critic and co-author of *Speaking of Words* and *The Copy Book*.

Contents

Acknowledgments

The completion of *Fionn mac Cumhaill* would have been impossible without the generosity and care of dozens of people. First among them is Richard Fallis, without whose encouragement the book would not exist; in addition, his innumerable suggestions all changed the final text for the better. Although David Krause spent less time with the text, his advice given in an informal conversation many years ago turned out to be vital. Grace Eckley's encouragement was essential in making a key decision. Several people read the text during different stages of development and made important suggestions about it; they include: Donald Dike, Paul Theiner, Pat Moody, and Paul Schneider. My colleague Donna Woolfolk Cross suggested important stylist changes.

People who helped in answering obscure questions include: Séamas and Étaín Ó Siocháin, E. Estyn Evans, Máire MacNeill Sweeney, Proinsias MacCana, Charles Bowen, George Brandon Saul, Philippa Nic an tSagart, Calum I. MacLeod, Margaret MacDonell, Samuel Diehl, and Sister Mary Kevin of Rathmines.

Lastly, I want to thank my wife, Patricia, who gave up more weekends than we can count and at least a half-dozen vacations while her husband searched through piles of little green books.

Syracuse, New York   JAMES MACKILLOP
Spring 1985

Introduction

Ben Lassiter: What's that book you're reading?
Robert Lassiter: It's a new book by an Irishman, James Joyce.
Ben: I don't care if it's by Fionn mac Cumhaill, don't let
   your mother see you reading it.

Beacon Hill
CBS-TV, 1975

Fionn mac Cumhaill is the hero of the most popular of the three cycles of Old Irish literature, the Fenian. Mention of Fionn's name begins in Irish or Gaelic tradition as early as the fifth century and continues to this day in Irish storytelling. In borrowing and permutations, Fionn—sometimes Anglicized as Finn MacCool—has also become a character in English literature.

For many twentieth-century readers the first association with Fionn's name is probably in Joyce's *Finnegans Wake,* a largely unread but widely known book. The title, embodying several puns, includes one calling out to Fionn to rise from a death-like sleep: Finn again wake. As I recollect, I was reading about such matters in Joyce's commentators when I determined to find out more about Gaelic heroic literature. I found more than I was looking for. Fionn's spoor could be found in many places far from Ireland. In a collection of folklore from Mabou, Nova Scotia, the village where my father was born, I discovered that Fionn had been one of the most persistent figures in the oral tradition of Scottish immigrants who had left the Highlands after the failure of the Jacobite rebellion. The link between my father's rural village and Joyce's *Finnegans Wake* was only one of the indications of how diverse a figure Fionn could be. Another one was in trying to determine the standard spelling of his name.

The spelling used here, Fionn mac Cumhaill, is standard in modern Irish, although Finn is preferred in Old Irish. The name is pronounced, roughly, "Finn MacCool," as the *h* following the *m* in *Cumhaill* indicates that is sounded as a *w*. The transliteration "Finn MacCool" has been used often in English and was favored by both William Butler Yeats and James Joyce. Admittedly, there is a logic in Anglicizing the name, just as we speak of "Florence" though we know it is *Firenze* to natives. But in Ireland, Anglicizations have carried a distasteful colonialist flavor since Home Rule was granted in 1922, and so we now conventionally refer to the great epic of Old Irish literature as the *Táin Bó Cuailnge* rather than *The Cattle Raid of Cooley*. The choices, Fionn and Finn, are only two of many that can be made. Because Irish has had four major dialects, none of which had standard spellings until modern times, the name may also be spelled Find, Feunn, Fin, and his patronymic with either a lower and upper case *m*—MacCoul, MacCumal, MacCooil. If these were not enough, his name may also be spelled differently in the two other languages of the Goidelic branch where his stories are also told, Manx and Scottish Gaelic; the most common Scottish variant is Fingal, although, as we shall see, most speakers of Scottish Gaelic never used it.

In the years I was reading about the hero, I asked several hundred people if they had ever heard of Fionn mac Cumhaill and, if they had, what they knew about him. As I did not foresee that an examination of their answers could be of any value here, it never occurred to me to keep a formal record of the kinds of people questioned or the patterns of their answers. There was no need to. The divergence in the descriptions I received confirmed what I was finding in my reading. Most people who could identify Fionn said that he was a warrior or hero of old Ireland. Some people, especially Irish immigrants of little education, were sure that he was an historical figure. Other people, such as the occasional college student who had heard of Fionn, thought that he was some kind of giant and about as probable as a character in a fairy tale. Those who made a more serious study of literature knew that he was somehow related to the Fingal of Macpherson's *Poems of Ossian* as well as the Finn of Joyce's *Finnegans Wake.* My colleagues at a Syracuse classical music station knew him from Mendelssohn's "Fingal's Cave" or "Hebrides" overture. One woman, the wife of a university professor in New York City, said that Fionn mac Cumhaill was a clown to amuse children and that Joyce had made adult nonsense out of what was meant only to be harmless play.

There was the problem. To some people, Fionn mac Cumhaill was a hero and to others he was a fool. Although Fionn was a figure in traditional Irish literature, we had learned his name in the English language as spoken in urban America. Could it be that Fionn's character had been split apart when his stories were translated into English?

My reading of the many citations of Fionn's name in several modern authors served to make the divergences in his character more graphic. William Butler Yeats portrayed him as a benign father in his first lengthy poem, "The Wanderings of Oisin" but also made him the villain of a curious play he had written with George Moore, *Diarmuid and Grania.* In Flann O'Brien's *At Swim-Two-Birds,* Fionn had been employed as a kind of anti-hero, parodying the pretensions of Irish nationalists, among others. If we look much farther afield, the stories of Fionn and his warriors provided analogues for a number of Arthurian romances, indicating that Fenian references could be found in English writing from medieval to modern times. Could it be that the incidence of Fenian allusions in English would provide a pattern unrelated to the portrayal of the hero in literature from the Irish language?

To answer these questions, I felt I had to write a history, not only of the character of Fionn mac Cumhaill as he appears in English writing, but of the mythic figure himself, as much as could be known about him historically, archeologically, and linguistically. Because he had appeared first in literature composed in the Irish language, I felt I had to outline what could be known from the translation texts from that language.

My first approach was that of the man who jumps on his horse and rides widely off in all directions. Few bibliographies existed on such subjects as Irish myth and legend as used in English, and so I began to compile my own. By asking people and visiting good libraries I soon had more material than could be read in a lifetime. If I had tried to deal with all the citations of Fionn's name, some of them cryptic and ironically allusive, I would be reading still. Instead, I tried to confine myself to narrative portrayals of the hero that seemed to have some rooting in Irish or Gaelic tradition. Even with this guideline I still had more than a five-foot shelf, although some of the items on that shelf were ephemeral and of slight critical interest.

As I read and sorted the materials, I could see that my work was resolving around five separate problems, which have become the five chapters of this book. First, I had to know how Fionn mac Cumhaill had emerged in Irish literature. For how long had he been written about? What was his characterization in Irish? Second, there had to be some measurement of him as a mythic figure. Was he but an adaptation of some Greek figure? Was he, as so many Irishmen felt, actually an historical figure? Once I had determined these questions, I could move forward to a consideration of Fionn mac Cumhaill in English literature. The more than one hundred treatments of Fionn in English appeared to sort themselves into three piles of unequal size. There were the heroic, now dealt with in chapter 3, of which the most considerable was James Macpherson's *Poems of Ossian* and its imitators, as well as certain Irish nationalist portrayals. Then there were the anti-heroic, with works by writers as diverse as William Carleton and Flann O'Brien in his *At Swim-Two-Birds*, the focus of the fourth chapter. And lastly there was Joyce's *Finnegans Wake*, a work so vast and complex as to require a chapter all by itself.

In living with this material for a long while, I found that I began to define some terms a bit differently than one might in ordinary discourse. To begin with, "Celtic" describes a family of languages but not a specific people of language; and although it entered English usage from learned discourse rather than common speech, it should not carry connotations of romantic grandeur, nobility, or magic. One language within the Celtic family is Irish, the principal language of Ireland historically that is still spoken by about 100,000 people. The Modern Irish word for the language itself is *Gaeilge*. A transliteration of this term, Gaelic, was used to describe the native language before independence in 1922; thus the language revival of the 1890s began under the sponsorship of the Gaelic League. After independence the government gave official recognition to the native language and used it in state documents, thus—Irish language. Since Ireland's independence "Gaelic" has more often described that language related to Irish and still spoken in four counties of the Highlands of Scotland; it is sometimes called "Scottish

Gaelic" to spare confusion. I have tried to avoid, in general, the term "Anglo-Irish," which most properly refers to the English settlers who ruled the island until the twentieth century and the literary tradition produced by such people as Swift, Congreve, and Goldsmith. Writing by Irish-born authors from William Carleton (1794–1869) and after in English I shall refer to as "English" because of its language, although I readily admit calling Synge and Lady Gregory "English" would be confusing in other contexts. I regret that we have never adopted the term "Anglophone" for English writers in countries where English is not the native language, much as writers who use French in Canada describe themselves as "Francophone," regardless of their ancestry, culture, or political choices, but I fear that my introduction of that term would become an irritant after a few pages.

Fionn mac Cumhaill has had a long life. First appearing with the beginning of writing in Ireland, he has had a continuing career in the imagination of Celtic-speaking peoples for more than a thousand years. As the Celtic languages have declined, he has found renewed vitality in English literature, appearing in writing of every century since the middles ages. Sometimes noble, sometimes foolish, he has enlivened poems, stories, plays, operas, and novels. His stream that begins in the bogs of Ireland and the glens of Scotland has entered the great river of western culture. In this longevity, and in the breadth, depth, and variety of his characterization, there are few heroes that can match him.

Fionn mac Cumhaill

The Myth of Fionn mac Cumhaill in Irish Literature

Although the English people had shared the British Isles with several Celtic peoples for fourteen centuries, English writers, by and large, did not discover the Celtic world until the sensational success in the 1760s of James Macpherson's *Poems of Ossian*, a bogus rendering of Scottish Gaelic ballads. Despite a critical rebuke from Dr. Johnson and much general controversy over their authenticity, the poems were widely read all over Europe and provided an introduction to Celtic literature for a score of important poets, critics, and tastemakers, including such diverse talents as Goethe, Blake, James Fenimore Cooper, and Matthew Arnold. Not many were taken by the intrinsic art of the poems; after all, Macpherson always described himself as a translator and virtually no one knew the language of the original. That they could be read at all was cause for celebration. Best of all for Macpherson's fortunes, *Ossian* appeared in the midst of a general European fashion for the primitive and ancient. In them, the reader could seize a literary tradition that had survived among somewhat backward people living on the fringes of modern society, a tradition so archaic that it provided a link between the present and the time of Homer.

The *Poems* was ascribed to Ossian because so many of the ballads Macpherson employed were composed in the persona of Oisín or Ossian, an old Celtic warrior and poet who sang the glories of a world recently lost to him. The most frequent subject of the poems, as Macpherson "translated" them, was Fingal, Ossian's father. In subsequent decades Fingal and Ossian would become widely celebrated figures in European literature, as would Ossian's son, the noble Oscar, whose name, for example, would be given to more than a half-dozen members of Scandinavian royal houses.

The Fingal of Macpherson's *Ossian* was based on a figure of traditional Gaelic literature, Fionn mac Cumhaill. As we shall see in chapter 3, there was some confusion in the minds of Macpherson and his contemporaries about the relationship of the Irish and Scottish Gaelic languages, and thus many early commentators, no matter what they felt about Macpherson's "authenticity," thought that there should be a distinction drawn between the Scottish Fingal and the Irish Fionn. The desire of scholars to know the background of the Macpherson question helped to lead to the development, especially in France and Germany, of the academic study of the Celtic languages. By the end of the nineteenth century a sufficient number of manuscripts had been edited and translated to demolish the pretensions of Macpherson and, more importantly, to give the rest of the Western world an understanding of the extent, complexity, and beauty of literature in the Celtic languages. Most of the effort in this first chapter will be to determine just what kind of character Fionn was in Irish and Scottish Gaelic literature so we can understand what transformations he underwent as he became a figure in English literature.

The two centuries of scholarship since the time of Macpherson have also given us a better understanding of the relationship between Celtic and English literature. Although the Celtic languages provide a paucity of loan words to English, we now know that there has been a steady transmission of Celtic themes and characters into English literature since early medieval times. As we shall consider in chapter 2, the archetype of Fionn mac Cumhaill is one of the many from Irish and Welsh literatures which have been adapted in the Arthurian legends. As far as we know, Fionn first appeared in English literature under his own name in John Barbour's Lallans dialect *The Bruce* (c. 1375). In the next four hundred years, until the coming of Macpherson, Fionn appeared in a large number of English chronicles and pseudo-histories and also in a number of works of imaginative literature reviewed in chapter 3. With the rise of English-language literature in Ireland, beginning in the early nineteenth century, we find almost a hundred depictions of Fionn mac Cumhaill, which shall be discussed in chapters 3, 4, and 5.

Fionn's many appearances in English literature fall into a number of seemingly disparate patterns. As we might expect, Fionn mac Cumhaill is presented as a magnanimous and brave defender of his people in quite a sizable body of works, including Macpherson's *Ossian*. Lady Gregory produced a more reliable concatenation of stories about Fionn the hero in *Gods and Fighting Men* (1904), but most of the other admiring portrayals of the figure have been in juvenile adventure fiction. Many serious writers who have dealt with Fionn have shown him in unflattering ways. As we mentioned earlier, Finn is the villain of W. B. Yeats and George Moore's *Diarmuid and Grania* (1901), and he adds comic commentary to Flann O'Brien's *At Swim-Two-Birds* (1939). Other authors who portray an unheroic Fionn include Austin Clarke, William Carleton, Eugene Watters, John Masefield, and Francis Ledwidge. Thus when his name appears as an allusion in the works of modern authors, as it does in several plays of Sean O'Casey and poems of Padraic Colum, we cannot always be sure of its intended reference. What are we to make of such a character?

Examining just what sense can be made of the different portrayals of Fionn mac Cumhaill in English literature is the purpose of this discussion. As we shall see, the apparent deterioration of the hero's character from the admirable to the despicable to the laughable exists outside of time, so that the many faces of Fionn can be seen in almost every generation. That we should see more of the heroic Fionn in one literary season and more of the contemptible or the laughable in another says more about changing literary tastes than it does about the hero.

Because the character of Fionn has seemed adaptable to poets and storytellers, many readers would call him a "mythic hero" just as certain historical figures—such as Napoleon or Wyatt Earp—appear "mythic" or larger than life as their narratives are continually retold, each time with a new investment of motivations and values from the literary creator. In order to measure the myth of Fionn mac Cumhaill in Irish or in English literature, we need some better guidelines for the definition of myth.

MYTH

The suggestion that the disconnected narratives of Fionn mac Cumhaill and his Fianna constitute a mythology would undoubtedly seem a presumption to many modern readers, especially to the Irish, most of whom know him through the storytellers among their country cousins in the *Gaeltacht* or Irish-speaking areas. For them the "tale" or "legend" of Fionn might seem more suitable. Even academics, usually more tolerant of presumption, may balk, more because of their concern for the current debasement of the word "myth." In a much-cited passage of *Hero With a Thousand Faces* (817, 1956, 382),[1] Joseph Campbell summarizes seven different definitions used in mid-century academia, many of which are not only mutually exclusive but contradictory as well. Because the present study is investigative and not polemical, I shall not seek to use one theory or definition against another but rather try to limit myself to the definitions of myth which have been used in the study of traditional literature.

In the eighteenth century, when the study of traditional literature began and the only traditional literature anyone studied was that of ancient Greece, the entire matter was much easier to handle. In the divisions of Greek literature made during the generation of Christian Gottlob Heyne (1729–1810) and Johann Gottfried Herder (1744–1803), "mythology" dealt with the origin of the world and of many, the vicissitudes of vegetation, weather, eclipses, the discovery of fire, and the mystery of death. Under this generalized definition, myth is distinct from legend in that the latter deals with figures people thought to have been historical, who may indeed have been, although their deeds are most likely invented or exaggerated. "Folktales" are purely imaginary and have no other aim than pure entertainment and thus make no real claim to credibility. All the stories of the Titans and the Olympians are therefore myths, from the narratives of creation found in Hesiod's *Theogony* to the romances of the gods, even those incorporating scandal such as the one describing Zeus's pederasty with Ganymede. The love of the non-Olympian Orpheus, on the other hand, may have been legendary, and the amatory and military conquests of King Theseus of Athens are more probably legendary. Many of the adventures of Odysseus, sometimes called myth because they are ancient, are actually folktales. The distinction is carried forth by Sir James Frazer and is given tacit support by such contemporary critics of myth as Northrop Frye. One of Frye's more succinct definitions of myth is "a story in which some of the chief characters are gods" (831, 1963, 30).

Under the strictest application of the criteria drawn from Heyne and Herder, it is difficult to argue that there is any surviving body of Celtic mythology at all. The prohibition against putting sacred beliefs in writing in Druidic mystery cults, coupled with early Christianization (fifth century), which sought to destroy profane "pagan" texts, has denied us the hope of finding a Celtic text with a picture of belief comparable to what we find in Hesiod's *Theogony*. This is not to suggest that there was never a Celtic religion or mythology; the handful of studies of Celtic mythology and religion are based largely on archeological artifacts and interpolations and extrapolations of contemporary texts from Roman and Greek authors. Thus in speaking of Celtic gods we do not know if they were anthropomorphic personalities like the Greek, mere *numina* like the Roman, or something much less. Marie-Louise Sjoestedt, in *Gods and Heroes of the Celts*, remarks that it is often difficult to distinguish between gods and heroes in early Celtic narratives, apparently because the dichotomy between mortals and immortals, an importation from the Mediterranean world, was not always honored by Celtic storytellers of different centuries, especially after Christianization (446, 1949, xiii).

Unquestionably, many storytellers have considered Fionn not only mortal but historical. This is a question considered more fully in the next chapter, but suffice it for the moment to say that a number of credulous, popular histories of Ireland, for example, Seumas MacManus' *The Story of the Irish Race* (1921), assert that Fionn is not the figment of anyone's imagination but a genuine historical personage. Among better-informed scholars the question of Fionn's historicity has not been seriously entertained since the late nineteenth ccentury. What is significant in the Irish peasant's tenacious belief in Fionn's historicity is that the hero is usually portrayed as an immortal who always lives in the present. Even as late as 1969, E. Estyn Evans came upon a farmer in County Cavan who spoke of Fionn and his men in the present indicative. "He's not a giant," the man said. "He's only five-foot six."

Such evidence suggests that Fionn is much more than a character in folklore and is at least a legendary hero, similar in status to, say, King Arthur of Camelot. Before we can argue that Fionn is more than a mortal, we must consider the kind of evidence open to us. Traditional literature in Irish, as in other vernaculars, is of two modes, the written or "manuscript," transmitted by literate poets, storytellers, and scribes, and oral tradition, which is transmitted by the unlettered. The term "unlettered" did not carry the pejorative implications of being ignorant or uncouth in earlier centuries, especially in Ireland where there was a professional class of trained but illiterate storytellers. As Gerard Murphy has pointed out in his Introduction to Volume III of *Duanaire Finn* (404, 1953), the manuscript and oral traditions can be demonstrated to exist side by side in Irish at least since the eleventh century. The figure of Fionn mac Cumhaill is essentially the same in both, even though the different traditions usually portray different aspects of his personality. The question of which came first, oral or written, is still moot, even though it has been the subject of much scholarly dispute for more than one hundred and fifty years; abundant argument exists to support both sides of the question in Irish as well as in other vernaculars. The relevance of reviewing the two traditions here is that most of the support for the contention that Fionn had divine origin is found in manuscripts written by the learned class.

Quite a bit of scholar's ink has been spilled in the last hundred years on the question of Fionn's divinity. Although there is so little unambiguous evidence as to limit positive conclusions, the subject cannot be shrugged off. Our assumptions about Fionn's origins have much to do with the classifications of Fenian narratives. If Fionn were an historical figure, as uninformed popular opinion has long supposed, or if he were only an aggrandized figure from folk imagination, then perhaps the stories about him would best be classified as legends. But if the persona of Fionn includes elements of the supernatural, then contemporary scholarship is more justified in thinking of him as a mythical figure.

In many stories, admittedly, Fionn does not seem like a god. He cannot control the weather, travel through time, or bring fire. There are no surviving prayers in Fionn's honor, no incantations, shrines, or votive paraphernalia. On the other hand he has what appear to be divinities in his genealogy, he has magical powers to foretell the future, and he may be able to overcome death.

Some of the most persuasive arguments for Fionn's divinity were given by T. F. O'Rahilly in his landmark study, *Early Irish History and Mythology* (431, 1946). In O'Rahilly's view Fionn was an anthropomorphized remnant of a Celtic god worshipped on the Continent and in the British Isles (pp. 271, 277–78). This same pre-Christian god was the original for the heroes of the other two cycles of Old Irish literature, Lugh Lámhfada and Cúchulainn. O'Rahilly's proposal has received wide acceptance from informed commentators but is based on linguistic and circumstantial evidence.

More compelling in O'Rahilly's discussion is Fionn's power of prophecy, which the hero can summon by chewing his thumb, an attribute he shares with Heracles, the Norse figure Sigurd, and the Welsh Taliesin. In a lengthy chapter devoted to prophecy and devination (pp. 318–40), O'Rahilly argues that Fionn was accorded the unique powers of *imbas forosnai* (roughly "foresight") and *teinm laída* (again, roughly, "break open the pith" or "superhuman intuition"). Within narratives Fionn wears his powers lightly. He does not exploit his gifts to win a high status in his society; instead, he is a leader among men because he excels at what all men can do—hunting and making poetry. When he does use his supernatural power, the effect is to disentangle him from a quandary or to free the narrative from an impasse. More significantly, Fionn's powers are the subject of debate between Patrick, when that saint becomes a figure in Fenian narrative, and the aged survivors of the Fianna, Oisín and Caoilte. Saint Patrick forbids the practice of *imbas forosnai* and *teinm laída* in an evangelized Ireland. The old Fenians lament the passing of pagan Ireland and champion the generosity and heroism of Fionn's time as against the Christian present.

The most certain divinity of Fionn's genealogy is Nuadu Argetlám, or "Nuadu of the Silver Hand," described in manuscript literature as the king of the Tuatha Dé Danann, the race of immortals who inhabited Ireland before the present generation of humanity arrived. Not only is Nuadu an immortal, but he is an Irish counterpart of the British god Nodons, whose cult flourished in Roman Britain and whose temple ruin may be found at Lydney Park, Gloucester. Nuadu's divinity does not automatically pass on to Fionn, of course, as many early historical Irish, including the entire Eóganacht federation of families in Munster, also claimed the same descent. This is little different from genealogies of ancient Greece in which a distinguished family, such as Erichthonius and his progeny of Athens, claimed descent from the virgin Athena.

A final indication of the residual belief in Fionn's divinity is his ability to overcome death. Fionn does face death, according to different stories, under different forms, a subject considered later in this chapter. Whether he faces death on the battlefield at the hands of many, or alone and slain by a single assassin, he is somehow taken away to a hidden place where he "sleeps" and will return to his people when he is needed. The same is true, of course, of such heroic figures as Arthur and Barbarossa, who are not perceived as gods. Folklorists classify such stories under the "Sleeping Warriors" or "Sleeping Army" motif, index number E502 in the Aarne-Thompson classification. The promise of Fionn's return found more reverence in the popular mind: there are more than thirty-five locations, in both Ireland and Gaelic Scotland, where Fionn and his men are supposed to be sleeping. Readers of *Finnegans Wake* will recognize that Joyce took a little-known Dublin variant of this motif to help structure that narrative. Joyce felt, as others have, that Fionn's ability to conquer death was not separate from the rest of his adventures.

Indeed, Fionn overcomes death in two identities, as himself, and also as Mongan, an Ulster petty king of the seventh century, described in the eighth-century narrative *Imram Brain*, "The Voyage of Bran, Son of Febal" (edited by D. Nutt, 567, 1895–97, vol. I, pp. 52; vol. II, pp. 6, 281). In a dispute with the court bard, Mongan allows himself to be portrayed as the reincarnated Fionn. The story is narrated by one of Mongan's warriors, alleging himself to be the reincarnated Caoilte. In the story Mongan/Fionn deals quickly with his enemies as, by implication, King Mongan will now.

The evidence when assembled does not prove Fionn's divinity, but it does suggest that if Fionn is not quite a god, he seems to be at least something more than a warrior-hunter-poet of a great mass of stories. Perhaps the safest judgment is that given by Alexander MacBain as long ago as 1894 (379, 100), when the impact of modern anthropology was first felt on the study of mythology:

> Fionn is, like Heracles, Theseus, Perseus, and other such persons of Greek Myth, a culture hero—probably originally a local deity raised to a national place. He is an incarnation of the chief diety of the race—the Mercury, whom Caesar tells us the Gauls worship—a god of literary and mercantile character. His grandson Oscar is a reflection of the war god, and other characters of the Fenian band no doubt correspond to the other personages of the Gaelic Olympus.

MacBain's analysis makes two points, one explicitly and other implicitly. The first is that Fionn compares with three great heroes of Greek mythology, all of them having some links to the divine. The second is the use of the term "culture hero," which is probably more apt to a Celtic context than in a Greek one. "Culture hero" was first used to describe figures in non-European mythology, such as the Coyote of California Indians or Gluskabe of those in the Northeast. Among the North American Indians there is not a clear demarcation between heroes and gods; a culture hero, whether worshipped or not, is distinct from others by the useful or good things he or she brings. Prometheus, for example, is a culture hero because he is a firebringer, not because he is a Titan. Among the Celts, too, there is no clear line between mortals and immortals. Fionn's status can be grasped by seeing that he is the center of an immense cycle of narratives, much as Heracles is. Fionn is a hunter, poet, seer, and warrior; for those who follow him, he is a benefactor. The persistence of his persona over more than a thousand years argues that his stories offered more than momentary diversion beside the turf fire.

Some questions about the accuracy of speaking of the "myth" of Fionn mac Cumhaill remain. Because the present study purports to say something about English literature, it should acknowledge that the word "myth" has acquired new implications since Joyce's *Ulysses*, Crane's *The Bridge*, or for that matter *King Kong*. Can the narratives of Fionn mac Cumhaill strike a response from our unconscious minds? Do they draw on a character who evokes a memory of the continuity of human experience? In short, do the stories of Fionn *function* as myth as well as meet the tests that distinguish myth from mere legend or folklore? They do. The stories of the Fenian Cycle are not only ancient and continuous but various as well. They embody supposed attributes of the Gaelic peoples: heroic, romantic, ribald, and even absurd. The working-out of these characteristics and values, over centuries and in different genres, is the labor of the next four chapters. A shorter route to the importance of Fionn as an embodiment of the unconsciously held value systems and beliefs of a suppressed nation is given to us by Joyce in *Finnegans Wake*. In it Fionn is among the first residents of the monomyth, the single narrative strand that unites all human experience.

THE CONTEXT OF IRISH LITERATURE

Thus far we have established only the externals of the character of Fionn mac Cumhaill. We know he is a figure of traditional Irish literature, sufficiently widely known to be recognized in an allusion today, and we know there is good evidence he is derived from a Celtic god. Such information alone would hardly justify the attention we are giving him, so that it seems a fair question to ask, "Who is—or was—Fionn mac Cumhaill? What does he do that sets him apart from other figures in traditional literature?" The short answer to those questions is that he is the leading figure in one of the great epochs of Irish literature, the focus of several thousand narratives we have called the "Fenian Cycle." An outline of the development of Fionn's character, the major responsibility of this chapter, cannot begin without understanding the place the Fenian Cycle holds in Irish literature. For reasons to be considered later, many scholars prefer to call the cycle "Finnian," in part to denote Fionn's central role in it, or "Ossianic," to underscore Oisín's persona as narrator in many of the tales, especially those from oral tradition. The Fenian Cycle is one of four major branches of narrative in Irish secular literature. The other three are called "Invasions" or "Mythological Cycle," the "Red Branch" or "Ulster Cycle," and the "Cycle of the Kings."

Of the four cycles the "Mythological" is commonly judged to be the oldest. The titling of this cycle, which is sometimes also known as the "Invasions Cycle," indicates that it deals with the origins of Ireland, but it does not mean that the others are less "mythological." Many of the narratives here are pseudo-histories, dealing extensively with the five legendary invasions of Ireland as reconstructed in the *Lebor Gabála,* "The Book of Invasions." Characteristically, much of this cycle is taken up with the recitation of genealogies of rather implausible families (kings sired by animals, multi-armed and multi-headed warriors, etc.). As is so often the case with fabulous histories such as Hesiod's *Works and Days,* the men of earlier days appear to be the champions of glory whereas the men of the present appear to be witless, cowardly, and crude. It follows then that the leading figures of this cycle are not the victors of the fifth invasions, those humans called Milesians; instead, most of the stories concern the Tuatha Dé Danaan, "the tribe of the goddess Danu," the imortals from the fourth invasion who linger to haunt the usually unimaginative, often hapless Milesians.

The narratives of the Ulster or "Red Branch" Cycle appear to be of later composition than the "Mythological" and are the best-known of all four to English readers, largely through the efforts of W. B. Yeats and his contemporaries. Much richer in character and episode than the earlier materials, the narratives of the Ulster Cycle are the product of disciplined court poets and storytellers. Yeats liked to think of them as "aristocratic" because of the patronage of the arts and education by such northerners as Ruaidhrí Ó Conchubhair, "Rory O'Connor" (fl. 1169), who founded a center of learning in Armagh. "Aristocratic" may seem a misleading description compared to French tastes at the opening of Versailles, but Ulster had been the leading province of Ireland long before the English invasion (1170), and the Ulster families were among the most cultivated in Ireland down to the time of the Flight of the Earls and the Cromwellian plantations of the seventeenth century. The Ulster Cycle includes not only the stories of Cúchulainn and Deirdre but also the "Irish Iliad," *Táin Bó Cuailnge*.

The cycle usually listed third is the Fenian, about which more later, and the fourth is made up of those stories about more or less historical figures that do not fit in the earlier three. Myles Dillon categorized these remainders as the Cycles of the Kings, if "king" is not too grand a translation for the Irish *rí*, denoting petty chieftains who ruled families in different parts of Ireland. The most celebrated of these kings was Brian Boru, who defeated the Danes at Clontarf (A.D. 1014). Other authorities have argued that the stories of Brian and his family should be called the Dalcassian Cycle, after their narrative region in what is now County Clare.

ASSEMBLING A HEROIC BIOGRAPHY OF FIONN MAC CUMHAILL FROM IRISH AND GAELIC LITERATURES

The third cycle is usually called the "Fenian," although some informed commentators wince at the term. Despite the similarity of phonology, "Fenian" does not refer to Fionn at all but instead derives from a confusion of *féni*, denoting the oldest, purest, or aboriginal inhabitants of Ireland, and *féinn*, a variant of *fiann/fianna*, implying Fionn's band of merry men. There are many other fianna than Fionn's, however, and the very concept of an independent caste of warrior-hunters may be much older than Irish tradition, having antecedent in the Gaulish *gaesatae* as described by Polybius (second century B.C.) and Roman commentators. What makes the word "Fenian" much more unattractive is that it was coined (in 1804) by the scholarly charlatan, Colonel Charles Vallancey, a man who also argued that the Irish language was derived from Phoenician. Informed readers shunned the word, and it probably would have disappeared if not used by the Irish-American political leader, John O'Mahoney, who adopted "Fenian" for the Irish Republican Brotherhood about 1858. Perhaps because of its political associations, "Fenian" is a term many modern readers recognize easily. Like "Quaker" and "Jesuit," it has become the standard reference despite the implications of its origins.

Rival terms for the cycle are neither more authentic nor more descriptive. "Ossianic," for example, is a neologism derived from Macpherson's spelling of Oisín. At one time it was used to describe all the irish literature that Macpherson pretended to translate; thus the first large-scale translations of early manuscripts were the *Transactions of the Ossianic Society* of Dublin, 1854–61. The term more accurately describes such works as the *Agallamh na Senórach*, "The Colloquy of the Elders," and subsequent ballad literature, beginning in the thirteenth century, in which Fenians surviving to the Christian era, usually Oisín or Caoilte, wrangle with Saint Patrick over the virtues of the old order.

As suggested earlier, the Fenian has been the most popular and widespread of all four cycles with Irish storytellers, in manuscript tradition and even more with unlettered storytellers. Alfred Nutt (415, 1910, 19) suggested that as much as 60 percent of all Irish native fiction is from this cycle, and Fenian characters and themes are widely celebrated in lyric, chronicle, pseudo-history, and proverb. Narratives of Fionn and the Fianna have been recorded in all the counties of Ireland as well as in the other two parts of the trifurcated Goidelic branch of Celtic languages on the Isle of Man and throughout Gaelic Scotland. Several dozen place names, such as "Finn MacCool's Pebble," "— Fingerstone," "Fingals' Cave," can be found in many parts of both Ireland and Scotland. Likewise, virtually every dolmen in Ireland has been called "The Bed of Diarmaid and Gráinne," though those primitive constructs, each a miniature Stonehenge, would be unsuited for sleep, much less lovemaking. John V. Kelleher has suggested that such mythological allusions in Irish place names have no more meaning than the many "Lover's Leaps" and "Devil's Washtubs" on the American map. But the preponderance of place names, such as the frequent naming of Fionn's seat of power at the Hill of Allen in Kildare, and great number of times in the narrative that Fionn's men are called the "Leinster Fianna," suggest that the homeland of the hero is somewhere along a line running southwest of Dublin from central Kildare to the Leinster/Munster border. Despite this, there is never anything regional about his characterization; the various aspects of his character do not appear to have any geographical pattern. And although different genre, different modes of transmission, and the passing centuries have wrought many changes in the particulars of Fionn's appearance, the archetype of the hero, as

Gerard Murphy has demonstrated, is recognizably continuous throughout (404, 1953, x1–1xi). This is not to say that the differences in Fionn's portrayals are not significant; indeed, charting and analyzing the changes in their presentations, especially as they appear in English literature, is the principal work at hand. Nevertheless, proceeding further, I want to stress that there is a discernible coherence and continuity in Fionn's character despite the disparity in his portrayal from one narrative to another.

Much of what gives Fionn's portrayal apparent stability through the thousands of narratives in which he performs is borrowed from the traditional European portrayal of kings, especially as they apear in fairy tale and romance. In common with unnumbered counterparts, Fionn is a brave warrior and leader of men, a stalwart defender of his country against all invaders, steadfast in battle and generous in victory. But there are distinctions in Fionn's kingship; he is the king only of his immediate followers, a *rígfhénnid*, and his power is nearly always represented as distinct from that of the *ardríg*, "high king," who is resident at *Temhair*, or Tara, northeast of what is today Dublin. When Fionn is a young hero the high king is Cormac mac Airt ("Son of Art"), with whom he maintains generally poor terms. Cormac, incidentally, has a much better claim to historicity than does Fionn (431, 1946, 130–40, *et passim*). The high king during Fionn's maturity is Cairbre or Cairbri ("of the Liffey"), Cormac's son, whose enmity for Fionn and his men grows with every episode.

In his separation and later isolation from royal power in Ireland, Fionn distinguishes himself from his counterparts in the other Irish cycles, Lugh and Cúchulainn. The French Celticist, Marie-Louise Sjoestedt, argued that Fionn's relegation to the countryside is what distinguished him most sharply from the more sophisticated hero, Cúchulainn. The myth of the Ulster hero is based on a heritage of an ordered society, of princes, scholars, and clerics, but the myth of Fionn derives from the men outside the tribe, the hunters, the woodsmen, and the soldiers-for-hire. Sjoestedt reminds us that the Fenian texts show that men are not born in the fianna; they acquire that status by choice and rigorous apprenticeship (446, 1949, 91, 82). Lacking other scholarly conclusions about the fianna, she asserts that they were originally a band of men who lived by hunting and plunder, roving the countryside under the authority of their own leaders. They trained as hunters from May 1 to November 1, *Bealtaine* to *Samhain*, and quartered where they could in winter. In the eyes of what established authority there was, the fianna were indistinguishable from guerillas. They may have been Irish counterparts of the Norse *berserkirs*. As evidence she suggests that *fían* has cognates in Old High German, Slavonic, Avestic, and Sanskrit, in each instance with words merging the notions of hunting and warring (p. 83). Thus she thinks that the tales which portray the Fenian heroes as appointed defenders of their country against foreign invaders are of later origin. Although Sjoestedt did not know of his work, Reidar Christiansen, writing several years earlier, provided evidence for her thesis in *The Vikings and the Viking Wars in Irish and Gaelic Tradition,* where he demonstrated that the historical episodes from the Norse invasions had become imbedded in Fenian stories of much earlier provenience (334, 1931). Cúchulainn does not fight Norsemen because the Ulster Cycle represents a different concept of the hero which does not make allusion to the realities of the countryside. At his most exalted moment in Irish literature, in the *Táin,* Cúchulainn does battle with Queen Medb and her warriors to retain possession of the Great Brown Bull of Ulster, all figures whose reality is no more likely than his. The distinction in Sjoestedt's summary is that: "The myth of Cúchulainn is the myth of the tribal man, the exaltation of heroism as a social function. The myth of the fianna is the myth of man outside the tribe, the release of gratuitous heroism. These two concepts do not contradict each other, but form an opposition like thesis and antithesis, two complimentary aspects of the racial temperament" (p. 90). And although she spoke only for Celtic tradition, Sjoestedt is also describing the Fionn mac Cumhaill of English literature, especially as he has been recreated in twentieth-century fiction such as *Finnegans Wake* and *At Swim-Two-Birds.*

In the Introduction to Volume III of *Duanaire Finn,* perhaps the most sustained and considerable study of Fenian literature ever published, Gerard Murphy agrees that two of Fionn's primary roles are hunter and warrior, which is demonstrated both in manuscript and oral texts from several centuries (404, 1953, pp. xlviii–liv). Murphy also argues that Fionn's role of seer is as much a part of his character over a comparable period of time, although this is less of a distinction since his power has analogues in the careers of Heracles, Sigurd, and Taliesin, as we have mentioned before. Fionn's power of devination comes from "chewing" his thumb, or placing it behind his upper teeth, a curious ritual which has been the subject of considerable speculation, including an entire book on the subject of Robert Douglas Scott (444, 1930). A character chewing his thumb, not identified as Fionn, also appears on a number of large Celtic

Crosses from the early Christian period, as Françoise Henry has observed (514, 1965, pp. 124, 139, 155).

A more important distinction, as Murphy shows us, is Fionn's ability to slay Aillén, "the Burner." According to the most frequently repeated story, Aillén harasses Cormac's court at Tara every November 1 at Samhain. As in *Beowulf*, none of the royal retainers can defeat the super-human power until the hero arrives from a land beyond the realm. Aillén burns down the palace and so might be seen as a more formidable opponent than Grendel, but Fionn's power proves to be greater. Fortunately, Aillén is not avenged by his mother. Again as in the Anglo-Saxon narrative, the hero wins the esteem of the royal household but does not become a part of it.

Although the oldest texts of the Aillén motif date only from the twelfth century, closer investigation of even earlier texts reveals that Fionn's opponents are non-human personalities whose "name, nickname, known character, habits, or story connect them either with fire in general, or more definitely with the Burner" (p. lxiii). For example, Fionn does battle with the three Fothadhs in a number of early romances, and further references to the Fothadhs, some of them highly ambiguous, can be found in narratives dating from as early as the seventh century. Although the Fothadhs are not always associated with fire in the narratives, an eleventh-century etymology of their name, viz. *fí-aeda*, i.e., "venom of fire," includes a description of them which translates, "They were a virulent fire in destroying clans and races." The genealogy of the Fothadhs includes, first, their father, Dáire Derg, or Dáire the Red, and their grandfather, Gnathaltach, whose epithet is *daig garg*, "fierce flame." The family line leads back ultimately to Nuadu, who is, coincidentally, Fionn's ancestor.

Another enemy of Fionn, who appears only in very early texts such as "Fionn and the Man in the Tree," is Dearg Corra moucu Dhaighre, whose name Murphy translates as "Red One of Corr[?] of the race of Flame." This "Red One," Murphy further explains, has the peculiar habit of jumping to and fro on the cooking hearth (p. lxiv).

The traditional enemy of Fionn mac Cumhaill in the prose romances of 1400–1800, and of most literature in English, is not so easily associated with fire or "the Burner." He is Goll of the Clann Morna and the Connacht Fianna who, according to one of the better known narratives of the cycle, *Fotha Catha Cnucha*, "The Cause of the Battle of Cnucha," has killed Fionn's father, Cumhal, and taken command of all the fianna of Ireland. In one of the tasks the young hero must undertake to prove himself, Fionn overpowers Goll and becomes the head of the Fianna Éireann. In some stories Goll is known as Áed or Aodh ("flame" or "fire"). There is no question of Fionn's killing Goll in the romances, but there is a persistent enmity between the two all through narratives in the manuscript tradition. One instance in English literature where this enmity is continued is *Finnegans Wake,* where Goll mac Morna is portrayed as a mysterious, incomprehensible, but unavoidable opponent. The several stories from oral sources which portray Goll as admirable or as a bosom companion of Fionn do not obscure the animosity in the oldest tradition.

In sum, Murphy's study of the early materials on Fionn as compared with most recent folklore shows that the irreducible components in Fionn's heroic character are: (a) his powers to slay "the Burner" and subsequently to overpower Goll mac Morna and become head of the Fianna Éireann; (b) his skill as a hunter; (c) his bravery as a warrior, especially in defense of his people; and (d) his ability to see into the future by chewing his thumb, an ability that allows him to be seen as a prophet or seer. These may be the four roots of his personality as it appears in the literature, but early tales, especially those written before the twelfth century, and oral folklore, even that composed and recorded in the twentieth century, do not develop personality of character as we understand those terms in the literature of the past three centuries. Nowhere is there a characterization of Fionn comparable to what we might have had if the myth had been adapted by Dickens, Balzac, or Strindberg. But to know anything of the fuller character of Fionn mac Cumhaill in Irish tradition, we must give some consideration to the vast, tangled body of ballad and romance composed, often extrapolated from earlier tales, between the twelfth and the eighteenth centuries.

Because the many narratives of Fionn mac Cumhaill are discontinuous, disparate, and widely dispersed, the full story of his adventures has never been told. There is no epic of Fionn; the closest approximation to epic in the whole cycle is the *Agallamhna Senórach,* which Oisín is the major figure and Fionn is a secondary character remembered from the distant past. Unlike Deirdre in "The Fate of the Sons of Usnech," or Cúchulainn in the *Táin* and two or three other narratives, Fionn does not appear as a major figure in any tale which has been of any great interest, either to critics or to adapters. I am excluding the "Pursuit of Diarmaid and Gráinne," in which Fionn plays a supporting role. Part of the continuity of Fionn seems to have been provided by the storyteller's feeling of having known the hero, as we have noted earlier, and his talent for expanding extemporaneously from the known. Unfortunately, there was no Malory in those times to weave together the known and the variants into one continuous fabric of narrative. The task is more difficult for a modern reteller of the tales in that he or she may now know too much about the hero, even though all the work of editing the texts has not been finished; nevertheless, the problem of determining the most authentic version of various stories would be an Herculean— if not Sisyphean—labor. As the eminent Norweigian folklorist Reidar Th. Christiansen has advised us, the mere description of the minutiae of difference between the manuscripts and their filiation is a super- human task (pp. 46–47).

If a complete and totally coherent retelling of Fionn's adventures is a superhuman burden, we can rejoice that a number of earthbound scholars have given us an interim solution, a kind of scenario of events, based on the apparent life of the hero. I say "apparent" not merely because there is no evidence that such a figure as Fionn mac Cumhaill ever lived, but more because there is none to suggest that Irish storytellers ever considered the concatenation of his adventures in apparently chronological order. A storyteller, or shanachie (Irish: seanchaidhe), in Kerry in the fourteenth century might have told a tale of Fionn in his maturity, while another in Meath in the fifteenth century might have told one of the hero's youth. The time of mythographers is outside that of chronologers. The only vital date of any kind we have for Fionn is given for the hero's death at the Battle of Gabhra, A.D. 283, recorded in the *Annals of Tigernach* (d. 1088) and inter-leafed in the *Annals of the Four Masters* in the seventeenth century (188, 1856, vol. I, p. 119). The dating in chron- icles and annals can be capricious, and those before the supposed date of the introduction of Christianity and literacy in A.D. 432 have little meaning. Within these severe limitations the most celebrated scenarist of Fenian narratives was Lady Gregory in *Gods and Fighting Men* (1904), more than half of which is given to this end. Her version is told in eleven chapters with sixty-four numbered episodes and is based largely on manuscript narratives which had recently been translated in such scholary Celtic journals as the *Transactions of the Ossianic Society* and *Revue Celtique*, as she acknowledged in rather incomplete footnotes. Where it suited her taste, she altered or aug- mented manuscript narratives with materials from oral tradition col- lected by Jeremiah Curtin, Douglas Hyde, and others, including some variants from Gaelic Scotland. Thus her final product was something never before seen anywhere, and it contained episodes which certainly would have sounded unfamiliar to almost any individual inheritor of Fenian tradition. Nonetheless, for her work in arranging these tales, and even more for *Cuchulain of Muirthemne* (1902), W. B. Yeats called her the Malory of the Irish Renaissance, a compliment as much indicative of the influence of her work as of its method of organization.

The extent of Lady Gregory's influence on English writing is a subject for consideration further elsewhere in this study, but for the moment we should acknowledge her dominance in a much smaller area, Fenian adventure fiction. Most of these works are of slight literary distinction and are remembered here because each of them attempted to fit the episodes associated with Fionn into a sequence. The first popular account in English of Fionn's adventures was Standish James O'Grady's *Finn and His Companions* (1892), a miscellaneous assortment of fantastic adventures, all taken from oral tradition. O'Grady's account is isolated in time and does not present any kind of developing or maturing hero as does Lady Gregory's. After *Gods and Fighting Men* there were five other novelistic accounts of Fionn's adventures. The first, Donald MacKenzie's *Finn and his Warrior Band* (1910), gave the stories a Scottish setting. A second portrayed the heroes in Irish Renaissance colorings with theosophic undertones: *Heroes of the Dawn* (1913) by Violet Russell, wife of George "AE" Russell. Two American authors who reshaped the narratives were Harold F. Hughes in *Legendary Heroes of Ireland* (1922) and Ella Young in *Tangle-Coated Horse* (1929); Young's version has been in print off and on for more than fifty years and is stocked in many public libraries. More recently, Rosemary Sutcliff produced an English (as opposed to Anglo-Irish) account in *The High Deeds of Finn MacCool* (1967). There is in addition a kind of fictionalized folklore collection by T. W. Rolleston, *The High Deeds of Finn MacCool* (1910), which suggests by its title that it deals exclusively with Fenian matters while actually treating of several cycles. All six later collections have at least three qualities in common with Lady Gregory: they blend manuscript and oral narratives, they consider Fionn's adventures a lifelong story, and they avoid most of the unseemly presentations of the hero, thus subverting the irony present in many of the Irish originals. But unlike Lady Gregory's work the six are, in varying degrees, geared for juvenile readership, much as O'Grady's was. This may have resulted from the Victorian convention of having children read Scott and Cooper novels, the implication being that heroic narratives from the past provided suitable life models for the young.

Two other attempts to weld the Fenian narratives into a whole were not compiled to be considered works of literature themselves. One comes from T. F. O'Rahilly in his *Early Irish History and Mythology* (431, 1946, pp. 271–81) and is concerned with distinguishing myth from history in pre-Christian Ireland; understandably, O'Rahilly restricted himself to manuscript materials. Seán Ó Súilleabháin, on the other hand, devoted himself entirely to oral tradition in his *Handbook of Irish Folklore* (432, 1963, pp. 588–97), a guide for collectors of living traditions, in which he compiled a thirty-six episode résumé of Fionn's adventures.

This still leaves the question: Just what did Fionn *do*? Lacking a manageable, coherent outline of Fionn's career I now summon the audacity to compile one here, for my present purposes. One of the first assignments is to find the Fionn most attractive to English-language writers over a period of centuries. The complete adventures of Fionn in Old, Middle, and Modern Irish literature must wait for another book, one much longer than this. What is presented here is taken from a reading of eight authors: S. J. O'Grady, Gregory, MacKenzie, Russell, Hughes, Young, Sutcliff, Rolleston, O'Rahilly, and Ó Súilleabhan, with references to some significant histories of Irish and Gaelic literatures such as Douglas Hyde (364, 1899), Aodh deBlacam (346, 1934), and Robin Flower (504, 1947).

Within limits, then, here are eleven key chapters of the Fenian Cycle, especially as they relate to English literature.

Genealogy and Birth

Fenian lore begins with the founding of Fionn's family, the Clan Bascna (*Baiscne, Baoisgne, Basca,* etc.), which grows to become the core of the Leinster Fianna. Leinster is the easternmost of Ireland's four provinces. The rival family of the Clan Bascna is the Clan Morna which is centered in Connacht, the westernmost of the Ireland's provinces.

In these narratives about the early rivalry of the families, the most important figure we encounter is Cumhal mac Trenmor, Fionn's father. Cumhal is killed at the Battle of Cnucha (modern: Castleknock, western County Dublin) by Goll mac Morna of Connacht, a catastrophe that brings a sharp reversal in the family fortunes; as a result, Cumhal's wife, Muirne of the White Neck, a great-granddaughter of Nuadu, flees into exile with the infant hero, Fionn mac Cumhaill.

The most important text in this chapter of Fionn's heroic biography is the manuscript tale, *Fotha Catha Cnucha,* "The Cause of the Battle of Cnucha," found in the oldest Irish codex, *Lebor na hUidre,* "The Book of the Dun Cow," dating from the early twelfth century. Although some variants of the story of Fionn's birth and departure into exile have been recorded in oral tradition, the genealogy and early life of Fionn has been of little interest to later storytellers, lettered or unlettered, and it has been ignored by English writers.

Boyhood Deeds of the Hero

After being reared in hiding, the youthful Fionn, then called Deimne, goes through a series of magical adventures which prepare him for his career as a great chief. The first of these is the Salmon of Knowledge episode: Finneigas, a druid, has been waiting for many years by the banks of a river for the appearance of the Salmon of Knowledge. In some versions Finneigas is waiting on the banks of the Boyne, a river rich in mystical associations ("Boyne" is from *Boann,* one of the principal early goddesses of Ireland), while other versions have the druid waiting at the falls of Assaroe on the Erne Estuary in County Donegal. There is perhaps no need to speculate on the significance of the salmon as the carrier of knowledge as there is a great body of lore associated with the fish all across the northern hemisphere, much of it identifying the characteristic leap of the salmon with inspiration, sexual energy, nimbleness, etc. The salmon has been especially important in Celtic tradition, both Goidelic and Brythonic, as a repository of Otherworldly wisdom. Finneigas succeeds in catching the long-awaited salmon and is proceeding to cook it when Fionn, quite by accident, burns his thumb on the salmon and nurses the burn in his mouth, thus inheriting the power of divination before the druid can.

Buoyant with the new confidence of his spiritual powers, Fionn sets about developing his physical skills and soon excels in running, jumping, swimming, handling of various weapons, and, in oral tradition, prowess in playing hurley or *camán,* Irish field hockey. While sporting with other young men, he acquires his heroic name when

THE MYTH IN IRISH LITERATURE

he is called "fionn," the Irish word for fair or white; Fionn is always represented as having blond hair and a fair, broad brow. He also acquires his special, magical sword from Lein (or Lochan), a smith of the gods, his aegis, a banner showing the likeness of the golden sun half-risen from the blue floor of the sea, and, most mysteriously, he wins a bag made of crane skin, *corrbolg*, which may represent the beginnings of the insular alphabet, *ogham*. Capping his boyish adventures, as recounted earlier, he overcomes Goll mac Morna to become unchallenged head of the Fianna Éireann, then goes to Tara and slays Aillén, "the Burner."

The most important Irish manuscript tale of Fionn's youth is *Macgníamhartha Finn*, literally, "The Boyhood Deeds of Finn," found first in the medieval *Psalter of Cashel*. The sequence of events we have described has been fairly popular in oral tradition; variants are recorded as late as the twentieth century, but the story of the youth of Fionn tends to become confused with parallel stories of other heroes, especially Perceval and the Welsh hero Peredur.[2]

English adaptations of the story of Fionn's youth have been quite numerous, including early chapters in the several juvenile retellings of Fionn's adventures as well as separate chapters in more than a dozen collections of Irish stories and folk tales. The most distinguished of these is certainly that found in James Stephens' *Irish Fairy Tales* (1920), which despite its title, devotes more than half its bulk to Fenian stories. Not all English adapters have been so admiring, however; Caeser Otway, an anti-Catholic evangelist and first editor of the peasant novelist William Carleton, wrote a burlesque of the "Salmon of Knowledge" story in his *Sketches in Ireland* in 1827.

Fionn the Resplendent Hero

After joining the two warring fianna, those of Leinster and Connacht, into the Fianna Éireann, Fionn quickly establishes his hegemony over the forests, streams, and open places of the four provinces of Ireland with his seat of power at the Hill of Allen (also *Almu, Almhain,* etc.) in County Kildare in Leinster. Almost immediately we encounter the paradigm of Fionn's character which made him the admired hero of the Goidelic peoples. As Gerard Murphy has pointed out in *Duanaire Finn*, Fionn is a hunter, warrior, and seer. He is also a poet of some skill; indeed, several poems ascribed to him, the best known of which is "In Praise of May," are still included

in anthologies of Irish poetry. In oral tradition he is also something
of an incipient civil engineer, building the Giant's Causeway, cutting
the pass at Glendalough, even working as far afield as the Grand
Canyon in the southwestern United States. Though usually in the
company of men, Fionn is occasionally portrayed as a lover; in
manuscript tradition he is more restrained, as in *Cath Fionntrágha*,
"The Battle of Ventry, or the White Strand," in which he is smitten
with the invading princess of Greece, overcomes her, but cannot
bear to take advantage of her. In oral tradition he is more bold; one
tale collected in Ulster has him steal the clothes of the queen of
Italy while she is bathing, and later sire three sons upon her (231,
1913, 91–92).

We also read of the leading men in the Fianna Éireann, a host
of immeasurable size. One text, *Airem Muintiri Finn*, "The Enumeration of Fionn's People" (143, 99–100), suggests that the hero was
surrounded by thousands of warriors, but a closer reading of the
narrative gives no more than thirty names. Across the breadth of
Fenian literature, only six figures from the Fianna appear with any
regularity. First, from his family, a son Oisín, and later his grandson,
Oscar (also Osgar, Osca, etc.), often called by critics the "Galahad
of the Cycle," and the embodiment of many of Fionn's aspirations
reborn. The more prominent non-familial Fenian is Goll mac Morna,
though his protryal ranges from the villainous in some manuscript
tales to the moral and physical superior to Fionn in some folk tales.
Caoilte (also Cailte, Keeltya, etc.) mac Ronain is the greatest runner
and jumper of the Fianna and a survivor with Oisín until the time
of Saint Patrick. Diarmaid O'Duibhne, a son-surrogate of Fionn's, is
the greatest lover of the Fianna; no woman who sees his "love spot,"
ball seirce, can resist him, even if Diarmaid would wish otherwise.
Finally, there is Conán Moal ("the bald"), a type for Falstaff and
Thersites, a sharp-tongued scold, the butt of most Fenian pranks
and, consequently, the comic relief in many early narratives.

Like popular heroes in much of world literature, Fionn is usually
best at what all men must do. And yet Fionn, because of flaws which
prefigure greater weaknesses to come, is frequently bested by his
men. Diarmaid is more attractive to women. Caolite is a better runner
and jumper. And both Oisín and Oscar often appear stronger and
more virtuous.

Irish texts detailing Fionn's heroic adventures from both manuscript and oral traditions abound through all centuries in which
Irish literature has been recorded. Indeed, many of the untranslated

texts feature the heroic Fionn and his men in pursuit of wild boar, rescuing maidens and their mothers, performing in contests of strength and skill, many of which are distinguished one from the other only by specific topographical references, "The Chase of Slievenamon," for example. The most significant appearance of the heroic Fionn in English literature is, of course, in James Macpherson's *Poems of Ossian*, based on rearranged Highland Gaelic ballad collections, elements of which are cognate with Irish ballads. Along with Macpherson came a half-dozen or so imitators, James Clark, the McCallum brothers, and others. Portrayals of the heroic Fionn also appear in the translations of such early and reputable scholars as Charlotte Brooke, notably the "Lay of Moira Borb" in her *Reliques of Irish Poetry* (1789). And allusions to the heroic Fionn are common in the writings of English authors from Sir Walter Scott (in *Waverley* and *The Antiquary*), and Thomas Moore, down to Padraic Colum. But as might be expected with the declining interest in heroic literature (Seán O'Faoláin speaks of a vanishing hero), most of the heroic depictions of Fionn mac Cumhaill in the past one hundred years have been found in juvenile literature. Surprisingly there are some specific omissions: there was no literature about Fionn produced by the Fenian movement, c. 1860–1900, despite the allusion in its naming.

Fionn the Defender of His Land and People

The most celebrated of Fionn's heroic roles in Irish literature is as a defender of Ireland. As Reidar Christiansen has shown in *The Vikings and the Viking Wars in Irish and Gaelic Tradition* (1931), there is an immense body of ballad literature based on historical predecents in which Fionn is portrayed doing battle with the savage Norsemen, or Lochlanns, as they are known in Irish, the men from beyond the sea. Norse influence in Ireland is the subject of a large chapter in every history of the island, and Norse influence infuses the culture of Gaelic Scotland at every level. Most informed commentators today agree that Fenian narratives predate the Norse invasions of the eighth century and after. One of the evidences for this is the Irish word for Scandinavians, *Lochlann*, cognate with the Welsh *Llychlyn*, was previously used for any invader, real or imagined, from beyond the Celtic world. Further, there is no longer much interest in the notion proposed by some German commentators, notably Heinrich Zimmer, that Fionn's characterization was borrowed from Norse invaders. The suggestion would not be worth commentary if James Joyce had not heard a précis of it from Zimmer's son in the early twenties and subsequently included Norse ancestry in the makeup of his Fionn archetype in *Finnegans Wake*.

Fenian stories in oral tradition, though dominated by Norse invaders when the stories are told in Ossianic frame, include a number of imaginative and allusive alternate invaders. For example, in a story called "The Chase of Glennasmol," Ireland is invaded by another Amazonian princess of Greece, armed wit a repertory of tricks, including the Circe-like power of lulling the Fenians to sleep— after which she destroys a hundred of them. One of the best known manuscript tales which portrays Fionn as a heroic defender of Ireland is *Cath Fionntrágha*, "The Battle of the White Strand" (also called "The Battle of Ventry," using the contemporary place name on the Dingle Peninsula in County Kerry that appears to be a corruption of *Fionntrágha*). This narrative, one of the longest and most tedious in the cycle, appears to be an Irish instance of the international tale of the "everlasting fight" (Aarne-Thompson 2300, motif 211). In it Dara Donn, variously identified as the Holy Roman Emperor, Charlemagne, or the king of Norway, invades Ireland. Fionn leads the defenders at the "White Strand," Ventry Harbor in Kerry, and the battle rages on interminably amid much slaughter. For some reason not apparent in printed texts of the story, the battle at Ventry Harbor seized hold of the imagination of the peasant storyteller and would not let go. Perhaps the *Cath Fionntrágha* was an invitation to lively histrionics on the part of the storyteller.

Fionn the repeller of invasions has not translated well into English; perhaps because the hero's character is so static in many of these tales, or perhaps because writers in English do not find the defense of Ireland quite so compelling. James Macpherson includes several episodes of Fingal (Fionn) doing battle with Lochlanns in the *Poems of Ossian*, but of course the country defended is Scotland, as seen through a Tory perception.

The Bruidhean Tales

The warrior Fionn is much more vincible when pitted against the supernatural powers of druids, magicians, and the like. After his initial establishment of power in the slaying of the Aillén, Fionn is successful in defeating supernatural power in only a handful of stories, notably the early manuscript tale from "The Book of the Dun Cow," usually known as "Finn and the Phantoms" (310, 1886). In this it takes Fionn and the Fianna an entire night to destroy an old hag with three heads on one thin neck, her husband with no head and an eye in the middle of his breast, and their equally charmless brood of nine children. In a whole series of tales, from both manuscript and oral tradition, Fionn is trapped in a magical dwelling and cannot get out without help. Following the conventions of those twelfth-century professional poets, the *filidh*, the stories of Fionn's entrapment always include with the same word, *bruidhean, bruidne*, etc., which cannot be precisely translated into English. The best approximations appear to be "palace," "hostel," or "dwelling" with Oz-like overtones of "enchanted" or "magical." Anne Ross has suggested that the *bruidhean* tales evoke the ancient Celtic mode of human sacrifice in which the victim is put inside a wicker container that is then set afire.

The most representative *bruidhean* tale is probably *Bruidhean Chaorthainn*, "The Hostel (or Palace, etc.) of the Quicken Trees," which Geoffrey Keating cited as long ago as 1633 to be typical of the "unhistorical" Fenian tales (195, 1908, II, p. 326). Midac, the son of the villainous Colga of Lochlann, was a boy whom the Fianna had raised as one of their own after they had found him during the defeat of the invader. Upon reaching manhood Midac left the hospitality of the Hill of Allen and took up residence at his "hostel" or "palace" on the Shannon, a gift from the Fianna. Midac invites Fionn and his men to a banquet, only to lure them into the trap of his enchanted dwelling; once inside the men find that they are fixed to their chairs and cannot cry for help from a window or raise themselves so much as one inch. Midac, it turns out, wants to contain Fionn while he conquers Ireland with the help of his grotesquely fantastic friends, Sinsar of the Battles, Borba the Haughty, etc. Fionn's children and grandchildren, some of them too young to attend the banquet, save the day, and slaughter the enemy as they ford a river; later, they pull their *paterfamilias* and the Fianna from their chairs, unharmed.

The *bruidhean* theme is found in texts as early as the tenth century and has been popular in both manuscript and oral traditions. Some of the better known manuscript tales are *Bruidhean Eochaid Bhig Dheirg*, "The Palace of Little Red Eocha," and *Bruidhean Cheis Choriann*, "The Enchanted Cave of Kesh Corran," this latter being among the most popular of all Irish prose romances of the late

medieval period. Kesh Corran, incidentally, is the best known hide-
way of Diarmaid and Gráinne. On the contemporary map it refers
to a cave about fifteen miles south of the town of Sligo, but in
earlier times, it may have referred to all of County Sligo.

The popularity of the *bruidhean* has never found a counterpart
among English writers. To be sure there are a fair number of translations, and at least a few of the collections of Irish traditional
narratives include a *bruidhean* tale; the juvenile collections of Fenian
tales, by Ella Young, and others, include at least one such tale, and
there is one *bruidhean* story in Charlotte Brooke's *Reliques*, but that
is the extent of it. The encumbered Fionn is not a part of English
literature of the past one hundred years either as a pathetic, comic,
or absurd figure.

Céadach and Other Helper Tales

Just as Arthur virtually disappears in a number of later Arthurian
romances, especially those which center on the exploits of Lancelot,
so too Fionn is peripheral to the action in a large body of tales found
mostly in oral tradition which concerns various helpers of the Fianna.
The most numerous of these concern a supernaturally gifted but
benevolent helper, or *giolla*, usually named Céadach. Murphy summarizes and coordinates twenty-five of these in an appendix to
Duanaire Finn III (pp. 177–88) and Bruford states that Cáedach tales
present the most popular of any theme in all of Irish folk tradition
and cites 128 versions from Irish and Highland sources (329, 1969,
123–27).

In the tales where the helper named Céadach is actually an
aid to the Fenians, his conventional task is to help defeat a magical
or giant opponent who puts his arm down a chimney; Céadach cuts
off the arm. This episode is, apparently at least, an analogue of the
fight between Grendel and Beowulf, and may be, as the eminent
Swedish folklorist, C. W. vonSydow, has argued, the source for it
(298, 1953, 183).

More pertinent to our immediate interests are the other tales
in which the Fianna is abused by the helper, such as *Tóraidheacht
an Ghiolla Dheacair* (which may be translated as "The Pursuit of the
Hard Gilly" or "The Difficult Servant"), and *Bodach an Chóta Lachtna*,
"The Churl in the Gray Coat," both of which are found in seventeenth-century manuscript redactions and numerous oral variants. In

the former an irritable and impudent servant coaxes the Fenians (but not Fionn) to sit on the swayed back of his enchanted roan and then runs off with them to the land beneath the waves. The Irish heroes are not only overpowered but also appear a bit absurd; in one Kerry variant they all pile on the back of the old horse and break it with their weight (324, 1969, 111). The "Churl in the Gray Coat" is the sea god, Manannán mac Lir, in disguise; he takes up the challenge of "Ironbones," son of the prince of Thessaly to run a race when the Fenians cannot muster a man. To the chagrin of the heroes, the churl makes no effort to run very fast, and instead sits down to eat blackberries, but nevertheless wins the race handily.

Despite their great popularity in Irish, the helper tales are uncommon in English. Lady Gregory and her imitators include the stories as threads in the whole Fenian fabric, and the "Hard Gilly" story is in at least two dozen collections of Irish folk tales, but other than James Clarence Mangan's early (1840) adaptation of "The Churl in the Gray Coat" there has been no individual English-language interest in this series of episodes. English interest seems to focus on Fionn and Oisín, their rise, which we have just considered briefly, and even more their fall.

The Fenians in Disgrace

In a passage cited above, Marie-Louise Sjoestedt described how the historical fianna of Ireland lived on hunting and plunder. In time, it would appear, their demands on the non-military population became onerous. Not only did the warriors have to be fed, clothed and housed, but they demanded the first option on all virgins in the community before they could be given in marriage. Perhaps for these barely substantial historical reasons, or perhaps because of a cloyed taste for the heroic, Irish storytellers also include in their repertory a considerable number of tales in which Fionn mac Cumhaill and the Fianna Éireann are pictured as something other than admirable. This non-heroic literature is in two modes; in some the Fenians, and Fionn especially, appear to be vicious, despicable brutes who degenerate their heroic ideal in pointless violence leading to their destruction in The Battle of Gabhra or Gowra, recorded by the annalists as having occurred in A.D. 283. In a second mode Fionn, only rarely with an accomplic or two, is made to appear just the

opposite of what he is in the heroic literature; in this second mode
he is cowardly and clumsy, but still something of a trickster.

Of the two non-heroic modes, the picture of Fionn mac Cumhaill
as villain is less common in both Irish and English. The most
important manuscript tale which portrays Fionn as a cruel rowdy is
probably the *Bóramha*, "Boromian Tribute," although Fionn is not
the only heavy in the piece (143, 1892, II, pp. 404–406). In oral
tradition, perhaps because of the lesser refinements of audiences for
the tales or perhaps because of the oral convention which frequently
portrays Fionn as a giant, we find a crude and cruel Fionn more
frequently.

The abused and comic Fionn is quite another matter indeed.
As seen in the *bruidhean* and helper stories, the leader of the Fenians
has a vulnerability to *contretemps*. The earliest reference to a comic
Fionn is in an eighth-century manuscript where the hero is attacked
by his son Oisín (141, 1910, 22–27). David Krause has speculated
in an insightful essay that a considerable body of literature has been
lost, in which Oisín has focused his Oedipal anxieties in order to
torment his father into a kind of farcial Laius. Such stories most
probably were suppressed by clerical scribes (313, 1966). Be that as
it may, in the literature which survives the comic and anti-heroic
Fionn seems disproportionately a part of oral tradition, so much so
that some scholars would identify that characterization with peasant
humor. Whether the comic Fionn is as old as the eighth century, as
Krause suggests, or only the creation of culturally dispossessed peas-
ants after the Flight of the Earls in the seventeenth century, the
comic Fionn is well established in English literature from the writing
of William Carleton as early as the 1830s to our own time, in Flann
O'Brien's *At Swim-Two-Birds* and Joyce's *Finnegans Wake*, both in
1939.

The Pursuit of Diarmaid and Gráinue

Of all the tales in the Fenian canon, the one with the greatest
critical reputation is also the one which bears the closest analogies
to international medieval romance narratives: *Tóruigheacht Dhiarmada
agus Ghráinne*, "The Pursuit of Diarmaid and Gráinne." Not surprisingly, it has been adapted in English more often than other
Fenian narrative, as a play, novel, narrative poem, and opera libretto.
So much attention has been devoted to it that it almost deserves to
be considered as a cycle by itself, especially as Fionn's role is nearly

always supportive to the main characters, the lovers. In all but one or two versions Fionn is cast as a most unattractive, vengeful, jealous cuckold.

Gráinne is the coquettish young dauther of Cormac mac Airt, the high king at Tara. For the convenience of her father she has been detrothed, and in some versions actually married to the now aging Fionn mac Cumhaill, who, when all of the texts are coordinated, has had something like thirty wives. The action begins when the Fianna Éireann is invited to Tara for a wedding feast and Gráinne for the first time sees Diarmaid, a favorite of the band and a surrogate son to its leader. Diarmaid is not only a handsome physical specimen but he is endowed with a magical "love spot," *ball seirce*, which makes him—literally—absolutely irresistible to women. Gráinne is immediately taken with him and although Diarmaid does not reciprocate, the two lovers flee from Tara and spend as many as the next twenty years travelling all of Ireland; Scottish variants, understandably, extend the itinerary to Scottish locales. Fionn and his men eventually find the lovers, usually in northwestern Ireland, often at Kesh Corran, and the disappointed old bridegroom entices the young warrior to join his old comrades in a boar hunt. The reforged bond between the men is short-lived when Diarmaid is injured by the boar and Fionn desists from a chance to save him.

The exact parallels with the stories of Naoise and Deirdre in the Ulster Cycle and Tristan and Iseult in European literature need hardly be mentioned except to say that the differences, such as Diarmaid's hesitance as a lover, are ultimately more interesting than the parallels.

Nessa Ní Shéaghdha has shown in the introduction to the best contemporary edition of a manuscript text that part of the uniqueness of the tale is that it incorporates and extrapolates from earlier Fenian narratives, some dating from the tenth century (162, 1967). The manuscript scenario of the tale, summarized above, apparently took form in the seventeenth century, but folk variants continued to appear until the twentieth century.

As I have said, "The Pursuit of Diarmaid and Gráinne," has been adapted in English more often than any other Fenian tale; further, the adapters have included such distinguished figures as W. B. Yeats with George Moore, Lady Gregory, Sir Samuel Ferguson, the ninth Duke of Argyll, and Austin Clarke, as well as a dozen lesser-known figures. The continued interest in the tale from writers in the different genre in both Irish and English is probably more indicative of the intrinsic merits of the narrative than of a public hunger for a villainous portrayal of the national hero of Ireland.

The Battle of Gabhra

Fionn and his men are recorded as having overcome many enemies and obstacles, animals, other Irish warriors, Lochlanners and other invaders, and when acting in unison, even supernatural powers. But the literature is divided on their success in the greatest of all heroic labors, the conquering of death. Many Irish storytellers never acknowledge that Fionn ever aged past maturity, much less died. For example, in the early modern manuscript tale, *Bruidhean beg na hAlmhaine*, "The Little Brawl at Allen" (143, 1892, II, pp. 382), Fionn performs feats of valor alongside his great grandsons Eachtach and Illan. In an oral tale of uncertain date, "The Chase of Slieve Guillean," Fionn is transformed into an atrophied old man by a jealous member of a trio of weird sisters reminiscent of *Macbeth* (25, 1904, 242–44). Later, with the help of the Fianna and another of the sisters, Fionn is restored; if he cannot quite conquer death he can muster the power to resist it.

Yet the annalists record a date for his death, and at least two stories depict the end of Fionn mac Cumhaill and the Fianna. In an article (396, 1897) that Kuno Meyer devoted to this subject we find that one version has Fionn decapitated (a significant mode of execution among the Celts from earliest times, as Roman writers observed) by Aiclech mac Dubdrenn at a battle named Áth Brea on the banks of the Boyne; this is first found in a tenth-century text by the poet Cinaed húa Hartacain and repeated by Tigernach (d. 1088) and subsequently by the "Four Masters" in the seventeenth century. This version is known to romance in at least one manuscript text, *Aided Finn*, "The Violent Death of Finn" (143, 1892, II, pp. 96–99) and three fragments. But the far better known version in romance literature is given in the text of *Cath Gabhra*, "The Battle of Gabhra (Gowra)" (144, 1853). Here the end of the Fenians is presented more dramatically. Along with the retreat from their heroic ideals which we suggested above, the Fenians begin to squabble among themselves; specifically, the Leinster Fianna revives the memory of wrongs it had suffered from the Clan Morna of Connacht at the Battle of Cnucha when Cumhal was killed. The reigning high king at Tara, Cairbre of the Liffey, resolves that he would rather die in ridding the country of the Fianna Éireann than try to rule an Ireland blighted by their immorality. Cairbre provokes the final conflict by killing Fionn's servant Ferdia, obliging Fionn to declare war. In the battle which ensues at Gabhra (Gowra, or on modern maps, Garristown in north-west County Dublin), the bloodbath is enough to rival that of the poorer Elizabethan horror dramas. The Fianna Éireann splits when Fer-tai of the Clan Morna falls in with Cairbre and fights his former comrades. Both sides use swords and spears, and the most common deaths are decapitations. Oscar, conventionally the most innocent of the Fenians, runs Cairbre through with his spear, and subsequently is killed by Cairbre's household guard within view of his grandfather. Fionn himself, although drawing blood on all sides with either hand, did not initially distinguish himself; he fulfills Cairbre's vision of him when he beheads the young son of Fer-tai, Fer-li, who stands alone against the host. One by one the Fenians fall, all except Oisín, who is not described at all, and Caoilte, the swiftest of runners, until Fionn stands alone. When the five sons of Urgriu come upon him with spears drawn Fionn knows he is defenseless and lets his aegis and shield drop to his feet, standing straight and unmoving as a pillar. Thus in death Fionn receives five wounds, not only like Christ but in keeping with conventions of Continental romance.

Although this version of Fionn's death is the best known in the early romances, it is by no means widely known or acknowledged across the body of the Fenian Cycle in Irish literature. Oral storytellers for the most part do not remember any tale in which Fionn is killed. Their view seems to be either (a) that he never engaged Cairbre in a final battle, or (b) he was wounded in an unnamed battle and now waits, "sleeping," at some specific spot, any of several caves all over Ireland and Gaelic Scotland, until he is again needed in the defense of his country. The reluctance of oral storytellers to speak of Fionn's death does not necessarily indicate a finicky unwillingness to deal with the distasteful, especially considering the buffoonish humor such tellers used to portray the anti-heroic Fionn. Instead, it seems more likely that folk tradition was presented with a dilemma by the Christian environment of Ireland, as seen in stories in the Ossianic frame. The reward of the unbaptized hero would be damnation. Yet even without the obstacle of revealed religion, storytellers seem to have difficulty in conceiving an end for Fionn and the Fianna. As Anton van Hamel points out, this is one of the distinctions between the Fenian and earlier cycles: "to Fionn and his warriors eternal bliss is unattainable" (356, 1935, 13).

Other than as a late chapter in Lady Gregory's work and that of some of her imitators, the story of Fionn's violent death in battle is unknown in English. Indeed, English writing knows of a different version of Fionn's death not found in Irish. Meredith Hanmer (1543–1604) records in his *Chronicle of Ireland* that Fionn died at an advanced age as a begger in great poverty.[3] The greatest significance of Fionn's death to English literature is, of course, that one alluded to by Joyce in *Finnegans Wake;* this is a little known oral variant on the "sleeping warriors" myth which would place Fionn's head under Howth, his body under Dublin proper, and his feet stretching all the way to Chapelizod.

Oisín in the Land of Youth

Explanations of why Oisín did not stand with his father and comrades in their annihilation are varied. The best known today is that he was seduced by a beautiful fairy woman, Niamh of the Golden Hair, who leads him to the Tír na nÓg, "Land of Youth." Although voyages to the Land of Youth or the Ever-Young are common in Celtic literature, just what happens to the fortunate who go there is not always clear, as David Spaan's dissertation has shown (604, 1970). The only known Irish text which treats with the narrative comes from an identifiable poet, Micheál Coimín (1676–1760), *Laoi Oisín i dTír na nÓg,* "The Lay of Oisín in the Land of Youth,"[4] which may mean that details have been individualized from a tradition we have lost. Coimín (anglice: "Comyn" or "Cummings") is airily unspecific about both Niamh and Tír na nÓg; apparently Oisín enjoys no sexual or other gustatory pleasures in the paradise of youth. For these or other reasons, Oisín grows bored after three hundred years and longs to return to the land of mortals. The Ireland he finds upon his return is domesticated and inhabited throughout by small men who bow to the authority of Saint Patrick and his bishops. As soon as Oisín, now a comparative giant, touches the earth when he tries to help some puny mortals lift a boulder, he is transformed to his actual age, thus appearing to be a semi-fossilized remnant of the past when he finally meets Patrick.

As Coimín's text is unique there is room for speculation that his narrative is the product of his own genius, especially as the name of Niamh is not associated with Oisín elsewhere in the cycle. Nevertheless, the episode of Oisín's survival to later times is extremely common in both manuscript and oral tradition. A completely loveless counterpart to Coimín's lay can be found in the oral narrative, *Fear ma dheiradh na Féinne,* "The Last of the Feni; or the Man Who Went to the Land of Youth" (261, 1908). Whatever his entanglement with Niamh, the Oisín who survives from a lost heroic time to compose nostalgic poetry in the glamourless present has several counterparts elsewhere in Celtic literature. Llywarch Hên, a sixth-century Welsh poet, laments the ruin of the great halls of Cyndylan and Urien. Likewise, Myrddin, a possible ancestor of the Merlin of the Arthurian legends, is credited with poems celebrating the heroic past of Wales, often championing pagan ideals against Christian.

In any case, Fionn's role is completely subsidiary to Oisín's in this segment of the scenario. We see him in Coimín's text as a benign, not an abused father, an embodiment of all that the younger hero has lost in time. This flattering picture of the older Fionn is not as important for Irish literature as it is for English, as W. B. Yeats's "Wanderings of Oisin" (1889), based on early translations of Coimín, has established the picture of an authoritative, refined, and pagan Fionn which may supersede that of any other in the minds of those readers who know Irish mythology only from its use in English poetry.

The Colloquy of the Elders

The Elders of the *Agallamh na Senórach,* the only text in the cycle which might be called epic in breadth and length, are Oisín and Patrick.[5] As mentioned often before, an elderly Oisín tells Saint Patrick of the adventures of the Fenians in pre-Christian times in the early manuscript, and further, this frame serves in oral tradition for the retelling of hundreds of different narratives. As these narratives in fact recapitulate many of the portrayals of Fionn mentioned in the previous pages, there are no new roles for him to play here. David Krause, in his essay, "The Hidden Oisin" (373, 15), feels that Oisín in the *Agallamh* has inherited a pugnacity from his disputes with his father. Thus when Saint Patrick affirms his patriarchal prohibitions he simultaneously assumes the role of a surrogate father and becomes an analogue for Fionn. This does not mean that we have even the beginnings of evidence that Fionn is actually identifiable with Saint Patrick, although it is worth mentioning that Oisín frequently remarks that his father had predicted the saint's coming;

further, both Irish and Scottish commentators have remarked on the confusion of Fionn and Saint Patrick in the folk traditions of their countries (626, 1902, 163; 392, 1929, 156–86). Except in the mind of Joyce writing *Finnegans Wake*, the association of Fionn with Saint Patrick is probably not worth pursuing.

Perhaps because of the relatively great size of the text of the *Agallamh* or because of the popularity of the Ossianic frame in folk tradition, the scenario of the "Colloquy of the Elders" has had a separate tradition in English literature, almost independent from the rest of the cycle. Macpherson's *Poems of Ossian*, to name but one example, are named for Oisín because their "translator" perceived them to have been composed by their persona. During the heyday of the Irish Renaissance, 1890–1920, at least two dozen poems appeared in periodicals with names such as "Oisín and Saint Patrick." An American poet, Mary Grant O'Sheridan, produced an entire volume of verse in 1922, *Lays and Ranns from the Folk-Lore of the Gael*, which is in fact an unstructured and highly interpretive "recension" of the translation by S. H. O'Grady. Darrell Figgis, one of the more secular writers of revolutionary Ireland, produced a novel based on the *Agallamh* in 1923 entitled *The Return of the Hero*, in which Saint Patrick becomes an anti-clerical effigy (23). But quite apart from translations, adaptations, or Irish tradition, Oisín, alias Ossian, is one of the most widely distributed figures of Western literature, certainly in excess of any other character of Irish origin. Even in American poetry he can be found as far afield as in the poetry of Robinson Jeffers, who published a poem entitled "Ossian's Grave" in 1933.

FIONN MAC CUMHAILL IN SUMMARY: A PARADOX

When confronted with the unfolding of heroic character in Irish tradition, Standish James O'Grady, nephew of the great translator, wrote in 1878 that "Heroes expand into giants, and dwindle into goblins, or fling aside the heroic form and gambol as buffoons" (422, 28). He was speaking of Fionn in particular, but he could have intended any of a number of figures in European tradition. What makes Fionn more distinctive is that the different parts of his character exist simultaneously in tradition. Perhaps because of his broad social appeal or perhaps because he was never ossified in one perfected romance which superseded all others, Fionn has remained alive in tradition, far in excess of any other Irish traditional figure. Because he remained alive in tradition, unlike Cúchulainn or even Arthur, there was never any need to revive him. He was both contemporary, familiar, and perhaps less than heroic, as well as ancient, revered and patriarchal. In contrasting Fionn with Cúchulainn, Padraic Colum wrote, "He is a folk-hero, crafty as well as brave, vindictive as well as generous" (18, 1943, 194). He is, in short, neither a contradiction nor only an accumulation of discontinuous personalities but rather a paradox. What is to be made of this?

To begin with we must look more deeply into the several competing theories which may help to explain the origin and progress of the Fenian Cycle. Thus far we have considered only a thin outline of events. Part of the continued popularity of Fionn mac Cumhaill in Irish tradition, as well as his frequent adoption by English writers, may be due to the language of myth in the different narratives which reaches into the unconscious of many sensitive individuals with the ordering of a popular literature.

2

The Dimensions
of the Myth of Fionn

ll myth is protean. Poets, however humble, give form to it. Forms often speak to us more clearly than do the myths themselves. That is why any myth when extracted from its literary form and measured only by means surviving artifacts seems equivocal or cryptic. The myth of Oedipus, for example, does not necessarily seem tragic when it is seen in Apollodorus, Hesiod, or Hyginus. In these non-dramatic sources it can be seen as a fragment from a local mystery religion or a lost chapter of Theban political history. Yet today we can have only a limited discussion of the myth of Oedipus apart from the form given it by Sophocles, who wrote in a neighboring province as many as seven or eight hundred years after the original narrative was composed. Most readers today would begin with Sophocles and look to earlier writers such as Hesiod only as a means for explication. As with Oedipus so with Fionn. Much of the last chapter was given over to the early literary records of Fionn in the Irish language. Subsequent chapters will examine the forms in which Fionn has been represented in the English language. The focus of this chapter is on the dimensions of the myth of Fionn as separated from specific renderings of it.

The antiquity and extensiveness of stories about Fionn invite some questions in any reader's mind. Couldn't there be a grain of historicity in all the storymaking? The belief that Fionn was an historical person persists in the popular imagination and has been entertained by at least a few learned commentators although the evidence for such a view is slight. Another common perception is that Fionn appears to resemble a number of other European heroes. The numerous parallels are hardly a coincidence, but it is no easy matter determining if Fionn was borrowed from them or they from him. Even the parallels with other Irish heroes, such as Cúchulainn and Lugh, are a puzzle, especially as the cycles of the heroes remain discrete in Irish tradition.

In his painstaking analysis of the ballads of the Fenian Cycle, the great Norwegian folklorist, Reidar Christiansen, remarked: "No attempt is made [in this study] to solve the problem of the origin of the cycle itself. There are several theories, but I do not believe any satisfactory answer can be given as to where, when, and why these countless tales gathered around Fionn mac Cumhaill" (334, 1931, 1). Christiansen spoke more than fifty years ago, and since his time several voices have been heard on the question of the origin of the Fenian Cycle, but they do not yet constitute a critical orthodoxy. As the dean of Irish studies in America, John V. Kelleher of Harvard University, has noted in several of his unpublished addresses, "There is no established body of critical literature in Celtic mythology; each student must begin at the beginning" (370, 1973).

Given these two admonitions, the student of Celtic tradition may be forgiven his measure of chagrin for so much as entertaining the question of the origin of Fionn mac Cumhaill and the Fenian Cycle. Yet it is not a question which can be dismissed. First, as Fionn is a traditional, a mythological figure, the surviving written record of him is only a thin shard of the greater whole of his reputation. Several critics have commented that part of our difficulty in reading older texts of Fenian narratives lies in the fact that their audience was presumed to know the details of the milieu in which they occurred and the conventional roles assigned different characters. For this reason we distort the myth of Fionn if we consider only the narratives of the hero and the literature, in either Irish or English, which repeat, adapt, or parody loosely formed oral narratives. A second, perhaps less worthy reason for considering the origin and development of the myth of Fionn is that so much of the critical material about Fenian matters is devoted to speculation about the origin of the cycle. Indeed, in the century and a quarter following the Macpherson forgeries, the search for an explanation of Fionn (or "Fingal") and Oisín (or "Ossian") was an obsession of Celtic scholarship.

Although the question of origins was an engaging one for a series of nonliterary reasons, some agreement on the provenience of the tales was necessary for the more lucubratious task of explicating the narratives in literary contexts. The question of Fionn's origin, whatever its implications for the ethnic rivalries of the Irish and Scots, was key in determining whether or not the narratives could be understood as myth, legend, folklore, or history. Put in blunter terms the question of Fionn's origin helps us to know if the Irish literature surrounding him is so much blarney about the pretensions of the past, or, as we hope to show, variations on a myth in literature, a subject for study comparable with the myth of Odysseus, Siegfried, Cupid and Psyche, Pyramus and Thisbe, or King Oedipus.

THEORIES OF THE ORIGIN OF THE FENIAN NARRATIVES

Although the review of the mare's nests and amphigouri conjured to explain Fionn's existence makes for some of the most delightful background reading to be found in this study, there is no need to indulge ourselves in considering too much of it here. Not only would such a review be much too vast for our space, but the subject has been adequately covered already, first by Alexander MacBain in "Who were the Féinn?" (379, 1894), and more recently, by T. F. O'Rahilly (431, 1946), and Gerard Murphy (404, 1953).

Of all the interpretations that scholars had to work to dislodge, the most tenaciously held, although insurrportable, is that common one assumed by many readers first encountering narratives of the hero—that Fionn mac Cumhaill was an historical personage.

Geoffrey Keating, the Herodotus of Irish historiography, working in the early seventeenth century, writes as though he believes that Fionn was historical, although he cautions the reader to reject fanciful and exaggerated stories about the hero, especially those from oral tradition. Eugene O'Curry, the first Irish textual scholar of manuscript materials, writing in 1855, holds almost identical views about the validity of Fionn's historicity (571, 1861, 303). Similarly, many of O'Curry's contemporaries in the first generation of Celtic scholarship also believed that Fionn was historical; John O'Donovan, editor of the *Annals of the Four Masters*, wrote, "I have always believed that Fionn mac Cumhaill was *a real historical personage* [italics his] and not a myth or a god of war . . ." (188, 1859, 285). W. M. Hennessy, editor of several important Fenian texts, accepted the popular opinion that "a person named Find [sic] MacCumhaill did live" but modified his position somewhat, perhaps under the influence of the then-dominant myth scholar, Max Müller, by asserting that "his history has degenerated into pure myth" (158, 1873, 87). Heinrich Zimmer went so far as to suggest that Fionn was based on an historical person who could be named, a Norseman who had settled in Munster, Caittil Find (d. 856). His agnomen "Find," while identical with one variant spelling of "Fionn," is derived from the Old Norse *Fiandr:* "enemy" (461, 1891).

Given the currents of scholarship in Greek and world mythology, the findings of Sir James Frazer, Andrew Lang, Bronislaw Malinowski, and others, it was never felt necessary for anyone to mount an argument to dissolve the notion that Fionn was historical. The numerous inconsistencies in the narratives, the complete scramble of chronology and the definite parallels with general European and world mythology were enough to confirm the suspicions of earlier skeptics by the end of the nineteenth century. Writing as early as 1881, Alfred Nutt was able to establish that many of the narratives of Fionn, especially "The Boyhood Deeds" fit the patterns outlined by J. G. von Hahn with his Aryan expulsion and return formula, in one of the first works in the new study of comparative mythology.

Of the sixteen-point outline for the career of the hero which von Hahn proposed, Nutt demonstrated that different retellings of the Fenian narratives would accommodate seven (410, 1881, 1–47). After presenting his arguments, Nutt could dismiss the likes of W. M. Hennessy in an aside, "So far from his [Fionn's] history having degenerated into a myth, his myth has been rationalized into history" (39). But the most important early study of the religious and ritualistic foundations of Celtic myth in general was Sir John Rhys's *Celtic Heathendom* (593, 1886), a non-polemical monument of recondite information, dispassionately edited and assembled. As the first professor of Celtic studies at Oxford, Rhys (1840–1915) helped take the study of Welsh and Irish traditions out of the hands of eccentrics. Rhys showed that the oldest Celtic traditions derived from the native or "heathen" religion and the figures of Old Irish romance were derived from gods whose worship was repressed by Christianity, an observation that made a profound impression on the young William Butler Yeats. Since the advent of Rhys and Frazer, the question of an historical foundation for the narrative of Fionn has not been seriously entertained by professional scholars, although as mentioned in chapter 1, the notion continues to appear in print. If some document or artifact should be recovered which irrevocably confirmed Fionn's vital dates in the third century, or even in the fourth, fifth, or sixth, this otherwise startling disclosure would be irrelevant in explicating Fenian literature, which underwent continuous development from the eighth to the nineteenth centuries, just as the establishment of Arthur's historicity in the sixth century would do little to aid our understanding of Arthurian prose romances, c. 1170–1470.

The rereading of world mythology that began concurrently with the publication of Sir James Frazer's *The Golden Bough* (1890–1915) extended to Celtic traditions. Frazer was the best-known of a generation of theorists, including Bronislaw Malinowski as well as the "Cambridge School" of Jane Ellen Harrison, Jessie Weston, and Francis M. Cornford, whose work linked mythology to ritual and ritual to religion. Though their work has long been subject to revisionist exception, Frazer and his contemporaries encouraged the readers of all world mythologies to look for religious roots for many heroes and heroic narratives. Within Celtic studies the first suggestion that the heroes of Old Irish and Old Welsh narratives might be divine came as early as Rhys's *Celtic Heathendom*. The most influential commentator to argue for the divine origin of Fionn is T. F. O'Rahilly in *Early Irish History and Mythology* (1946), as cited in the last chapter. To repeat, O'Rahilly felt that Fionn, Lugh, and Cúchulainn were all based on the same divine hero and that they were discrete literary characters only because their stories were told in separate cycles. The key episode that both indicates a divine origin and links them together is that all three do battle with and slay a monstrous one-eyed destroyer. In the case of Fionn, it is the Burner of Tara. Lugh kills the terrible Balor in *Cath Maige Tuired*, "The (Second) Battle of Mag Tuired," and Cúchulainn kills Goll mac Carbada.

The question of the fianna, taken separately from Fionn or the Fenian Cycle, is much easier to address. Freelance bands of roving warrior-hunters have been recorded in Celtic societies since ancient times. The Greek historian Polybius described Gaulish warriors known as *gaesatae* at the Battle of Clastidium (222 B.C.), who came from north of the Alps to aid tribes already settled in Italy. Because they were not a part of the peoples they defended, Polybius glossed their name as "mercenaries." A more likely translation is "spearmen"; cf. Old Irish *gae:* spear, javelin; Scottish Gaelic *gath;* Modern Welsh *gwayw.* The economies and social structures of Gaul and ancient and medieval Ireland may not have been identical, but for various reasons bands of landless warrior-hunters, known as *fiann* (Old Irish *fían*), plural *fianna* (Old Irish *fíana*), continued to exist in Ireland over the centuries, as many records testify. Much of the evidence indicates they were not mercenaries nor were they held in contempt. Further, their recognition in the Brehon Laws implies they were not a subject group nor were they foreigners.

Returning to the literature itself, two commentators, Eoin MacNeill and Gerard Murphy, have profferred explanations for the original of the Fenian Cycle itself. Of these MacNeill is probably the better known, in part because he was an active Irish patriot in the years 1916–22, and was once a political rival of Eamon de Valera. His thesis is found in the introduction at an edition of *Duanaire Finn* (291, 1908), the seventeenth-century text from the oral tradition which he began to edit after 1900 but later had to abandon. Gerard Murphy, a generation younger, completed the work of editing the manuscript and placed MacNeill's explanation in the introduction to the third volume forty-five years later in 1953.

MacNeill was impressed that references to the Fenian Cycle are scanty in such great Irish codexes as the *Lebor Na Huidre,* "The Book of the Dun Cow" and *Lebor Laighneach,* "The Book of Leinster", although he knew from chronicle that the stories were known in earlier centuries. Further, he knew that successive historical invaders had pressed into service the survivors of earlier cultures. From this he deduced, plausibly enough, that the Fenian narratives had originated among the peoples subjected by the last invaders of Ireland, the Q-Celtic or Gaelic people, who referred to themselves in manuscript as Milesians, after an assumed eponymous founder, Míl Espáne or Miled. He would assign the origin of the cycle to an earlier people known as the Iverni, or in a Latinized form, Ivernians, who are often identified with the Builg or Fir Bolg, a P-Celtic people who once lived in what is today Belgium and were culturally linked with the Britons whom Caesar conquered.

Although MacNeill was not supported by the work of such contemporaries in Celtic scholarship as Kuno Meyer and A. T. Nutt, he had no rival in his work with Fenian manuscripts, and thus his speculations were accepted in a number of influential texts. For example, MacNeill's theory was promoted by Eleanor Hull's *Textbook of Irish Literature* (1906–1908), which was in wide use after independence came, and also by the important Irish medievalist, Edmund

Curtis (or Eamon Curteis), as in his article, "The Age and Origin of the Fenian Tales" (344, 1908).

Gerard Murphy's explanation of the origin of the Fenian Cycle is based in the distinctions between different literary castes in early Ireland, specifically the succession of influence from the elite order known under the general name of *vates* to the humbler bards. A brahminlike professional class of priests, poets, and seers had existed in Celtic civilization from earliest times; indeed, the term *vates* comes from Roman commentators. In Ireland the *vates* were represented by two bodies: the *brehons*, or jurisconsults, and the learned savants, the *filidh* (also *filí*) who, shorn of priestly duties after the introduction of Christianity, were entrusted with the care of national traditions, literature, and scholarship. In literature the term *filís* and *druis* are frequently interchanged, suggesting that the claim to powers of divination persisted among the *filidh* until a late date. In general the *bard*, despite the luster that loanword has acquired in English, appears to be simply a poet and a versifier, somewhat comparable to the *joglar* or *jongleur* in Continental tradition, whereas the *filidh* are more comparable to the *troubador* who composed aristocratic poetry. During much of the history of pre-Christian and pre-Danish Ireland, the two bodies existed side-by-side, with the bards taking a lesser position and the learned *filidh*, whose training lasted twelve years and required the mastery of at least three hundred and fifty tales, taking the more aristocratic. The *filidh* appear to have lost their discipline and subsequently their power during the Norse invasions, but the less rigorous bardic schools survived until the seventeenth century. Secular poetry and prose narrative, indeed, the body of the narratives in the Ulster Cycle, could be traced to the *filidh*, while the Fenian narratives came largely from the lesser literary order, the bards.

Murphy's criticism of MacNeill's theories was judicious and scrupulously polite, acknowledging that it had been "brilliantly presented" and "widely accepted" (pp. 211–12). The older scholar had, nevertheless, misdated a number of texts, had overlooked the importance of folk tradition, and had misunderstood the nature of the fianna. The fianna were not only Gaelic or Q-Celtic Irishmen but they were freemen, not bondsmen, and further, their narratives predated Norse invasions. In demonstrating these statements, Murphy not only disposed of much of the work of MacNeill, as well as the justly maligned Zimmer, but also of another Continental upstart, Anton van Hamel, who, in the Rhys Memorial Lecture at the British Academy in 1934, had argued that the Fenian narratives, like the

Arthurian legends, were in origin "exemplary myths" (his own term) used to instruct timorous Irishmen during the time of invasion (511, 1934).

Murphy also dismisses suggestions one still encounters in print, such as those of David MacRitchie (394, 1889; 393, 1893), that Fionn was a Finn from Finland; or Alfred T. Nutt (413, 1891; 415, 1910, etc.) that the Fenian cycle was only romantic legend; and of George Henderson (358, 1904–06) that the cycle was mythology merged with stories of the historical Caittil Find.

All of this should not suggest that the question of the origin of Fionn or his cycle is settled. As with speculations about the origin of the Arthurian legends, unequivocal evidence is hard to come by. But Schliemann-like quests to "prove" the existence of literary figures has not been a fashion in early Irish archaeology. Somewhere, somebody might be looking for Noah's Ark, but there seems to be little point in rummaging around the Hill of Allen for the spear of Fionn. Instead, the undertakings of our own generation incline toward trying to make sense of the reader's reception of traditional narratives as interpreted in a series of schools: structuralism, deconstruction, semiotics, etc.

Whatever the origin of the cycle itself, the development of the narratives in literature is easier to trace. The oldest narratives are the *laoidh* or lays, a form considered briefly in chapter 1. Although many of the *laoidh* survive only in fragments, they are readily accessible, along with some chronicle accounts and prose narratives, in Kuno Meyer's *Fianaigecht*, (1910) etc. Interest in Fenian material, as Murphy shows, must have been considerable in oral tradition from very early times, and it becomes a more important theme in manuscript tradition in the eleventh century, a demonstrable fact which prompted one writer, J. J. O'Kelly, to argue that Fionn was a creation of the eleventh century (222, 1913, iii). Indeed, the heroic and literary Fionn is very largely the creation of the eleventh century, like his many heroic counterparts in Germanic, French, and Slavic traditions. The greatest work of the Fenian Cycle, the *Agallamh na Senórach*, apparently dates from the twelfth century. The greatest proliferation of texts from the manuscript tradition occurred in the subsequent two centuries, reaching highest volume in the late fifteenth century. Although the evidence for such dating comes from sound and spelling changes and may appear to be controvertible, the evidence from the social and political history of Ireland supports textual evidence. The princely patronage of poets which grew in the generations after the defeat of the Danish (1014) to the invasion of the Norman lords (1170) was redoubled when the invaders were Gaelicized and became more Irish than the Irish temselves. In addition, there seem to be no historical allusions introduced later than the twelfth century. For example, Fionn and his men travel on foot and never use horses. Further, although they fight innumerable Norsemen, some of whom are cognate with verifiable historical figures, they never so much as encounter an Englishman or a Norman. Development in the oral tradition is obviously more difficult to demonstrate but, significantly, the elaborate sophistication of the poems in the *Duanaire Finn*, committed to paper by Irish *émigrés* in the Spanish Netherlands after their defeat in the Elizabethan wars, gives every indication of a rich and developed heritage. Even without the *Duanaire Finn*, we have the evidence of Irish and Scottish Gaelic balladry, in which Fionn is the leading figure; the ballad traditions of most countries originate during the eleventh and twelfth centuries, reaching their apogees during the fifteenth and sixteenth. The most significant contemporary testimony to the popularity of the Fenian Cycle in the sixteenth century comes from a dedicatory letter Bishop Carsewell of Argyll wrote for a prayerbook published in 1567. The good bishop complained that his couontrymen were more interested in listening to the idle tales of Fionn and his heroes than they were in hearing of the Christian God (413, 1891, xi).

In subsequent centuries the myth of Fionn mac Cumhaill was to receive much greater development, both in Irish and Gaelic and, as we shall see, in English. This is to be expected as it parallels the development of other important figures from medieval and renaissance popular literature, King Arthur, Robin Hood, Roland, El Cid, etc. What makes the Irish tradition unique, specifically as it relates to Fionn, is that the narratives have never died out and are alive until this very day, despite successive waves of cultural repression and Anglicization during the Plantations, the Cromwellian wars, penal laws, absentee landlordism, rack-renting, and all the rest of the litany of horrors in the Irish nationalist's indictment of English oppression.

LINGUISTIC AND CULTURAL FOUNDATIONS
OF THE ARCHETYPE OF FIONN MAC CUMHAILL

The name "Fionn," as noted earlier, employs the Irish *fionn*, which means "white" or "fair." The modern Irish form, Fionn mac

Cumhaill, can be traced to the Old Irish *Find mac Umaill*, as Kuno Meyer has demonstrated (397, 1911). Under any form, and there may be more than two dozen, the donation remains constant. Colors are used most infrequently for the naming of men in heroic literature and are more often applied to animals, e.g., Achilles' horse Xanthus, "yellow." Alexander MacBain has speculated that the root of *fionn* may be found in the Celtic noun *vei*, shorter form *vi*, or the verb form *veid* and *vid*, which translate "know" and "to know." The Old Irish verb *finnaim*, "to know," seems more certainly from *veid/vid*. This would give *fionn* the force of "wise" or "learned one," which would suit the character of a seer, poet, and utterer of proverbs (379, 1894, 78).

Writing sixty years after MacBain, Gerard Murphy found the root for *fionn* in the Gaulish *vindos* and *vindonos*, again "white" and "fair." He argues that the evidence of Gaulish placenames indicates that there was a Continental Celtic god whose name began with *Vind-*. There were several *Vindonissas* on the ancient map from which derive the modern Windisch in the Swiss canton of Aargau and the French Vendresse in the Ardennes. There were several *Vindobonas*, two of which the Romans renamed *Augustobona* and *Iuliobona*, but another retained its Celtic form through Roman occupation to become the Austrian Wien, or in English, Vienna (404, 1953, xxxi–xxxiii; 405, 1961, 8). The Continental Vind- could be the ancestor of both the Irish Fionn mac Cumhaill and the Welsh Gwyn ap Nudd. Vind- appears to be identical, as Myles Dillon has shown, summarizing the research of M. Tierney and Máire MacNeill, with the Continental Lugh, commemorated in fewer surviving placenames, *Lughdunum Remorum* (Modern French, Lyons) and *Lugudunum* (Modern French, Laon) (494, 1967, 13). These onomastics give further support to O'Rahilly's assertion that Lugh and Fionn as well as Cúchulainn, have a common ancestor.

Mac Cumhaill or *mac Umaill* is much less ambiguous, as *mac* has meant "son" in Old, Middle, and Modern Irish. As mentioned earlier, *Cumhaill* is the genitive form of *Cumhal*, the name given to a number of figures in Irish tradition. Fionn's father was Cumhal mac Trenmor, the leading figure of the narrative, *Fotha Cath Cnucha*, discussed in chapter 1. Earlier speculations that Cumhal may be associated with Camulos of the Túatha Dé Danann, and, in turn, with the Mars-Camulos of Roman Britain, and further with the Old King Cole of nursery rhyme, seem overly ambitious and unfounded.

"Fingal," the variant from Highland Scottish tradition, is apparently only the name Fionn plus an epithet *na Ghal*, "of valor." The alternative etymology seems less likely, that "Fingal" is somehow a borrowing from *Rí Fionnghall*, "King of the Fair Strangers (or Norse)," a title once borne by the Lord of the Isles. One of the several reasons this is unlikely is that "Fingal" was recorded for "Fionn" from the early fourteenth century, and the lordship of the Isles was created only in 1354 and forfeited to the Scottish Crown in 1493. In any case, Fionn or Fingal has no connection with the Irish place name "Fingal," denoting the plain in County Dublin running north from the River Tolka. The etymology of this name is apparently *fine gall*, or "land of strangers." At one time this "Fingal" could denote the entire English settlement of the Pale, and thus the "Fingallian dialect" was the somewhat debased English spoken by settlers in Ireland. Not surprisingly, Joyce saw a link between Fionn and the placename Fingal while hero-building in *Finnegans Wake*, and at least one commentator (434, 1982) sees Ossianic echoes in Samuel Beckett's story "Fingal" (1934), which is set there.

In any case, Fionn, "The Fair," may be a title rather than an actual name; certainly it is not his name from birth. As common with other heroes, the name is awarded to the figure after a characteristic feat; cf. Heracles, "Glory of Hera," who was first known as Alcaeus or Palaemon, and Cúchulainn, "The Hound of Culann," who was first known as Sétanta. According to the twelfth century *Macgníamhartha Finn*, the hero was first known as Demne Mael, or in later texts, Deimne Maol, and still later in oral tradition variants as Domhnach (from *damnat*: little doe?). Demne Mael had won a victory in a swimming contest, or, as in oral variants, a shinty or field hockey match, and had killed a rival who challenged his winning. Impressed, a spectator cried out, "Who is the fair boy?" *"Có é an giolla fionn?"* Demne Mael's nurse answers for him and tells the others that he is the fair (or white) one, Fionn. As for the epithet Mael, J. F. Nagy has recently shown (407, 1981) that Demne/Fionn's shorn hair indicates his affinity with druids and druidical types such as poets and craftsmen and thus company with those who have close contact with the otherworld.

Of all the theorists of mythology of the late twentieth century, the one whose views have had the most influence on Celtic studies has been Georges Dumézil (1898–). As detailed in dozens of titles beginning in 1924, Dumézil's system is sometimes called the "New

Comparative Mythology" because it draws heavily on different traditions from Indo-European culture, especially Roman, Iranian, and Indian. Dumézil's book most concerned with Celtic culture is *La troisième souverain* (497, 1949), but his ideas have been more widely disseminated in a well-known but still controversial book, *Celtic Heritage*, by Alwyn and Brinley Rees (590, 1961). According to Dumézil, all of early Indo-European society was divided into three classes that were served by a fourth. The first is the sacred (in India *brāhman*); the second, warrior *(kṣatriya)*; and the third, farmer *(vaiśya)*. Although the military flavor of much of Fenian training might seem to associate them with the second function or division, Rees and Rees (p. 145) class Fionn and his cycle with the third function and only allow affinities to the second. Assignment to the third function does not mean, however, that Fionn and his fianna were hard-laboring farmers. Instead, the third function denotes primarily fertility, which can include fruitfulness in human beings, animals, and plants, but also food, wealth, health, peace, and the fruits of peace. Although this is not the place to file a brief for Dumézil, his theories fit well with the division of the three cycles of Old Irish literature, as understood by O'Rahilly and Murphy. Further, they explain how in the Ossianic dialogues that Oisín and Caoilte champion both Fionn and the beauties of nature while contending with Saint Patrick.

Although the arguments for Fionn's divine origin are persuasive, there has been no explication of the relationship between the figure's religious functions and his later characterization in literature. This question is unlikely to be resolved given our present information because we lack a knowledge of the ritual from which the romances were spun. Of all the motifs associated with Fionn's character the ones most likely to be rooted in his divine origin are his slaying of the burner Aillén, and the sucking and chewing of his magic thumb of prophecy. As we have mentioned, Fionn shares the motif of the thumb with Taliesin and Sigurd as well as with Heracles. The controversial Robert Graves has suggested that Heracles was associated with the thumb to the same extent that Achilles was associated with the heel. The wild olive, which was brought by the Hyperboreans to Olympia and used in the crown of victory after the seventh Olympiad (seventh century B.C.), belongs to the top joint of the thumb, supposedly a seat of virility, and therefore called "Heracles." In Greek tradition, Graves asserts, the fingers were personified by the Dactyls who had associations both with magic and the casting of spells (834, 1955, 185–86). A much more reliable commentator,

Patrick K. Ford, sees a different significance in the thumb. The Old Irish word for thumb, *ordu*, may also signify a morsel of something, especially of meat. This may explain why Fionn gains the gift of prophecy from other means in different stories. In some variants he eats magical hazel nuts, or the hazel nuts may have been eaten by the salmon before it is caught. Still, the thumb motif is persistent, especially when the thumb is thrust into Fionn's mouth. In one variant Fionn gains prophetic wisdom from three fairy women but later smashes his thumb while passing through the door of the fairymound (352, 1977). Though Ford does not mention it, the eating of a special small piece of meat, such as that of a white snake, is Type 673 in the Aarne-Thompson international motif index (964, 1977, 83–85). If these associations of the magic thumb are correct, they would support hypotheses of Fionn's divine origin and his later characterizations as poet, seer, and hunter.

Another aspect of the magical thumb motif is that it can be represented easily outside of written texts. No less an authority than Françoise Henry believes that Fionn may be represented in the relief adorning a pre-eighth-century High or "Celtic" Cross near Slievenamon, County Tipperary, a mountain long associated with the hero (314, 1965, 124, 139, 155). The High Crosses are products of the early centuries of Christianization in Ireland. That the pre-eminently Christian crosses should contain pagan iconography may be all the evidence we need to suggest that the Christian church played an important role in transforming the Celtic god into a hero of chronicle and romance.

Because of the paucity of surviving artifacts associated with the myth of Fionn, the motif of the bitten or sucked thumb is virtually the only unambiguous item of Fenian iconography. Fionn has no emblem which can be associated with him throughout the narratives, although some scattered evidence suggests that the dog may have been. The dog in Irish trdition was free of the pejorative, grotesque, and absurd associations it has in the English language; Cúchulainn is, after all, the "hound" of Culann. As a hunter Fionn is constantly with dogs and obviously holds many of them in deep affection. The most trusted of Fionn's dogs are Bran and Sceolang, who are mentioned frequently in the narratives, especially those in oral tradition; the stories of how Fionn won them have been among the most popular in modern Irish folklore. Whatever their value in modern tradition, the two dogs are theriomorphic cousins of Fionn as John Reinhard and Vernam Hull have shown (437, 1936). Their evidence tells that the two dogs metamorphosed from two fellow hunters, while retaining the closeness of blood relations with the hero.

Although dogs may not be found in Fenian iconography in Ireland, they are featured prominently at the Romano-Celtic shrine at Lydney Park, on the west bank of the Severn in Gloucestershire. The figure worshipped here is Nodons, a probable cognate of Nuadu, and an ancestor of Fionn's. He is portrayed as surrounded by dogs, much as Fionn would be at the Hill of Allen, home from a day of hunting.

Another element in the development of the archetype of Fionn which may lend itself to an anti-Christian animus comes from his portrayal as a poet. Early Celtic society afforded a place of honor for poets, as we have already considered, and the power of naming, telling, and describing was often considered mantic as well. This association explains in part the brahmin-like status of the *filidh* in early Irish society. Fionn is nowhere portrayed as a member of the *filidh*, but some of their prestige appears to have been transferred to him. As we mentioned in the previous chapter, the *imbas forosnai* and *teinm laída* are two techniques of divination which are Fionn's prerogative, powers which the hero does not share with other figures. The term "technique" is preferred here as it alludes to the well-known definition of shamanism by Mircea Eliade, "technique of ecstasy." Again, in the literature which survives, Fionn is not a full-fledged shaman, and in most of the heroic literature in Irish he seems reluctant to use what power he has; nevertheless, some small survival of shamanistic power is his because he is a poet.

It was suggested earlier that Christian scribes may have helped transform Fionn into a literary hero, but determining the role of Christian belief in the actual narratives is, however, quite another matter. Excluding for the moment the *Duanaire Finn*, a seventeenth-century redaction from oral tradition, most narratives in which Fionn is a protagonist show barely a trace of Christian influence, even in passing allusions. The absence of Christian ideas or references in the manuscript tradition was a cause of concern to such early scholars as John O'Donovan. Contrast the commonplace criticism of *Beowulf* that such Christian references as "a son of Cain," etc., have been interpolated by monastic amanuenses. Monastic Christianity came much earlier to Ireland than to Germanic Europe and, as elsewhere, writing was initially a clerical franchise. The great codices, *Lebor na hUidre*, "The Book of the Dun Cow," and *Lebor Laighneach*, "The Book of Leinster," were monastic productions. Similarly in oral tradition, in which the tales were kept alive by a people who were elsewhere characterized by their piety, we find only the slightest influence of Christianity. The Scottish folklorist George Henderson has quoted a Gaelic reciter, William Robertson of Tobermoray, in showing that the fianna had neither priest nor minister—nor Friar Tuck, for that matter—among them (358, 1905, 2). Fionn's Fianna spend most of their energy in hunting and fighting in the open fields, pastimes more evocative of European polytheism than Hebraic monotheism. Beyond resisting the influences of Christianity, the narratives of Fionn appear to have influenced Christian tradition; Eleanor Hull demonstrates that the pseudo-saint, Moling, finds his origin in the Fenian Cycle (518, 1928, 301).

If Fionn does not often meet an apostle of the Gospel, his son Oisín more than strikes the balance. Oisín survives the destruction of the Fianna, perhaps in A.D. 283, and lives on to meet Saint Patrick, apparently some time after A.D. 432, the year in which Patrick was traditionally thought to have been consecrated bishop and sent to Ireland. Most often, Oisín is an adversary of Saint Patrick, resistant to proselytizing, and a dogged champion on the virtues of the old order which find their apotheosis in his father, Fionn. Nevertheles, according to the twelfth-century *Agallamh na Senórach*, Fionn foretold the coming of Saint Patrick. We also learn that he made an act of Christian faith before his death, though this last is introduced rather absurdly, as Myles Dillon observed, for the edification of the fairies. Oral literature in the Ossianic frame, moreover, is a vast repository of anti-clerical feeling. In this tradition, as J. A. MacCulloch observed, Saint Patrick is usually portrayed as sour and intolerant in contrast to Fionn, whose memory Oisín cherishes, and who is seen as splendidly free, an enemy of guilt and repression (382, 1911, 40). Alfred Nutt speculates that the association of Fionn with anti-clericalism, though it pervades oral tradition in the Ossianic frame in collections from as early as the *Book of the Dean of Lismore* (1527) to the most recent collections he knew (c. 1910), is a later accretion which originated in Scottish Gaelic literature, with its heavy infusion of Norse anti-Christian sentiment, and that Scots bards and storytellers carried the motif of the association back into Ireland (415, 1910, 34–35).

All of this should not imply that Fionn is absolutely fixed as an anti-Christian figure. In the *Duanaire Finn*, the incidental introduction of Christian motifs is commonplace. In lay number 50, "The House of Morna Defend Fionn in Hell" (vol. II, pp. 168–74), the

hero does battle with Satan and his demons and is defeated, despite
the help given by Fionn's mortal enemies, Goll and the rest of the
Clan Morna. After sixty years an angel releases him so that he might
visit Oisín and tell of the son's salvation. Gerard Murphy feels that
this lay is the exception that proves the rule, not only for the Fenian
Cycle but for pre-Christian Irish literature more generally, as it is
one of the very few solid treatments of the Celtic *sidhe*, or fairy
otherworld (vol. III, p. cii); the obvious comparison with the Christian
infernal otherworld suggests the story is not Irish in origin. In other
oral tradition Fionn's Christianization is more ironic; George Henderson records an episode from Scottish Gaelic tradition titled "Fionn's
Baptism," in which the hero drowns some schoolboys at the bottom
of a pond (358, 1905, 140–41).

Whatever the actual story of the archetype of Fionn as handled
by Christian redactors, the associations of his name in a Christian
context, in literature of the past three centuries, both Irish and English,
are unmistakably pagan and antagonistic to Christian belief. For
example, consider the widely known poem attributed to Oisín, "The
Blackbird of Derrycairn." It has been translated more than a dozen
times in recent decades; this is from Seán O'Faoláin (124, 1938, 93):

> Ah, when Finn and the Fian lived,
> They loved better the mountain than the monastery:
> Sweet to them was the blackbird's speech.
> As for your bell's tongues—they despised them!

In summary we can see that the cultural foundations for the
archetype of Fionn are in the earliest experiences of the Irish people
and that the subsequent elaborations upon and aberrations of that
archetype cannot obscure the continuity that is central in his characterization.

THE HEROIC FIONN MAC CUMHAILL AT APOGEE

As we considered in Fionn's heroic biography, the hero is
consistently seen in three roles throughout the manuscript tradition:
those of hunter, warrior, and seer. The union of these three roles

may appear unlikely in English or other European tradition because of the experience of feudalism and the development of culture in commercial centers from the high medieval period and after. In Ireland, however, the social and economic experience of the centuries from A.D. 900 to A.D. 1500 was uniquely different. The basic political unit was the *túath*, a word which means basically "a people" and cannot be defined in terms of territory. It is frequently compared to the Greek *polis*, incorrectly translated as "city state," in part because both made government a personal matter for each citizen. Although the ruler of the *túath* is a *rí*, an apparent cognate of the Latin *rex*, he was not a king, as many contemporary genealogists assert, nor even a lord of the manor, at least to the extent that he governed territory. In the ninth and tenth centuries there were about one hundred *túatha* in Ireland in an economy more concerned with herding and livestock than with agriculture. Not only was feudalism foreign to Ireland but cities were as well, and both were introduced by foreigners, the former by the Normans and the latter by the Danes. In such a society it is not surprising that the most admired and cultivated men spent a good deal of time in the field, especially as Ireland was rich in game and relatively easily traversed on foot; thus Fionn is a poet and a hunter. Ireland was also characterized by continual internecine warring, also to be expected in a herding society without territorial stability, and thus Fionn is a hunter-warrior-poet.

The position of the hunter-warrior-poet in Ireland before the Norman invasion bears some analogues to that of the *scop* in Germanic Europe in the time of the *comitatus*. Certainly there is none of the gentility of the chivalric tradition. The behavior of many early Irish heroes, as Alan Bruford observed, might have shocked Froissart. Women are treated like men if they take up arms, defeated enemies are often decapitated and their bodies looted, and human life is the customary price of vengeance. This is common in the more "aristocratic" Ulster cycle, as well as in the Fenian and others. The refinement that appears in manuscript literature was apparently introduced by the class of poets known as *ollamh* (English, ollave), who were themselves poets who hunted and fought with their *rí*. As considered earlier, the Fenian stories may find their provenience among the bards or *bairdne* instead of the more highly trained *filidh*; nevertheless, in the centuries subsequent to the writing of the great codices and the Norman invasion, Fenian narratives were part of the repertory of the *ollamh*, the most esteemed order of *filidh*. An example

of the later identification of the *ollamh* with the Fianna can be seen
in the rules for Fianna membership outlined in Keating's history;
along with the expected demands on the candidate's manliness, his
courage and athletic prowess, is the stipulation that he have the
taste for poetical composition. He must not only learn the rudiments
of prosody, but he must also be able to compose according to the
rules laid down by the *ollamh* (195, 1908, 333–35). Admittedly the
war ode, *rosg catha*, takes precedence in composition, but the greater
repertory of the *ollamh* includes poetry of love, the celebration of
nature, and lyrics on much tenderer subjects.

In the manuscript tradition, subsequently, the accretions to
Fionn's character are fitting to his triad of roles. As befits a hunter
and warrior, he competes in athletic competition, succeeding most
often as a runner, jumper, and swimmer. Other members of the
Fianna might best him in individual matches, but he is often represented as the finest all-round competitor in Ireland. As befits a
leader of men, he often demonstrates that he has guile, though he
does not become the trickster that he sometimes is in oral tradition.
And although he has a number of wives, he is not often represented
as a lover. The family role which best suits him, because so many
of the tales are told in Ossianic frame, is that of father.

Oisín's vision of his father is sometimes aberrated with Oedipal
anxieties, to be considered at length in chapter 4. Despite this, Fionn
is still often portrayed as the embodiment of the pre-Christian Irish
ideas of bravery and generosity. In an often cited passage from the
Agallamh na Senórach, Oisín's companion Caoilte speaks of Fionn
with Saint Patrick. When the Saint asks, "Was he a good lord with
whom you were,/Finn mac Cumahill, that is to say?" Caoilte replies,
"Were but the brown leaf/Which the wood sheds from it, gold,/
Were but the white billow silver,/Finn would give it all away." And
when Patrick continues, "Who or what was it that maintained you
so in your life?" Caoilte answers, "Truth that was in our hearts, and
strength in our arms, and fulfillments in our tongues" (143, 1892,
104).

The Fionn of oral tradition has a much more wide-ranging
career. As Seán O'Faoláin has observed: "Fionn must have been a
Godsend to the folk storytellers. Given a hero, authenticated and
accepted by long tradition, there was little to check the endless
stringing of adventure after adventure on his neck, taking the incident
both from the universal lore of the *seanchuidhes* ["shanachies," or
storytellers] and from the treasure-chests of imagination and expe-

rience" (420, 1930, 162). In this, O'Faoláin adds, Fionn enjoys the
fate of Alexander, whose name has lived among the peasantry for
more than 2000 years, and who has conquered more lands in legend
than were known of in the geographies of his day.

As the elaboration of Fionn's character is "endless," and in this
O'Faoláin is congruent with other commentators on the Fenian cycle,
Christiansen, MacNeill, and Murphy, there is no need to enlarge
upon the heroic biography found in chapter 1, except to point out
that the additional roles of giant, engineer, trickster, and later buffoon,
are typical of the oral tradition.

FIONN MAC CUMHAILL AND OTHER EUROPEAN HEROES

There was a time that when any informed reader encountered
a new mythology, he or she expected to find counterparts to already
familiar gods. Such a perception predates the many competing theories of mythology of our own time. Julius Caesar, north of the Alps,
described "Gaulish Mercury," "Gaulish Jupiter," etc. Thus Cúchulainn
was once known as the "Celtic Heracles" and Angus the "Celtic
Apollo." Once nineteenth-century scholars abandoned the search for
the Ur-myth, the absolute original version that would explain all
variants, several commentators began to notice that there were thousands of parallels in the careers of heroes from widely divergent
cultures; among the earliest such theorists was J. G. von Hahn (837,
1876). Since then there have been several other mythographers,
notably Otto von Rank and Joseph Campbell, who have delineated
a paradigm of the hero's career. Rather than pit one theory against
another, our purpose here is to find a tool which allows us to frame
Fionn against other European figures. Comparison with Asian and
North American heroes seems too large a question now, especially
as there is no suggestion of borrowings or loans of different motifs.

Lord Raglan provides a twenty-two point formula in his study
The Hero (859, 1936). Although *The Hero* is in part a polemic for
the now highly unfashionable ritual theory of myth of the "Cambridge
School," Raglan's formula can be used without reference to his
questionable hypotheses. At best Raglan gives us a starting point on
which to focus comparisons with other heroes. The formula runs
less than a full page (859, 1956, 175–75):

1. The hero's mother is a royal virgin;
2. His father is a king, and
3. Often a near relative of his mother, but
4. The circumstances of his conception are unusual, and
5. He is also reputed to be the son of a god.
6. At birth an attempt is made, usually by his father or maternal grandfather, to kill him, but
7. He is spirited away, and
8. Reared by foster parents in a far country.
9. We are told nothing of his childhood, but
10. On reaching manhood he returns or goes to his future kingdom.
11. After a victory over a king and/or a giant, dragon, or wild beast,
12. He marries a princess, often the daughter of his predecessor, and
13. Becomes king.
14. For a time he reigns uneventfully, and
15. Prescribes laws, but
16. Later he loses favor with the gods and/or his subjects and
17. Is driven from the throne and city, after which
18. He meets with a mysterious death,
19. Often at the top of a hill.
20. His children, if any, do not succeed him.
21. His body is not buried, but nevertheless
22. He has one or more holy sepulchres.

By coordinating various sources which he does not identify, Lord Raglan rates a number of important figures, both mortal and immortal, from traditional literature. Allowing one point for each coincidence with his formula, Lord Raglan gives the highest score to King Oedipus who, when variants on his narrative are included, meets all twenty-two points. From the Mediterranean world the following figures also match very well: Theseus (20), Dionysus (19), Perseus (18), Romulus (18), Heracles (17), Bellerophon (16), Jason (15), Pelops (13), Asclepius (13), and Apollo (12). Moving north into the rest of Europe Lord Raglan finds that King Arthur merits nineteen, Llew Llaw Gyffes, the Welsh hero, seventeen; Robin Hood, thirteen; and Sigurd/Siegfried, eleven. Outside European tradition he cites only two heroes, presumably because he feels he has demonstrated his case. Watu Gunung, the Javanese hero, matches the formula on eighteen points, and Nyikang, from the Upper Nile, matches at fourteen.

If we do not distinguish ancient and modern sources or those from manuscript or oral tradition, we find that Fionn also does well against Lord Raglan's formula.

In most accounts Fionn is the son of Cumhal mac Trenmor and Muirne Man-chaomh, "Murna of the White Neck," who is descended from the god Nuadu Argetlám and therefore (1) "royal," although we have no word of her virginity prior to conception of Fionn. Cumhal was a "king of battle," *rígfhénnid* (2), and more than one modern commentator has argued that he may, like his son, be derived from a Celtic immortal (5). The usual manuscript accounts tell us nothing of Fionn's conception, Irish prudery perhaps omitting such information, but variant texts supply us with possible analogues. Christiansen tells us of a ballad version of *Fotha Catha Cnucha*, "The Cause of the Battle of Cnucha," in which Fionn is seen as a byblow of the womanizing Cumhal, begotten during a visit to Lochlann (334, 1931, 21–22). There is no evidence of incest in Fionn's conception, as Otto Rank sugggests there should be in *The Myth of the Birth of the Hero* (861, 1952) and as Lord Raglan clearly expects, but in the one story we have, from ballad tradition, there is at least the unusual circumstance of illegitimacy (4). This does not mean that the suggestion of incest is absent from the narratives, however; T. F. O'Rahilly analyzes genealogical tracts in which Fionn, under another name, Finn mac Gleoir, marries Muirne as well as another figure who is sometimes described as his mother, Torba or Tarbda (431, 1946, 276).

Following the defeat of Cumhal and his Fianna at Cnucha, Fionn is born to dreary expectations, after which the young hero finds his life threatened (6) and is spirited away (7), and lives under the name of Demne. Manuscript tradition tells us nothing of his childhood (9), but oral tradition supplies us with the names of at least three nurses and foster parents (8): Bodhmall, the female druid; "The Grey of Luachair," Liath Luachra, and Cumhal's sister; "Speedy Foot," Los Lurgann, whom the young hero wears to a shinbone, making her the eponymous daemon of Lough Lurgan, the ancient name for Galway Bay.

As recounted, Fionn does go on to his "kingdom" (10), becoming the *rígfhénnid* of the Leinster Fianna, and he slays Aillén, the burner of Tara (11). Manuscript and oral tradition assign more than two dozen wives to Fionn, several of whom are princesses (12), although none is the daughter of his predecessor, Cumhal, which would necessitate his marrying his own sister. Fionn's favorite wife is usually

thought of as Sadb or Saba, the mother of Oisín, a Danann princess
who was transformed into a hind. Another wife, Tasha of the White
Arms, was the daughter of the king of the fairy. The two daughters
of Cormac mac Airt, the high king or *ardríg* of Ireland at Tara, are
also associated with Fionn. The more comely of the two daughters,
Gráinne, is betrothed to the hero. Further, another sister, Ailbe, either
marries Fionn and dies or is given to Fionn in consolation for the
loss of Gráinne. Although there is no kingship in the modern European sense in Ireland, as we have considered, Fionn as *rígfhénnid*
has a seat of power (13) at the Hill of Allen. He does not govern
territory, but he does prescribe laws of his Fianna (15). Fionn's
Ireland never knows peace, but to the extent that his rule at the
Hill of Allen is untroubled and unchallenged, it might be said that
he reigns uneventfully (14).

That Fionn loses favor with Cormac, the high king, and most
of the people of Ireland (16) is one of the continuing paradoxes of
Fenian tradition. Fionn's death is never presented as mysterious,
however, and contrary to Lord Raglan's expectations, the various
sites given for the hero's final battle are all on flat land.

Fionn's progeny are numerous, but neither the most eminent,
Oisín, nor the most courageous, Oscar, his grandson, can succeed
him as head of the Fianna (19). This loss is part of what gives so
much of Fenian literature its characteristic mood of retrospection.

In the three principal accounts of Fionn's death, recounted in
chapter 1, the final blow struck at the hero is of decapitation, following
the ancient Celtic practice of taking the heads of slain enemies.
Nowhere do we read of his being buried, although several sites in
Ireland and Celtic Scotland have been claimed as his burial place.
To the extent that these sites have been popular attractions they are
sepulchres (21), although sepulchres in the Mediterrnean sense were
unknown in medieval Ireland. Traditionally, Slieve Guillean in County
Armagh, a place name rich in Fenian associations, has had the most
widely respected claim to be Fionn's burial place, although another
claimant is Knockfin, near Westport in County Mayo.

This means that Fionn may be awarded seventeen of a possible
twenty-two points, far too many for coincidence, making him a
counterpart of such figures as Lord Raglan has named: King Arthur,
Theseus, Heracles, etc. It would seem that Joyce had chosen wisely
in assigning an important role to Fionn in *Finnegans Wake*. Yet this
is not to argue that Fionn is invisible, an indistinguishable persona

in the monomyth. Further, we have no indication from Irish tradition that the millions of people who have known of Fionn's exploits looked upon his as just another of the thousand faces of the universal hero. Traditional literature still provides him with enough individuality to allow us to distinguish him from all other heroes, even while he resembles a number of them in certain respects. For this reason we shall presently consider, briefly, some of the other figures from European traditional literature who seem to bear the closest relationships to Fionn mac Cumhaill, starting with the Irish, and then to successively more distant traditions, the Brythonic or Welsh, Arthurian, Norse, and finally Greek.

In oral tradition the heroic figure of Fionn is sometimes confused with the historical king, Brian Boru, the victor over the Norsemen at the Battle of Clontarf, A.D. 1014, whose exploits are celebrated in the Dalcassian of the Cycles of Kings. E. C. Quiggin has argued that the *chasons de geste* which emanated from the Irish victory became a part of the *omnium gatherum* of Fenian literature, *Cath Fionntrágha*, "the Battle of Ventry" (419, 1935, 51). More playfully, both Fionn and Brian are credited in oral tradition with ripping up a divot of turf in Ulster and throwing it into the sea, thus creating Lough Neagh and the Isle of Man at the same time.

As the aging, thwarted lover of Gráinne, Fionn can be compared with Conchobar mac Nessa, who suffers a similar refusal from young Deirdre. The old king's rival is Naoise, who, along with his brothers, flees with Deirdre to Scotland. Conchobar, like Fionn, pursues, kills his rival lover, and takes his betrothed back with him. Yet we would be hasty in suggesting that Fionn can be identified with Conchobar as both figures can as easily be compared with King Mark in the Tristan and Iseult story.

Saint Patrick, the historical personage of the fifth century, is also a figure in Irish tradition, indeed, as he enters into "colloquy" with the aged Oisín, he becomes a figure in the Fenian Cycle. In a provocative essay David Krause has argued Saint Patrick serves as a surrogate father for Oisín, and that Oisín's disputatiousness is a key aspect of his character which can be traced back to his reviling of his actual father, Fionn, in an eighth century fragment, all of which are part of a tradition repressed by the clerical franchise on scribal transmission (373, 1966).

In popular tradition as well, the two looming figures from the distance share common attributes. The virtual cliché that Saint Patrick rid Ireland of snakes and monsters has also been ascribed to Fionn, not only in Ireland but also in several poems in the Scottish Gaelic *Book of the Dean of Lismore* (1527). Standish J. O'Grady repeats the association in his fanciful *History of Ireland: Heroic Period* (422, 1878, 33), as does the more scholarly Patrick Weston Joyce in *Social History of Ancient Ireland* (522, 1903, 514). Similarly in topographical lore, W. G. Wood-Martin records traditions in which stones with similar V-shaped marking are alternately described to Fionn and Saint Patrick (626, 1902, 163).

Evidence for comparisons with figures from Brythonic or Welsh tradition is harder to come by. The two bifurcations of the insular Celtic world have been separate since earliest written record, and the surviving languages are radically different in phonic system, as neophytes to the study of either language are at pains to learn. Once the differences between Irish and Welsh are comprehended, the relative lack of parallel between the figures of comparable mythical narratives is more understandable. Fionn shares the motif of the divining thumb with Taliesin, for example, but that leaves them far from identical. Taliesin has more poems ascribed to his pen than his biography can credit, albeit many of them were not committed to paper until the sixteenth century, a full millennium after his death. A much more magical figure, Taliesin underwent numerous metamorphoses, becoming an eagle and a salmon, and tasted the magical salmon while under the persona of Gwion.

The Welsh figure who is far more often compared with Fionn is Gwyn ap Nudd or ap Nuada, as mentioned earlier. Although Gwyn is a shadowy figure in Welsh tradition, in no way a match for Fionn in the measure of his fame, the suggestion that the two may be counterparts was first made by Thomas Powel in 1884 (433). The eminent Celticist Kuno Meyer dismissed the suggestion shortly after (400, 1884), and for a time the linking of the two figures seemed mere sophistry based on the similarity of their names. More contemporary scholarship, however, has located a passage in which Gwyn is also referred to as a "magic warrior huntsman," and Gerard Murphy has found still another link in that both hunt a beast whose name translates as "Lord Boar" (404, 1953, xxvi). This information was of much utility to Murphy who sought to demonstrate Fionn's divine origin, but it is found so sparsely in the surviving narratives of Gwyn ap Nudd that there is little else we can use in the explication of literature, Welsh, Irish, or English.

Perhaps because the topography of Wales differs dramatically from that of Ireland, there seems to be no tradition of hunter-poet who roams with his band of men through the hinterlands, fending off enemies, and all the while cultivating a rigorous aesthetic in poetry. To this extent Fionn has no counterpart whatsoever in Welsh traditional literature, as opposed to Welsh mythology. The suggestion that the British/Welsh militia leader Dwledig haunts the countryside much as Fionn does, first proposed by Duncan Campbell in 1888 (330), has long since been dismissed by Alfred Nutt and other scholars.

In actual narratives, as opposed to figures in narratives, *Macgníamhartha Finn*, "The Boyhood Deeds of Finn", bears a certain resemblance to the youthful exploits of Pwyll, Prince of Dyfed, as recounted in the first book of the *Mabinogion*, as the Welsh scholars W. J. Gruffydd and Rachel Bromwich, among others, have suggested (470, 1965, 212). The young prince is a hunter who grows in perception as he comes to know more about the spirit world. He does not, however, burn his thumb on cooked salmon. Pwyll goes forth to his kingdom, Dyfed, the Welsh name for Pembrokeshire, meets, most dramatically, the beautiful Rhiannon, who bears him a son, Pryderi. Marriage and fatherhood come to many heroes, and in outward appearance the elements in Pwyll's career do not suggest any incidents in the biography of Fionn, who, it will be remembered, knows little of romantic love and does not reign with a queen as consort. Pwyll, further, wins the title, Pen Annwn, "Head" or "Lord" of the "Otherworld," which would suggest parallels with a number of other Irish figures. Fionn was not the lord of a *sidhe* nor king of the fairies.

Both Welsh and Irish stories are often cited as sources and analogues for the many Arthurian legends. A generation ago Roger Sherman Loomis made a career of finding Celtic "sources" for almost every narrative and motif in Arthuriana. And today, though many of Loomis's more ambitious claims have been disregarded, it has become a scholarly commonplace that many of the Arthurian and Fenian narratives were alive in popular tradition over several centuries among both the Celtic and Saxon populations who lived only a few hundred miles from one another, albeit not speaking each other's languages; further, Welsh, Irish, and English stories appear to share a number of common elements in characterization and narrative structure. Because our focus is on the archetype of Fionn and not the enumeration of his adventures, the focus should be limited only to those Arthurian figures who are most often suggested as analogues, Perceval, King Mark, and Arthur himself.

The first scholar to demonstrate that the narratives of Fionn had contributed to the development of the story of Perceval was Arthur C. L. Brown in *The Origin of the Grail Legend* (629, 1918–35). In Brown's view the key element was Fionn's youthful revenge for the killing of Cumhal, the father he had never known. Although most Irish scholars, such as T. F. O'Rahilly and Gerard Murphy, have accepted Brown's analysis, R. S. Loomis, surprisingly, did not. In his widely known *Celtic Myth and Arthurian Romance* (1927), Loomis objected that weapons differed significantly in the two narratives, Fionn's and Perceval's, and implied that Brown's case required further study (633, 1927, 244–45).

Fifteen years later a student of R. S. Loomis's, Sheila McHugh, without making reference to Brown's work, devoted a master's thesis toward demonstrating that the youthful adventures of Fionn were the basis of *Sir Perceyvelle*, the fourteenth-century metrical romance of mixed Midland and Northern Middle English dialect, which is preserved in the Thornton Manuscript at Lincoln Cathedral. McHugh's line of provenience follows that proposed by Loomis for the general development of the Arthurian legends in his *Celtic Myth and Arthurian Romance*, although she makes extensive citations of texts. Toward the end of her essay, McHugh provides a flow chart to summarize her thesis. The ultimate source was "The Boyhood Deeds of Fionn," which influenced the development of Pwyll, Prince of Dyfed, which in turn was transferred to Brythonic Brittany from whence no manuscripts survive. Breton minstrels carried the originally Irish motifs and narratives throughout France, influencing the Perceval and *La bel inconnu* tradition, from which Anglo-Norman minstrels carried the stories to the north midlands of England (635, 1943, 73). McHugh argues further that French tradition was so rich that it returned influences to Celtic Britain, helping to form the Irish folktale of the "Big Fool," in Irish *Eachtra an Amadáin Mhoir*, a narrative which had long been considered a part of the Fenian cannon, although no Fenian names appear in it.

In an authoritative review of the published thesis, Gerard Murphy chided the American for being so selective in her arguments and for neglecting Brown, but allowed that ". . . when Miss McHugh . . . concludes that 'the Irish *Macgníamhartha Finn* represents Perceval *enfances* in its fledgling state,' no Irish scholar is likely to differ seriously from her" (635, 1948, 370). Thus it seems to us that Fionn, though he never quests for the Grail, may be associated with the youthful Perceval, that most innocent of heroes, a link which Joyce was to exploit in *Finnegans Wake.*

The episodes of "The Pursuit of Diarmaid and Gráinne" form the most dramatic of all Fenian narratives. The fugitive young lovers, the vengeful but authoritarian thwarted old man, have been irresistible to a millennium of listeners in a number of languages. The characters in the European romance of Tristan and Iseult provide the most available counterparts. As in the Irish story, the disappointed aging lover, King Mark, plays only a supporting role, although the greater proliferation of the European tale has allowed him a wider variety of characterization as in Thomas the Rhymer's *Sir Tristrem* in which he is seen rather sympathetically.

The stories are unquestionably related; what is to be demonstrated is whether one is older than the other, although both appear to have classical antecedents. As regards the development of medieval literature the argument has run in favor of an Irish origin, largely because the oldest fragments of the Diarmaid and Gráinne story can be traced to the ninth century. The Irish origin was first suggested by Eleanor Hull in 1908 (360, p. 59) and was developed at some length by Gertrude Schoepperle in her *Tristan and Isolt: A Study of the Sources of the Romances* (641, 1913). Subsequently, the argument in favor of the Irish origin, despite some revisions (475, 1955, 189–242), and despite the admission that the European story has reached greater literary excellence, appears to be standard. Thus Fionn may be associated with the cuckold Mark as well as the questing Perceval, a paradox ready-made to serve Joyce's ends in *Finnegans Wake.* And as King Mark is very likely only a persona for Arthur, we have the beginnings of a link with a greater king.

In dealing with literatures as vast as the Fenian and the Arthurian, and figures as protean as Fionn and Arthur, heroes who were invested with many of the achievements of numerous namesakes and historical figures, we should inevitably find analogues too numerous to mention. For this reason it is common to read of Fionn described as the "Irish Arthur." As we have considered, both Arthur and Fionn score well against the formula of Lord Raglan. With this in mind, it is surprising to see how little critical attention has been given to explicating the relationship, far less than that given to the relationship between Fionn and Perceval, which initially looks much more tenuous. The most substantial study of the question is in Anton van Hamel's sprawling Rhys Memorial Lecture to the British Academy in 1934, titled somewhat misleadingly, "Aspects of Celtic Mythology." In van Hamel's view five points in the comparison of Fionn and Arthur are salient (511, 1934):

A. Both are great boar hunters.
B. Both slay monsters.
C. If necessary, both Arthur and Fionn intervene in the super-natural world.
D. Both ward off foreign invaders.
E. Both release prisoners.

It could be added that both were men among men, both were surrounded by about a dozen faithful warriors, and both were cuck-olds. More individualized motifs such as the sword in the stone or the divining thumb do not find counterparts in the opposite tradition, and thus we expect that the Irish and the British figures should never be confused.

Continuing without citation of specific sources, van Hamel fur-ther asserts that both traditions had their origin in ancient Celtic religion, that remote, largely unstudied evanescent sphere from which no texts survive. This hypothesis might, however, stand; what irritated other scholars about "Aspects of Celtic Mythology" was van Hamel's additional assertion that the reason Fionn and Arthur evolved from Celtic myth was that there were no gods in the Greek or Hebrew sense. Instead, van Hamel suggests, Celtic myth, uniquely in Europe, was "exemplary," i.e., educative, and thus the greatest personalities in the tradition were supreme heroes and not immortals. In answer to this Gerard Murphy devotes an appendix in his edition of *Duanaire Finn*, dismissing the "exemplary myth" theory with the abundant evidence that there were Celtic gods, although allowing that Irish and Welsh myths are exemplary in the older sense, much as prayers are. At the same time he leaves the ties between Fionn and Arthur unassailed (404, 1953, 213–17).

As the Germanic speaking peoples and the Celtic speaking peoples have lived in close association for almost two millennia, not only in the British Isles but throughout Continental Europe and Scandinavia, one would expect to find the cultural traditions of the two peoples highly mixed. The physical anthropology of the two peoples indicates they are presently barely distinguishable. The descendants of formerly Celtic speaking peoples now inhabit Bavaria, Flanders, Denmark, much of England, and Iceland. Similarly, most modern Irishmen, including most of the longtime "Irish" residents of County Dublin, and most Highland Scotsmen, derive from Scandinavian antecedents. In this context the speculations of Schultz and Zimmer as to the Norse origin of the archetype of Fionn, as well as Joyce's credulous adherence to them, are entirely understandable, though more careful reading has refuted them.

An additional problem in considering the relationship between Irish and Germanic traditions is the paucity of Germanic texts. The standard sources of the mythology of the Teutonic peoples are the so-called *Eddas*, the "Elder" in verse and the "Younger" in prose, both of which were recorded in Iceland, a country discovered by Irish monks in the eighth century, whose first settlers, Danish and Norwegian chieftains, had Irish concubines.

In such a confused milieu, one looks for analogues rather than the influence of one tradition on the other. The Norse figure most often cited as a corollary of Fionn's is the great hero Sigurd of the *Volsunga Saga*. As mentioned previously, several commentators have noted Sigurd's sharing of the motif of the divining finger. E. O. G. Turville-Petre, one of the present generation's most authoritative scholars of Norse tradition, has reaffirmed earlier study of the comparison. He explains: "It has often been noticed that some of the Norse legends have affinities with the Celtic ones, which are too close to be explained by chance or by common Indo-European inheritance. No Norse hero resembles the Celtic ones as closely as does Sigurd, and the Celtic legends may help us to understand him" (867, 1965, 41).

After Sigurd killed the dragon Fafnir, he took out the heart and roasted it. Impatiently watching it cook, he prodded it with his finger, and burning himself he put the finger in his mouth. At once, according to a text entitled *Reginsmál*, he understood the language of birds.

The other Fenian motif which Sigurd shares is his birth from a doe, although this is not attributed to Fionn but rather Oisín, whose name means literally "fawn."

Turville-Petre also points another corollary between Fenian and Norse traditions. According to an episode in *Feis Tighe Chónain*, "The Feast of Conan's House," and not found elsewhere in Fenian narrative, Fionn gained his power of divination from the three daughters of Bec. While guarding the door of a *sidhe* which the hero and two companions sought to enter, the eldest daughter accidentally spilt water from a bowl of precious water into Fionn's mouth. This suggests to Professor Turville-Petre the blood of Kvasir, divine mead, upon which Odin relies, and which looses the creative powers of Norse poets. This additional assertion does not confuse the consideration of Irish-Norse analogues but rather suggests that Fionn may be seen as the counterpart of a god as well as the counterpart of a hero, which substantiates the arguments for the hero's divine origin put forth by O'Rahilly and Murphy.

Professor Turville-Petre's allusion to the common Indo-European inheritance in mythology leads us, at last, to Greek tradition, the mythology whose study is most often included in the standard Western curriculum and is thus usually the first that a reader would know. Many of the techniques for the study of mythology in general have come from the sustained academic scrutiny of Green mythology, and, initially, many readers expect the figures from non-classical mythology to behave like some old Greek or Roman figure. In this the reaction of Matthew Arnold speaks for many (466, 1867, 51):

> The very first thing that strikes one, in reading the *Ma-binogion*, is how evidently the medieval storyteller is pillaging an antiquity of which he does not fully possess the secret; he is like a peasant building his hut on the site of Halicarnassus or Ephesus; he builds but what he builds is full of materials of which he knows not the history, or knows by a glimmering tradition only.

In the first decades of the Irish revival in the nineteenth century, many commentators thought they had perceived the Greek mythological building blocks which had been pillaged in the construction of Fionn mac Cumhaill. Standish James O'Grady opined that Fionn's poetical skills reminded him of Apollo (63, 1892, 80). To Lady Gregory, otherwise so insightful and useful in her study of Irish tradition, Fionn's divining thumb suggested Prometheus because the power had been snatched from a druid who knew the forbidden powers of the gods (355, 1904, 89). Fionn's pursuit and retrieval of his lost betrothed Gráinne suggested Orpheus and Eurydice to David Fitzgerald (350, 1884, 243), but in that it includes a boar hunt it reminded John Campbell, the ninth Duke of Argyll, of Calydon (7, 1908, 138). As in the search for faces in clouds, we may have as many answers as we choose.

Fionn mac Cumhaill being the hero of an extensive popular tradition, we find the closest corollary in the Greek hero most celebrated in popular tradition, Heracles, and subsequently in the figure who derived much from him, Theseus, who is rightly called "The Athenian Heracles." As already considered, Fionn shares the divining thumb with Heracles; and concurrently Fionn, Heracles, and Theseus match well with Lord Raglan's formula. Fionn must remain subservient to Cormac mac Airt in much the same way that Heracles must serve Eurytreus. Like Fionn, both Heracles and Theseus are subjected to a period of disenchantment from storytellers in which they become subjects of abusive fun. In an appendix to his edition of *Duanaire Finn* entitled, "Antiquity of Many Irish Folktale Motifs," Gerard Murphy reviews many more arcane examples (loss of hair while cutting one's self from a monster's belly, etc.), and concludes that episodes from a variety of Greek sources have gravitated toward the Fenian narratives (404, 1953, 194–96) and that the preponderance of examples from the tales of Heracles may only be coincidence.

CONCLUSION

Although the intent of this chapter has not been polemical, reviewing many of the aspects of Fenian tradition should give the kind of data which would satisfy the criteria for many different definitions of myth: linguistic, cultural, religious, anthropological, and literary. With the evidence we have just considered we could argue that the surviving narratives and lore of Fionn mac Cumhaill constitute a myth because they behave like other materials which are called "myth." The archetype appears to be as old as the Celtic languages, and it survives into the present. As late as April 1974, an American folk collector in County Donegal recorded narratives of "Fionn agus na fianna" from a shanachie who spoke of the hero as though his story had just begun.[1] In this it appears that Fionn is a mythical figure in ways which his more jaded counterparts are not. The appeal of Fionn's myth is unconscious, and literary allusions to him appear spontaneous and uncontrived. Put another way, much of the information considered in this chapter has not been formally available to the many poets and storytellers, in both Irish and English, who have written of Fionn. The ultimate dimensions of the archetype of Fionn mac Cumhaill have been in their imagination.

3

The Heroic Fionn mac Cumhaill
in English Literature
From the Beginnings to Macpherson's Ossian and After

ionn mac Cumhaill's heroism was conventional in Irish literature. An Irish poet trained in the fifteenth century would
master phrases of Fionn's nobility just as he would learn
others for Achilles' prowess, Croesus' riches, and Orpheus's
harp of gold. This can be seen in proverbs, the artifacts of
conventional wisdom. In these we find that Fionn acquires the
attributes of nobility and magnanimity as a matter of course, as T.
D. MacDonald shows in his *Gaelic Proverbs* (280, 1926, 136–37),
which devotes an entire chapter to the Fenians. The first proverb is
spoken in Fionn's persona:

> Fuil mo namh ch d' dh'iarr mi riamh,
> Na'm bu mhiann iris falbh an sith.
> (The blood of my enemy I ne'er did seek,
> Were he but willing to depart in peace.)

> Or:

> Cha d'thug Fionn riamh blar gun chumhan.
> (Fionn never fought a fight without offering terms.)

Confidence in strength, benevolence, and wisdom has been maintained in the twentieth century as Lady Gregory shows in her English-
language records of Irish peasant belief, the Kiltartan Books (258,

1909, 70–71). An anonymous countryman speaks: "Finn mac Cumhaill was a great man. Every hair of his head had the full strength of a man in it. He was a very nice man, with fair hair hanging down his back like a woman; a grand man he was. When he would chew his little finger he would know all things, and he under stood enchantments as well . . ."

Other examples of the permanence of Fionn's heroic identity come abundantly from Irish oral tradition, in part, it would appear, because so many Fenian stories continued to be told in Ossianic frame in which Oisín might wax nostalgic about his father. But they are harder to find in English; those that can be found are older and not often read in these post-heroic times.

The greatest portrayal of the heroic Fionn in English is James Macpherson's *Poems of Ossian,* where his name is "Fingal," an alternate form of long standing. The greatness of *Poems of Ossian* is measured by its impact on culture and literature, not by its intrinsic artistic merit. Macpherson had such an effect on English perceptions of the Celtic world that he divides six centuries of borrowings into those that came before and those that came after.

THE HEROIC FIONN MAC CUMHAILL
IN ENGLISH BEFORE MACPHERSON

When the English reading public first encountered young James Macpherson's *Fragments of Ancient Poetry Collected in Highlands of Scotland* . . . in 1760, later expanded to the *Poems of Ossian,* they could not recall having read anything quite like it. Until that time, as now, most Englishmen were content to remain quite ignorant of the traditions of those benighted regions of the British Isles beyond the periphery of Anglo-Saxondom. The manners of the Welsh and the Irish did not make them attractive to London tastes, and the Scots Highlanders had been more than a nuisance in their tenacious backing of those otherwise forgotten reactionaires, the Stuarts. Nevertheless, these warlike, poor, and uncouth peoples were not without some historical fascinations; earlier in the century Edward Lhuyd, an Anglicized Welshman, had demonstrated that the Welsh, Cornish, Irish, and Scots Highlanders were the survivors of the ancient Celtic tradition and thus provided a disagreeable but nonetheless living

link with the classical past. With little experience on which to base
a critical judgment of *Ossian*, many informed readers could do little
better than to rely on their pre-formed cultural and political attitudes.
The reactions of Samuel Johnson, whose pronouncements all but
fixed the place of Macpherson in the lower depths of English literature,
are instructive. By his own admission Johnson knew little of the
Celtic languages, even on such an elementary point as the close
relationship between Scottish Gaelic, or "Erse," and Irish. He assumed
further that Highlanders had never written their language and that
no manuscripts in it would be forthcoming, although some had been
available since the early sixteenth century and many were produced
in the generation preceding *Ossian*. In Johnson's judgment, therefore,
Poems of Ossian were the grossest of frauds, complete fabrication; he
wrote, "I believe they have never existed in any other form than
that which we have seen" (662, 1930, 107). In response to one of
Macpherson's defenders, Dr. Hugh Blair, Johnson denied that the
Poems of Ossian exhibited any internal evidence of antiquity; asked
if he thought any man of the modern age could have written such
poems, Johnson replied, "Yes, Sir, many men, many women, and
many children" (648, 1953, 280).

Rather than abuse Dr. Johnson for his lack of diligence in
ferreting out such recondite information as the history of earlier
Fenian manuscripts in Irish and English, information so much more
accessible to us today, the modern reader should see his judgment
as evidence that there was no Fenian tradition in English until that
time. Indeed, many otherwise informed readers still feel that Macpherson introduced the archetype of Fionn to English writing, but
they are in error. The scholarship of recent years has uncovered
more than a dozen references and allusions to Fionn, not so many
as to make a tradition, certainly, but enough to demonstrate that the
heroic figure of Fionn mac Cumhaill or Fingal had impressed itself
on the English-speaking imagination before the eighteenth century.

In all of the early references to Fionn in English, the hero never
loses his native language; he is always Goidelic, either Irish or Scottish
Gaelic. All of the references and allusions to him appear to have
originated outside of Anglo-Saxondom and fall mostly within two
rather narrow traditions: the courtly literature of the kingdom of
Scotland, and more extensively, the English-language histories of
Scotland and Ireland. The former may not, initially, appear English,
and the latter may not seem literature, but on closer scrutiny, we
see that Royal Scots is a dialect of English and that the writing of

history before William Robertson or Edward Gibbon often required a poet's imagination.

Scots dialect or Lallans, the language spoken by many common people there, is distinguished from the English spoken south of Cumberland by its heavy influence from the Scandinavian languages, particularly Danish. Contrary to popular misunderstanding, Scots dialect includes very few words of Gaelic etymology and only negligible Gaelic influence in phrasing and syntax.

The other language of Scotland, Gaelic, has been spoken by an ever-decreasing population north of the Grampians in the counties of Argyll, Inverness, Ross and Cromarty, and portions of Perth. Much of Gaelic Scotland had been part of the sovereign principality of the Lord of the Isles from 1354 to 1493 and retained a kind of feral independence under clan leadership down to the crushing of the second Jacobite rebellion in 1745. In addressing an English ear the Celtic poet or storyteller in Scotland spoke to his countryman, not his conqueror, as would be the case in Ireland. Not surprisingly, then, Fionn appears in English as recorded in Scotland before he does elsewhere.

The Scottish literary tradition begins with John Barbour (1316–1395), archdeacon of Saint Machar's, Aberdeen, who includes a reference to Fionn in his great work, *The Bruce* (84, 1894, 43–84), a narrative poem celebrating the war for independence fought by Robert Bruce, James Douglas, and others in 1307. Speaking of the absent Bruce, the Lord of Lorne alludes first to Goll, whom he calls "Golmakmorn," and says "he . . . was wone to haiff fra Fyngall his menge, rycht swa."[1] As there is only this line and no more, we can see that Barbour portrayed the Lord of Lorne, presumably from Gaelic Argyll, expecting his listeners to be acquainted with the Fenian heroes, and further, that Barbour demanded as much from his readers. In this small allusion we mend some of Macpherson's tattered honor: not only was *Ossian* not a complete fabrication, as the evidence of the two previous chapters shows, but the name "Fingal" was not a solecism or neologism.

More often read today, despite their remoteness in time and the difficulty of their dialect for modern readers, are the so-called "Scottish Chaucerians." Two of these, William Dunbar (1465–1530) and Gavin Douglas (1474–1522), spoke of Fionn mac Cumhaill, as did their contemporary, a more popular poet, David Lyndsay, or Lindsay (1490–1555). Although each of these poets makes only a passing reference to Fionn, each reference, taken individually, makes

a substantial contribution to the knowledge of the hero outside Irish
and Gaelic traditions. In Dunbar's interlude, "The Droichis [Dwarf's]
Part of the Play," which is, incidentally, the earliest specimen of
Scots dramatic verse (c. 1500), a comic dwarf claims descent from
"Fyn Mackoll" through Gog Magog (91, 1958, 103). Gavin Douglas,
writing in the "Palice [sic] of Honour" (before 1522; 90, 1874, vol.
I, p. 65), describes Fionn as both Irish and possibly divine:

> Great Great Gowmakmorne and Fyn Makoul, and
> how They suld be goddis in Ireland as they say.

Writing sometime later than Douglas, Sir David Lyndsay gives different evidence for a possible belief in Fionn's divinity; he has a
pardoner selling some of the ancient hero's relics (95, 1871, vol. II,
p. 107):

> Heir is ane relict land and braid of
> Fyn Mac Coull the richt draft blaid
> With teith and al togidder.

The relic, it appears, is an enormous jawbone, in itself a motif
Reidar Christiansen has traced among Gaelic-speaking residents of
the Hebrides in the twentieth century (334, 1931, 62).

Writing in Scotland coeval with the Chaucerians was Hector
Boece, or, as he preferred, in Latinized form, Boëthius (1465–1536),
a rector of Aberdeen, associate of Erasmus, and the leader of the
revival of learning in his country. Boece's Latin history of Scotland,
Scotorum historiae a prima sentis origine, etc. (1526), contains many
fabulous narratives, including that of Macbeth and Duncan, which
passed into Holinshed's *Chronicles* and thence to Shakespeare. Drawing on as many as a half-dozen manuscript histories from the previous
two centuries, Boece regarded Fionn with critical scrutiny overcome
by credulity. Fionn mac Cumhaill, or as the name appears in Latin,
"*Finianum filium Coeli* fyn mak coul, *vulgari vocabulo*," was a Scotsman
who lived about the time of the advent of Saint Patrick and, as
Boece saw it, at the beginning of the Iron Age in the British Isles,
around A.D. 431–32. As in Scots Gaelic oral tradition, Boece's Fionn
is a giant and a hunter, and, the author notes, a great many stories
are told about him, much in the manner of King Arthur (85, 1946,

418). Because Boece's reputation as a man of learning (ironically, Johnson speaks admiringly of him on several occasions in *Journey to Western Islands of Scotland*) and perhaps also because his *History* was published in Paris, his account of Fionn may have reached more readers in the sixteenth and seventeenth centuries than any other from Scotland. One measure of wide readership can be seen in Geoffrey Keating's rebuke, in his Irish-language history of Ireland in 1633, of Boece's giving credence to folk accounts of Fionn's great size (195, 1908, 330–31).

Fionn continues to be a celebrated figure in Scots Gaelic tradition all during this time, much as in Ireland, and although the tradition is severely attenuated with the "clearances" or forced depopulation of the Highlands, or from the defeat at Culloden to about 1840, he can still be found in folk narratives recorded in the twentieth century. As noted in the previous chapter, Bishop Carsewell of Argyll and the Isles had deplored the popularity of the Fenian narratives among his flock in 1567, complaining that the stories were a rival to the Gospels. A century later, in 1684, Reverend Kirk, a Gaelic translator of the Psalms, included this note in the introduction (665, 1894, 105):

> Little volume, go boldly forth
> Raise whom ye reach to pure and godly strains,
> Hail the generous land of Fingal's heroes
> The Highland tracts and Isles of Hebrides.

For the most part there is little distinction between the Fionn of Irish tradition and the Fionn or Fingal of Scots Gaelic tradition, although, as might be expected, the Scottish tradition occasionally includes experiences not found in Irish history. W. A. Craigie records the work of a Scots Gaelic bard named Muchanach who speaks of the fair play of Fionn and the Fenians in a ballad about the massacre at Glencoe (1692), contrasting it with the perfidiousness of the Lowlanders (337, 1908, 134). Additionally, Craigie cites numerous popular poems of the sixteenth century in Scots dialect to demonstrate that "Finn Mak Coul" was a name much associated with the Highlanders. Although numerous collections and translations of Highland narratives were made in the mid-eighteenth century, Fionn's characterization became almost inseparable from Macpherson's conception of him in *Ossian*, a work which exploits and misrepresents tradition.

Yet the unmuddied stream could still be found by the persistent, as Sir Walter Scott demonstrated on several occasions in the Waverley Novels. Scott in his youth was much taken with Macpherson, but he knew from his own researches that there was a Highland tradition celebrated long before *Ossian*. In *The Antiquary* (1816), Hector MacIntyre, a Highland officer, recites a bit of a Fenian ballad set in Norse invasion times. In *Waverley* itself (chapter 44, 1814), Scott describes the genealogical pretensions of poor Highlanders who would find ancestors in Fionn and Cumhal. Elsewhere in the work, Scott repeats a "battle Song" of purported ancient origin, where one line in the last stanza reads:

> Be the brand of each chieftain like Fin's in his Ire!
> May the blood through his veins flow like currents of fire . . .

In the instances where Fionn entered the English language from Scottish tradition, as we can see, there is little ambiguity about their heroic conception.

Turning from Gaelic-English influences we find that the development of English writing in and about Ireland has a separate and substantially different history. Here English was the language of an invading people, little given to *belles-lettres* of any kind, and thus the first descriptions of Fionn mac Cumhaill appear in histories and pseudo-histories. The first invaders to come from England in 1170 were actually French-speaking Anglo-Norman nobles, who did not suppress the native culture but instead infiltrated the existing feudal system, eventually becoming dominant landowners in many parts of the country. Successive waves of immigrants, increasingly more Anglo-Saxon and English-speaking, came to Ireland and occupied comparable social and economic positions down to Elizabethan times, although they became gradually more absorbed in the native culture until they were, in some instances, more Irish than the Irish. Subsequently, early Anglo-Irish literature from 1200 to 1582 is almost exclusively religious and political. The most enduring work about Ireland from the invading culture during pre-Elizabethan times is unquestionably the Latin *Topographia Hibernica*, "Topography of Ireland" (c. 1200), by the Welshman Giraldus Cambrensis. Although numerous commentators have suggested they see veiled Fenian allusions in Giraldus, we find only a mention of "Raunus," who may be identical with the "roanus," another name for the Fenian runner Caoilte, mentioned by the seventeenth-century historian Hanmer.

The first English-language discussion of Celtic heroic narratives taken from Irish sources is found in *The History of Ireland* (c. 1571), written in Douai by the English Jesuit, Edmund Campion (1540–81), an Oxford-trained scholar and brief resident of Dublin who was later tortured and executed in the Tower of London. Taking some narratives from the *Agallamh*, Campion deals with a number of Fenian personalities, including Caoilte and Oisín, but neither depicts nor alludes to Fionn (101, 1971, 24–38). Campion's *History* is written in a most unfortunate style but evidently found some readers as it is listed as a source for the Irish volume (VI) of Holinshed's *Chronicles*. Campion is also distinguished by a reprimand from Keating (195, 1908, 328–29).

Shortly after Campion, the anonymous author of *The Book of Howth* also retold some Irish heroic narratives, although in this instance the Fenian are more prominent. The work begins with a genealogy of Fionn and Oisín and includes dialogues between Oisín and Saint Patrick, one of which is an account of Fionn's three-day battle with a giant, where the hero relies more on guile than his superhuman strength (83, 1871, 8–9). This is the first suggestion in English that Fionn might be something other than a pinnacle of courage, valor, and strength, a theme which is not developed again in English until the nineteenth century.

Coming later in the same decade as Campion are the famous *Chronicles* of Raphael Holinshed (1577) in six volumes, the last two of which deal with Scotland and Ireland. The Scottish volume (V) contains the only indexed reference to "Finmacoll the great hunter," derived from Boece, but the Irish volume (VI) provides several unindexed examples. Being sixth in the series, the Irish volume carries the name of its commissioner, Raphael Holinshed, although it is signed by, and presumably fully edited by, Richard Stanihurst (or Stanyhurst). Only thirty when the volume was published, Stanihurst readily admits his reliance on his "friend and inward companion," the Jesuit Edmund Campion, so we may assume that much of the information in Stanihurst's contribution to the whole actually came from the beleaguered cleric. Whoever was the real author, the text contains some family allusions to Fionn and includes this commentary after a discussion of the festivities at the Hill of Tara (99, 1808, 39): "The Irish historians hammer manie fables in this forge of Fin mac Coile and his champions, as the French historie dooth of king Arthur and the knights of the round table. But doubtlesse the place seemeth to beare the shew of an ancient and famous monument."

As Holinshed's *Chronicles* is one of the best-known titles issued in Elizabethan England, one might have expected that Stanihurst's account of Fionn would have reached a wide audience, but such does not appear to be the case. Stanihurst, like his "maister" Campion, was not blessed with a workable style (his infamous translation of the *Aeneid* was so ridiculed it was abandoned after the fourth book) and the *Chronicles* are not often read today, apart from those passages selected as background for Shakespeare, and the last complete edition of the six quarto volumes, more than 600 pages each, was in 1808.

The greatest of all the Elizabethan historians, William Camden (1551–1623), founder of the first chair of history at Oxford, also drew on Irish sources in his Latin history *Britannia* (1586), first translated into English by Philemon Holland in 1607. Camden devoted considerable attention to the ancient heroes but also reported on the contemporary attitude toward them in Ireland: "They [the Irish people] think the souls of the deceased are in communion with famous men of those places, of whom they retain many stories and sonnets, as of the gyants Fin-Mac-Huyle, Osshin Mac-Owim, and they say through illusion, that they often see them" (86, 1695, 1048).

Of all the pre-eighteenth century histories and pseudo-histories dealing with the character of Fionn the only one which develops extensive narratives of the hero is the *Chronicle of Ireland* by Meredith Hanmer (1543–1604), published posthumously and bound together with Campion's *History*, by Sir James Ware in 1633 (98, 1971). Hanmer was an Anglican clergyman who went to Ireland in 1591 and remained there until his death. He evidently acquired little if any Irish; his account is marked with numerous errors and specious scholarly argument, and seems to have relied most heavily on the English language *Book of Howth*, c. 1570–75, mentioned above. For example, the Fianna Éireann was known in the *Book of Howth* as "Fin Herin" and "Fyenerryne," but in Hanmer it became a warrior, not a band of warriors, and was then called "Fin Eryn." To compound this folly, Hanmer further speculates, in anticipation of Heinrich Zimmer and James Joyce, that "Fin Eryn" is actually of Danish origin, coming from the Norse form, Fin *Eric*. In a recounting of the battle of "Fentra" (apparently from Ventry, *Fionntrágha*), Hanmer's Fionn leads the Danes, who have become, *mirabile dictu*, the allies of the Irish, and together they take on the combined forces of Scotland, Cornwall, Normandy, Germany, Spain, and other non-allied Danes. Curiously, all the while that Hanmer confuses prose romance with

history, he carefully excises apparently anachronistic chivalric references, and derides all old Irish history as ridiculous. And with his
distortions and misunderstandings, Hanmer does nothing to enlarge
the heroic figure of Fionn; the hero is still a hunter, warrior, and
defender of his people, but he seems shorn of his poetic and ritualistic
powers.

During the remainder of the seventeenth century, and continuing
through the first six decades of the eighteenth until the advent of
James Macpherson, many more depictions of the heroic Fionn appeared in English, but because they are generally one of two continuing types I shall deal with them in summary. Most printed sources
dealing with the Irish past came from two separate historical developments: the general rise of commerce, prosperity, and literacy
which brought, willy-nilly, more published translations of Irish-language materials, and also the massive increase in the numbers of
English settlers coming to Ireland in the Stuart and Cromwellian
Plantations and rewriting the history of the country to suit their own
shortsightedness. The first undistorted translations of Fenian narratives came in Conall Macgeoghan's *Annals of Clonmacnoise* (1627),
though they apparently reached only a few readers (186, 1896).
Roderick O'Flaherty presented many more heroic narratives, though
fewer Irish ones, in his Latin *Ogygia*, etc., in 1685, a book which
reached many readers, including, as we shall see, James Macpherson.
O'Flaherty's volume provides the first non-Irish-language version of
the narratives of Diarmaid and Gráinne (98, 1793, 242). And in 1723
Dermod O'Connor translated and published in London the monu-
mental *History* of Geoffrey Keating. Had these texts been made
available to Dr. Johnson, he would have been obliged to revise his
case against Gaeldom in general and against Macpherson's integrity
in particular.

In the later English-language histories the credulity of earlier
centuries was continued, but not without challenge. The Irish Fran-
ciscan Peter Walsh produced *A Prospect of the State of Ireland*, etc.,
in London (1682), in which he argued for the historicity of Fionn
and other figures from romance (100, 1682, 51–53). He was attacked
by Sir Richard Cox, an Irish judge and strong Protestant, the later
Lord Chancellor, in *Hibernia Anglicana*, etc., published in London
(1689), the same year as the celebrated Orange victory at Londonderry
and a year before the Battle of the Boyne. Cox stands at the head
of the anti-Irish traditin in literature by suggesting that any Irish
claim to an heroic past is a ridiculous pretension. In the same year

James Farewell in *The Irish Hudibras, or Fingallian Prince*, etc., portrayed Fionn as having been sent to the Christian hell (92, 1689,
85). The ridicule of Irish heroic narratives was, of course, the slightest
burden the native population had to bear following the passage of
the Penal Laws, also in 1689, although it was not until the ninteenth
century that the anti-Irish animus produced extensive abusive portraits
of Fionn in English.

As admitted at the outset of this discussion of early references
to Fionn in English, they are not so numerous nor so extensie as to
form a tradition, and Dr. Johnson can be excused for overlooking
them, even those in Boece, Holinshed's *Chronicles*, and the Scottish
Chaucerians. Indeed, many of them are difficult to locate today. Two
aspects of these early references seem, in summary, to be important.
First, the Fenian stories seem better known and more attractive to
English writers than those from the other Irish cycles. For example,
there is no suggestion of the Deirdre narrative, in later times the
most celebrated Irish mythical narrative in English writing, until
Hugh MacCurtain's *Brief Discourse* in 1717, a work which in other
details is heavily dependent on Walsh's credulous and derided history
of 1682. Secondly, the early English-language presentations of Fionn
are predominantly heroic, with little variation from the character of
older oral tradition in Irish and Scottish Gaelic; the two slight exceptions would be the guileful Fionn in the *Book of Howth* and the
settler-conceived Fionn who appears after 1689. There is little in
these early references to suggest that Fionn mac Cumhaill could
expand to become the universal figure of *Finnegans Wake*, and perhaps
he would never have offered much to the English-speaking imagination if he had not received the enormous attention that followed
the publication of *Fragments of Ancient Poetry Collected in the Highlands of Scotland and Translated from the Galic or Erse Language* by a
twenty-four-year-old country schoolmaster.

JAMES MACPHERSON'S *OSSIAN* AND FINGAL

The first place many modern students of literature encounter
the name of James Macpherson is in a footnote to Boswell's *Life of
Johnson*. Johnson did not think Macpherson was much of a translator
or poet. His altercation with Macpherson, because of its heat, and

because of the wit of Johnson in gaining the upper hand, is included in even the briefest selections of the whole. Johnson abused Macpherson's purported translations soon after he had read them, basing his judgment on their aesthetic merits alone. In the first years after the *Fragments'* publication Johnson felt no need to mount a case against them, and it was not until ten years later that Macpherson knew of the great critic's dismissal of the enterprise. A series of letters followed, in which Macpherson's language was no more intemperate than Johnson's, until finally, in February 1775, Johnson understood that he had received a physical threat from the Scotsman; we cannot know for certain if this is true as Boswell did not see the contents of the letter and it has not survived. As Macpherson was then thirty-nine, and Johnson sixty-six, the older man decided to defend himself by, first, buying a cudgel six feet in length ending with a knob three inches in diameter, and second, more effectively, by denouncing the younger man in a short letter, the last paragraph of which reads:

> What would you have me retract? I thought your book an imposture; I think it an imposture still. For this opinion I have given my reasons to the public, which here I dare you to refute. Your rage I defy. Your abilities, since your Homer, are not so formidable; and what I hear of your morals, inclines me to pay regard not to what you say, but to what you shall prove. You may print this if you will.

Few modern readers share Johnson's moral perspective, but to most Macpherson appears a bully. And as many would share Johnson's distaste for Macpherson's style, they are likely to join in the assumption that the *Fragments,* later expanded into the *Poems of Ossian,* is a fraud concocted to exploit a credulous public. To dismiss Macpherson and his translations so easily is to miss one of the most phenomonal chapters in the development of our literature.

Macpherson was a publicly immoral man, as Johnson had charged, though that would more likely add to his reputation than detract from it, had he lived today. He never married, but acknowledged at least five illegitimate children from different women, and these progeny argued over his considerable estate until the mid-nineteenth century in a debate which rivalled that over the authenticity of *Ossian.*

His later profligacy contrasted with his origin and background. He was the son of a Presbyterian farmer in Ruthven at the edge of the impoverished and largely Catholic Scottish Highlands. Perhaps because of their religion, the Macphersons spoke English instead of Gaelic, and in the repression which followed Culloden, the old language was an unlikely one for a proud and ambitious boy to study. A middling student, Macpherson attended King's College, Aberdeen, and, for a shorter period, Marischal College, Edinburgh, but did not receive a degree. By the time his *Fragments* appeared he had taught school in rural Inverness, published some undistinguished poetry, and tutored the children of the rich, which gave him access to people of fashion and influence. To help finance his travel with the privileged he corrected printer's proofs, which gave him access to Edinburgh's publishers.

Macpherson's attraction to the translation of Gaelic poetry may have come from the example of Jerome Stone, whose poems appeared in the *Scots Magazine* during the winter of 1755–56. Whatever his debt to Stone, Macpherson was certainly not the first young Scotsman who hoped to make a literary reputation by using the poetry of the recently defeated Highlanders. After toying with a few verses Macpherson was encouraged to consider more extensive translations and eventual publication by John Home, an aristocrat and playwright (*Douglas*, 1756), who later served as an heroic model in Scott's *Waverley*.

The publication of the *Fragments* was an unprecedented success, first in Edinburgh and later in all of England. Never before had an upstart, a country schoolmaster, won the favor of so many established writers, the critic Hugh Blair and the philosopher David Hume in Scotland, and two of the most esteemed poets in England, Thomas Gray and William Shenstone. Popular and commercial success brought more fragments, the epic-length "Fingal" in 1762, and the second epic "Temora" in 1763, completing the corpus. The full collection of two epics and twenty fragments was not published under the title *Poems of Ossian* until 1765. If the *Fragments* had been a success, *Ossian* was a sensation. *Ossian* was read and admired by dozens of the most esteemed writers in the English language, including Blake, Byron, Scott, Coleridge, Thomas Jefferson, James Fenimore Cooper, Henry David Thoreau, Elizabeth Barrett Browning, and Matthew Arnold. *Ossian*'s influence in Europe, especially Germany, Scandinavia, France, and Russia, has taken three bibliographies to chart. Goethe has one character in *The Sorrows of Young Werther* (1774) say that Ossian had banished Homer, and later Goethe himself translated two fragments and wrote numerous imitations in German. Napoleon took an Italian translation with him to Moscow. The work inspired more than a hundred paintings and at least fifty short musical works by such composers as Schubert, Mendelssohn, and Brahms, and at least a dozen operas. Macpherson's success in asserting that Fionn under the name of Fingal, was one of the great heroes of western literature had the short-term effect of introducing Fenian names to many literatures. But a more important result, as we shall see, was one he had not anticipated, the bringing of learned scrutiny to the literature of the Celts, a scrutiny which ironically helped to deny his claim to authority.

Though he evidently considered himself a personal success, Macpherson's reputation as a poet began its decline in London with the publication of his translation of Homer in 1773. After he appeared to get the worst of the dispute with Johnson, calls grew louder for the originals on which his translations were based, manuscripts which he freely cited but could not produce. The posthumous publications of his "originals" for *Ossian*, literally retranslated into Gaelic, did little to satisfy his detractors, and, except among diehard Scots nationalists, the star of James Macpherson began to set, never to have another dawn. Urban-bred nationalists kept the book in print during much of the nineteenth century with such projects as stocking every parish school in the Highlands so that children "might know their heritage," but in city and country alike it had a steadily declining readership. The consideration of the authenticity of Macpherson's translations, at first a partisan quarrel among equally ill-informed parties from Scotland, England, and Ireland, has taken two bibliographies to chronicle and continues to our own day among less choleric scholars.

In Macpherson's *Poems of Ossian*, which, by the way, are neither in verse nor much devoted to the exploits of Ossian, Fingal is uncontestably the dominant character. He is the protagonist in the two *soi-disant* epics, "Temora" and "Fingal," and is mentioned prominently in all but three of the fragments, a central figure in some and an aging Arthurian presence in others. Macpherson's first premise, that all of the narratives have been composed by Ossian, or Oisín, coheres with the premise of the ballads and other narratives from oral tradition in Ossianic frame in which Fionn's son recounts the deeds of by-gone days to the proselytizing Saint Patrick. Accordingly, in two of Macpherson's fragments, "Carric-thura" and "Calthon and Colmal," Ossian is portrayed addressing his poems to an unnamed "culdee," though the narrator does not imply any polemical intent as in the Irish and Gaelic versions. Given these allowances for the differences in focus, we can see that Macpherson's Fingal is some kind of adaptation of the heroic Fionn mac Cumhaill.

Fingal's family is especially close to Fionn's. His father, Comhall (cf. Cumhal), was slain before the action of the poems begins by a member of the Clan Morni (cf. Morna). In battle Fingal calls upon the memory of an even earlier ancestor, Trenmore, just as Cumhal is "mac Trenmor." Ossian, as mentioned, is Oisín, and his son Oscar uses a form of the name Osca/Oscar/Osgr, frequently found in Irish and Gaelic traditions. Tall and fair, Fingal looks much like Fionn mac Cumhaill. At one point Fingal is thought to have married the daughter of Cormac, king of Ireland. She is here called Ros-Crana instead of Gráinne. Familiar 'members of the Fianna appear under slightly altered forms of their names; Dermid is obviously Diarmaid and Co-Alt is Caoilte. Macpherson's Gaul MacMorni is based on Goll mac Morna, the conventional adversary of Fionn in the manuscript tradition, and here, as in the smarmy bonhomie of the oral tradition, is made the trusted ally of the hero. In "Temora" Fingal does battle with Cairbar, much as Fionn is at war with Cairbre of the Liffey. The name "Temora" itself appears to be adapted from the Irish name for Tara, Temair, Temhair, etc. Even the hero's dog, here represented as a greyhound, is called Bran. Additionally, two of the fragments in which Fingal does not figure prominently are also close to narratives from Irish and Gaelic tradition. Dar-Thula, the heroine of the fragment of that name, is Deirdre, and Cathon is much like Connla, son of Cúchulainn, who is killed unknowingly by his father in an Irish version of the Sohrab and Rustum tale. Finally, Cuthullin, alias Cúchulainn, appears as an Irish hero in a number of the narratives, but he is uncharacteristically weary and ready to defer to Fingal's greater power. These last three examples, it should be pointed out, are from the Ulster Cycle and are not recorded in Irish as infiltrating the Fenian Cycle until the twentieth century, and then most infrequently.

In saying that Fingal was "some kind of adaptation of the heroic Fionn" the hesitation is not simply one of colloquial diction. Many of the elements in Ossian have no antecedent in any Irish tradition or history. Macpherson continually stresses that Fingal is a Scotsman and that his realm is centered in Morven, whose capital is Selma. Macpherson's Morven, which sometimes seems to encompass all of Gaelic Scotland, should not be confused with the historical Morven, more often Morvern, a barren region in Argyll north of the Sound of Mull. His Selma is a great city somewhere on the west coast of the Highlands, where the largest metropolis known to history is Oban (a municipal borough with a population [1961] of 5759). Fingal wears armour as Fionn never does and as would have been unlikely for any British warrior of the third century. Fingal also commands a fleet though the Celts built only coracles in pre-medieval times. On land, the warriors of Morven do battle with two Roman legions, although no Imperial Romans are mentioned in Irish or Gaelic tradition. The historical Romans, in contrast, far from coveting the infertile Highlands, built two walls to insulate themselves from its inhabitants.

The greater question of the "authenticity" of the *Poems of Ossian* has been the subject of considerable study. Surveying all the scholarly energy expended on the question of Macpherson, we find at least four supportable points: (1) No one in the middle of the eighteenth century really knew what folk tradition was; (2) Fionn/Fingal was richly celebrated in Highland tradition, and there were enough collections available to Macpherson to ballast several *Ossians*; (3) many passages in *Ossian* bear a close comparative analysis with collections of Highland ballads; and (4) we do not know precisely how Macpherson envisioned his work.

The modern study of folk tradition began with the Brothers Grimm, whose first published work appeared in 1812. Even at the advent of their work all folk traditions were called "popular antiquities," implying a distorted, inarticulate memory of the distant but actual past. New understanding of the phenomena did not call forth a new term until 1846 when the English antiquarian, William John Thoms, first used the word "folklore." The Irish historians Roderick O'Flaherty and Geoffrey Keating, whose work had been recently translated, both argued that Fionn was an historical figure of the third century, A.D. Macpherson would later dispute their claim to the Irish origin of the Fenian narratives, but he saw no reason to challenge their dating or their euhemerism, that delusion which attracts so many fledgling students of popular traditions. For these and other reasons, as Derick Thomson observed, "It is perhaps not impossible that Macpherson was, in fact, under the impression that he was collecting the *disjecta membra* of an old Gaelic epic" (684, 1952, 12).

The scattered Fenian members Macpherson might have found in the Highlands were far more extensive than Dr. Johnson had supposed. Ignoring the evidence from modern folk collectors considered in the first chapter, we have the testimony of Martin Martin, whose travel record of the Hebrides, *Description of the Western Islands*, was published in 1703. Martin speaks repeatedly of "Fin-Mac-Coul": "This gigantic man is reported to have been general of a militia that came from Spain to Ireland, and from thence to those islands. . . . The natives have many stories of this general and his army, with which I will not trouble the reader" (553, 1884, 152). Further evidence may be adduced from Tobias Smollett, admittedly one of Macpherson's allies, who, in *Humphrey Clinker* (1771), says that "the poems of *Ossian* are in every mouth" and describes an antiquarian who can "repeat them all in the original Gaelick. . . ." Further, and again contrary to Dr. Johnson's understanding, the Fenian oral traditions of the Highlands had been recorded in at least seven manuscripts before the publishing of the *Fragments* in 1760. Two of these manuscripts had themselves been published, and others were widely circulated among the cognoscenti. The Fenian narratives published by Sir James and Duncan MacGregor in *The Book of the Dean of Lismore*, a work in many ways comparable to the *Duannaire Finn*, marked the beginning of written Scottish Gaelic literature. More recently, Jerome Stone, of Dunkeld in the eastern Highlands, had collected and published a large number of Fenian poems in the widely circulated *Scots Magazine* (1755–56). Macpherson is known to have examined some of the earlier unpublished manuscripts, especially those of Reverend Alexander Pope, a minister at Rea, Caithness (1739), and Reverend Donald MacNicoll, minister at Lismore, Argyll (1755). In addition, between 1760 and the completion of "Temora" in 1763, Macpherson collected, with the assistance of the antiquarian Captain Morison and the Laird of Strathmashie, a number of manuscripts which he reportedly used, and later, evidently destroyed; a knowledge of the existence of these documents subsequently helped to fuel the controversy over *Ossian*'s authenticity, but they have never been recovered.

Just what relationship passages of the *Poems of Ossian* bear to traditional Gaelic poetry has also been the subject of much discussion. Scholarly detractors of Macpherson, more numerous than his champions, have derided the gross howlers in his handling of the language, mistaking such elementary matters as the definition and gender of common words in everyday Gaelic. His conversational Gaelic, even during the heat of the authenticity controversy, was studded with curious blunders. Added to this are the implausible conventions and the improbable diction he attributes to the Gaelic author, Ossian. For example, many of the fragments begin with phrases suitable to a Cecil B. DeMille epic, "A tale of the times of old! The deeds of other years! The murmur of the streams, O Lora!" (exclamations his). In the face of this bathos, several commentators have labored to show that, despite the portents to the contrary, Macpherson's *Ossian* does bear numerous parallels with bona fide Gaelic tradition. Macpherson had not helped matters by producing bogus evidence to support his claim to authenticity; the manuscript *Dana Oisein Mhic Fhinn,* a contemporary translation of *Ossian* into Gaelic, published posthumously, only gave evidence of his prevarication. Henry MacKenzie produced all the then available evidence in the *Report of the Highland Society of Scotland* in 1805, including numerous post-*Ossian* collections of Gaelic Fenian narratives, but they did not overturn Dr. Johnson's judgment. In view of Macpherson's claim that *Ossian* was a third-century composition, nothing less than a genuine word-for-word Gaelic manuscript would suffice.

Boswell probably spoke for the general informed English opinion in the *Life of Johnson* (1791), when he said that the question of *Ossian's* authenticity had become "very uninteresting," and subsequently it was relegated to the toils of ill-informed, provincial fanatics until the rise of Celtic studies on the Continent almost a century later. Our contemporary understanding of Macpherson's reliance on sources comes from Loys Brueyre (1887), Ludwig Stern (1895), and the Scottish Celticist, Derick Thomson, whose *Gaelic Sources of Macpherson's Ossian* (1952), a work already cited, incorporates all earlier examination of the question. In recalling upwards of a hundred passages, Thomson shows that Macpherson continually achieves a distant echo of Gaelic heroic verse. One example describes Cuthullin (Cúchulainn) at the beginning of "Fingal." The Irish hero is greeted by Moran, the son of Fithil:

> "Rise," said the youth, "Cuthullin, rise; I see the ships of Swaran. Cuthullin, many are the foe: many are the heroes of the dark-rolling sea."
> "Moran!" replied the blue-eyed chief, "thou ever tremblest, son of Fithil: Thy fears have much increased the foe. Perhaps it is the king of the lonely hills coming to aid me on Green Ullin's plains."

The Gaelic passages Thomson chooses for comparison are from the collection of Reverend James Maclagan, who, contemporary with Macpherson, lived in different villages in the western and eastern Highlands. Letters from Macpherson complimenting Maclagan on the quality of his text have survived. Part of Macpherson's charade was that he already had in his possession a copy of the actual third-century manuscript of Ossian; when he found what he liked in the ballad collections of emergent folklorists, whose work he exploited, he would praise them for the authenticity of their supposed survivals. Fortunately for our understanding, seventy-five pages of the Maclagan manuscripts were preserved and published in 1894 (236, 1894, 295–370). Thomson's translation of Maclagan reads as follows:

> Arise, Hound of Tara, I see an untold number of ships, the undulating seas full of the ships of the strangers.
> A liar are thou, excellent doorkeeper, a liar art though today and at every time; that is but the great fleet of Moy, coming to help us.

In Thomson's view Macpherson took considerable pains in composing *Ossian*, especially in "Fingal." In many cases Macpherson has dovetailed the action of two and more narratives, eliminating catalogues and other rhetoric suited to oral recitation and adding episodes and details from still other stories. We can never look for literal translation in Macpherson, as his earlier readers did, and in general, "it is not easy to assess what is disingenuous and what is written in good faith and bad judgment" (684, 1952, 14, 42, 71).

Macpherson was, of course, one of several would-be literary antiquarians of the eighteenth century. From our point of view he seems to compare unfavorably with his later contemporary Thomas Chatterton, whose forged medieval lyrics reveal a fresh and enlivening talent. The uniqueness of the *Poems of Ossian* is that they are at root genuinely traditional and archaic, but their author presented them, or was seduced by public pressure into presenting them, as something older than they were, a lost Gaelic *Iliad*. His dishonesty would have been matched by any English forger who stapled together ballads of Robin Hood and passed them off as the Nottingham *Beowulf*, though that would have been more difficult to do as English tradition lacks the obscurity and longevity of the Gaelic. Because no record of Macpherson's private views of his work survive we have only his public imposture on the poems, a pose which met the popular misconceived reception to the *Fragments* and *Ossian*. Just how Macpherson found himself in that position is a subject of speculation. John S. Smart in his then comprehensive (1905) and unfriendly study of Macpherson believes he was a confidence man from the moment he met John Home, using his "translations" as a route to a life of corrupt ease. Knowing that Macpherson abandoned *Ossian* and Gaelic studies at the age of twenty-seven, except to defend his completed works, and that he was an opportunist in later life, we can hardly dismiss such a judgment. On the other hand, T. Bailey Saunders, Macpherson's biographer, argues that he did not misrepresent his intentions until he was asked to and sees him as a victim of his own success. Had he behaved differently, Saunders asserts, Macpherson would compare well with Chatterton, with Bishop Percy, who dealt rather cavalierly with ancient poetry in his *Reliques* (1765), with Elias Lönnrott, whose concatentation of Finnish popular poetry has been accepted as the *Kalevala* (1835), the lost national epic of that country, or even with Snorri Sturluson, the Icelandic Christian whose confused record of Norse mythology in the prose *Edda* (c. 1225) is still our best source on that subject. More affirmatively in Macpherson's favor, the great linguist W. A. Craigie has written: "Had the same thing been done by one of equal genuis at an earlier date there might have been a great Gaelic epic not inferior in interest to those of Greece or later Europe" (338, 1899, 262). Arthur Koestler ponders the question of Macpherson in his *Act of Creation* (1964), asking if the poetic quality of the work itself is altered by the fact that the poems were not written by Ossian the son of Fingal, but by James Macpherson (663, 1964, 402–403). How else could a work which most modern readers find dull have, in Koestler's quotation of an older edition of the *Encyclopedia Britannica*, "done more than any single work to bring about the romantic movement in European, and especially in German, literature. . . ." John V. Kelleher has answered that question in saying that Macpherson was a poetical genius; a third-rate writer, but still a genius (370, 1973).

Macpherson's *Ossian*, whatever its artistic demerits, gives to the archetype of Fionn mac Cumhaill a fuller, more detailed characterization than it had yet received in any one work in Irish, Scots Gaelic, or English. Part of the reason for this is that the poems, in the midst of their many pretensions, are actually works of prose fiction. They lack the precision and tension we associate with the modern short story and the thematic and character development of even eighteenth-century novels. Instead, they seem more like the Renaissance novella or English novel in the generation of Aphra Behn. In common with this earlier, rather prolix form, *Ossian* gives the enumeration rather than the analysis or development of character. Fingal does not receive the kind of development he would have received in a novel of the 1760s because the *Poems of Ossian*, accurately reflecting the disorder in collections of Gaelic ballads, lack not only thematic but also chronological development. The *Poems of Ossian* are so fragmented that different editors, including the most recent, have arranged the fragments differently without troubling to comment on it.

Fingal is, nevertheless, consistently drawn, in part because of Macpherson's efforts to maintain the sham of the persona of Ossian, a point of view he sometimes received intact from those ballads we describe as, in reattributed phrasing, spoken in "Ossianic frame." Ossian being a dutiful and obedient son, Fingal is always portrayed as powerful (he is frequently called the king), responsible, proud, stately, sometimes grave and solemn, but not ambitious or cruel. Malcolm Laing in the introduction to the Edinburgh edition of 1805 summarized Fingal's persona thus: ". . . wise and prudent as Solomon, strong and terrible as Achilles; early in love like Rinaldo; mild and affectionate as the pious Aeneas, yet exempt from all that was reprehensible in their characters" (p. xliv). Remembering Gerard Murphy's delineation of Fionn's permanent core of distinctions, we find that Fingal too is a warrior, hunter, and poet, though not in the same proportions as in Irish tradition, manuscript and oral. Fingal is almost constantly at war, pursuing new conquests, righting new wrongs, never cloyed with any victory. He is much more bellicose than the Fionn of Highland ballads, although both are the product of a society which was, down to 1745, as warlike as any in Western Europe. Still, Fingal does hunt, as in Book VI of "Fingal," but he does it more as a digression from battle than as an end atavistically sacred in itself. Similarly, Fingal is a patron of poetry and song, particularly the lament for those slain in battle, and the narrator frequently implies that Fingal is himself a poet, though no specific works are ascribed to him in *Ossian*. Throughout the work, actual composition always seems the province of the bards. Fingal lacks Fionn's magical thumb and powers of divination, but he does seem to retain some of the power to heal, not magically but pharmacologically. In a note to Book VIII of "Temora," Macpherson tells us that "Fingal is very much celebrated in tradition for his knowledge of the virtues of herbs."[2]

Most of the descriptions of Fingal come in conventional apostrophes at the beginning of narratives of adventure. Here, for example, is one ascribed to the bard Carril as he recounts, to Cuthullin, Fingal's adventures in Lochlin (cf. the Irish Lochlann), which includes the death of his beloved, Agandecca, the sister of his enemy, Swaran.

> "Fingal! thou dweller in battle," said Carril, "early were thy deeds in arms. Lochlin was consumed in thy wrath, when thy youth strove with the beauty of maids. They smiled at the fair-blooming face of the hero; but death was in his hands. He was as strong as the waters of Lora. His followers were the roar of a thousand streams. . . . His big heart swelled with pride; the death of the youth was dark in his soul. For none ever, but Fingal, had overcome the strength of the mighty Starno. . . . (61–62).

Macpherson always tells rather than shows. The diction of *Ossian* is thick with figures of speech, but precise imagery, especially visual imagery of people and events, is nonexistent. Thus Fingal, like most of the characters in the work, comes before us pre-formed and subjectively judged. We are always told how to react to his virtues of courage and heroism. The opportunities for irony in such a character can hardly be discussed. Unlike Fionn mac Cumhaill, Fingal never falls from grace, never takes a pratfall, and never suffers vilification.

Yet Macpherson allows Fingal a richer emotional life than his counterpart in traditional literature. Fingal has a much more abundant love life than does Fionn, and he shows much deeper grief. He has a romantic presence and attractiveness allowed only to Diarmaid in the traditional narratives. We can see this in the fragment "Comala," named for the Orcadian princess who falls in love with Fingal after seeing him at a wedding feast, and, consumed in a violent passion, disguises herself as a youth so she might follow him into war, which leads to her destruction. Fingal is successful in his love of the daughter of Cormac, king of Ireland, here called Ros-Crana instead of Gráinne, and she later becomes his only wife. As suggested in the previous paragraph, Fingal was the star-crossed lover of the beautiful princess from Lochlin, Agandecca, one of Macpherson's inventions. Fingal has two romantic encouters with Agandecca, and in the second she warns the hero of an ambush the Lochlinners plan for him. After Fingal annihilates his attackers, Agandecca's father, the dastardly Starno, "pierces her side with steel." No beautiful maiden ever dies for love of Fionn, and though he is recorded in genealogies as having mated with more than two dozen women, most of his sexual encounters with lovely ladies are depicted as carrying more dangers than pleasures.

More importantly, and from our perspective most characteristically, the Fingal of Macpherson is a man of feeling, an epitome of the mid-eighteenth century morbid sentimentality that sighed at the *Sentimental Journey*, wept over *Pamela*, and trembled with Young's *Night Thoughts* and Balair's *Grave*. Appropriately, then, Fingal is more concerned with mourning the dead than with celebrating victory although Macpherson presents him as suffering no significant defeats. Maudlin morbidity is general in the *Poems of Ossian*, but in "Temora," where it is gratuitous, exaggerated, and awkwardly juxtaposed with contrasting emotions, the ubiquity of gloom is absurd. The tone of the epic is set early in Book I when we see Oscar killed. As in traditional Fenian literature, Macpherson's Oscar is an admirable young hero of romantic promise. His early death, like that of Adonis and Balder, underscores his beauty, and may have helped to make his name popular all over Europe, from the royal families of Germany and Scandinavia to the Wilde family of Dublin. Many first readers of *Ossian* may have shared grandfather Fingal's grief:

> How long on Moi-lena shall we weep? How long pour in Erin our tears? The might will not return. Oscar shall not rise in his strength. The valiant must fall in their day, and be no more known on their hills. Where are our fathers, O warriors! The chiefs of the times of old? They have set like stars that have shown. . . . Thus shall we pass away, in the day of our fall (p. 231).

Subsequently, other warriors of Morven go forth and win great victories while Fingal holds his might in reserve, waiting for the greater battle with the archvillain, Cathmor. In Book III, Gaul Fillan, a brother of Ossian, returns to the Caledonian camp to celebrate yet another victory. Rather than join in the feasting, Fingal is still of a mind for grieving, not for Oscar cold in his grave, but instead for

a companion of childhood who was killed almost incidentally in the
recent battle:

> My soul feels a want in our joy. I behold a breach among
> my missing friends. The head of one tree is low. The squally
> wind pours in on Selma. Where is the chief of Dun-lora? Ought
> Connal to be forgot at the feast? When did he forget the stranger,
> in the midst of this echoing hall? Ye are silent in my presence!
> Connal is then no more (p. 262).

The action of "Temora" continues and the warriors of Morven
gain on the blackguardly Cathmor, but at an increased price: Fillan,
Ossian's brother, is killed. At last, when the Caledonians meet
Cathmor in contest, Fingal, the mightiest of the host, must come
forth to the fray. Just as he is to enter battle, he passes Lubar's cave
where Fillan lies buried, and in a nonce-ritual he stops to think of
his fallen son:

> Then grief stirred the soul of the king, like whirlwinds
> blackening on a lake. He turned his sudden step, and leaned on
> his bending spear.
> He came, and looked towards the cave, where the blue-
> eyed hunter lay, for he was wont to stride, with morning, to
> the dewy bed of roe. It was then the tears of the king came
> down, and all his soul was dark. But as the rising wind rolls
> away the storm of rain, and leaves the white streams to the sun,
> and high hills with their heads of grass: so the returning war
> brightened the mind of Fingal (pp. 318–19).

His toll of tears paid, Fingal goes on to meet Cathmor, and
victory is his in just a few paragraphs. Celebration ensues, but Fingal
will not be given over to vulgar merry-making. He closes the action
of the epic by giving over his spear, the spear inherited from his
grandfather Trenmor, in the passing of power from age to youth,
an acknowledgement that Fingal will withdraw and wait for death
away from war.

The sentiment which the informed reader of the twentieth
century finds so mawkish in Macpherson is apparently the same one
which in earlier generations contributed to Ossian's prestige. As late
as one hundred years after the initial publication, the fey morbidity

of the *Poems of Ossian* was attractive to, of all people, Matthew Arnold, who chose as an epigram for his *Study of Celtic Literature* (1867) a line from the fragment "Cath-loda," which runs, ". . . they came forth to war, but they always fell" (p. 14). Arnold's choice of this line no doubt reflects his admiration for a recognition of the dangers of life which contrasted with the shallow optimism of his contemporary bourgeois imperialists, but his judgment, as well as his entire essay, has been scorned by many Celticists because of his lack of knowledge of Irish or Welsh and his reliance, apparently inevitable, on James Macpherson. This is not to say that the fatalism and sentiment which drips in Macpherson cannot be found in actual Celtic literature. Speaking in defense of Arnold's insight, Rachel Bromwich, one of the most eminent Welsh scholars of our own day, suggests that the line "they went forth to war, but they always fell" could have been found in a translation of the sixth century *Gododdin* in which the bard Aneirin speaks of the British warriors who fell at the battle of Catraeth with a recurrent fatalism which is no less despondent than Macpherson's (471, 1965, 19).

In the evidence reviewed here so briefly, it should be clear that some of what Macpherson exploited from Gaelic ballads is, in itself, actually traditional, or, more broadly, that it is actually representative of Irish and Gaelic tradition. Instead, the reason we must look upon Macpherson's work as an episode in English literature is, put most simply, that it distorts Irish and Gaelic traditions, not only in the matter of the characterization of Fionn mac Cumhaill but in the greater matter of representing the *weltanschauung* of the traditional poet in the Celtic languages. An effective contrast to the vision of Macpherson is that of his Irish contemporary Brian Mac Giolla Meidhre (*anglice,* Merriman, 1747–1805), whose *Cúirt an Mheáin Oich* ("The Midnight Court," 1781) is an earthy, humorous, colloquial, multi-leveled satire which both in Irish and English translation has been one of Ireland's most frequently banned works. A measure of Macpherson's representiveness can be seen in J. F. Campbell's great collection of Highland Fenian ballads, *Leabhar na Feinne*, in which only a six-page appendix is devoted to "Heroic Gaelic Poems, like Macpherson's Ossian" from the total of a 224-page volume (236, 1872). Another editor, such as Derick Thomson, would doubtless provide Macpherson with a higher percentage of the total, but Campbell's implicit criticism, that the bulk of Highland Fenian ballads are of substantially different tone and theme than the epics and fragments of the *Poems of Ossian*, still stands.

Our modern understanding of *Ossian* encourages us to read the work as if it were anonymous, eschewing all questions of authenticity and the intentional fallacy which dominated earlier criticism of it. The manifest shortcomings of Macpherson's prolix style, visible in the citations above, make it unlikely that the *Poems of Ossian* will see a revival in our lifetime, barring a campy interest in eighteenth-century morbidity. Our perspective, however, does allow us to measure the work as an expansion of the literary use of myth and an adumbration of things to come. In the *Poems of Ossian* the author's infusion of contemporary tastes and values is an anticipation of Tennyson's *Idylls of the King* and Homeric poems, and, ultimately, of Joyce's *Ulysses*. Macpherson's more considerable accomplishment is that he took the archetype of Fingal, which he thought to be ancient, and transformed it into a paradigm of contemporary taste. In his hands Celtic myth became literary myth in English. Fingal is not only a hero of sentiment, he is also the resident of an ontologically self-sufficient Newtonian universe; for all the mists and clouds in Morven there are no gods to be worshipped or feared. The portrait of life in Macpherson's *Ossian* is like the classicism of the blue and white Portland vases Josiah Wedgwood began to produce in the late eighteenth century. Like the figures in relief on the vase, or like the characters in Jane Austen's novels, Fingal and the warriors of Morven live in a world without droughts, plagues, social disorders, or any economic upheavals. If their heroism or grief is exaggerated it is because of its isolation in the text. This portrait of the Fenian hero and of the world of the Celtic imagination was to be a lasting one.

THE RIVALS, HEIRS, AND MENDERS
OF THE *POEMS OF OSSIAN*

As it has already been the subject of several book-length studies and numerous articles, the question of the impact of Macpherson's *Ossian* on English literature and culture will not long concern us here. The immediate impact of the Ossianic taste for exotic, sentimental gloom produced the short-lived Celtic Revival (to be distinguished from the Celtic or Irish Renaissance more than a century later) among such writers as Thomas Gray, Henry Brooke, Macpherson's ally John Home, and a host of lesser writers, as E. D.

Snyder's study, *The Celtic Revival in English Literature*, has shown (603, 1923). John J. Dunn's dissertation investigates the role of *Ossian* in British Romanticism (655, 1966), and F. I. Carpenter has studied the vogue for *Ossian* in America (651, 1931). Other writers have studied the ties between Macpherson and Blake, Wordsworth, Byron, Thomas Jefferson, and Thoreau. It can be argued that the writer most indebted to Macpherson's imaginative world is the American novelist James Fenimore Cooper; many details in Cooper's novels, including such trivial ones as the taboo against snapping twigs in the forest that won Mark Twain's celebrated scorn, are of Fenian origin. It may be that any number of Cooper's woodland heroes are really Fingal and Ossian transmogrified in the new continent (660, 1969).

Putting these aside, we shall instead confine ourselves to those works appearing in the wake of *Ossian* in which the characters of Fionn or Fingal are actually depicted. In all of these, some supporting Macpherson, others imitating him, and at last, still others correcting him, there is little development of the personality of the hero from the outlines limned in *Ossian*.

The unprecedented success of the *Poems of Ossian* inevitably encouraged other obscure young would-be littérateurs to exploit the rich resources of Highland Fenian tradition. "Popular antiquities", as we have considered, were not yet understood as folklore, and in the Gaelic Highlands, they were still plentiful. By 1810 a dozen collections of Fenian narratives, mostly ballads, had been gathered from Gaelic storytellers and singers, many of which would serve other translators, real and ersatz, even though the texts were not published until the late nineteenth century. Our contemporary understanding of the mythical foundations of Fionn and his cycle was not possible until scholars, most of them Continental, learned to read the earliest manuscripts. Meanwhile Macpherson had created the framework in which much bogus literature and history would easily fit. Actually, the originator of bogus Gaelic literature in the mid-eighteenth century was Jerome Stone, whose freewheeling translations, noted earlier, spurred Macpherson initially. Stone's "translations," while not as eclectic or inventive as Macpherson's, cannot be described as either literal or conceptual, and they do not treat of Fingal or Fionn.

The first of the volumes to appear which compares with *Ossian* is John Clark's *The Works of the Caledonia Bards, translated from the Original Galic* [sic] (1778), a work often referred to as *Caledonian Bards*, or *Morduth*, after its best-known character, which set the pattern for subsequent enterprises. Far from challenging *Ossian*'s authenticity, Clark, who had once been a student of Macpherson in Badenoch, defended Macpherson and claimed that both his and his teacher's works had survived from ancient times. According to Clark's pretext, Morduth was a later king of Caledonia who authorized the bards, principally one named Douthal, to compose the poems which he, Clark, was now bringing to English. Understandably, Fingal plays a small role in the narratives; one reference gives the etymology of his name as "white" or "fair." *Caledonian Bards* was a much less ambitious work than the *Poems of Ossian,* and its prose was much harder going; Nigel MacNeill called it "turgid nonsense" (392, 1929, 336), although an admirer, Mrs. Grant of Leggan, put a portion of the book in verse.

More ingenious than Clark, or for that matter, Macpherson, was the scholarly minister of Argyllshire, Dr. John Smith, whose *Sean Dana le Oisian, Orran, Ulann,* etc. appeared in 1787. A fine student of Gaelic, Smith translated into that language the *Shorter* [Anglican] *Catechism* and the entire *Old Testament,* as well as having edited the Gaelic Psalter; he had also written a *History of the Druids,* a life of Saint Columba, a study of Gaelic antiquities, as well as a work on ecclesiastical discipline. Knowing this we are hard put to explain why he includes a defense of Macpherson in an appendix. Smith's Ossianic poems appear bound with Gaelic "originals." Derick Thomson has explained that Smith first wrested English prose narratives from Gaelic ballad manuscripts and later translated the prose back into the original language (683, 1958, 180). The author of *Poems of Ossian* lacked the perspicacity and apparently the skill to produce such "originals" on his own, and, indeed, he was still laboring with a comparable forgery when he died nine years after the publication of *Sean Dana.*

Smith is more authentic than Macpherson to the extent that he keeps all his narratives more strictly in the persona of Ossian, much as the Gaelic ballads do, instead of digressing into other cycles as Macpherson does with "Dar-thula." In keeping with this premise, Smith's Fingal is already dead when the action of the first narrative begins, and thus the only salient distinction between his and Macpherson's Fingal is that Smith's is more an embodiment of the lost days gone by.

The MacCallum brothers, Hugh and John, were resourceful enough to raise a subscription to publish their *Original Collection of the Poems of Ossian, Orrann, Ulin, and other Bards, Who Flourished in the Same Age* in 1816. Their work is a step toward a genuine translation of Gaelic materials, but the authors unfortunately succumbed to the continuing Ossianic expectations of the Scottish reading public. Like Clark and Smith they defended Macpherson's translations, and following Smith's lead they produced, in a very small press run, line-for-line Gaelic originals for their English text. Drawing from the many new collections of Gaelic ballads, the MacCallum brothers included a number of serviceable translations of common Highland ballads intermixed with their spurious poetry.

The MacCallums' *Fingal* shows a number of departures from the others of recent construction. Like the hero of traditional ballads, their Fingal is a poet-warrior, as in the second chapter of the work where he sings a war chant to rouse his men to repulse the Scandinavian invaders. More significantly, the MacCallum brothers portray Fingal and his men in something less than an admiring light. In this third narrative in the collection, Fingal is shown as old and unlucky in love; when he is rebuffed by a maid whose affection he desires, he sings of his youth when he was a better lover. In the following section, the Fingalians are insulted not to be invited to a feast, and in reaction, leave the country to form an expedition to Lochlin. Perhaps the most lasting contribution from the MacCallum brothers was their critical introduction, which attempted to give scholarly support to the Ossianic associations of the colonnaded Staffa Island in the Inner Hebrides, where there is one of the many Fingal's Caves. Through this association Fingal was commemorated in Mendelsson's alternate title for his *Hebrides Overture*, "Fingal's Cave" (1829).

Although Smith, Clark, and the MacCallum brothers supported Macpherson's claims to have uncovered the poetry of a lost civilization, they are his rivals in that they produced additional books which claimed the same descent. Their efforts did not exhaust the impulse which was continued as late as 1841 by a Highland émigré in Canada, Patrick MacGregor, who "corrected" Macpherson in a retelling of the *Poems of Ossian*, but as no later work in this vein does anything to expand an understanding of the character of Fingal, we may ignore them.

Macpherson's influence spread far beyond Ossianic questions, encouraging a generation of would-be interpreters of the remote past. There is, for example, a "Welsh Macpherson," Edward Williams, who, in the 1790s under the name of Iolo Morganwg, created a body of sham medieval poetry, including eighteen poems in Welsh which he ascribed to the actual fourteenth century poet, Dafydd ap Gwilym, and succeeded in having included in a 1789 edition of Dafydd's poetry. Departing from *belles-lettres*, we find that the Irish rivals of Macpherson, as John V. Kelleher has suggested, were the "twin plagues of Irish historiography," Colonel Charles Vallancey (1721–1812), and more importantly for our questions, his colleague, Sylvester O'Halloran (1728–1807), whose several repetitive histories of Ireland, 1772–1778, relied more on intuition and divination than on antiquarianism or scholarship (370, 1973). Their foolishness pursued such questions as whether the Irish might be the lost Tribe of Israel. But they also gave us the neologism "Fenian."

Quite apart from the sham antiquities and Macpherson's rivals was another body of literature, all of it *belles-lettres* rather than psuedo-scholarship, which also appears to draw from the imaginative world of the *Poems of Ossian*. Several writers, many of whom are still anonymous, might be called the heirs of Macpherson because they inherit the romantic attractiveness of long ago Morven without troubling to construct a specious apparatus to convince readers they are being treated to something preserved from a lost world. Among these were the dramatizers of *Ossian*. Ironically there were more of these on the Continent and in Scandinavia where from 1780 to 1820 there were at least a half-dozen operatic libretti based on Macpherson's text, one of the least forgettable being Jean François LeSueur's *Ossian; ou les bardes* (1804). For the English dramatic imagination, it would appear, the endless heroics of ancient Caledonia were less stageworthy. There is record of only one dramatic presentation of Fingal and that was in an anonymous, short choral masque published in London in 1815.

Although we do not know the author or original performance date of *The Druid, or Vision of Fingal; a Choral Masque*, the copy which survives includes the names of performers and musical accompaniment; judging by the silence from historians of the English theater of this period and the intrinsic banality of the tetrameter couplets, *The Druid*, seventeen pages long in published form, was less than a success. Taking the characters, Fingal and his wife Roscrana, and the setting, the hall of Selma, from Macpherson, *The Druid* begins at a victory celebration which, characteristically, Fingal feels too much grief to join. Asked the cause of his woe by Roscrana, Fingal answers that his victory can never be complete. Sometime in the future

When Fingal's race, the race of song,
Shall sink amidst that current strong,
And silence brood where Bards in Selma sing,
And fluttering ivy climb where hands the tuneful string (p. 6).

Roscrana calls in an unnamed druid, who, unlike the simpler bards of *Ossian*, has the power to divine the future. He says, first, that the Highlanders will outlive the Romans, but that there will be centuries of wars and contentions, and culminating them all, the French Revolution:

The halo leaves the royal head,
To helmets grim the mitres grow,
The lawn is dy'd with murder red,
And at carousals lewd and dread
The batter'd chalices o'reflow (p. 12).

Fingal still wishes that his eyes could pierce the veil of the future, but he is otherwise emboldened, and the masque ends in four choruses from assembled warriors which include, among other things, an invocation to "Wodan! O God of our Fathers" and this propitiation of the hero:

Fingal! raise thine arm on high!
Strike aloud the sword on thy shield of Oak,
That it reach th'oppressor's ear,
And with with-ring palsy strike his arm:
Let thy voice be heard amidst our fountains
And return in echoes from the mountains (pp. 16–17).

The author of *The Druid* seems to equate Romans with Napoleonic Frenchmen and ancient Caledonia or Albin with modern Albion, and he puts Fenian narratives in the service of bellicose nationalism; ironically English nationalism, for the first time.

In Ireland, meanwhile, there was a different response to Macpherson's success. Along with the bona fide translation of Fenian materials came a criticism of the *Poems of Ossian* which did not dispute their authenticity but instead attacked the Scottish setting of the poems. Representative of this response was the popular *History of Ireland* by Thomas Moore, the only English Romantic poet of any standing who contributed to the myth of the heroic Fionn mac Cumhaill in English (557, 1835, 133, 137). The heroic vision of Moore's *Irish Melodies* (1808–34) was in its way as untraditional as that of *Ossian*, although it came two generations later. The *Irish Melodies* are, of course, short lyrics rather than sustained heroic narratives, and the details have been modified by incipient Celtic philology, at first sham, but, as time passed, more informed. An example of the accuracy of Moore's vision can be seen immediately in his naming the warriors of the Ulster Cycle the "Red Branch Knights." In the original texts, the Ulster heroes, *curadh*, are not comparable to the high medieval, chivalric knights, *ridire*. Moore presented a lasting portrait of heroic Ireland in such poems as "The Harp that Once Through Tara's Halls," based on materials from the Ulster Cycle, but he was not especially attracted to the Fenian Cycle. One of the few exceptions is "The Wine-Cup is Circling" which describes festivities at the Hill of Allen (here "Almhim"). Fionn is seen:

> . . . mid his heroes reclining,
> Looks up, with a sigh, to the tophied wall,
> Where his sword hangs idly shining (1895, 218).

The repose of the Fenians (here "Finians") is shattered by invading Danes, familiar foe:

> While remembering the yoke
> Which their fathers broke,
> 'On for liberty, for liberty!' the Finians cried (60, 197–98).

Again we see Fionn politicized, only this time he seems a champion of the principles of the French Revolution rather than their adversary.

The most sustained Irish response to Ossian is the anonymous *Fingal, A Fine-Eirin*, a lengthy (164 pages) narrative poem in five cantos published in London in 1813, a forgotten work which has not, to my knowledge, been the subject of any critical discussion. The author has drawn on information in Keating and O'Halloran but has no pretenses about what he is doing. "Let none then despise the endeavour, however humble, now made, even by the aid of fiction, to throw light upon the former manners and customs of one of the oldest and noblest nations of the earth" (4, iv). Like Moore, the author does not call Macpherson a fraud, but he challenges the expropriation of Fingal (not here called Fionn) to Scotland. In taking the "aid of fiction" to reach the world of the ancient Fenians he invents a new cast of characters with Macphersonic names including Veivion, the lovely young maiden who is the leading character of the poem; Carthollan, a good Irish king, a villainous usurper of Tara (here "Tarah"), Marthon, of whom one of his subjects remarks, ". . . curs'd be that hour. When Marthon strode to kingly power" (p. 47). Fingal does not appear in the first four cantos, in which we learn of unrequited love, scheming high priests who live in the dream luxury of Coleridge's Kubla Khan, and the need for unity between Carthollan's kingdom, Emania (after Emhain Macha, the ancient capital of Ulster whose remains are near the modern town of Armagh) and Tarah. While not present, Fingal is the subject of much con-versation; he is here a conflation of the Fionn of Irish tradition with some of the sentiment of the *Poems of Ossian*, plus a few innovations. For example, he is a warrior in the service of Tarah, but somehow he has been isolated from royal power, does not stand at the head of the armies, and is away in the country. Like Macpherson's Fingal, he is distinguished by his grief:

> Fingal's great spirit glow'd no more,
> No bonds of amity he form'd;
> He griev'd, but no man knew his owe;
> It seemed as heav'n in wrath had storm'd
> And laid a beauteous Fabril low (p. 131).

Perhaps to personify his sorrow, Fingal is here described as dark, the only time he is presented as other than fair-haired.

When Fingal at last appears he is in disguise, but his com-manding virtues are immediately manifest to the faithful:

> His ample shield, his dark-plumed helm,
> His look that might a host o'erwhelm,

His giant voice he raised on high—
'Come sons of Tarah, round the throne' (p. 136).

Straightaway Fingal restores virtue, light, and order. He finds the
bloodstained knife with which Marthon had killed a faithful retainer
and locks him up for life without a trial. Assuming the throne himself,
Fingal tells Veivion to put off her woe and makes the plans to unite
her with a prince of Tarah and, subsequently, to merge the kingdom
with Emania.

There were, in addition, other responses to Machperson's *Ossian*,
by translators who did not rival his misrepresentation and poets who
did not inherit his imaginative vision. These were the writers who
sought to mend the misimpressions of Irish and Gaelic literature
created by the success of the *Poems of Ossian*. Among the ranks of
the menders are the more than dozen collectors of Highland Fenian
narratives. Their work, much of it not published until the late
nineteenth century, was the first extensive collection from the folklore
of the Celtic peoples of the British Isles who, within a century,
became largely English-speaking and thus were cut off from their
heritage. Many of these collectors were Macpherson's partisans and
had hoped to prove the *Poems of Ossian* the genuine lost epic of the
ancient Celts; their monument in scholarship is the *Report of the
Committee of the Highland Society of Scotland* (1805), largely edited
by Henry MacKenzie, which collated numerous manuscripts and
reached a conclusion in accord with our present understanding of
Macpherson's efforts.

Eventually the vitality of Fionn, the Celtic warrior-hunter-poet,
overcame and displaced the gloomy sensibility of Fingal, the eighteenth-century hero. The effort to restore Fionn, as well as other
Celtic figures, was conducted by three disconnected generations of
Irish translators from the 1780s to the 1850s. The three generations
were first the old Anglo-Irish gentry, who sometimes took a paternal
interest in the peasantry; second were the nascent Celticists whose
enthusiasm sometimes overcame their weak grasp of the language;
and third, the men of learning who, by the mid-nineteenth century
sought to meet the then current standards of scholarship in England
and on the Continent. The turbulence of Irish social life shaped and
limited the work of early revivalists. The prosperity of the time of
the Irish Parliament ended abruptly with the Act of Union (1800),
followed by an economic decline that reached its nadir in the Famine

(1844–47). A country that was not allowed to rule itself and could not always feed its people did not always have time for scholarship.

The Ascendancy discovery of traditional native poetic tradition apparently began with Charlotte Brooke's *Reliques of Irish Poetry* in 1789. I use the qualifier "apparently" because *Poems Translated from the Irish Language* (London, 1782) by one Charles Wilson does not survive although its existence is testified to by Sir Walter Scott and others. Charlotte Brooke was one of the twenty-two children of Henry Brooke, an Anglo-Irish man of letters in Georgian Dublin. Charlotte Brooke's versification, while less than arresting, avoids the tiresome mannerisms of Macpherson and company. She evokes neither the diction nor the rhetoric of Irish and evinces no anticipations of the distinctive Anglo-Irish tradition in poetry that began in the generation of J. C. Mangan and Sir Samuel Ferguson. Nevertheless, her *Reliques* does include a handful of Fenian poems that do portray the hunter-warrior-poet unsullied by the banalities of contemporary taste. Her poem, "The Chase," depicts Fionn in the familiar *bruidhean* enchantment wherein nature is seen as much magical as it is enticing.

Responses to Brooke's *Reliques* were slow in coming, as much because of the lack of patronage for Celtic study as for lack of media for publication. The Gaelic Society of Dublin, under the musically named Theophilus O'Flanagan, included several Fenian poems in its *Transactions* (1808), the only volume published. In time such popular publications as *The Christian Examiner, The Dublin Penny Journal,* and *The Irish Penny Journal* as well as the Ascendancy *Dublin University Magazine* provided outlets for Irish language materials. Fenian subjects were often featured. Translators of many of these poems and stories are anonymous, but among them was James Clarence Mangan whose Fenian story, "The Churl in the Grey Coat," appeared in *The Irish Penny Journal* in 1840. Two collections of early translations were William H. Drummond's *Ancient Irish Minstrelsy* (1852), taken mostly from oral tradition, and John Hawkins Simpson's *Poems of Oisín, Bard of Erin* (1857). Although many of his materials had been collected in Ireland, some from very old manuscripts, Simpson, heavily influenced by the nefarious Colonel Vallancey, subsequently assumed the absurd position of trying to uphold Macpherson even as he refuted him in his translations.

The work which made the decade of the 1850s the landmark separating the imitators and correctors of Macpherson from everything that came later was the six volumes of translations appearing in the *Transactions of the Ossianic Society,* 1853–61. The four scholars who worked on the translations, Nicholas O'Kearney, Standish Hayes O'Grady, John O'Daly, and Owen Connellan, were all products of informal training in the Irish language, but they knew what they were about. Of the scholars, some, like Connellan, were given to eccentric excesses, such as believing that Irish was identical with Etruscan, whereas others, like Standish Hayes O'Grady, were fully competent linguists who went on to make further contributions to scholarship later in the century. All of the volumes in the *Ossianic Society* series are dual language editions, although the provenience of manuscripts is not always clear. In general the translations were the best then available, and although many passages would today be translated differently, each volume of the series, though superseded, is still usable. In addition to the translations, each volume contained extensive notes, sometimes equal in length to the works they described. And of the six volumes, five presented the heroic hunter-warrior-poet Fionn mac Cumhaill. The darker Fionn appeared in the sixth volume, *The Pursuit after Diarmaid and Gráinne*, although, curiously, the editors did not feel they needed to explain the lack of coordination with the more admirable figure in the other volumes. Perhaps because the juxtaposition of jealous cuckold with hunter-warrior-poet would be familiar to anyone who knew the Irish traditions it required no commentary at that time. The misconceptions of the Macpherson era could no longer be entertained, although the definitive rebuttal of his imposture would not come for a few more decades, and the authenticity question was now clear to anyone who cared to examine it. As Fenian narratives were Irish in origin, variants of them had proliferated in the Gaelic Highlands, and not the other way around. The hero of those narratives was far more diverse than anyone seen in the *Poems of Ossian*. The heroic Fionn mac Cumhaill was now accessible to the urban writer in Ireland, be he Anglo-Irish or a Celt who had lost his native language.

Within a few years more manuscripts, including those from the other heroic cycles, stories of Cúchulainn, Deirdre, the Children of Lir, etc., would be translated from the oldest manuscripts, demonstrating to the Irish writer, oppressed and increasingly an alien in his own land, that he was the heir of great body of fabulous literature, at root a mythology, the figures of which were not the homely creatures of the folklore which survived in the cabins dotting the boglands of the country but rather the survivals of ancient gods now in their twilight.

FIONN MAC CUMHAILL IN
THE IRISH RENAISSANCE AND AFTER

Although the Irish Literary Renaissance is conventionally portrayed as an isolated cultural phenomenon in which an elite guard of poets, many of them theosophists, found a common cause with the oppressed Catholic subclass, we can now see it as an Irish example of a general European pattern. The characteristic lassitude and sweet despair of the "Celtic Twlight" have cognates in the tastes of the contemporary aesthetes and decadents of more urbanized countries. At the same time the "Twlight's" Celticism seemed to insist on a national uniqueness existing from earliest times. Although the "poets and dreamers," in Lady Gregory's phrase, were more interested in bringing literary distinction to provincial Dublin, absent since the time of Dean Swift, than they were in politics, their movement runs parallel to, even while indifferent to, the nationalist drive for the establishment of an independent republic. A similar kind of cultural and political nationalism can be found in other European heirs of ancient tradition which had not yet become nation-states. In Italy the drive for national unity brought with it the *risorgimento*, a renewed celebration of that country's distinctive and rich tradition in art and literature. In Germany the rise of nationalism was warded by a legion of fastidious scholars who saw in Germanic tradition the oldest and purest stream in European culture, a heroic tradition which would find its greatest contemporary commemoration in the titanically egotistical music dramas of Richard Wagner. Even in moderate England, men like Augustus Pugin and William Morris looked to the distant past for a style and taste more attractive than that of the sometimes sordid present. What set the Irish example apart from those elsewhere was that the traditions of distant epochs still lived in the remote and unfashionable corners of the country, the *Gaeltacht*. The traditions of the popular national hero, Fionn mac Cumhaill, came more readily to the lips of folk reciters in the Irish-speaking districts than any other, and, as we have seen, Fenian myths were the first from the early manuscripts to be revived, yet when the authors of the new revival of letters looked for a patron-hero, a Siegfried, they chose instead the hero of the aristocratic Ulster Cycle which had been lost to popular tradition for several centuries, Cúchulainn.

What made Fionn unsuitable for revival after so much effort
had been expended to extricate him from the misconceptions of
Macpherson and his contemporaries? It may have been that his name
was a commonplace, already too heavily invested with popular, not
to say vulgar, associations that made the Fenian hero too pedestrian
for the Kelmscott-Gothic tastes of the earlier Irish Renaissance. It
could be argued that because Fionn still lived, he could not be
revived, or that any attempt to restore him to his medieval heroic
splendor was bound to include the popular colorations he had received from the peasantry. Further, Fionn became the butt of those
who, for one reason or another, opposed the pretensions of emergent
Irish nationalism. Beginning as early as the 1820s, and including
such well-known contributors as William Carleton (1794–1869), an
anti-heroic Fenian tradition had been developing in Anglo-Irish literature which made Fionn appear a bumpkin and a buffoon. This
is not to say that no new heroic Fenian literature was produced.
Even before the *Transactions of the Ossianic Society* appeared there
were several examples of a revived heroic Fionn mac Cumhaill. For
example, James Clarence Mangan, who had produced some of the
most memorable translations from Irish, such as his most famous
poem, "The Dark Rosaleen," also composed an original "Lament for
the Fianna" (c. 1840), filled with the heroic retrospection which
characterizes the Fenian Cycle in Irish. Yet for the most part, though
the checklist of heroic Fenian portrayals in literature of the Irish
Renaissance is fairly extensive, more often writers for children, historians and essayists, belletristic writers of lesser talent were attracted
to the heroic Fionn.

An apt illustration of the conspicuous absence of heroic Fenian
literature can be seen in the history of the secret society known as
the Fenians, a body which had previously been known as the I.R.B.,
alternately the Irish Revolutionary and the Irish Republican Brotherhood, who adopted the mythological name in 1858. It is because
of their popularization of the word "Fenian" that it is used for the
cycle of Irish literature, despite its being a solecism. After adopting
a form of his name, the Fenians took no further interest in Fionn
mac Cumhaill. For example, there is not one mention of Fionn in
the rallying songs of the movement, collected in Stephens' *Fenian
Songster* and *Fenian War Songs* (both 1866). Paradoxically, one of the
most familiar, or most anthologized, portraits of Fionn came in some
nationalist verse written by Thomas D'Arcy McGee, an émigré who
became a member of parliament in Canada where he denounced the

Fenians and was subsequently assassinated in 1868. McGee's "The Celts," while hardly the kind of poetry that would find much critical favor today, was reprinted dozens of times and was a longtime standard in Irish high school textbooks. In the fourth stanza McGee deals with the Fenians of literary traditions, and incidentally makes Oisín the son of the married Fionn and Gráinne:

> Of these was Finn, father of the bard,
>   Whose ancient song
> Over the clamour of all change is heard,
>   Sweet-voiced and strong.

After the assassination, Evan MacColl, a Scots Gaelic poet who had also emigrated to Canada, wrote an English verse in which he decried McGee's murder and charged the Fenians with betraying the brave tradition of the Fianna.

In the absence of an epic, novel, drama, or lengthy narrative poem depicting the heroic Fionn we find instead the fanciful prose histories of Ireland by Standish James O'Grady. Not to be confused with his uncle Standish Hayes O'Grady the translator, fourteen years his senior, Standish James O'Grady (1846–1928) was a Protestant journalist, essayist, and author of boys' historical adventure fiction who is sometimes called "The Father of the Revival." In several volumes of history, O'Grady dealt with heroic Fenian narratives most extensively, first in *History of Ireland: Heroic Period* (1878), in which he approached the past "through the medium of tales, epical or romantic . . . with the subject of bringing remote times and men vividly before the mind's eye," and, later, with the slightly more conventional *History of Ireland: Critical and Pilosophical* (1881). Neither of O'Grady's histories appears to owe much directly to Macpherson, perhaps because petty ethnic rivalries made the *Poem of Ossian* Scottish and therefore foreign. O'Grady wrote that his first interest in ancient Ireland came from reading the (bogus) histories of Sylvester O'Halloran, who drew much from the milieu of *Ossian.* O'Grady's method was entirely different from Macpherson's; although not well-informed about the Celtic past he never pretended that he was writing anything but a subjective account of materials he took from the previous generation of Irish scholars, Eugene O'Curry, John O'Donovan, George Petrie, etc. Writing with verve comparable to Dumas *père* and Rafael Sabatini, O'Grady did much to raise the imaginative possibilities of many figures in old Irish mythology. Fionn was not an initial favorite, however, possibly because O'Grady could not ignore the debasing accounts of contemporary folk traditions.

Perhaps because of the irony he saw in Fionn's character, O'Grady did little in his histories to expand the archetype of the hero beyond what already existed in Irish-language texts. What he may have neglected in the histories he compensated for in his boys' novel *Finn and His Companions* (1892) and in the subsequent *The Masque of Finn* (1907). Following the tendency of most Victorian popular fiction never to recount anything untoward, O'Grady puts his stories in the mouth of Caoilte, here spelled Caelte, the great Fenian runner, who has survived with Oisín from heroic times but has been baptized and has become a pious Christian. All the badgering of Saint Patrick has been excised, and instead Caelte seems positively deferential. He remarks that the Fianna could speak the truth even though they had not known the True God because "we had truth in our hearts, strength in our hands, and discretion in our tongues" (62, 1892, 17). Their adventures seemed dedicated to good manners and probity. Like Moore, O'Grady prefers to see the old Irish heroes infused with the good graces of chivalry. After a character named the Curmudgeon refuses the Fianna the hospitality of his castle, Finn and his companions press the question, and the Curmudegeon decides to consent. In a short time he reforms his bad ways, joins the Fionna on their travels, and at the end of the chapter returns to his wife as a refreshed and renewed warrior; a fresh growth of thick black hair has replaced his baldness. O'Grady's Finn is much like the hero from Irish literature. He is still a kind of *rígfhénnid*, an uncrowned king of the forests. He is still a champion of poetry and music, has the gift of prophecy, and lives at the Hill of Allen. We see him first as the paternal leader of the Fianna, and later in the book we read fairly straightforward accounts of the episodes from the *Macgníarmhartha Finn*. In short, O'Grady's hero in *Finn and His Companions* is the warrior-hunter-poet of tradition cleaned and dressed up to meet the demands of rectitude on a Victorian Sunday. And though the book has long been out of print and is stocked in only a few libraries today, it was once hailed by William Butler Yeats as sixteenth on his list of "Thirty Best Irish Books."

In O'Grady's *The Masque of Finn*, there is a substantially different hero, although he follows a scenario derived from the later chapters of *Finn and His Companions*. This can be explained, partly, by its being directed toward a different audience. Written "sometime after" the boys' novel, *The Masque of Finn* was first performed on the grounds of Lady Desart's estate, Aut-Evin, Kilkenny, on the banks of the Nore. In his introduction, O'Grady owns that his *Masque* is modeled on Milton's *Comus* and also shows that he has become aware of the interpretations of Celtic myth that John Rhys and others were then bringing to light: "Were I to hazard an opinion of my own, I would suggest that the Fians were originally the gods of some very ancient pagan Irish religion—Finn and the Clan Basna the celestial gods, and the Clan Morna the earth gods, personifications of the ruder forces of nature" (64, 1921, 14). The Finn of the *Masque* is changed additionally because he is a character in a drama, and the narrative frame in which his story is told to Saint Patrick is deleted. When the action begins, a defeated Fianna, still dispirited seventeen years after the Battle of Cnucha, await their deliverer, the as-yet-unnamed son of their old leader, Cumall (*sic*). Finn appears, in fulfillment of prophecy, but is not recognized as he is disguised as a beggar. He brings with him gifts of ale and food and the decapitated head of Luchat Mael, here described as Cumall's usurper. The beheading motif, fairly common in Irish manuscript and oral tales, is usually omitted in children's versions. In a number of passages later in the piece Finn is portrayed as a pagan messiah bringing redemption to the captive Irish. For example, after Finn convinces the greedy Nod (an invented character personifying miserliness, first seen in *Finn and His Companions*) that he should share his wealth with the Fianna, the reformed villain praises the hero of unwalled Allen thus: "Our walls challenge the enemy and our locks invite the thief. This is the day of new things; this is the day of the wisdom of Finn" (p. 67). In the final scene of the *Masque* when Finn has been rescued from a *bruidhean*-like enchantment in a *sidhe*, the chorus of Fianna and converted enemies sings Finn's praises with such lines as (pp. 81–82):

> Prince of hunters, feasters, fighters,
>   Seek thee nobler spheres of fame,
> Be the heart and soul of Erin,
>   Be the manhood of the Gael.

> Let thy spirit with their spirit
>   Mingle till some mighty birth,
> Brings the Irish hero savior
>   Of the nations of the earth.

Because he deleted the ironic aspects of Finn's character that he had acknowledged in his histories, O'Grady gives the Finn of the *Masque* the maximum heroic investment the archetype would know in the Irish Renaissance or, for that matter, anywhere in English literature. But before bestowing too many laurels to the work we should remember it was all but ignored by O'Grady's contemporaries. It was performed in the country, not at the Abbey Theatre, and has not provoked one line of commentary, neither by Ernest Boyd, who devoted a chapter to O'Grady in *Ireland's Literary Renaissance* nor in Phillip Marcus's monograph (1970), the only lengthy study of O'-Grady's works.

If the heroic Fionn mac Cumhaill of O'Grady's *Masque* had little impact on the literature of the time, other portraits of the hero were becoming readily available. In the last two decades of the nineteenth century many more translations, some of them so bowd-lerized and mutated as not to resemble the originals, appeared to receptive audiences. In 1879 Patrick Weston Joyce published his *Old Celtic Romances*, rivalling O'Grady's histories as the protocataractal work of the Irish Revival. Slightly under half the total bulk of the collection is given over to Fenian narratives, all severely emended and written in rather pallid academic prose. Fionn is just another figure from the ancient past, and he is seen in both flattering and unflattering portrayals. Similarly, about a third of American folklorist Jeremiah Curtin's *Myths and Folktales of Ireland* (1890) was devoted to Fenian narratives. Indeed, virtually all of the three to four dozen collections of Irish traditional narratives published since the 1890s include at least some Fenian narratives. Most of them, especially those from nationalist editors or those preparing editions for children, tend to delete the stories portraying Fionn as the buffoon of oral narratives, or the jealous, vengeful cuckold of the Diarmaid and Gráinne story, or the pest of Tara as he appears in the later Irish manuscripts. The different faces of Fionn could be seen in the more scholarly and less contentious translations which also began to appear about the same time. Dozens of Fenian texts were studied in the Continental journals, *Revue Celtique* (founded 1870) and *Zeitschrift für celtische Philologie* (founded 1897). In 1892, Standish James O'-Grady's uncle, Standish Hayes O'Grady, produced one of the finest collections of Irish heroic manuscripts ever seen, *Silva Gadelica*, a work not yet superseded. Such texts were much too demanding for popular reading, but they gave non-Irish-speaking scholars the evidence needed to investigate Fionn and his heroes as mythological figures.

Concurrently the poets and playwrights of the Irish Renaissance were becoming more interested in the darker Fionn. The dramatic opportunities of the narratives portrayed Fionn as a villainous heavy outweighed the possible denigrating implications to the Irish male psyche.

Falling somewhat short of S. H. O'Grady's scholarship, but much more comprehensive than Standish James O'Grady's adventure stories, were the several works of that grand mistress of logistics in the Irish Renaissance, Lady Isabella Augusta Persse Gregory. The story of how Lady Gregory, Protestant, artistocratic, widowed, approaching middle age, could have restructured her own life and then become the mother-hen to a generation of young writers is itself a kind of myth. Although it must have seemed unlikely to her contemporaries, Lady Gregory was the perfect popularizer: she was learned and cultivated enough to avoid the malarky about the Irish past propounded from the time of Macpherson and his heirs, Colonel Vallancey and Sylvestor O'Halloran, and she was approachable and colloquial enough to be able to speak to all classes of the Irish populace. Her reading and the force of her personality were enough to encourage those with greater talent than her own to consider the beauties of Irish folklore and myth. For the popular reading public she provided two quite readable texts of the old narratives, *Cuchulainn of Muirthemne* (1902), and more important for our purposes, *Gods and Fighting Men* (1904), about two thirds of which is given to Fenian narratives. Lady Gregory tried to make up for the absence of an epic of Fionn mac Cumhaill by weaving together recent translations of Irish texts until she had produced one more or less coherent narrative. In notes accompanying the text she identifies her sources, including the six volumes of the *Transactions of the Ossianic Society*, S. H. O'Grady's *Silva Gadelica*, and the many volumes of *Revue Celtique* and *Zeitschrift für celtische Philologie*. She took what she liked from these, emending and rephrasing as she went, and where she found linkage between different episodes deficient she drew from recent collections of oral tales such as Douglas Hyde's *An Sgealuidhe Gaelhealach* (1897), from some of her own collections from Counties Clare and Galway, as well as a number of Scottish Gaelic collections such as J. F. Campbell's volume issued as part of the Ossianic controversy, *Leabhar na Feinne* (1872), his more extensive *Popular Tales of the*

West Highlands (1861) and Lord Archibald Campbell's great collection of Highland folklore, *Waifs and Strays of Celtic Tradition*. She even reached back for some passages from Hanmer's *Chronicle of Ireland*. Lady Gregory's method owed nothing to Macpherson and differed essentially from O'Grady's; not only could she exploit another generation of scholarship, but she was determinedly more objective. Her imagination assembled what appears to be a coherent order; O'Grady's led him to improvise what he could not find. Consequently, O'Grady's heroes have the dash and vigor of nineteenth-century adventure fiction, whereas Lady Gregory's prefigure the peasant luminosity of Synge's characters. Though each motif and episode is taken from a Celtic text of some kind, Irish or Scottish Gaelic, manuscript or oral tradition, the final result is like nothing ever seen before in any language. To this extent the eleven chapters and sixty-three episodes Lady Gregory devotes to Fionn and his Fianna might well be considered more the product of her own taste and genius than of tradition.

Lady Gregory's creations have been the subject of considerable comment, but one of the most interesting is that of Stephen L. Gwynn which appeared in 1903 before *Gods and Fighting Men* was published (510, 1903, 38–58). Gwynn shows that Lady Gregory worked to eradicate some of the redundancy of the original trans-lations; she also threw out many of the formulaic phrases that grate on modern ears as well as such grotesque details as the seven pupils which glare from the eyes of different heroes. For the student of mythology, of course, such a loss is critical, as pleasing as it may be to the modern reader. But in any case, Lady Gregory is, as Gwynn shows, more faithful to texts than Macpherson was. Here, first, is a passage from the early twelfth-century "Book of the Dun Cow" translated by Whitley Stokes: "Now Conall Carnach escaped from the Hostel, and thrice fifty spears had gone through the arm which upheld his shield. He fared forth till he reached his father's house, with half his shield in his hand, and his sword, and the fragments of his two spears. Then he found his father before his garth in Taltin." And here is her version of the same passage: "Conall Carnach, after he got away, went on to his father's house, and but half his shield in his hand, and a few bits left of his two spears. And he found Amergin, his father, out before his dun in Tailltin."

Unlike S. J. O'Grady's Fenian adventure novel, *Gods and Fighting Men* focuses on the Fianna rather than its leading hero. Beginning with the coming of Fionn to knowledge at the salmon pool on the

Boyne, it proceeds through a reconstructed chronology to the Battle of the White Strand (Ventry), many huntings and enchantments, and on to the developments of the more unattractive sides of the hero's character. Eight episodes are given to the Diarmaid and Gráinne story, and subsequently we see what Lady Gregory calls "The Wearing Away of the Fianna," their defeat at Gabhra, and finally Oisín's dialogues with Saint Patrick. She allows Fionn to grow in villainy, but does not suggest, as a modern plot would require, that the change in his character grew from some defect in personality or from any experience he had endured. Although she draws on many folk sources, Lady Gregory never allows Fionn to appear clownish; most of the humor of Fenian literature entirely vanishes except for the inclusion of the Giolla Decair or "Hard Gilly" episode. In short, Lady Gregory's Fionn mac Cumhaill is not an inflated heroic figure, nor is he an expansion of the pre-existent archtetype. He is the figure from Irish and Gaelic tradition made rather more respectable, a selective assembling of motifs very likely recognizable to most of the professional poets and scribes of bardic times.

Lady Gregory's efforts with Fionn mac Cumhaill found many imitators. Because of her success and fame she could not have been ignored by any of the later retellers of the Fenian narratives, and thus we shall not invest much time trying to distinguish nuances in their modes or characterization. All of them appear more directed toward the juvenile reader; for example, the spellings of names are simplified and less authentic than those used by Lady Gregory. Most of the books make some claim to authenticity, usually in a note referring to the *Transactions of the Ossianic Society* or *Silva Gadelica*. In Scottish folkorist Donald A. MacKenzie's *Finn and His Warrior Band* (1910), all of the locations are Scottish and there seems a greater reliance on folklore than manuscript, but the model is clearly *Gods and Fighting Men* and not the *Poems of Ossian*. The poet and translator T. W. Rolleston deleted such stories as the "Pursuit of Diarmaid and Gráinne" from his *High Deeds of Finn MacCool* (1910) because he felt that these portrayals were inconsistent with the heroic Fionn and contained a "certain sinister and depressing element" making them unsuitable in a collection intended largely for the young. No prude, Rolleston is also remembered as the champion in Ireland of Walt Whitman, with whom he exchanged a number of letters. Violet Russell, the wife of George "AE" Russell, in *The Heroes of the Dawn* (1913) and, much more, James Stephens in his *Irish Fairy Tales* (1920), accentuate the divining talents of Fionn, attributing to him some of the spiritualist beliefs they themselves held. Indeed, Stephens, the only one of these storytellers to ignore the later career of Fionn, makes the hero into a model of himself, a somewhat Blakean celebrator of nature and a vigorous athlete. Stephens has Fionn speak a line often cited as summarizing the author's aesthetic. When the Fianna contest over who can find the most beautiful sound in nature, Fionn responds that he loves "the music of what happens." American author Harold F. Hughes retold a number of Fenian narratives, emphasizing swashbuckling adventure, in *Legendary Heroes of Ireland* (1922). One of the few to include the folk story "The Legend of Knockmany," here called "Finn and the Scottish Giant," Hughes succeeds in transforming the comic Finn into a more heroic champion. In the hands of an American lady, Ella Young, in *The Tangle-Coated Horse* (1929) and an English one, Rosemary Sutcliff, in *The High Deeds of Finn MacCool* (1967), the stories are again retold primarily for their intrinsic entertainment value, with an ever-receding flavor of the originals.

Yet the several popularizations of Fenian stories did not establish Fionn mac Cumhaill as a national hero of the same degree as Cúchulainn; for example, it was Cúchulainn's picture that Yeats hung in the lobby of the Abbey Theatre and it was Cúchulainn whom Yeats depicted as stalking the G.P.O. at the Easter Uprising in 1916. The influence of S. J. O'Grady, Lady Gregory, and their imitators, like that of Howard Pyle in his much earlier *Merry Adventures of Robin Hood* (1883), was directed toward the more popular, less literary imagination. This can be seen in the naming of the Gaelic *Jugendkorps* Countess Markievicz established at her estate in the second decade of the century; she called them "the Fianna." In the "Cyclops" chapter of *Ulysses*, Joyce cites one Joseph M'Carthy Hynes who appeals for the resuscitation of the ancient Gaelic sports and pastimes practiced morning and evening by Finn MacCool (p. 317). More visibly, the political party Eamon deValera organized in 1926 from the factions of Sinn Féin who opposed signing the treaty with Britain establishing the Free State, the party which has dominated Irish politics for the better part of the last sixty years, is the Fianna Fáil, usually translated as "Soldiers of Destiny," a continuing heroic Fenian allusion.

The central focus of our attention, Fionn mac Cumhaill, is not, of course, the only hero of Fenian literature. In oral tradition the narrator of Fenian adventure is, by convention, Fionn's son Oisín, or as Macpherson fixed it for many English speakers, Ossian. Thus the first large-scale translations from Fenian literature were by the "Ossianic Society." In the stories from oral tradition Oisín or sometimes Caoilte is seen in colloquy with Saint Patrick, most often on the subject of values. Oisín had pursued Niamh to Tír na nÓg, and on his return found the country given over to the new Christianity and his old comrades vanished. Saint Patrick praises a succession of virtuous souls while Oisín lauds Fionn. Over the centuries the Irish-language stories became a reservoir of anti-clerical sentiment which does not always spill over into English.

Such narratives of Oisín, owing nothing to Macpherson, began to appear in the 1840s and attracted such diverse talents as C. M. O'Keefe (1880), Aubrey T. DeVere (1884), Stephen L. Gwynn (1903), John Varian (c. 1910), and James Stephens (1910). The American author Thomas Wentworth Higginson, friend of Emily Dickinson, produced "Usheen in the Land of Youth" in 1898. Measured against these, the two most interesting accounts of Oisín and Patrick are William Butler Yeats' "Wanderings of Oisin" (1889) and the secularist-nationalist Darrell Figgis' *Return of the Hero* (1923).

"The Wanderings of Oisin," the first important poem of the twenty-four-year-old William Butler Yeats, has been, like all the longer works in his canon, the subject of intense scrutiny. Yeats used translations of *Laoi Oisín in dTír na nÓg*, "Lay of Oisín in the land of Youth" (c. 1750) by Micheál Coimín, who had drawn upon bardic tradition. Spurred by the arguments of John Rhys in *Celtic Heathendom* (1886) diagnosing the figures in Old Irish narratives as euhemerizing Celtic Gods, Yeats saw in Coimín's poem a vision in which all of life is cast symbolically, a view compatible with his own. Coimín's themes, old age versus perpetual youth, mortality versus immortality, change versus changelessness, were adumbrations of those that would become some of Yeats's most persistent concerns. In adapting the scenario, Yeats enlarges the differences between Oisín and Patrick, making Fionn the source of forgotten wisdom from the time outside of time. For example, near the end of Book II of the 1889 text, Oisín recounts his memory of Fionn to Saint Patrick after he had become glutted with a hundred years of feasting on the Island of Victories:

> The hundred years had ceased;
> I stood upon the stair: the surges bore
> A beech bow to me, and my heart grew sore,
> Remembering how I stood by white-haired Finn
> The hare leaped in the grass. (lines 226–30)

Rhys's insights into the origin of Celtic mythology have been confirmed by more recent scholarship, but because the old Irish myths had been transmitted by Christian poets down to modern times, Fionn had not been portrayed as incorporating magical, divinely inspired power in English since the time of Gavin Douglas in the early sixteenth century. If the heroic Fionn was too coarse to be the national hero of Ireland, in Yeats' view, he might instead be enshrined in Oisín's memory as a beacon of spiritual order amid the hated fasting and prayers of the world ruled by Patrick's "brazen bell."

An even greater investment was made in Oisín's memory of Fionn by Darrell Figgis' *The Return of the Hero* (1923). One of the most colorful Irish writers from the early part of this century, Darrell Figgis (1882–1925) took an active role in the Irish struggle for independence. In 1914 he helped to smuggle in the first guns from Imperial Germany to the Irish Volunteers and later spent some time in prison on another political charge. After the Anglo-Irish Treaty, he helped to draw up the constitution of the Free State. His polemical novel, *The Return of the Hero,* was originally published in 1923 under the pseudonym, "Michael Ireland." Figgis committed suicide in 1925, but his book was republished five years later in America, where it received a warm critical reception by such writers of distinction as E. E. Cummings. As Figgis explains in an appendix, *The Return of the Hero* is based on a comparative reading of the earliest manuscripts of *Agallamh na Senórach,* "The Colloquy of the Elders." And even though there are many ancient manuscript antecedents for most of Figgis's episodes, a first reading of *The Return of the Hero* will show how their meaning is transformed. The patron saint of Ireland, here called by the Irish name Padraic mac Alphurn, and his twelve bishops are monsters of repression as would be conceived in a Freudian nightmare. The bishops, especially one named Iserninus, have little patience with Oisín's pagan naiveté and insist that he accept his guilt from Original Sin and also recognize that Fionn and all the Fianna must be in hell because they were not baptized. Blissfully unconcerned, Oisín, when he first sees Patrick, mistakes him for a druid. When asked about his father, Oisín replies, following the original manuscripts, "Were but the brown leaf which the wood sheds from it gold, were but the white billow silver, Finn would have given it all away" (p. 30).

The bishops heatedly attack Oisín's attitudes on sexuality, his laconic insistence that the flesh need not be scourged. In his defense Oisín continually cites Fionn's humanity and generosity. The bishop

Auxilius worries aloud that Oisín's resistance will destroy the mission to Ireland. "Men would fly from us like the plague. They would say we were bringing a responsibility to them that they did not desire. . . . Instead of emancipating them from sin we would be merely endowing them with its penalties. Our strongest argument would be turned against us. Salvation would become a menace" (p. 153). The answer Auxilius would give is to bury the memory, the myth, of Fionn: "We have already seen the effect of such an idea on this preposterous old hero. He said he would die in innocence. Naturally. Everyone would determine to die in innocence, and then what hope would there be of organising the Church? My dear brethren, I urge you to consider this. We cannot be too firm. It is even essential for the future of the Church that Finn mac Cumhall be bound in hell" (p. 153).

A theological committee decides that Oisín could not go to hell if he dies in pagan innocence, but he could go, joining his father, if he acknowledges his guilt and is baptized. Accepting this paradox he asks for baptism to join the Christian church. Preparing to meet his father, Oisín gives this paean to Fionn: "Childlike and wise, happy and grave, simple and fearless in his welcome of all simple and fearless things, proud and wild and unashamed, he had, unlike these bishops, never expected earth to put itself out of the way to suit his preconceptions" (p. 181).

The neo-paganism of Figgis' hero would seem more at home in the novels or anthropological writings of D. H. Lawrence than in Irish bardic tradition, but when we remember the vogue for the surviving primitive in all the arts during the first part of the century, one should expect that surviving Celtic traditions should serve, at least once, such an end.

Figgis's *The Return of the Hero* came out one year after Joyce's *Ulysses*, and since that time ideas about myth, literature, and myth-in-literature have not been quite the same. Additionally, twentieth-century literature since World War I has not been rich in heroic themes, and thus we should not be surprised that there has not been a sustained, inventive treatment of the heroic Fionn mac Cumhaill in English, barring the juvenile fiction by Ella Young and Rosemary Sutcliff and the special case of *Finnegans Wake*. What treatment there has been, though of marginal interest, includes a rock opera, an Off-Broadway play, and a short story. O. B. Miller's 1939 narrative, "Finn MacCool, the Greatest of Civil Engineers" (58, 282–97), purports to be folklore collected from Irish workers on the U.S. transcontinental railway, but as the author does not cite sources and includes in Finn's crew such ersatz folk characters as Paul Bunyan, the story may be an example of what Richard Dorson called "fakelore." In the story Finn/Fionn puts his magical thumb to his lips to gain the strength to dig the Grand Canyon while working in the employ of Old Man Mazuma (from the Yiddish for "money"). The folk-rock opera titled "Fionn mac Cumhaill," featuring the musicians known as Planxty, with script and lyrics by the Kerry writer Sean McCarthy, was performed at the Edinburgh Festival, September 1974. Despite warm popular reception, "Fionn" has not been published or recorded. Finally, Frank Hogan's "Finn MacKool, the Grand Distraction," opened at the Theatre de Lys in New York, September 29, 1975. The play, which has not been published, portrays a powerful Irish-American family, clearly based on the Kennedys, which is active in finance and politics.

In the absence of sustained narratives, the heroic Fionn lives on in countless allusions, in which he has served any number of causes. I say "countless" because I no longer bother to record them, but friends are continually finding them in such diverse materials as cowboy books, hunting guidebooks, and Allied propaganda in World War II. Two from Ireland's most distinguished authors will serve in the place of thousands. In *Red Roses for Me* (1943), Sean O'Casey, the sometimes Marxist chronicler of Dublin's slums, has two Irish girls talking about which regiment of English soldiers had the most attractive uniforms, when a third, Finnoola, speaks for Ireland and revolution: "What would a girl, born in a wild Cork valley, among the mountains, brought up to sing the songs of her father, what would she choose but the patched coat, shaky shoes, an' white hungry face of th' Irish rebel? But their shabbiness was threaded with th' colours from the garments of Finn Mac Cool of th' golden hair."

O'Casey's late contemporary, the poet Austin Clarke, had a different political agenda. As a champion of Irish antiquity, Clarke became, especially in his later years, a scourge of land developers and suburbanization, as if condominiums were somehow a betrayal the heroic past. In "The Loss of Strength" (1961) his anger takes a Fenian turn. He envisions the destruction of the Hill of Allen in Kildare, where Fionn had hunted, in order that stone might be found for new roadbeds. In such a world, it would appear, heroic Ireland is not only dead and gone, but even the marker is crushed and recycled.

CONCLUSION

When all of the portrayals of the heroic Fionn mac Cumhaill in the English language are tallied, our most spectacular finding is that, like the Fionn of Irish literature, he is long-lived. Excluding the figures from the Old and New Testament, we could very likely not find another character who appears in a national epic in 1375 (The Bruce) and a rock-opera in 1974. The consistency of the character is more difficult to chart, perhaps because "hero" is so often a subjective and honorific description. The hero of Irish literature is a hunter-warrior-poet, but in English he can be anything the scribe wants him to be: a god, a fighter, an embodiment of morbid sensibility or an exemplar of Arnoldian sweetness and light, a conservative adversary of the French Revolution of its liberal champion, a well-mannered proto-Christian and master of probity or a fleshly neo-pagan, an emblem of bucolic simplicity or a civil engineer, a herald of the distant, romantic past or a signal of what we are to lose in the present. The mythic hero is a palimpsest the poet carries with him, on which he writes and rewrites the definition of "hero" as he goes. This does not mean that Fionn's projection is limitless. Like the sea-divided Gael from whom he springs, Fionn is more rural than urban, rough-hewn rather than refined, and reputedly not much of a lover. Yet there have been dozens of writers in the English language over the past six centuries who have looked upon Fionn mac Cumhaill as a personality to be admired. We shall see in the next chapters that a number of influential writers, James Joyce, W. B. Yeats, Flann O'Brien, and William Carleton, present us with a grotesque, vicious, and guilty figure, but though their work invites critical attention, far more than the Poems of Ossian, Finn and His Companions, The High Deeds of Finn MacCool, etc., the heroic Fionn mac Cumhaill is a part of living tradition in English literature.

4

The Insulted and the Injured

Fionn mac Cumhaill in
William Carleton, Flann O'Brien, and Others

Seán O'Faoláin describes an impassioned political orator before an audience of workingmen in the early Irish Free State period (c. 1926). Like the literary nationalists of the generation before him, the man on the stump made frequent references to the past glories of the Ireland that was almost lost under English domination. But to his surprise and chagrin, the speaker found that his audience broke into a loud roar of laughter when he spoke of Irish glory in terms of Fionn mac Cumhaill (419, 1935, 45). Such is the popular testimony to the degraded hero of modern Irish tradition in the English language. The clownish Fionn is frequently dismissed by folklorists, apparently with embarrassment, but he is not to be denied. O'Faolain also tells of a story Yeats once heard in which Fionn was on his way to police court when he fell over a cock of hay. Clearly the heroic characterizations explored in the last chapter do not by any means tell the whole story.

The non-heroic characterizations of Fionn are not simply the product of twentieth-century irreverence but have apparently been coeval with the heroic from the beginning of Fenian tradition. As we considered in the last chapter, a guileful Fionn exists in English as early as the anonymous sixteenth-century *Book of Howth*. At the end of the seventeenth century such English settlers as Richard Cox and James Farewell heaped ridicule on native Irish traditions, including the most popular of Irish folk heroes. And even in those

stories from oral tradition which would celebrate Fionn's great deeds
he is conventionally less than supreme in his attainments. Although
a fast runner, he is never as fast as Caoilte, one of the Fianna. Oisín
and Diarmaid can beat him at chess. In time, much of Fionn's prowess
as a warrior seems to pass to his grandson, Oscar. As Padraic Colum
once observed, Fionn's character is permanently flawed, crafty as
well as brave, vindictive as well as generous (18, 1953, 194).

This chapter examines how the different faces of Fionn emerge
from Irish tradition and continue in English writing. Some writers,
such as William Carleton, borrow themes from folk tales insulting
to the heroic Fionn of the nationalists. Flann O'Brien shows a Fionn
abused and made absurd by modern vulgarity. And a series of more
than a dozen writers portray an injured Fionn, vengeful at the loss
of his betrothed, who relentlessly pursues two young lovers until he
can see one of them, his surrogate son Diarmaid, die from grisly
hunting wounds.

But the archetype of Fionn mac Cumhaill is, in Whitman's
phrase, large enough to hold contradictions.

THEORIES OF THE INVERSION OF THE HERO

For many writers in Irish tradition the differing faces of the
hero Fionn mac Cumhaill, magnanimous warrior, comic buffoon,
vengeful cuckold, do not present a problem. Standish James O'Grady
undoubtedly spoke for many when he said: "Heroes expand into
giants, and dwindle into goblins, or fling aside the heroic form and
gambol as buffoons . . ." (422, 1878, 28). Fionn had been admirable,
laughable, and contemptible for as long as anyone could remember,
like a figure in a Bavarian barometer, not a contradiction but a
succession of personalities which come, somehow, from nature. No
one seemed to ask before the twentieth century why Fionn had a
variety of characters whereas other heroes, such as Lugh or Cúchulainn, did not. In the twentieth century, perhaps because so many
traditions seem to be dissolving, we are less willing to accept without
question, even when our answers are less than conclusive. In analyzing Fionn's fall from grace and dignity, there are at least four
ways of looking at the blackened hero.

Fionn may have been understood to have three personalities at some undetermined time before the development of literary traditions. T. F. O'Rahilly in his landmark study *Early Irish History and Mythology* says that there are three Fionns who were heroes of superhuman accomplishment. The first was the Midland Fionn. The second was the Fionn of the Lagin, an early people who gave their name to Leinster, Ireland's most easterly province. And the third was the Fionn of the Érainn, a P-Celtic or non-Goidelic people who lived in the south of Ireland from the time of Ptolemy's map of early Ireland (second century A.D.). Although the Fionn of romance and story was disassociated from them, various special pedigrees were invented to accommodate him (431, 1946, 275). Eleanor Knott remarks that the phrase "land of the three Finns" *(na dtrí bhFionn)*, served as a conventional name for Ireland in the bardic poetry of Tadhg Dall Ó Huiginn (1550–91) and may identify the three Fionns mentioned in Keating's genealogies (530, 1926, 342). Then again, the name "Fionn" or "Fair One" may be a title even as Deimne acquires the honorific *fionn* before assuming his father's heritage as head of the Leinster Fianna, becoming Fionn mac Cumhaill. An example of the honorific use of the title "Fionn" can be seen in the Ulster Cycle: three brothers-in-law of Conchobar mac Nessa (through either Clothru or Eithne), Bres, Nar, and Lothar, who are called the "Three Finns" or "White Ones" of Emhain Macha (381, 1918, 90). Although the three-faced Fionn is not found in Fenian tradition proper, several Celtic divinities appear in triads and may once have been identical. There are, for example, three gods of craft, Goibniu, Luchta, and Credne, and three gods of poetry among the Tuatha Dé Danann, Etan, Cairbre mac Etaine, and Aí mac Olloman. Additionally, Brigit is usually seen in three aspects, much as many classical figures are, e.g., Artemis-Selene-Hecate. If one accepts the three-fold classification system deriving from Indo-European society as shown by Georges Dumézil and others, one might expect that almost any mythical figure might be seen as part of a triad if enough is known about him. It may be that Fionn shows a different face in different stories because he is literally three persons and can find a physical correlative in the enigmatic tricephalic heads which have been found at different archaeological digs in Ireland; the best-preserved of these comes from Corleck in County Cavan and is now displayed in the National Museum in Dublin.

The least controversial approach to the different personalities in Fionn's character is based on an observation of the popularity of his traditions. Fionn is not the central figure in one of the great epics of Irish literature, as Cúchulainn is in the *Táin Bó Cúailnge*, which fixes him in the storyteller's repertory. Compare, for example, the stability of Achilles in the *Iliad* with the mutability of Heracles. The wrath of Achilles became a fixed part of the narrative of the *Iliad* in the ninth century B.C. and remained a fixed part of his heroic character through all antiquity. The most notable addition to his story was the episode of Thetis dipping him as an infant in the Styx, an item scribbled in the margin of the text by an anonymous scholiast. But Heracles was not the center of any one lengthy narrative, and his character underwent many transformations from story to story in different regions of Greece. By the time of Periclean Athens, Heracles had become a stock figure in slapstick comedy. In Aristophanes' *The Frogs*, for example, he is largely motivated by gluttony and lust. It is this variety of characterization, Aristotle observes in *The Poetics*, that makes Heracles an unsuitable subject for epic.

In an Ireland which has known no Periclean age the impulses for humiliating the hero are much greater. Fionn is initially more vulnerable than his counterparts Cúchulainn and Lugh because his narratives have been a part of the repertory of the *déclassé* bards instead of the more estimable *filidh*. When the remnants of Ireland's native aristocracy abandoned the island in the Flight of the Earls in the early seventeenth century, most of the ancient traditions atrophied, but the Fenian cycle survived in the mouths of impecunius bards until it passed into the folklore of the Anglicized peasantry in the nineteenth century. Without patronage the professional bards and their successors, the shanachies (from *seanchaidhe*: antiquarian, historian) and storytellers needed only to meet the uncultivated tastes of small farmers and tradesmen in the impoverished and ever-shrinking *gaeltacht*. It could be argued that a suppressed people who knew only failure in revolution were in need of a hero; to fill that need the heroic stories about Fionn did survive, as we have considered. But as everyone now knows after a generation of television, a popular artist—even one of great skill and refined taste—cannot long survive if he exceeds the limited taste of the audience which supports him. Thus we see that the conception of Fionn's character in oral tradition becomes not so much popular as demotic. The Fionn of oral tradition is no longer capable of poetry; his courage seems more often vain, bullying, or self-deceiving. By the early nineteenth century, contemporary with the proliferation of the stage Irishman in the writings of Samuel Lover and Charles Lever, Fionn's story had acquired a number of English-language tales in which the hero blunders through ludicrous adventures, one of which requires him to dress as an infant and hide in a cradle to evade his pursuer. Some of these tales seemed so at odds with the heroic Fionn to Seán O'Faoláin that he called them "spurious," although other chapters of the hero's story of popular provenience are not dismissed because of their origin. Further, there is nothing spurious about the *bruidhean* tales in Irish in which the Fenian hero is humiliatingly trapped in a magical house and cannot struggle free under his own power, tales which have had little appeal to Irish popular traditions in the English language.

If the paradoxical hero-buffoon Fionn mac Cumhaill seems implausible to O'Faoláin, the same bifurcated figure evidently presents no problems to those members of the Irish peasantry reared in traditional literature and culture. The juxtaposition of the contrasting elements in Fionn's character is one of the continuing motifs in *Finnegans Wake*. As befits Joyce's use of the paradoxical Fionn we find that the hero-buffoon is not merely Irish but also nationless. Because the merger includes two separate stock figures from the ancient world (*hero* is a Greek word, and the Italian *buffone* from which "buffoon" derives is a translation of the Greek *bomolochos*) we can hardly assert that the hero-buffoon is universal, but we do find that he is widespread in popular traditions. In his study of myths in modern popular culture Raphael Patai speaks of the hero-buffoon as a common figure in comic books and television serials (856, 1972, 216–19). In this literature, written by professionals but popular to the extent that it is directed toward tastes which are excluded from the elites of wealth, power, and cultivation, we find a hero who combines popular aspirations with mass man's long term understanding of his own shortcomings. Hundreds of such figures have appeared in rather ephemeral popular literature, one of the most memorable of which may be Buster Keaton, especially as seen in his best-known film, *The General* (1926). The script for the film was taken from the adventurous narrative of William Pittenger, who, during the American Civil War, helped to steal an entire train from the Confederacy, subsequently winning the first Congressional Medal of Honor; but in Keaton's film the episode seems more absurd than courageous. In this and other examples it could be argued that heroic and buffoonish are subjective appraisals, more so than in classical literature, but it is demonstrable in any case that a popular audience can readily accept a hero who takes pratfalls.

An Irish audience may even prefer that its heroes do pratfalls. As John V. Kelleher (526, 1975) once pointed out, some of the most admired figures in Irish history have attracted scurrilous anecdotes told as counterparts to the stories of deeds that won the figures honor. Prominent among these is the Catholic populist leader, Daniel O'Connell, a continent family man, who is sometimes portrayed as a prolific philanderer. An oft repeated story has it that one could not throw a stone on any street in Dublin without hitting one of his unacknowledged children. A similar libel has been attached to dozens of other Irish figures and may be a survival of the belief that great leaders must have great fertility. As such stories do not diminish O'Connell's stature, Kelleher has suggested that the heroic and comic figures are inextricably one.

Although the instances of the comic portrayal of Fionn are more common in English than in Irish, and seem generally more popular than learned, making them consequently more modern than ancient, the antecedents of the hero made foolish can be found in the earliest texts. This leads to a consideration of the third explanation of the transformation of Fionn's character, asserted by David Krause in his essays "Rageous Ossean" (1961) and "The Hidden Oisin" (1966) and expanded in *The Profane Book of Irish Comedy* (1982). In looking for the origin of the comic Fionn and the abused Fionn, Krause disregards the questions of the rivalry of the bards and *filidh*, as well as the more knavish portrayals of the hero in Irish literature.

Instead, Krause looks to an eighth-century manuscript whose English title is "The Quarrel Between Finn and Oisín" (141, 1910, 22–27) for a definition of Fionn's character as seen in relation to his son. Although Oisín conventionally speaks admiringly of his father when in dialogue with Patrick, Krause argues, his antagonistic attitude toward the saint derives from the filial rebelliousness he showed in "The Quarrel Between Finn and Oisín." In short, Oisín's incipient Oedipus complex leads to his obstreperous and boisterous energies directed toward Saint Patrick in the Fenian stories told in Ossianic frame.

The main thrust of Krause's argument is that the Ossianic dialogues form a vast literature, much largely lost, which celebrates the joys of the pagan world of nature and berates the repressions of foreign Christianity. He sees Oisín as the first subversive against the strictures of Holy Ireland, the ancestor of a figure who runs through Irish culture and literature down to modern times.

Although Krause deals only secondarily with Fionn, what he has to say is provocative. If Oisín plays Oedipus in "The Quarrel of Finn and Oisín," then Fionn is Laius. And whereas Oedipus is a tragic figure, the reviled father is subject for comedy. Krause draws on such Freudian critics as Stanley Tarachow and Martin Grotjahn (836, 1957), Vivian Mercier's *Irish Comic Tradition*, as well as a reading of ancient comedy to argue that a stock comic figure from earliest times is the old man who "refuses to act his age." Such a stereotyped figure as the circus clown tramp represents a depreciated father figure. So it is with the clownish Fionn of later tradition, who, it must be admitted, is often seen as a father.

Krause's thesis seems like a contradiction, but it can be resolved. Oisín reviled Fionn and made him a figure of fun, and then he spoke admiringly of him to Patrick. But, implies Krause, Oisín did not make Fionn the paradigm of the old values until Fionn had disappeared from the scene and was replaced by Patrick.

As it has been presented here only summarily, Krause's thesis must sound speculative, and it has not always been received warmly. Nonetheless, it is grounded on the scholarship of the most reliable Celticists. Both Kuno Meyer, who edited the best modern edition of "The Quarrel Between Finn and Oisín," and T. P. Cross (340, 1950, 176–82) have seen the quarrel between father and son as a humorous burlesque of the Sohrab and Rustum story. Gerard Murphy (404, 1953, xcvii–xcix), as Krause readily acknowledges, was reluctant to see burlesque in "The Quarrel" because he was disinclined to consider comic or burlesque themes valid for learned Ossianic poetry. Yet James Joyce, who apparently knew none of this, portrays the humiliation of H. C. Earwicker, the hero-dreamer (who has a trace of Fionn in him), in the filial rebellion of Kevin and Jerry (alias Shaun and Shem).

Thus far we have considered treatments of the comic Fionn as he is perceived in the popular imagination. Whether the comic Fionn is the product of the derogated traditions following the Flight of the Earls in the seventeenth century or is the result of the Oedipal (perhaps Laiusal) humiliations delivered by his son, Oisín, theories which incidentally could easily be synchronized, we have ignored the contributions of the individual artistic talent or experience. Concurrent with the declining fortunes of the Irish language came the rise of the English settlers in Ireland who had a taste for the abuse of native traditions. As noted in the last chapter, James Farewell's

Irish Hudibras, or the Fingallian Prince (1689), etc., puts Fionn in hell, without the benefit of any Ossianic anti-clerical irony. Although the low regard which the Scots and English settlers reserved for the native population was manifest in the penal laws of the eighteenth century, it did not find sustained literary expression until the nineteenth century and the advent of the stage Irishman. The Anglo-Irish writer most interested in travestying traditional narratives was the evangelist Caesar Otway (1780–1842), remembered today as the patron of William Carleton, the premier Irish novelist of the first half of the nineteenth century. In his own day Otway was the *bête noir* of Irish nationalists for his publication of scarifying anti-Papist "true stories" in his proselytizing *Christian Examiner.* Otway shows considerable interest in the implausible details of a number of Fenian tales in his *Sketches in Ireland* (1827). Some of the satires Otway retells, "Fin M'Coul and the Hag with the Finger," e.g., needed few editorial alterations to appear grostesque to English and Anglophile readers. The story which Otway most relishes concerns Fionn's winning of bravery and wisdom, the catching of the salmon of knowledge. The setting is now Croagh Patrick in Connaught, a less romantic location than the conventional falls of Assaroe or the Bend of the Boyne; additionally, Fionn must now compete with King Cormac to win the prize. Otway's readers took such delight in the story that it was reprinted five years later in the Dublin popular press. And over a century later the story turned up as a comic tale in an English collection of fishing stories.

    In summary, the comic and anti-heroic Fionn may be able to exist concurrently with the heroic because his personality was multiple to begin with, because of the social and artistic decline of Irish popular tradition, or because of Oedipal humiliations inflicted by the Ossianic narrator. Certainly one strain of the comic traditions originates in Protestant travesty of Irish culture. All four of these analyses may contribute within a limited degree, or, it must be admitted in modesty, the final answer may lie in an approach which we have not yet anticipated.

FIONN MAC CUMHAILL IN
"THE LEGEND OF KNOCKMANY" AND ITS VARIANTS

    Of all the tales in English about Fionn picturing him as an absurd figure, the one with the widest circulation is usually known by the title given it by William Carleton, "The Legend of Knockmany" (1845), named for a hill in Carleton's native County Tyrone. Carleton (1794–1869) was a novelist and storyteller, of course, and not a folklorist, but he sprang from the Irish-speaking peasantry and knew volumes of peasant lore, including oral traditions that dated to earliest times, more, most probably, than any other Irishman who wrote novels. As Carleton's "Knockmany" was written after his conversion to Protestantism and during his subsequent career with the fierce anti-Papist Caesar Otway, he unquestionably altered his vision of the Irish past, but his immediate circumstances hardly seem to diminish his credentials as a contributor to Fenian literary tradition in English.

In Carleton's "Legend of Knockmany," Fionn (here spelled "Fin M'Coul") is at work on the Giant's Causeway when he hears that another giant, named Cucullin (sic), spelled without the aspiration in the second syllable, in on his way for a match of strength between them. Let us not be troubled that Cúchulainn is the hero of another cycle and does not usually appear in Irish Fenian literature, oral or manuscript, because this may be a case of mistaken identity. Fionn returns home to his wife Oonagh at Knockmany, quaking with fear, sure that he is going to be "skivered like a rabbit" by his enemy. Oonagh is more confident, knowing that the rival giant's power resides in the middle finger of his right hand, and so sets about to outwit him. She has Fionn dress as a baby and hide in an unnamed son's cradle, while she prepares to bake bread in which she has inserted granite stones. Giving false hospitality to Cucullin, who is annoyed at not finding Fionn home, Oonagh offers Cucullin the granite bread. After trying twice to eat the bread, losing teeth in each attempt, Cucullin refuses to take another bite, at which point Oonagh offers another loaf, this one without the granite insert, to Fionn whom she blandly describes as her baby. Fionn, of course, has no difficulty in eating at all, which leaves Cucullin amazed and apprehensive about confronting the father of such a child. Cucullin now wants to leave Knockmany, but not before feeling the teeth of such an astonishing infant. Readying for the climax, Oonagh invites Cucullin to place his magic finger well into Fionn's mouth. Fionn immediately bites the finger off, jumps from the cradle, and makes short work of the rival giant—now debilitated. The hero is again victorious, but at the price of showing us his cowardice, chicanery, and buffoonery; a hero who has been disguised as a baby by his wife has been made a fool, no matter what happy purpose it may serve. There are many other examples of Fionn's guile as a trickster, but in no earlier narrative is he so absurdly anti-heroic.

Carleton's version of this story is but one, the best-known and most widely circulated. Yeats, for example, includes it in his *Irish Fairy and Folk Tales*. In addition, it has been adapted and anthologized a number of times, often without credit to Carleton. The next best-known version comes from Patrick Kennedy, the early folktale collector, who published an Anglo-Irish version of what is obviously the same tale in his *Legendary Fictions of the Irish Celts* in 1866. A number of details are changed: for example, the loaves of bread become griddle cakes, and the rival giant is induced to play a game of fingerstones, but the outcome of the action is the same. The most important variant is that the rival giant is not Cúchulainn but rather an unnamed Scotsman who wades across the Sea of Moyle on the trajectory of the Giant's Causeway.

The rival giant is also a Scotsman in a version Frederick Marryat puts in the mouth of an Irish character named O'Brien in his *Peter Simple*, first published in 1834. To confuse matters further Fionn is here called "Fingal," and the speaker must deal with charges that the Fenian tales are Scottish rather than Irish. Also significant is the reduction of the violence in the tale; the rival runs off as soon as he sees that Fionn can eat the loaves of bread. Fionn is less of a fool here because the idea for the infant disguise is his, not his wife's.

In part because there is no Irish-language folk recording of the tale older than Carleton's version, and also because of the tone of it, some commentators have declined to consider "The Legend of Knockmany" a part of the Fenian canon; indeed, this is one of the stories O'Faoláin calls spurious. Such a judgment overlooks folk recordings of the tale, as, for example, one found in Ulster in the early twentieth century by Elizabeth Andrews, in which the rival giant is Goll mac Morna (231, 1913, 91–95). The Scottish folklorist J. F. Campbell recorded a Gaelic variant from the Hebrides in the 1860s where Cúchulainn, described as a member of the "Feinn," is challenged by Garbh MacStairn, a figure known elsewhere in Highland tradition as a Lochlannic or Scandinavian champion. In recounting the story Campbell notes the similarity with Carleton's "Knockmany," and comments that the narrative is "old, Ossianic, mythological, and Celtic," common to both Ireland and Scotland, and available in print and oral tradition (242, 1890, vol. III, pp. 198–99). Furthermore, the American folklorist Thomas E. Oliver has identified the story as an analogue of the old French tale of deception usually known as "Maistre Pierre Pathelin" (424, 1909, 412–14). Additionally, a third analogue exists in the Fenian cannon, the minor tale of "Gilla na Grakin and Fion MacCumhail," in which the conventionally comic Conán Maol harasses Gilla and subsequently is deceived much as the rival giant is in "The Legend of Knockmany." Thus we can see that the tale is rooted in folk tradition no matter how much it may have been modified by Carleton or some unnamed County Tyrone shanachie.

Somewhat earlier than Carleton's "Knockmany" was another version of the same story appearing in the pages of the *Dublin Penny Journal* (6, 1833, 327–28). It is anonymous, attributed to an author known only as "Q," and has not been the subject of any critical commentary. Although the tone of the version, also known as "The Legend of Fin-Mac-Cool," suggests an author from the landlord class, the congruity of detail with Carleton's and other versions of the story suggests a lost original from folk tradition. As with Kennedy's, Marryat's, Campbell's, and Jeremiah Curtin's versions, there are numerous minor variations in detail, such as a change of location to Ballynascorney in County Dublin, but there is also one exceedingly important one. This time the other giant comes from Scotland again, but he is Oisín, or here, "Ussheen," Fionn's own son.

Does this version supersede the others? Since it was not widely circulated and in that there is no published antecedent from folk or learned tradition, we may be inclined to answer no. Yet Cúchulainn, the rival giant in Carleton's version, is from a cycle of Irish literature, a distinction which shanachies have honored until most recent times. And if the rival giant were originally Cúchulainn or an unnamed Scotsman he would be most unlikely to find a substitute in the protagonist's son, especially as the scenario includes a wife/mother and another child's crib. Even if Oisín was introduced to the story by a Gael-baiting member of the Ascendancy who had hoped to make Irish tradition appear more grostesque, the Oedipal aggressions of Fionn's son have a precedent which, as David Krause has reminded us, dates from the eighth century. If the *Dublin Penny Journal* version is not the original then it is certainly the most interesting variant. In it we can see substantiation for three of the theories of the comic Fionn. The hero is reduced to the peasant's milieu, a small cottager rather than a hunter-warrior-poet; he is the object of an Oedipal attack; and the tone of the narrative is set with Anglo-Irish disdain for native traditions.

In any case, no matter which of the versions is the most authentic, the Fionn of the "Knockmany" story and its variants is not only comic but anti-heroic. Whether he is facing his own son or an intruder from another cycle or from another part of the Celtic world, Fionn loses his dignity but prevails nevertheless. Perhaps the greater critical curiosity in this matter is not the origin of the story but rather its continuing popularity all through the nineteenth century to our own times, even among the belligerent Irish public that rioted at the imagined indignities to the nation in *The Playboy of the Western World*. The attraction of the Knockmany story may have been a means of offering an alternative to the reluctant nationalists from the native culture. Like the Czechs at the other edge of the Germanic world who in modern times made a national hero of the Good Soldier Schweik, some Irishmen could see that stealth and guile, not to mention silence and cunning, were useful to a people who lacked the physical and financial power to overcome visiting giants sure to win in a test of strength. Whereas some could intellectually arm themselves with the hyperbolic heroic tradition of the past and prepare for a struggle greater than they may be able to sustain, there were certainly others, men whose names do not live, for whom unheroic silence and cunning were preferable to exile. The myth of Fionn mac Cumhaill is rich and diverse enough to serve both ends.

Although the buffoon Fionn is often celebrated in public-house anecdote, he does not appear as frequently on the printed page. Even in the hands of such as Samuel Lover, one of the creators of the stage Irishman, Fionn is not abused or satirized. Lover did include a long, comic digression about Fionn in one of his tales, but the satire is directed against the bombast of the credulous storyteller who believes Fionn can cut through a mountain with his sword (41, 1831), an episode of such widespread currency in actual folk tradition it has been included in the *Encyclopedia Britannica*. Similarly, the witless dialect stories of Patrick Joseph MacCall, *Fenian Nights Entertainment* (1897), present comic tales of Fionn in which the humor is directed more at the credulous narrator than at the protagonist. In one, "Fionn MacCumhaill and the Princess," the national hero of Ireland is seen competing for the hand of a princess when he is asked to try to chew a mouthful of oatmeal and whistle at the same time. Refusing to respond to such a demeaning contest, Fionn throws a rock "as big as a castle" over a mountain. When this does not win the princess's hand, he throws three more, the last one sailing over Dublin "scrapin' the nose of Howth."

The comic Fionn is less available as a literary allusion. One of the very few is to be found in a poem by Francis Ledwidge (1891–1917), a rather Georgian Irish poet, frequently compared with Rupert Brooke, who was killed in the British Army in World War I. In his post-humously published "A Dream Dance," the poet's reverie takes him to a ball given by Maeve where he dances with Deirdre the fair until interrupted by the boorish Fionn (40, 1919, 229):

> How loud was the laughter of Finn
> As he blundered about thro' a reel,
> Tripping up Caoilte the thin,
> Or jostling the dreamy Aleel.

Except for the "Knockmany" story, the comic or anti-heroic Fionn found less favor with nineteenth-century writers in English. The nineteenth was not only the century of Carlyle's vision of the hero, but it was also the century of nationalism. And Irish nationalism was one of the more humorless varieties. But the twentieth century, when the hero "vanished" in O'Faoláin's phrase, there was more taste for the comic and the absurd. The fullest expression of the absurd, still wedded to the heroic, is in Joyce's *Finnegans Wake*, a work that requires a bit more preparation to approach. A more accessible portrayal of the comic Fionn appears in the other great Irish novel of 1939, Flann O'Brien's *At Swim-Two-Birds*.

FIONN MAC CUMHAILL IN
FLANN O'BRIEN'S *AT SWIM-TWO-BIRDS*

Some first readers have seen *At Swim-Two-Birds* as the twin of *Finnegans Wake*. Not only because of the coincidence of date and nationality but more because both are complex, multi-leveled, filled with allusion and linguistic calisthenics, the two works are frequently paired. The author of *At Swim-Two-Birds*, under another name, even appears in *Finnegans Wake*. But on closer look, *At Swim-Two-Birds* is really no more forbidding than, say, *Tristram Shandy*. Though still little known to many informed readers, the author called "Flann O'Brien" (1911–66) has attracted a distinguished and dedicated following. An English writer in *The Spectator* compared him with Borges and Robbe-Grillet (722, 1968, 36). While this is not the time to fix his station in modern letters, O'Brien was a dextrous linguist and a challenger of novelistic form. He was also an elusive trickster, not only in his art but in his life, even to such matters as his proper name.

Born plain Brian O'Nolan in Strabane of a middle-class, Irish-speaking family, the writer came to be known by a series of pseudonyms. He sometimes used the Gaelicized form of his name, Brian Ó Nualáin, under which he wrote the most admired satire in twentieth-century Irish, *An Béal Bocht* (The Poor Mouth) in 1941. He was best known during his lifetime as journalist under the pseudonym Myles na gCopaleen (or, Anglicized, Gopaleen), which translates into English as "Myles of the Little Horses." The original Myles was a trickster in Gerald Griffin's *The Collegians* (1829) and Dion Boucicault's popular dramatization, *The Colleen Bawn* (1860). As both Griffin and Boucicault have been widely known in Ireland, the literary character of Myles is readily identifiable by many readers there; thus the references to Myles in *Finnegans Wake* (192.26–27, 246.19, 343. 11–12) may not actually indicate Brian O'Nolan. At various times and in different media, he also wrote as Brother Barnabas, John James Doe, George Knowall, Matt Duffy, and Count O'Blather. The name readers outside Ireland are most likely to recognize, Flann O'Brien, was used for the novels, *At Swim-Two-Birds, The Hard Life* (1961), *The Dalkey Archive* (1964), and *The Third Policeman* (1967). A number of quite plausible explanations have been given for O'Nolan's having taken the pseudonym "Flann O'Brien," too complicated to review here. But as O'Nolan had a master's degree in Irish Studies, he certainly knew that one of the best-known Flanns of early literature was Flann mac Lonáin (d. 893), who was called "the devil's son" during his lifetime for the bite of his satires.

As O'Nolan/O'Brien's first literary efforts made little initial impact, he worked as a civil servant, a job he detested, and wrote a tri-weekly column for the *Irish Times* known as "Cruiskeen Lawn." Written under the Myles pseudonym from 1940 until his death, "Cruiskeen Lawn" became one of the most widely read columns in the history of Irish journalism. None like it has ever appeared anywhere else. Myles employed cross-linguistic puns, jokes in Old Irish, phonetic transcripts from Homeric Greek, and a continuing series of shaggy dog stories about the adventures of Keats and his friend Chapman. When his international reputation began to rise after the republication of *At Swim-Two-Birds* in 1960, it was difficult for many Irishmen to think of O'Nolan as a novelist who had been a journalist instead of the other way around.

Although *At Swim-Two-Birds* was published at the recommendation of Graham Greene, it was largely ignored by reviewers and the informed reading public. One exception was the twenty-six year old Dylan Thomas who provided later publishers with the memorable blurb, " . . . just the book to give your suster if she's a loud, dirty, boozy girl" (721, 1939, 78–79). O'Brien's friend Niall Sheridan carried a copy of the book to James Joyce in Paris, which, Sheridan asserts, was the last book Joyce read. The copy survives in Joyce's small library left behind in Paris and is described in the collection's catalogue as *"livre tres aime de Joyce."* Almost forgotten in the turmoil of World War II, *At Swim-Two-Birds* was republished through the efforts of several English writers, including Philip Larkin and John Wain.

Despite its relative accessibility, *At Swim-Two-Birds* defies facile summary. The pretext of the book is this: O'Brien wrote a novel in which the first narrator is an unnamed student at University College Dublin, a kind of Irish Oblomov, who would prefer to spend most of his time lolling and daydreaming in bed. The student is writing a novel about a tenant in the seedy Red Swan Hotel, Dermot (from the Irish Diarmaid) Trellis, who is voluntarily bedridden, but whose imagination has narrower limits than the student's. Trellis invents a few characters and borrows some others, including Fionn mac Cumhaill and some figures from pulp fiction, and proceeds to write his own novel until his various characters tire of his shortcomings and sit at the end of his bed like Mamalujo in *Finnegans Wake* and begin to write a book about him. O'Brien helps us with this contrivance by declaring at both the beginning and the end of the novel that this is indeed what he is doing.

A number of seemingly peripheral matters initially taunt the reader with suggestions of absurdist obfuscation. For example, the book begins with chapter 1, but there are no later chapters. This is not a printer's error: O'Brien evidently planned it this way. The first narrator is never identified, a device O'Brien used in later novels. And then there's the matter of the title, four simple English words which make little sense in this arrangement. About a third of the way through the text,[1] O'Brien provides the reader with some help: "Swim-Two-Birds" is a translation of the Irish placename, Snámh-dá-én, mentioned in the medieval narrative of *Buile Suibhne*, "The

Frenzy (or Madness) of Sweeney," a summary of which is retold in the context of the novel through the persona of Fionn. As described in the *Metrical Dindshenchas*, a compendium of traditional lore of places, the poetic gazetteer of Ireland, *Snámh-dá-én* lies along the Shannon, a few miles south of the once great monastery, Clonmacnoise (198, 1935, vol. 5, p. 202). The site is resonant with implications from episodes in early Irish culture. Within the medieval narrative of *Buile Suibhne Geilt* the placename of *Snámh-dá-én* does not appear to be the site of any memorable adventure; Sweeney observes a series of domestic activities, clerics reciting their *nones*, and a woman giving birth to a child. A closer reading of the text will reveal, however, that after passing *Snámh-dá-én* the protagonist is a changed man in ways he has not anticipated: he becomes more gentle, pious, and humble (580, 1913, 33).

The three levels of consciousness in *At Swim-Two-Birds* are separate from one another and are pierced only infrequently and then most tellingly by the persona of Fionn, here called Finn MacCool. The first level of consciousness is described by the unnamed narrator who lives in the world perceived by the common senses; he knows fatigue and hunger, suffers the depredations of his anti-intellectual peasant-Catholic uncle, and faces imminent and intimidating examinations at the National University. Although it would be presumption to identify him with O'Brien/O'Nolan, he shares some of the author's literary tastes at the time of composition—Joyce, Gide, and Huxley.

The second and third levels of consciousness, that of Trellis and his subsequent creations, are most closely intermixed; both inhabit a world of atrophied imagination. Although he insists that his literary concerns are moral, Trellis hungers for great popular acclaim and would willingly write pornography for the promise of an audience. A nationalist *ad absurdum*, Trellis will read only books with green covers. Among Trellis' fellow tenants in the Red Swan are a number of tedious louts, some of whom have come in from the streets, and others who appear to have come from the pages of pulp fiction. Finn MacCool is also one of the residents of the hotel, and some unemployed leprechauns live in the cellar. Trellis' literary master is a William Tracy, an improbably conceived Irish writer of Western romances who introduced Irish locales for many of his tales of cattle rustling and adventures; Tracy's "Ringsend Cowboys" (named for Dublin's Coney Island) roam through the Red Swan Hotel, taunting Trellis, muscling their way into his creation. Trellis' creations in the third level of consciousness are implausible caricatures, Pooka MacPhellimey, "a member of the devil class" (p. 9), named for the *puca* of Celtic tradition, and John Furriskey, born at the age of twenty-five with a knowledge of physics, who is an incarnation of evil.

The reader can perceive order in this seemingly dadaist conundrum, first, in a wink to Proust, and, second, in the continuing allusion to Old Irish tradition, specifically the narratives of Finn. In an early description of Finn MacCool parodying the hyperbolic excesses of heroic tales, the student narrator interrupts, saying, "I hurt my tooth in the corner of my jaw with a lump of the crust I was eating. This recalled to me the perception of my surroundings" (p. 10). In a cuisine as impoverished as the Irish, O'Brien cannot find *madeleine*, but his piecrust is enough to remind us that the novel's swirl of history, social and literary criticism, and morality stream from his consciousness. The Fenian context which the piecrust episode punctuates is but one of a series appearing through the first half of *At Swim-Two-Birds*. Finn MacCool appears to both the student narrator and to Trellis, lives in the Red Swan Hotel, and talks with the Ringsend Cowboys. As the personification of diverse national aspirations, Finn MacCool, whom many of the "Plain People" of Ireland would like to believe historical, is himself an incarnation of the real and the fantastic, and his innovative portrayal in *At Swim-Two-Birds* serves as a cement between the different levels of the book.

The first appearance of Finn in the novel comes in the mock-archaic hyperbole interrupted by the Proustian digression, cited above. The student narrator disparages the ancient national traditions: "Finn MacCool was a legendary hero of old Ireland. Though not mentally robust, he was a man of superb physique and development. Each of his thighs was as thick as a horse's belly, narrowing to a calf as thick as the belly of a foal. Three fifties of fosterlings could engage with handball against the wideness of his backside, which was large enought to halt the march of men through a mountain-pass" (p. 10).

After the lump of crust reminds the narrator of his surroundings, he is detained by the things of his world for five pages, but when he can return to the "kingdom of his mind" (an allusion to Sir Edward Dyer, d. 1607), Finn appears again, unsummoned: "Finn MacCool, a hero of old Ireland, came out before me from his shadow, Finn the wide-hammed, the heavy-eyed, Finn that could spend Lammas morning with girdled girls at far-from-simple chessplay" (pp. 15–16).

This introduces a ten-page "incursion into ancient mythology," as the narrator tells us in his own rubrics, " . . . from my typescript descriptive of Finn MacCool and his people, being humorous or quasi-humorous" (p. 16). The student narrator's Finn speaks in his own voice:

> I will relate, said Finn, when the seven companies of my warriors are gathered together on the one plain and the truant clean-cold loud-voiced wind goes through them, too sweet to me is that. Echo-blow of a goblet-base against the tables of the palace, sweet to me is that. I like the gull-cries and the twittering together of fine cranes. I like the surf-roar at Tralee, the songs of the three sons of Meadhra, and the whistle of MacLughaidh. These also please me, man-shouts at a parting, cuckoo-call in May. I incline to like pig-grunting in Magh. Eithne, the bellowing of the stag of Ceara, the whinging of the fauns in Derrynish. The low warble of water-fowls in Loch Barra also, sweeter than life that. I am fond of wing-beating in dark belfries, cow-cries in pregnancy, trout-spurt in a lake-top (p. 16).

O'Brien/O'Nolan, whose master's thesis is on nature in Old Irish poetry, evidently writes a most loving parody of the style of the old texts. His friend Niall Sheridan tells us that he indulged himself with them and, unrestrained, would have unbalanced the book with them; Sheridan adds that these passages were the ones which most delighted Joyce (701, 1971, 86). The pseudo-Fenian parodies are not only a stylistic tour-de-force, with syntactical inversion, kenning-like compounds, and convoluted genitives, but they provide the student narrator with a text for defining the difficulties of finding reality in language. Whereas the parodies are as concrete as a policeman's report, they also have shown the inaccessibility of an actual Finn behind the narratives. O'Brien will not allow us to accept the somewhat genteel, Tennysonian heroes of the Protestant translators of the Irish Renaissance, Douglas Hyde, S. J. O'Grady, and company. And neither does O'Brien shrink from the hyperbole of old Irish tradition. Thus would he measure Finn MacCool's nose: "The caverns to the butt of his nose had fulness and breadth for the instanding in their shade of twenty arm-bearing warriors with their tribal rams and dovecages together with a generous following of ollavs and bards with their law-books and their verse-scroll, their herb-pots and their alabaster firkins of oil and unguent" (p. 19).

In this early apparition to the student narrator, Finn tells his men that he is a great warrior and storyteller, but when asked to recount a number of well-known narratives from the sublime to the humorous, including the *Táin Bó Cuailnge*, he replies in the phrasing of translations from the old texts, "I cannot make it." But Finn knows what to make of himself; with a peasant arrogance greater than he has in the Ossianic ballads he sees himself as superior to the Christian god: "Who has heard honey-talk from Finn before strangers, Finn that is wind-quick, Finn that is a better man than God? Or who has seen the like of Finn or seen the living semblance of him standing in the world, Finn that could best God at ball-throwing or wrestling or pig-trailing or at the honeyed discourse of sweet Irish with jewels and gold for bards, or at the listening of distant harpers in the black hole of evening?" (p. 23–24).

Finn knows that he is more than the hunter-warrior-seer of the Hill of Allen, and in what must have sounded like absurd exposition of the vanity of the hero, O'Brien delineates the archetype in monomyth (p. 24):

> I am an Ulsterman, A Connachtman, a Greek, said Finn,
> I am Cuchulain, I am Patrick.
> I am Carbery-Cathead, I am Goll.
> I am my own father and my son.
> I am every hero from the crack of time.

Yet Finn knows that in the modern world he is abused, " . . . is without honour in the breast of the sea-blue book . . . is twisted and trampled and tortured for the weaving of a story-teller's book web." It is not the oppressive British nor pre-technological economy that disgraces the Irish past but rather the country's artists and intellectuals: "Who but a bookpoet would dishonour the God-big Finn for the sake of a gap-worded story?" (p. 24). But Finn's decline and abuse are a part of his story for he also accuses the story tellers of bringing pain and destruction to characters in two of the most tragically moving stories in Irish tradition, the transformation of the Children of Lir into swans and the exile of Mad Sweeney, made to roost in a yew tree. "Indeed, it is true that there has been ill-usage to the man of Erin from the book-poets of the world and dishonour to Finn, with no knowing the nearness of disgrace or the narrowness of death, or the hour when they may swim for swans or trot for ponies or bell for stags or croak for frogs or fester for the wounds on a man's back" (p. 25).

Finn is considerably more subdued when we next encounter him as a tenant of the Red Swan Hotel in the second strata of *At Swim-Two-Birds*. Along with the various Ringsend Cowboys and a number of working class louts, Finn is "hired" by Trellis, the would-be popular moralist, because of his now venerable appearance and experience to play the stern father to Peggy, a domestic serving girl, and to chastise her for transgressions against the moral law. This may be a suggestion that the last home for the heroic is in the working class, authoritarian father. But Finn cannot serve; even as he is introduced it is revealed that an elderly man, Finn himself, has already assailed Peggy's virtue (p. 85).

Finn still has a chance to recover some of his dignity. He could tell a story; he is hectored by the crude and witless Shanahan and Lamont, who address the hero as "Mr. Storybook," into reciting the tale of *Buile Suibhne Geilt*, "Mad Sweeney Among the Trees." Finn's reading of the narrative is not only faithful to the published scholarly translations, but it is also one of the most moving passages in all of *At Swim-Two-Birds*. The Suibhne narrative includes the only reference in the book to Snámh-dá-én, "At Swim-Two-Birds," the place on the Shannon where Sweeney undergoes his subtle transformation, thus putting the key to the whole in Finn's hands. In traditional Irish literature Finn would not have told the story as it is not found in the Fenian Cycle. Furthermore, *Buile Suibhne Geilt* has an emotional delicacy and philosophical subtlety not found in most Fenian stories.

Before Finn can complete the story he is interrupted by his loutish companions who would rather hear something more suited to their own tastes, something from the poet of the people, Jem Casey, who, Finn is advised, "was a poor ignorant laboring man but head and shoulders above the bloody lot of them, not a man in the whole country to beat him when it comes to getting together a bloody pome [sic]—not a poet in the whole world would hold a candle beside him" (p. 103). Jem Casey's most enduring refrain is the porter-drinker's anthem, "Your pint of plain is your only man," a line which O'Brien took from Patrick Purcell, a Dublin personality of an earlier generation.[2]

After listening to chorus after chorus of clichéed doggerel Finn tries to respond with poems from the Sweeney story, but he begins to blither, reducing himself to defense against unworthy adversaries. They are tolerant, however, and one of them, John Furriskey, Trellis' creation, encourages Finn to continue his story, "Let him talk . . . it'll do him good. It has to come out somewhere" (p. 110).

Finn's persistence flags, and after an interval of about fifty pages, Mad Sweeney himself appears, reciting heroic poetry in a face-off with Jem Casey, the proletarian poet, who responds with verse in the same meter. Meanwhile Finn, wearily patient while derided, continues to reappear periodically through the rest of the book. We learned that he was made a cuckold when his "wife" Gráinne, here spelled "Granya," ran off with Diarmaid, identified here with Dermot Trellis (p. 200). In a description of a "day from the life of Finn," we see the elder hero idling away his time playing chess, watching young boys playing ball, and sleeping (p. 214).

Most of the rest of the action of *At Swim-Two-Birds* is taken up with Dermot Trellis' dealings with his several characters. He creates Sheila Lamont who is so ravishingly beautiful that Trellis cannot resist raping her, thus producing the bastard son, Orlick Trellis, who quickly joins the evil characters Pooka MacPhellimey and John Furriskey. When the "seeds of evil, revolt, and non-serviam" (p. 214) are sown in his heart, Orlick, who inherits a modicum of literary ability, begins to write a novel about his father, Dermot Trellis, to seek revenge for his wronged mother. In a scene pointedly reminiscent of Joyce's Nighttown, Dermot Trellis is put on trial for his life before a court and jury made up of his own characters plus Mad Sweeney and Finn MacCool (p. 281). Just before Trellis is to be found guilty and executed, his servant fortuitously burns the pages of manuscript which give life to the vindictive characters, and the creator escapes; thus ends the novel-within-the-novel. Meanwhile the student narrator has won his bachelor's degree from the University College, Dublin, and *At Swim-Two-Birds* ends with a short passage introduced with the rubric, "Conclusion of the book: ultimate" (p. 314), containing a short philosophical essay on the association of death and the number three.

At Swim-Two-Birds is a novel of manifold implications, only a few of which offer any critique of the Fenian narratives of Irish tradition. O'Brien's most salient ideas give criticism of the novel form itself, as in the student narrator's anticipatory manifesto for the anti-novel, which begins with *At Swim-Two-Birds'* most quoted line, " . . . a satisfactory novel should be a self-evident sham to which the reader could regulate at will the degree of his credulity" (p. 33). The implicit cultural criticism of the Fenian passages is certainly one of the major themes of the whole work. O'Brien's comic Finn does battle on two

fronts; his heroic grotesquery is a blot on the pretensions of the
Gaelic Leaguers and their allies. The mythic Finn behind the ancient
narratives is too distant to serve as a basis for determining a twentieth-
century Irish identity. On the other hand, the abused Finn of Trellis'
"novel" would speak of the beauties of the knowable past in Irish
literature, but his words are lost in the blighted present, a present—
in the Free State period (1939)—that was dominated by populist
philistines descended from the mobs who had jeered Yeats, Synge,
and O'Casey. The implications of this are clear: those who would
enshrine the past isolate it from the present as much as do those
who would denigrate it. But O'Brien's Finn is not merely the past,
a relic of less harried times; instead, as a deathless but aging mythic
hero, an Irish Tithonus, he speaks the poetry of the past in precise
and unjaded imagery. His absurdity is not of O'Brien's making, it is
the condition of poetry in a world of plaster statues and pulp-fiction
heroes.

For all its games and tricks, At Swim-Two-Birds seems to be
devoted to one of the great themes of the conventional novel, the
dichotomy between illusion and reality. As Philip L. Coulter has
suggested, the central tension of the novel is between the alternating
reality of the narrator's external world and the fantasy of his internal
world, expressed in his own fiction (701, 1971, 13). Finn first appears
"in the kingdom of his mind," the narrator portrays him as a
continuing, many-sided fantasy, reflecting, buffeted by, but never a
part of the real world.

In sum, At Swim-Two-Birds is not diverse and fragmented but
unified. If O'Brien's purpose had been only to comment on the
archetype of Fionn, his book would hardly have attracted such wide
acclaim. If it were only a critical exercise in the aesthetics of fiction,
it would have little interest to us here. Instead, one purpose com-
pliments the other. As V. S. Pritchett has commented, O'Brien reduces
the total of Irish literary tradition, Mad Sweeney, Finn MacCool, and
Jem Casey, leaving only farce. He seeks to knock the regionalism
out of Irish literature by exaggerating it (719, 1960, 250). At Swim-
Two-Birds makes the de-provincialized, deflated Ireland a proper
setting for the contemporary absurd. The Red Swan Hotel already
houses Finn MacCool, leprechauns, and comic book heroes; it could
as easily accommodate Vladamir and Estragon from Samuel Beckett's
Waiting for Godot. Through his use of an anti-heroic Ireland, O'Brien
has a means of approaching the post-Joycean novel. The novel is
multi-leveled to allow us to probe the changing meaning of Irish

tradition and the Irish ego. As T. S. Eliot advises, O'Brien cannot deny or annihilate tradition, only modify the way we see it from our place in time. In *At Swim-Two-Birds* Finn MacCool, an embodiment of old Ireland, lives and dies simultaneously.

FIONN MAC CUMHAILL IN ADAPTATIONS OF THE STORY OF DIARMAID AND GRÁINNE

As noted in chapter 1, the story of the pursuit of Diarmaid and Gráinne has been, in both Irish and English, the most popular narrative in the Fenian Cycle. Its appeal reaches not only to peasant shanachies and to nationalist translators but to more disinterested poets, critics, and scholars as well. The adaptations in English are so extensive as to constitute a tradition in themselves. There are, depending on how one classifies them, upwards of twenty.

Although there is a brief summary of the action of the Diarmaid and Gráinne story in chapter 1, a more extensive review of the principal episodes could serve us well here. The title of the narrative in Irish, *Tóruigheacht Dhiarmada agus Ghráinne*, classifies it as a conventional "pursuit" in the repertories of early bards and story tellers. If we assume that the various fragments of the narrative can be reconstructed chronologically, the first episode in it would be the curse put on Diarmaid in his childhood. Diarmaid was the lawful son of the chieftain Donn Uí Duibhne (or "O'Dyna") and the uterine brother of a bastard fathered by Donn's steward. When Donn killed the bastard brother in a rage, by squeezing the child between his legs, the steward cursed Donn, saying that the murdered son in the shape of the boar would pursue the living one, Diarmaid, until vengeance was met. Not all versions include this episode, but Diarmaid is conventially forbidden to eat pork or to hunt the boar.

Most versions of the story begin at the betrothal feast of Fionn and Gráinne, at which the coquettish Gráinne first espies Diarmaid, one of the most filial of Fionn's men, and succumbs to his irresistable *ball seirce* or "love spot." Gráinne urges Diarmaid to take her away from Tara, which he does, and the lovers spend the next year, or, as in some versions, the next twenty years, fleeing across all of Ireland; Scottish Gaelic versions have them flee through an additional series of Highland and Hebridean locales. One analogue of the story's popularity is the conventional name for the hundreds of dolmens in Ireland as "the bed of Diarmaid and Gráinne," although most of them would be unsuitable for sleeping, let alone lovemaking. Diarmaid is initially a reluctant lover, speaking frequently of his uneasiness at having violated the code of the Fianna and affronted Fionn. Most of the other members of the Fianna, notably Oisín, do not share Fionn's anger and instead sympathize with the lovers. In all versions the menacing Fionn eventually finds the lovers, usually at Céis Chorainn (English: Keshcorran) in County Sligo, whereupon he invites Diarmaid, out of respect to the codes of the Fianna, to come on a hunt of the wild boar. Diarmaid is not long at the chase when he is disemboweled by the boar, sometimes by the boar's tusks and sometimes by his bristles. As Diarmaid lies mortally wounded, Fionn comes and stands over him, gloating that he wishes all the women in Ireland could see how the beautiful young man looks now. Diarmaid asks Fionn to make use of his magical hands; just as he has the power of divination in his thumb, so too he can heal the wounded by carrying water in his cupped hands. Fionn carries water three times and allows it to slip through his fingers each time, after which Diarmaid dies. When Fionn brings this news to Gráinne her grief is shortlived. In most versions she betrays the memory of Diarmaid and returns to live with Fionn as his wife.

Irish-language redactions of the story frequently include additional episodes during the pursuit of the lovers which are dropped in most English language versions. These include Gráinne's desire for and Diarmaid's quest of magical, youth-restoring berries from the quicken or rowan tree, a comical chess game in which Diarmaid drops rowan berries on strategic squares of a chessboard, thus allowing Oisín to beat Fionn, and combats with various giants and drawfs. Such folkloristic details seem to obfuscate the inherent drama of the love triangle of Fionn, Gráinne, and Diarmaid.

The dramatic possibilities for Fionn's role in the narrative are not initially promising. Not only is cuckoldry demeaning for the national hero of Ireland, but his vengeance in pursuing the lovers, his characteristic emotion in the story, seems inconsistent with the Fionn mac Cumhaill of other stories. On the face of it there appears to be little an English-language poet could do with the characterization of Fionn here, not simply because the hero is now the third member of a love triangle but also because he seems separated from the archetype we have been discussing.

This is not to say that Fionn's persona lacks the dynamism to assert itself more dramatically. For example, Gaelic shanachies in the Outer Hebrides have a repertory of riddles conventionally ascribed to Fionn and Gráinne, dealing with such puzzles as, "What is blacker than the raven?" (Death); "What is sharper than a sword?" (The reproach of a foe), etc. As the Scottish folklorist J. F. Campbell has commented, no matter who is the questioner or answerer, Gráinne represents quick wit and beauty while Fionn represents a more mature wisdom (242, 1893, vol III, 46–48). Diarmaid is never a party to the riddles, which suggests that considered by themselves, Fionn, hunter-warrior-poet, and Gráinne, daughter of the high king at Tara, manifest enough tension to sustain some kind of dramatic presentation, a possibility never realized in English.

To understand what possible connection the Fionn of the "Pursuit of Diarmaid and Gráinne" has with the rest of Fenian literature we must investigate further the scholarship dealing with the origins of the story. To begin with, what is the origin of the narrative itself and how did it happen to become a part of the body of Fenian literature? Because the narrative in its earliest forms, *Aithed Gráinne*, "The Elopement of Gráinne," etc., dates from earlier than the ninth century, inquiries into provenience lead easily to speculation. The eminent Celticist R. A. Breatnach in his study of the narrative declined to deal with its origins at all (325, 1958). Less cautious readers have several hypotheses from which to choose. For example, Sir John Rhys in his epoch-making study, *Celtic Heathendom*, argued that the story was originally a solar myth. Evidently writing under the influence of Friedrich Max Müller's now discredited essay of *Comparative Mythology* (1856), Rhys saw Gráinne as a goddess of the dawn, Diarmaid as a solar hero, and Fionn, by asserting that he is the counterpart of the Welsh Gwyn and therefore "king of the fairies and of the dead," as the king of darkness (593, 1898, 146). Another theorist whose ideas lie beyond the periphery of accepted mythological scholarship is Robert Graves, who sees the rivalry between Fionn and Diarmaid as another manifestation of the continuing ritual combat between the sacred king and his tanist, or apprentice, heir-apparent, and prospective executioner (834, 1955, vol. 1, p. 72). Most Celticists look upon Graves as an interloper and pariah and therefore usually do not comment on his scholarship, but a study by G. F. Dalton, "The Ritual Killing of Irish Kings," supplies information which suggests that the sacred king/tanist theory may require further investigation from cultural anthropologists and archaelogists: the presence of the apparent vegetation motif of the quicken (or rowan) tree and its berries, which may provide the renewed youth Gráinne desires, and which are used to foil Fionn's chess game with Oisín, would be a concomitant function of the sacred king of the grove (486, 1970).

Like Graves and a number of more accepted commentators on Irish tradition, Alexander H. Krappe, the eminent linguist and folklorist, sees a key to the story in the motif of Diarmaid's death from the boar, a fate he shares with Adonis and Tammuz. The Babylonian Tammuz was the lover of the great goddess Ishtar, and in the subsequent Phoenician and Greek retellings of the story, Adonis became the lover of, first, Ishtar and, by adaptation, Aphrodite. On Olympus Aphrodite was married to Hephaestus, but her most usual lover and virtual consort was Ares. Thus the love triangle for Adonis included Aphrodite (or Venus) and her elder, rough-mannered, quasi-husband Ares (or Mars), not only in Greek and Roman tradition but also in those of many exotic peoples under Roman influence. Krappe believes the narrative became a part of the Fenian cycle through the association of Ares/Mars with Fionn, the hunter and warrior (372, 1936), although he is at a loss to explain the cultural linkage. The route from late Roman to Old Irish literature is much easier to trace today. The introduction of Christianity around A.D. 432 also meant the initiation to Roman culture. Although Ireland was outwardly cut off from the Mediterranean after the legions departed Britain in A.D. 450, Roman learning was pervasive among Ireland's first literati, the Irish monks, as Robin Flower describes in *The Irish Tradition* (497, 1947, 2–10). More recently William B. Stanford has shown how profound and complex were the Irish ties to Rome in *Ireland and Classical Tradition* (606, 1976). And when we remember the residual anti-clericalism in many Fenian stories, we understand how a monkish scribe recording secular literature in the great codexes and elsewhere might have found delicious revenge by including the cuckolding of the unchurched Fionn mac Cumhaill.

The reminder of the Deirdre analogue from the Ulster Cycle is instructive. The aging and rejected betrothed in that narrative is Conchobar mac Nessa, who, like Fionn, is usually seen as a most admirable figure in other stories from the cycle. Indeed, when compared with Conchobar, Fionn seems a more likely cuckold as he had already suffered Oedipal abuse in the Ossianic poems and more general denigration in the oral tradition. When we recall that Diarmaid, as a member of the Fianna, is a son-surrogate for Fionn just as Naoise, the young lover of Deirdre, has a filial relationship with Conchobar, we are reminded of David Krause's insights mentioned earlier in this chapter: that the rebelling son (Oedipus, etc.) is usually tragic just as the usurped father (Laius, etc.) is comic or absurd. Fionn, the aging, spurned lover of Gráinne is absurd, if not comic, sharing much with the conventional middle-aged lovers in such comedies of manners as those by Marivaux, Congreve, or Boucicault. He is also a threatening figure, not only because of his vengeance, but also because his age is a reminder to the lovers of what they will become in time.

The fifteen to twenty adaptations of the Diarmaid and Gráinne story in English do not, alas, include any masterpieces, celebrated or neglected. Most of the poems and plays are by lesser authors, perhaps justly forgotten, and those from more compelling authors, Yeats and George Moore, Lady Gregory, Austin Clarke, Sir Samuel Ferguson, and John Masefield, are secondary works in their respective *corpora*. What distinctions we can make among the several versions of the story are posited on the ambitions the different writers held for it, the diverse purposes they would have it serve. Whereas at least a dozen writers, most of them narrative poets, retell the story of Diarmaid, Gráinne, and Fionn more or less straightforwardly, evidently relying on its intrinsic appeal for readers as one of Ireland's hallowed legends, a smaller group of writers have regarded the story as a genuine literary myth, a record of the continuity of human experience. The following discussion will look at the storytellers first, with special attention to the most notable of them, Austin Clarke in his *Vengeance of Fionn*, and then continue with those writers who took more freedom in reshaping the narrative, Lady Gregory, Yeats, and Moore, and E. R. Watters, a narrative poet of the present generation.

The first poet to adapt the narrative in any manner was the Protestant Anglo-Irishman, Sir Samuel Ferguson, whose 114-line "The Death of Dermid" appeared in 1865 (221, 153–60). Though little read today, Ferguson was a fitting poet to introduce the story to polite literature as he had launched an Ascendancy taste (which, after many decades, became a vogue) for the Old Irish narratives with his Deirdre poem, "The Death of the Children of Usnach," thirty-one years earlier. Unlike Charlotte Brooke's *Reliques*, Ferguson's poetry was a contemporary expression. Heavy with the liabilities of mid-Victorian aesthetic, paraphrasis, Wardour-street archaism, and conventional moralizing, Ferguson's "Death of Dermid" is nonetheless passingly interesting in that it takes the form of dialogue between Fionn and Diarmaid from which Gráinne is excluded. The passage, as Ferguson freely acknowledges, is taken from S. H. O'Grady's translation in the *Ossianic Society Transactions*, and begins with Fionn's scornful address to the fatally gored young hero (p. 154):

> It likes me well at last to see thee thus.
> This only grieves me, that the womankind
> Of Erin are not also looking on:
> Such sight were wholesome for the wanton eyes
> So oft enamoured' of that specious form:
> Beauty to foulness, strength to weakness turn'd.

The model for Fionn's viciousness is in the original text, and although Ferguson's beginning on this note might seem to emphasize the darker Fionn, the poet actually humanizes the hero's vengeance. When Fionn allows the saving water to slip through his hands it is because he remembers his lost Gráinne. When Diarmaid reproaches him, Fionn speaks of his own pain (p. 155):

> How at these hands canst thou demand thy life,
> Who took'st my joy of life?

But Diarmaid's death is not to be tragic. When Fionn fails with the third handful of water, Diarmaid has a vision of "that Just One crucified/For all men's pardoning," and he dies with a smile on his face.

The vitality of the conventional Fionn of the love triangle prevails through more than a dozen different refashionings of the same Irish story, despite continual restructuring of the accidents of his person and station. In her "The Pursuit of Diarmuid and Gráinne" (1887), Katherine Tynan Hinkson, one of W. B. Yeats' first colleagues in the Irish literary revival, speaks of Fionn as "the king of Ire," as he never is in Irish tradition, but fixes his character in the image, "gnarled like an oak." Another poet and early disciple of Yeats, Nora Hopper, transformed the narrative into rhythmic prose in her *Ballads in Prose* (1894), in which a modern-dress persona named Maurice Cahill envisions Gráinne in a dream and senses that the soul of

Diarmaid is reanimate in him. Employing a style which Phillip Marcus has characterized as "extreme deconcretization" (551, 1971, 267), Hopper relegates Fionn to the background where he is barely perceivable but still menacing. Three years later the ninth Duke of Argyll, John Campbell, provided a libretto for Hamish MacCunn's opera, *Diarmid*, sometimes known as *Diarmid and Ghrine*, in which the role of Fionn is sung, predictably, by the baritone. Lord Campbell diffuses some of the tension of the triangle with such characters as Freyja, the love goddess from Norse mythology, a Macphersonically-named Eragon, king of the Norsemen, and a daughter of Fionn, Eila, whom, Gráinne (here "Ghrine") charges, Fionn prefers to his young betrothed. And as would befit a grand opera by a nobleman, the trappings of the scenario are considerably enriched; when Fionn refuses Diarmaid the saving waters he uses a golden cup instead of his bare hands. But seven years later the same story could also serve the popular and sentimental poet, Anna MacManus ("Ethna Carberry"), who divided the narrative into two rhythmic prose tales for her "slender volume," *In the Celtic Past* (1904). Writing for a general audience at a time when populist nationalist sentiment was asserting itself with renewed vigor, MacManus included some attempts to lighten Fionn's character. She invented a series of episodes in which Fionn aids Gráinne's father, Cormac, king of Tara, and has his praises sung by the bards. Seeing her betrothed so honored, Gráinne, uncharacteristically, gazes lovingly upon the aging hero. But at the death of Diarmaid, Fionn is still present, vengeful and unaiding, as the young hero dies.

The longer narrative poem has been something of a literary fossil in the twentieth century, which makes it all the more surprising that there should have been seven poems treating of the Diarmaid and Gráinne story, four of which merit some attention.[3] Of these, three, by Austin Clarke (1917), J. R. Anderson (1950), and John Masefield (c. 1957), render the narrative fairly conventionally, while a fourth, by E. R. Watters (1964), is so unconventional it should be considered separately. Describing a poem's narration as "conventional" does not, of course, presuppose a critical position on it but rather provides a means to approach it; the poems by Clarke, Anderson, and Masefield are all comparable, and Clarke's is easily the most interesting, Masefield's the least. The poet laureate was eighty when his *Story of Ossian* was issued on phonodisc, an unfortunate medium for so windy an enterprise. Another distinction of Masefield's effort is that it portrays Fionn as the prime mover of the tragedy, greedy for power and wealth, hoping to marry Gráinne for his own gain (57, c. 1957):

> All this began because Fionn wished to wed,
> He was lonely, old, and covetous of power,
> He dreamed of empire with himself as head,
> With eastern Éire pledged to him as dower . . .

Masefield's Gráinne has some of the unattractiveness of Irish versions; she is as "beautiful and graceful as a snake." Her father, Cormac, barters her off to Fionn in a marriage Gráinne finds more hateful than death. Other changes are slight, such as when Oisín and Niamh are introduced to diffuse the tension, or when Fionn is humanized slightly when trying to have Diarmaid taken alive and returned to his tent.

The 180-page *Pursuit of Diarmuid and Graunia* of J. R. Anderson (1950) is obviously much more ambitious and considerably more successful. John Redwood Anderson was an English schoolmaster of what he described as "American descent." Though it has not attracted much crittical attention, the blank verse narration of his poem, interspersed with unrhymed lyrics, offers the reader many small pleasures. As befits Anderson's milieu, his *Pursuit of Diarmuid and Graunia* eschews all the marvellous elements of the Irish story and, instead, supplies the lovers with deeper psychological motivation. His Graunia is in love with Diarmuid long before she is betrothed to Finn and, indeed, agrees to the marriage only as a means of bringing the Fianna into the royal household at Tara. Anderson's Finn is more brash; when Ae Beg on Avin, a new character created from the traditional Conán Maol, mocks the pregnant Graunia, Finn abruptly takes off his head with a stroke. Something of a Casanova, Finn verbalizes his memories of previous loves. Finn's attraction for Graunia is more lustful than loving, a lust which is rekindled at the climactic boar hunt. After Diarmuid is gored, Finn goes to console Graunia in the final scene of the poem. She is dry-eyed, leaving the reader with the unmistakeable impression that when a year passes, a suitable time for mourning, Graunia will accept her once-thwarted lover Finn.

This leaves the most distinguished of the verse narratives, *The Vengeance of Fionn* of Austin Clarke. Although still not widely known in North America, Clarke was the most admired of Irish poets after the death of Yeats. His *Vengeance*, published when he was twenty-two, was sufficiently well received to win the young author an invitation from the exiled James Joyce in Paris. A product of the transition from the late Georgian taste of the pre-war era and the coming taste of Eliot, Pound, and the later Yeats, the *Vengeance* combines a lovely lyricism and rich imagery from the Irish countryside with a discordantly ironic characterization of the principals. Clarke's lovers are not young but middle-aged, ugly, and jaded. Employing a restructured chronology he evidently borrowed from the much inferior poet, Herbert Trench, in his *Deirdre Wed* (1901), Clarke begins the narration with a reconciliation between the aged Fionn and the aging Diarmaid, who are about to begin the hunt for the boar. The familiar elements in the story, the betrothal, the elopement, flight, etc., are seen in flashback as Fionn and Diarmaid pursue the fatal boar. The vengeance of Fionn cited in the title is not immediately apparent; the old hunter, initially bitter, is ready to be reunited with his former friend and claims to be too old to refire his unrequited love:

"Let be, for I am Old,"
He cried, "foolish and old. What have the old to do
With dreams the heated sinews of youth, no spears
Or staghunts weary, beget. His words can woo
No woman to him whose body is bent and cold."
Proudly he towered through the mountain air,
"Old . . . Old . . . the whitlow, this thing for women's tears,
A moment's blood drop; no more! Who'll snarl, rage,
Whelping his wounds? I am of that old dark breed
That's gone, begotten from the fire that's hid
In the loins of the cold rocks."[4]

Clarke includes some vivid descriptive passages of Diarmaid and Gráinne's first celebration of their love, but as that love has become a distant memory, the theme of *The Vengeance of Fionn* deals more with love's futility. Diarmaid knows that the white Gráinne of his memory now has breasts of leather (pp. 271–72). Clarke's Fionn, whose eyes have a boar-like glint, has an allegorical dimension: he is the pursuer the lovers could never escape, the hunter whose weapon is the grim scythe.

Throughout the poem Clarke's handling of the juxtaposition of memory and the present is economically deft. The flashbacks are not disgressions from the development of the central theme but rather contributions to it; the past modifies the present. The pain of their boredom and their apparently loveless marriage is intensified when juxtaposed with a reminder of the lovers' expectations at the time of their flight and exile. This is most poignant in the scene where two anonymous young lovers comment on the death of Diarmaid, just occurred offstage. The maiden speaks (p. 308):

> "And I saw poor Gráinne in the sunlight,
> Wrinkled and ugly. I do not think she slept.
> My mother says that she was beautiful,
> Proud, White, and a queen's daughter long ago,
> And that they were great lovers in the old days—
> Before she was married—and lived in hilly woods
> Until they wearied of the rain and cold.
> I do not want to grow so old like her.
> O it is best to be young and dance and laugh
> And sing all day and comb my sleepy hair
> In the startime, and never, never grow old.
>
> O shiny dew,
> O little creature of the air,
> Youth only is wisdom and it is love."

Although we do not see the principals at the end of the poem, Clarke has made the denouement implicit within the narrative. The gray and gaunt old Fionn is hardly a rival of Diarmaid's, even now, yet he is Gráinne's only release from her now loveless marriage (p. 285).

> "Stern is his will,
> Swift is he to love, swifter to kill.
> Gladly to the grianan[5] I will go,
> My maids will loose my hair and quiet as sleep,
> Barefooted with the moonlight I will creep
> Into his couch."

The romantic attraction that Clarke's Gráinne voices for Fionn is but another irony in *The Vengeance of Fionn*, assuring us that the old hero will not be attenuated into a symbol. As Clarke places him in a richly imagined outdoor setting, a vision of nature closer to the Irish Fenian poems than any of the other adaptations of this story, the Fionn of *The Vengeance* is a convincingly real, mortal warrior and hunter whose retribution is the atrophy and death no one can escape.

Although Austin Clarke did not produce another full-length adaptation of the narrative he made frequent allusions to it throughout his career, including it in his autobiographical sketches, *Twice Around the Black Church* (1962) and *Penny in the Clouds* (1968). His most sustained use of allusion is in his novel, or "prose romance," *The Bright Temptation* (1932), chronicling the initiation into love of a young scribe, Aidan, and a girl, Ethna, in medieval Ireland. Clarke, ever the scourge of Irish puritanism, treats their affair as something beautiful and good, a parallel of the love of Diarmaid and Gráinne, thus making an oblique commentary on the repressive sexual morality of Free State Ireland.

Despite the archetypal dramatic conflict of the story, and despite Yeats' assertion that Irish drama was rooted in the Fenian cycle,[6] the pursuit of Diarmaid and Gráinne has not been well served on the stage, even in comparison with the limited successes of verse narrative. Of the three published dramas in English that employ the story, not one raised favorable comment when it first appeared, and only Lady Gregory's *Grania* (1912) is of such quality as to merit a revival, even by amateur groups. The plays have another trait in common, which may or may not bear on their relative failures, the mollification of the aging, vengeful cuckold, Fionn mac Cumhaill.

The least considerable of the three is *Last Feast of the Fianna* (1900), a one-act play and the first dramatic endeavor of Alice Milligan, a minor but competent poet of the early Irish Renaissance. The play's historical distinction is that it was the fourth dramatic production of the revival. Merging elements of the Diarmaid and Gráinne story with that of "Oisín in Tír na nÓg," *The Last Feast* is set in an unnamed banquet hall, apparently at the Hill of Allen, where Fionn and his returned queen, Gráinne (here "Grania"), preside. During the banquet the Fianna are visited by Niamh of the Golden Hair, who first invites Fionn to come with her, and, when he refuses, asks Oisín. Though clearly intended as a serious drama, *The Last Feast of the Fianna* could be, when placed against the rest of Fenian literature, produced as a comedy. Not only is Oisín Niamh's second choice, but Fionn's love for Gráinne, now his wife, takes some unexpected forms. He has forgotten her choice of a different mate in youthful folly, but he chides her for her present jealousy. "Hold your peace, Grania, for the stranger [Niamh] is about speaking. I see you cannot endure beauty in another woman" (p. 52). He is more declamatory in his rejection of Niamh who offers the promise of eternal life to any man who makes love to her (p. 53):

> "You would not invite me to fly from Death with waving arms, with winning words, if you had known, as is known in Eri, how I have sought Death more than women. In my life of ages since boyhood, Death and I have always been comrades. . . . O fairy woman of the music, tell this to the lords of life, that Fionn Mac Cumhal follows Death, whom even the De Daanans [sic] fear. I will face the terror that men dread. I will unveil the secret mystery, and if Death is more terrible than life, at least I will not cry out in fear."

For all his patriarchal authority, Fionn gradually withdraws from the conflict, which focuses on Oisín and Niamh. Once the decision to leave is made, Fionn's last speech laments Oisín's departure (p. 55). Gráinne, who is peripheral to most of the action, speaks her farewell as a still embittered stepmother.

One year after Alice Milligan's *Last Feast of the Fianna*, the Irish Literary Theatre, an ancestor of the Abbey Theatre, produced one of its most curious if not most successful plays, George Moore and W. B. Yeats' *Diarmuid and Grania*. Although not published for fifty years,[7] the play has raised considerable critical interest, apparently because of the circumstances of its production and from Moore's comments on the play in his autobiography, *Hail and Farewell*. Actors were imported from London for the production, and incidental music was commissioned from Sir Edward Elgar, the leading British composer of that time, whose "Funeral Music for Diarmuid" is still performed. Moore, then forty-six and well established, and Yeats, thirty-six but confident of his future, were incompatible collaborators. Moore wanted Gráinne to be the daughter of a king, and Yeats wanted her to be a peasant. Moore wanted prose, and Yeats wanted poetry. Lady Gregory, who had provided a scenario for the project (27, 1901), mediated. In a moment of exasperation, Yeats suggested that Moore write a play in French which Lady Gregory would translate into English; Taidgh O'Donoghue would translate this text into Irish, which Lady Gregory would put into English. Then, rejoined Moore generously, Yeats would put style into it. When the production was a failure, apparently because of the weaknesses in the company, both authors abandoned the play, and it was later thought to have been lost. Yeats saved the manuscript, showing it with some pride to Lennox Robinson in the late thirties. And though it appears to bear Moore's hand more distinctly, it can be studied in relation to Yeats's other work and is included in the Variorum edition of his plays.

Diarmuid and Grania, subtitled "A Three Act Tragedy," is sufficiently long to include the major episodes in the narrative, from the betrothal of Gráinne and Fionn to the death of Diarmaid. Several of the scenes and many of the characters have been modernized along the lines Moore suggested in *Hail and Farewell*. As Yeats has requested, the lovers are familiar with peasant life; for example, in the third act when we see where the lovers have been living in domesticated exile, Diarmaid is shearing a sheep. As the realist Moore wanted, over Yeats's objections we may presume, all elements of the supernatural have been expunged; Gráinne's attraction for Diarmaid comes not from his "love spot" but is, instead, foretold in a dream. Likewise, Fionn no longer has the power to save Diarmaid from death with the healing water, and it is ambiguous whether his vengeance or Diarmaid's clumsiness deprives the wounded hunter of a draft of quite ordinary water from Fionn's helmet. More importantly, the lovers seem to share an idealism that hungers not simply for escape but for an ordered and more perfect life, a motivation not suggested in the various Irish redactions of the tale. Because the theme of the difficulty or even folly of attempting idealism in this world was present in other works of George Moore, in his plays *The Strike at Arlingford* and *The Bending of the Bough* as well as in such novels as *Evelyn Innes* and *Celibates,* and because the dialogue has such prosiness, commentators on *Diarmuid and Grania* have argued that it is more Moore's play that Yeats's.

The Fionn mac Cumhaill of Moore and Yeats is an unattractive husband for Gráinne, not so much because of his age as because of his coarseness. In the initial exposition of the play a retainer in the royal household tells of Fionn's heroic deeds in the hunt and in battle, much to Gráinne's civilized distaste. When she first speaks to her father of her unwillingness to marry Fionn she mentions "going away into the woods." Cormac acknowledges, "Maybe you think Finn [sic] too rough a man to marry" (p. 1180).

But the Fionn we see upon the stage is a subtler character than Gráinne has described, with all the guile and duplicity of a conventional lounge lizard. He denies that he suffers any jealousy for the loss of Gráinne and claims that he is angry at Diarmaid only because he broke oath in leaving the Fianna. Later, in the final scenes of Act II, he acknowledges to Gráinne that he pursues the lovers because he genuinely does hate Diarmaid. Similarly, Diarmaid anticipates that Gráinne, as conceived in this play, may hold a lingering affection for Fionn; earlier in Act II, before they admit that their love for one another has atrophied, Diarmaid asks Gráinne if, were he to die, she would become Fionn's wife (p. 1195).

By the final scene in Act II, Gráinne is indeed ready to return to Fionn. Even before the fatal boar hunt, Diarmaid knows that there can be no peace between Fionn and him because they both still love the same woman (p. 1204–1205). Diarmaid would prefer to settle with Fionn in a duel, but he relents when Fionn accuses him of lacking the courage to hunt the boar. Fionn knows that Diarmaid is "fated" to be killed by the boar, as he acknowledges to Gráinne after Diarmaid is gored and dying before them. Knowing Diarmaid cannot be saved, Fionn is more protective of Gráinne, saying he will not leave her side and will protect her from danger (p. 1218–1219). Gráinne asks that Fionn join her in mourning, and cries out to her father that one of the great heroes of Eri[n] has been killed and deserves the worthiest of funerals. When she leaves the stage, Fionn agrees and offers the best of his horses to be killed in sacrifice with Diarmaid's horse so that "he may have nobler horses when he awakes" (p. 1222). These respects paid, Conán comes to Fionn with the last line of the play, "Grania makes great mourning for Diarmaid, but her welcome to Finn shall be the greater" (p. 1222).

Gráinne is dominant in Moore and Yeats's play as she is in Lady Gregory's outline for it. But as Lady Gregory would not have counseled, Gráinne incorporates an almost medieval anti-feminism in her self-indulgent inconstancy. Gráinne's role puts special demands on the actress playing it, demands which, commentators tell us, Mrs. F. R. Benson, wife of the company's director, could not meet in the first and only productin of the play, October 1901. Lennox Robinson and Joseph Holloway blame her performance for the play's reputation as a failure.

But even if the company had succeeded in acquiring the services of their first choice, Mrs. Patrick Campbell, the première actress of the British stage at that time, the play would very likely have met only limited success. The script as we read it has enough weaknesses to sink it, such as a tendency for excessive exposition in which more

Fenian lore is remembered than we need. The play is rife with a heavy-handed and self-conscious dramatic irony which has, for example, some retainers nailing a boar's head to the wall as the curtain rises. The weakness which would most likely prevent its revival today is in the dialogue which has not stood the test of time at all well. Here are the lovers squabbling over Diarmaid's rejoining of the Fianna for the hunt of the boar (p. 1212):

Grania: Kill me if you will, kill me with your sword, here is
            my breast.
Diarmuid: You would have me kill you. Maybe if I would kill
            you all would be well.
Grania: Hold fast my hair, draw back my head and kill me.
            I would have you do it. *(Pause)* Why do you not do
            it? If you would go to this hunting, you must do it;
            for while I live, you shall not go.

A transformed Gráinne is manifestly the dominant character in Lady Gregory's *Grania*, a play which, despite many excellences, was never performed during the author's lifetime. Although *Grania*,[8] a three-act drama, also derives from the same summary provided Moore and Yeats, it is a distinctly different play. Like the earlier collaboration it begins at a splendid Almhain, or Hill of Allen, which is not to be found in Irish tradition, but now there are only the three characters of the triangle instead of a company of servants, retainers, warriors, etc. More significantly, Gráinne is now the constant stalwart who is caught in the emotional tangle of two men, both of whom appear to be her inferior in wit as well as courage. Anthony Farrow calls her a "Celtic Hedda Gabler" (80, 1974, 10).

Considerably reduced in Lady Gregory's play is Diarmaid who is such an absurdly timid lover that he has not so much as kissed Gráinne in the seven years of their exile. The only tension Lady Gregory allows him is a somewhat boyish guilt for having broken the code of the Fianna in running off with Gráinne. He is also troubled with himself for having allowed an interloper, "the King of the Foreigner," to kiss Gráinne without responding in defense of his own honor. After he is wounded by the boar Diarmaid is more attentive to his former leader Fionn than to Gráinne, whom he virtaully ignores. His death speech begins with the declaration of how foolish any man would be to give up his friend and master for a woman (p. 42). When Fionn invites her to return with him to Almhain she agrees, responding that she sees no reason to spend the rest of her life as a widow when so much of it was lost as a virgin.

Following Anthony Farrow's suggestion that Lady Gregory's Gráinne is the Celtic Hedda Gabler, Diarmaid, her consort if not her lover, becomes something of Hedda's inane husband, Tesman, and Fionn, the thwarted lover, no longer a symbol of aged decrepitude, becomes an approximation of Hedda's unrealized lover, Eilert Lovborg. In direct contrast to the Fionn of Moore and Yeats's play, Lady Gregory's Fionn is gentle and considerate. In an early speech to him, Gráinne praises his virtues: "I had an old veneration for you, hearing all my lifetime that you are so gentle to women and to dogs and to little children, and you wrestling with the powers of the world and being so hard in war" (p. 14). Gráinne speaks unknowingly to Fionn of her unaccountable love for Diarmaid (from the love spot, which has been rationalized as a wound), and Fionn, before the young man can speak, rashly accuses Diarmaid of betraying him. Gráinne says she is the cause of her infatuation with Diarmaid, who seems unwilling to refuse her affection, but the two men continue to argue; when Fionn faints at the end of Act I, the "lovers" flee.

Seven years pass before the beginning of Act II, in which Fionn appears at Diarmaid's camp disguised as a beggar, claiming to have been sent by Fionn himself. Without showing any concern for his lost betrothed, Fionn in disguise chides Diarmaid for having broken his vow to the Fianna and for tolerating the kiss given Gráinne by the "King of the Foreign."

In Act III, set in the afternoon of the same day, Fionn identifies himself to Gráinne and asks her to return to him, not so much for his disappointed love as for his hurt pride. In a speech which echoes the solar theories of John Rhys, Fionn tells Gráinne of the attraction he is sure she must feel for him: "I tell you, my love that was allotted and foreshadowed before the making of the world will drag you in spite of yourself, as the moon above drags the waves, and they grumbling through the pebbles as they come, and making their own little moaning of discontentment" (p. 326). Although Gráinne says she hates Fionn for the unnatural bond he has sworn Diarmaid to, she hears Fionn swear that he has kissed every spot she has set her foot in Ireland and knows his great passion. She contends with Fionn on the question of who is a better lover, he or Diarmaid, and is about to call in the younger man as a witness when his body is carried in from the boar hunt. After a moment of bitterness and regret, she agrees to go with Fionn to Almhain in a speech cited above. As the final curtain approaches, Fionn and Gráinne hear jeering laughter from soldiers off-stage, and as Fionn picks up his newly rebetrothed and carries her out, the laughter ends abruptly. The irony of the final exit is twofold; Gráinne simultaneously quashes the rough-mannered Fianna and, implicitly, all the anti-feminists in Ireland outside the theater.

Lady Gregory's *Grania*, which she included among her tragedies, seems a comic variation on the conventions of the Diarmaid and Gráinne story. But it is a coherent variation of the peculiarly Irish feminist theme which runs through much of her writing. Her Gráinne, based on the supposedly fickle harpy who betrays both husband and lover, embodies the frustrations of a woman who suffers a society dominated by peasant values. Lady Gregory's Fionn and Diarmaid are clearly caricatures of the loveless and guilt-ridden Irishmen who value boyish camaraderie among themselves to the mature love they might share with a woman. In the end Fionn is only barely preferable, but he would rather kiss her footprint than her lips.

This leads us at last to the final adaptation of the Diarmaid and Gráinne story, E. R. Watters' *Weekend of Dermot and Grace* (1964), the only work which restages the action a modern setting. Eugene Rutherford Watters began his literary career in Irish under the name Eoghan Ó Tuairsc, producing fiction and drama as well as poetry. He did not begin work in English until he was past his fortieth birthday. Published at a time when the audience for book-length narrative verse has apparently disappeared, his *Weekend of Dermot and Grace* has thus far received only perfunctory critical commentary. The poem is set in Dublin, August 1945, a few days after the dropping of the bomb on Hiroshima, a time and theme Watters explored in his Irish poem *Lux Aeterna*, also published in 1964. The *Weekend* is narrated by the sardonic Dermot who runs away with Grace, a bored Dublin shopgirl, to remote Donegal, Watters' native county. Other mythological figures are similarly attenuated. Oscar, usually a glamorous figure in Fenian literature, becomes tedious Uncle Oscar who fought the Black and Tans and from whom the protagonists would like to be preserved.

The one figure enlarged in Watters' treatment is Fionn, who expands to include much of the outmoded, paternal past, the historic nightmare from which the lovers are struggling to awake. Dermot speaks of him (p. 3):

"Hide us from dead wisdom.

He is laid in a tremulous tomb of the wind's making,
Eyes blinded under passionless lids
May no longer arraign us with their come-down to earth,
Only his stud glimmers where it is transfixed."

What is Watters' Fionn? Dermot answers us (pp. 34–35):

"Finn is the gash of the footlights hung
Between our eyes blinded with radiation and the guessed
Vast auditorium where only a shirtstud gleams,
Half believed in, one half dream.
Finn is a kind of plainsong
Bearing along in its many charactered swell
The year half-blinded and the strenuous limbs
Between the two profundities.
Half believed in, half believed in,
Heaven the blue untried, the tide-grey will.
Now Finn is form, a scherzo movement
Wrestling with the apathetic windy power
That unconfined in sinew, gut and string
Would lose itelf in the last
Vast auditorium where as a shirtstud gleams
Blue light of the last star,
Ply within ply shaping it as a flower."

And further (p. 35):

"Half believed in and half dream,
He shuts us in a solitary confinement
Behind anonymous eyeballs watching the years as they straggle
Bar after slanting bar on a whitewashed wall
Across the initials of a nameless ageing [sic] man . . ."

Watters' Fionn/Finn is the mythic hero without an euhemerist
gloss. He is not pegged to some possibly historical warrior at Almhain
but is instead an almost insubstantial figure created from the experiences, the fears and oppressions, of the Irish past. His continuing

unfolding story gives shape to a modern identity threatened by atomic holocaust. Finn carries the dead wisdom of the past, and capture by him is a fate the lovers dread equally with an entry into the deadeningly empty future.

Yet Watters' Finn is more substantial than a mere symbol. He is "Mr. Finn that bald nailbiter of an architect" (p. 6). He is in his middle fifties, wears a fine-clipped beard, and issues his thunderbolts with a ball-point pen. The lovers cannot flee him as he is pursuance itself. Though previously a hunter and warrior, the modern Fionn mac Cumhaill has no need to leave the city. His continuing imagistic leitmotif is the shirtstud which catches light and can always be perceived through the dimness, in a darkened theater or in the open evening air. Watters' Diarmaid knows that the myth has condemned him (p. 37):

> "I have carried the doom of him about with me since dawn
> Cracked the delicate dim
> Withdrawal of our tented sleep."

Despite such foreboding, *The Weekend of Dermot and Grace* is not a pessimistic work; raddled with Christian symbolism, the poem finds an end in conventional Roman Catholic belief. For example, the poem is divided into three parts titled "Friday," "Saturday," and "Sunday." The lovers depart in gloom on Friday, the day of the Crucifixion, and return on Sunday, which simultaneously recalls the first Easter as well as Easter 1916. The horror of disintegration, death, and seemingly utter failure are transformed into rebirth and wholeness through the great Christian mystery of the first Easter rising which Roman Catholics believe they continue through the Mass. It is no printer's error that leaves the last line of the poem unpunctuated: "Bretheren pray that my sacrifice" (p. 45). For Watters, as for Eliot of the *Four Quartets*, history is now and his own country, Ireland not England. "A people without history/Is not redeemed from time, for history is a pattern/Of timeless moments."[9] Fionn/Finn is composed of timeless moments in Irish history, filled with glory and folly, and Dermot can escape him with Christian Grace, the pun fully intended, in apprehension of the still point of the turning world, where the dance is.

CONCLUSION

Fionn mac Cumhaill, like all mythic figures, is protean. Not limited to the heroic uniforms sewn for him by James Macpherson and Standish J. O'Grady, he can be the clown in Carleton, the ridiculous anachronism in Flann O'Brien, or the villainous avenger of the Diarmaid and Gráinne stories. Whereas the comic, peasant Fionn of the "Legend of Knockmany" might appear initially to have nothing in common with the vaporous pursuer of *The Weekend of Dermot and Grace*, the many Fionns have more in common than their names. All are rooted in the heroic tradition. There could hardly be a comic Fionn if there were no hero to deride, denigrate, or parody.

Whichever theory of diminished hero is the most plausible, we should recognize that each manifestation of Fionn mac Cumhaill that has been examined in this chapter has emphasized, to some degree or other, his age. Fionn the thwarted lover of Gráinne may be based on a model taken from the classical world or the Levant, but unlike Ares, the cuckold consort of Aphrodite, or Mars, who is abandoned by Venus, the Fenian avenger is an old man. The words of the sixty-three year old Yeats could have been spoken through the mask of Fionn mac Cumhaill:

> What shall I do with this absurdity—
> O heart, O troubled heart—this caricature,
> Decrepit age that has been tied to me
> As to a dog's tail?[10]

The archetype of Fionn mac Cumhaill is large enough to accommodate contradiction. The next line in Whitman's famous quotation accepting his own contradictions is that he is large enough to contain many multitudes. And so it is with Fionn, as we shall see in our discussion of *Finnegans Wake.*

5

Fionn mac Cumhaill
in James Joyce's *Finnegans Wake*

E.
Estyn Evans, the Irish social scientist and folklorist, once observed that Americans look upon *Finnegans Wake* as a handbook and guide to Irish culture.

His statement has irony worthy of the *Wake* itself and would certainly have won Joyce's admiration. First, there is the comic irony in the suggestion that *Finnegans Wake*, a notorious *ne plus ultra* in obscurity, could serve as a handbook for anything. The secondary irony, probably a weary one for a scholar of Irish traditions such as Evans, is that many Americans can sustain an interest in Irish language and culture only so long as they provide some kind of gloss for the works of W. B. Yeats and James Joyce. The American Joseph Campbell appears to have taken his first serious interest in Irish myths and folklore about the time of his early explication of *Finnegans Wake*, the famous *Skeleton Key*. At the same time Evans' remark can be taken literally: *Finnegans Wake* makes a more extensive use of Irish tradition than any work of fiction ever published. In its pages may be found a gallery, albeit apparently disordered, of figures from the Irish past, from Saint Patrick and Fionn down through Parnell and Kitty O'Shea, and ordinary, otherwise anonymous Dubliners of Joyce's own time. The *Wake*'s use of Irish tradition takes into account the historical, the mythical, and the legendary, the public and the intimate, the celebrated and the suppressed, the remembered and the forgotten. It seems likely that many Americans would never have read the exploits of the seventeenth-century pirate Grace O'-Malley, nor ever known the legendary associations in Irish placenames (e.g., Chapelizod—"Chapel of Iseult") had they not tried to unlock the secrets of *Finnegans Wake*.

More than any other work cited here, *Finnegans Wake* is a Celtic book. It is, of course, also an international work, as the various glosses of Scandinavian, German, Italian, Slavic, Volapük, etc., vocabularies have demonstrated. There are no formal criteria that make a book Celtic or Irish, nothing comparable to what can make an opera Italian, a miniature Persian, or a farce French. Nor are the mere questions of setting, language, character, and theme enough to secure a literary work's nationality, although *Finnegans Wake* provides a Celtic answer to each of these questions. The essential Celticness of *Finnegans Wake* is most easily perceived when measured against the distinctiveness of Celtic tradition. Here, for example, is the judgment of the art historian Paul Jacobsthal in distinguishing emergent primitive Celtic art from the established orderliness of the Greek (520, 1944, 10): "to the Greeks a spiral is a spiral and a face a face and it is always clear where one ends and the other begins, whereas the Celts 'see' the faces 'into' the spirals or tendrils: ambiguity is a characteristic of Celtic art. . . . It is the mechanism of dreams, where things have floating contours and pass into other things."

Such a passage could easily be included in a commentary on *Finnegans Wake*, especially the last line. The mechanism of dreams, the things with floating contours which pass into other things, can be discerned all through Irish tradition from before *The Book of Kells*, despite the presence of the occasional realist. For this reason, the reader of traditional Irish literature has prepared himself for some of the demands Joyce makes on the reader of *Finnegans Wake*. Consider, for example, some of the information about Fionn outlined in our first and second chapters. The very name "Fionn" comes in as many as two dozen forms, including "Fingal," which puns with a placename from the north of County Dublin in an area once dominated by Protestant settlers, which, in turn, puns with the Modern Irish word *fionghal*, "fratricide," or "murder." Further *fionn* in Modern Irish meaning "white" or "fair," may not be an actual name at all. There are "Fionns" in other cycles, such as the three brothers-in-law of Cúchulainn, the "Three Fionns of Emhain." Our hero, first known as *Demna, Deimne,* or *Dohmnch,* won the name "Fionn mac Cumhaill." Joyce finds an additional confusion with the name as it puns with the Modern Irish *fion*, "wine." Early Continental etymologies for his name link him with the placenames of Vienna and the Canton of Windisch in Switzerland. Once we outline his persona in Irish literature we find he may be identical with Lugh or Cúchulainn. Common people in Ireland have long wished to think of Fionn as historical, although no evidence exists to support such a claim. Some of his more incredible adventures, however, link him with genuine historical figures from Irish tradition such as Brian Boru, the victor of Clontarf, or even Saint Patrick. Going outside Irish tradition we find that Fionn may be identical with such diverse figures as Theseus of Athens, Gwyn ap Nudd, Sigurd of the Volsungs, King Mark, or King Arthur. Because his name means "fair," Fionn can be associated with the conventional Irish phrase for a fair maiden, *cailín bán*, or "colleen bawn"; and the Irish pronounciation of his name, *Fionn* as "fewn," is much like the first syllable of the English word "funeral." In any event Irish orthography has always been highly flexible and accommodating, just as Joyce's spelling in the *Wake* is kaleidoscopic. Furthermore, as the repertories of most shanachies are composed in the historical present, we could expect to hear stories of Fionn juxtaposed in which he appears successively as a youthful hero, a mature defender of his people, a poet, a marauding parasite, a cuckold, a butt of crude and tasteless jokes, and a clown. Not confined to his own cycle, Fionn is reincarnated as King Mongan in Ulster literature. One reincarnation may have been only the beginning. As explained by the allegorical euhemerism of Giovanni Battista Vico (1668–1744), a "mythic" figure is one drawn from human experience who lives anew in each generation. Just as Odysseus could walk the streets of modern Dublin as an advertising salesman, so too can Fionn mac Cumhaill be reincarnated uncountable times. Recognizing all these elements and ideas Joyce inherited from mythic scholarship, we should be less intimidated by, for example, the transmogrifications of H. C. Earwicker into Persse O'Reilly. "Earwicker" is close to the name of the insect earwig, which is *perce-oreille* in French, which, in turn, sounds like "Persse O'Reilly" when pronounced in Dublin English.

This kind of tortuous explication will not be a feature of the last chapter of this study. Commentators on *Finnegans Wake* have already filled several five foot shelves with studies, and if David Hayman's 15,000-word explication of one sentence in the work is the measure (751, 1958), many libraries full are yet to come. Such study is not to be dismissed because reading *Finnegans Wake* is a collective enterprise of no ordinary kind. For this reason I shall assume that anyone reading this chapter has already spent some time with *Finnegans Wake*, with or without critical assistance, and recognizes some of the basic assumptions of the work, the reliance on Vico's *Scienza Nuova*, the importance of night and the dream, and the "circularity" of the narrative. Further, I shall assume that my readers understand the cross-linguistic punning and games playing of *Finnegans Wake*, even though the different languages and games may not always be evident. For the present our task will be to determine how Joyce made use of the myth of Fionn mac Cumhaill in *Finnegans Wake*. As we have followed the thread of the archetype of Fionn through the forests of Irish and English literatures, so do we now try to follow Fionn's vein through the finely grained marble of the *Wake*.

JOYCE'S PERCEPTION OF FIONN MAC CUMHAILL IN IRISH TRADITION

Some casual readers of James Joyce assume that the nightmare of history from which Stephen Dedalus would like to awake is Irish rather than Western or human. To them, it seems that when Stephen chooses exile along with silence and cunning at the end of *A Portrait of the Artist*, this must mean exile from his native land. Also memorable is the response Joyce's Gabriel Conroy in "The Dead" gives to the Gaelic nationalist, Miss Ivors, "O, to tell you the truth . . . I'm sick of my own country, sick of it." But to take such passages as an indication of Joyce's actual feelings is to confuse the author with his creations, a snare for the incautious. Joyce, in fact, remained fascinated with Irish affairs throughout his lifetime in exile. He may have lacked stamina for Irish politics and the Irish struggle for independence, but he was indefatigable in his championing of aspiring Irish writers and artists. His four principal works of prose fiction and his one play are all set in Ireland, regardless of how critical their view of Irish customs and character.

Standing between Joyce and Irish tradition were the literary nationalists of the Gaelic Revival. We need only survey the parodies of the "Cyclops" chapter of *Ulysses* to see that Joyce portrays the movement as fundamentally anti-intellectual. English was the language of urban Ireland by Joyce's time, not Gaelic or Irish, and the translations of the texts from the older language, including interminable narratives of blood-thirsty, unreflective warriors and kings, offered little to the imagination of a faithless, arrogant young aesthete like Joyce. The narrator of the *Portrait* sounds more like the actual Joyce in his description of the peasant nationalist, Davin: "His nurse had taught him Irish and shaped his rude imagination by the broken lights of Irish myth. He stood towards this myth upon which no individual mind had ever drawn out a line of beauty and into its unwieldly tales that divided themselves as they moved down the cycles in the same attitude as towards the Roman catholic religion, the attitude of the dulwitted serf" (p. 181).

Although Joyce would appear ready to reject his Irish identity, it would not release him, as an oft-cited passage, also from Book V of the *Portrait*, implies (p. 189):

> The little word "tundish" seemed to have turned a rapier point of his sensitiveness against his courteous and vigilent foe. He felt with a smart of dejection that the man to whom he was speaking was a countryman of Ben Jonson. He thought:
>
> —The language in which we were speaking is his before it is mine. How different are the words *home, Christ, ale, master,* on his lips and on mine! I cannot speak or write these words without unrest of spirit. His language, so familiar and so foreign will always be for me an acquired speech.

Without identifying the author with Stephen Dedalus, we can see from these citations the dimensions of Joyce's difficulty in reconciling himself with a tradition. Neither the native language of Ireland nor the English of Great Britain are his languages. Neither could he use the idealized but bogus Irish-English recently concocted by Lady Gregory, Douglas Hyde, and J. M. Synge, all members of the Protestant Ascendancy. Joyce did, however, accept the genuine popular Irish-English tradition of Dublin, especially as manifested in the city's music halls, most notably in the songs of a Trinity College educated engineer, Percy French (1854–1922). Many of French's songs and parodies have become so popular they are frequently mistaken for anonymous popular songs; those that Joyce admired, judging by their inclusion in *Finnegans Wake*, include "Phil the Fluter's Ball" and "Come Back Paddy Reilly (to Ballyjamesduff)." Joyce did not find Received Standard English so foreign that he could not use it in *Dubliners*, the *Portrait*, or *Ulysses*, in his letters, or in conversation. If there was to be an Irish rival to George Ade or Finley Peter Dunne, he would not serve. Joyce had immeasurably grander ambitions for the pun-loving demotic *patois* he had known from his childhood: he would use it as the basis on which the ambitious punning of *Finnegans Wake* would be constructed. Although many questions about the *Wake* are the subject of continuing critical argument, this linking of Joyce with the popular spoken language of Dublin now seems an accepted commonplace.

Joyce's taste for Percy French offers an explanation of how Fionn mac Cumhaill came to play such an important role in the construction of *Finnegans Wake*. Fionn is the only one of the important figures from the national mythology who survives in modern popular tradition. The mythological figures of the Abbey Theatre dramas, Deirdre, Conchobar, and Cúchulainn, had been lost to popular culture and were revived by an elite coterie of writers who celebrated a sanitized version of the national tradition. For Yeats and his followers the only roles that could be found for Fionn was as the father of Oisín and the lover of Gráinne. The buffoon Fionn of popular tradition would never find a home in the Abbey Theatre. Yet from Joyce's point of view the popular caricature of the national hero of Ireland must have been what made him exploitable in *Finnegans Wake*.

The question of just how much Joyce knew about Irish tradition, specifically the Irish language and the several narratives translated from old texts, has been the subject of extensive inquiry by much more qualified authorities than the present writer. In the view of Vivian Mercier, Joyce's knowledge of the Irish past was quite sketchy. Mercier finds Joyce's Irish reference library, catalogued after his death, to be "pathetically inadequate." Most of the Irish works contained in the library were secondary sources, many of the most unscholarly kind, such as those written for secondary and even primary schools (554, 1962, 235–36). John V. Kelleher, the dean of Irish scholars in America, feels that Joyce's knowledge of Irish tradition in *Finnegans Wake* is taken from his own sometimes capricious memory, and that Joyce probably knew much less than the professors who seek to explicate the *Wake* with the Irish sources at hand. Kelleher thinks that Joyce's principal source of information on Fenian matters was Lady Gregory's *Gods and Fighting Men* (1904), from which a sentence in the *Wake* (219.10) is "almost certainly" taken (754, 1971, 167). More recently Danis Rose and John O'Hanlon have shown (768,

1980) the extensive use Joyce made of the American compilation of translations of Old Irish texts, T. P. Cross and C. H. Slover's *Ancient Irish Tales* (1936). Citing evidence from the notebooks, corroborated by the testimony of Jacques Mercanton, who visited the author in 1938, Rose and O'Hanlon demonstrate that Joyce worked in dozens of references to Fenian stories from Cross and Slover during the final weeks of the composition of *Finnegans Wake*.

Joyce's knowledge of the Irish language was considerably more substantial, despite the several suggestions in the *Portrait* that the young artist had little time for the study of it and dropped it after only one lesson. To clarify the question of language, Stanislaus Joyce in *My Brother's Keeper* tells that James Joyce studied Irish intermittently for two years before he left Ireland (753, 1958, 171). And whether or not Joyce was a diligent student of Irish, he did know a vast number of words as shown by the lists of them that can be drawn from his writings. By including loan words, place names, and direct translations Brendan O Hehir counts twenty-two in *Dubliners*, one in *Pomes Penyeach*, sixteen in *A Portrait of the Artist as a Young Man*, two in *Exiles*, and well over two hundred in *Ulysses* (765, 1967, 333–53). A more conclusive measure of Joyce's interest in and knowledge of Irish comes in O Hehir's *Gaelic Lexicon for Finnegans Wake* which runs 331 pages, including about 5,500 entries. This work gives substance to Joyce's assertion, cited in the "Scribbledehobble" notebook, that the three most used languages in the *Wake* are English, Irish, and Norse, the three languages which, in that order, contribute to Dublin English. O Hehir makes no claim that Joyce was a profound scholar of Irish; indeed, Joyce's spellings indicate he knew little of the reforms in Irish orthography instituted after he left Ireland in 1904.

There seems to be no question that Joyce knew from childhood something about the narratives of Fionn mac Cumhaill. In my own limited researches I have yet to encounter an Irish man or woman who could not identify some aspect of Fionn's career, even after the assault of international, commercialized pop culture. Joyce mentions Fionn in the Cyclops chapter of *Ulysses* when Mr. Joseph McCarthy Hynes is quoted as making an appeal for the resuscitation of the ancient Gaelic sports and pastimes, "practised morning and evening by Finn MacCool" (p. 317). Later Joyce makes reference to the "Tribe of Finn" in a catalogue of Irish heroes (p. 323). And although Joyce has no occasion to make mention of mythological figures in his two

earlier works of fiction, he does include Fenian allusions in both
Dubliners and the *Portrait*. For example, in the famous final paragraph
of "The Dead," Joyce begins the description of the snowstorm thus:
"Yes, the newspapers were right: snow was general all over Ireland.
It was falling on every part of the dark central plain, on the treeless
hills, falling softly on the Bog of Allen and, farthur westward, softly
falling into the dark mutinous Shannon waves" (p. 223).

The Bog of Allen is, of course, adjacent to the Hill of Allen,
whose best-known resident has been Fionn. Given the context of
the story, the reference to the bog seems more appropriate. On the
other hand when young Stephen Dedalus returns to Dublin from
Clongowes Wood College the first landmark he seems from the train
window is the Hill of Allen (p. 20).

There are, in addition, further elements in Fenian tradition which
would have made it attractive to Joyce in writing *Finnegans Wake*,
although we cannot demonstrate that Joyce knew them. For example,
the Hill of Allen is a feature of a larger geological region known
traditionally as Magh Life, "the Plain of the Liffey," from which the
headwaters of the Liffey flow. As it is now a commonplace of *Wake*
explication to associate the Liffey, the water of *Life* (a cross-linguistic
pun which includes "whisk(e)y," *uisce beatha*, also the "water of
life"), with all rivers and all femininity, and therefore ALP, it would
be fitting to have the Liffey flowing from the same plain that includes
the traditional home of Fionn mac Cumhaill, so easily associated
with HCE.

Whatever Joyce's interest in the Fenian narratives before he
began work on the *Wake* we know that some measure of his desire
to portray Fionn as the hero of Dublin and not only of Ireland was
based on bogus scholarship. As noted in chapter 1, Joyce heard of
Heinrich Zimmer's speculations on the Norse origin of Fionn's archetype from Zimmer's son, the Oriental scholar, in Paris in 1921,
although the assertion was first put forth more than thirty years
earlier and had long since been discredited. Joyce had no interest in
Zimmer's scholarly reputation because the Norse origin theory was
so useful for associating Fionn mac Cumhaill with H. C. Earwicker,
who is an Irishman of Scandinavian background. There seems little
use in berating Joyce for being intrigued with an informal summary
of Zimmer's thesis any more than we would chastise Shakespeare
for using the unreliable history found in Holinshed's *Chronicles*. The
more immediate question should be to find out what kind of character
Joyce wished to make of Fionn.

FINDING A ROLE FOR FIONN MAC CUMHAILL IN THE *WAKE*

When the time comes for some harmless drudge to compile a *Cliff's Notes to Finnegans Wake*, the easiest chore will be to explain how Joyce named it. The book's title comes from a street ballad of the nineteenth century, most probably of Irish-American origin but known in Ireland as well, which includes the conventional apostrophe for the possessive, "Finnegan's Wake." The name of Tim Finnegan, the protagonist of the ballad, evokes that of the traditional hero Fionn mac Cumhaill in both English and Irish spellings. The stem of the Irish name Ó Fionnagáin includes *fionn*, "white" or "fair," although there is no indication that the family makes any genealogical claim on the hero. Very early in the text Joyce insures the association of the two Fionns: "Hohohoho, Mister Finn, you're going to be Mister Finnagain!" (5.9–10)[1] In the original ballad, Tim Finnegan, a hod-carrier, arrives at work one day slightly under the influence of alcohol and subsequently falls from a scaffolding and apparently dies. His friends collect his body, wrap it in a clean sheet, and, following the conventions for an Irish wake, place fourteen candles at his feet and a gallon of porter at his head. Finnegan's friends, wife, and relatives assemble for the wake, making the appropriate protestations of grief amidst the general liveliness of the wake, and in time a scuffle breaks out in which a thrown gallon of whisky spills on Tim and awakens him. In Joyce's *Wake* Tim Finnegan is described as a "dacent gay-labouring youth" (6.23), and while he is still believed dead his mourners keen, "Macool, Macool, orra whyi deed ye diie?" (6.13). Because Tim Finnegan does not die but, as in the euphemism, only sleeps, *Finnegans Wake* is the dream he could dream, although it seems most unlikely his unconscious mind would ever store all that is in the book. The title, therefore, includes a number of puns, some which came with the title and some which Joyce manufactured. The first comes because Tim Finnegan awoke at his own wake; Finn, short for Finnegan, again wakes. But as Tim Finnegan's name also implies an association with Fionn mac Cumhaill, the title can also be read as an address to the universal human archetype: [All the] Finn-agains [among us,] Wake! Joyce builds this second pun by removing the possessive apostrophe, perhaps the most famous omission of punctuation in modern literature.

Much said thus far is widely known, even to people who have never opened a copy of *Finnegans Wake*. Fionn's association with the

Wake is furthered by the third paragraph of the first page, one which
has been analyzed so often it has become a kind of Rosetta Stone
for the rest of the text.

> The great fall of the offwall entailed at such short notice the
> pftjschute of Finnegan, erse solid man, that humptyhillhead of
> humself prumptly sends an unquiring one to the west in quest
> of his tumptytumtoes: and their upturnpikepointandplace is at
> the knock out in the park where oranges have been laid to rust
> upon the green since devlinsfirst loved livvy (3.18–24).

   Much of this is especially appropriate for Fionn mac Cumhaill's
"erse solid man," a hero of Erse literature and an arse in popular
tradition. Many readers subsequently gloss "humptyhillhead" as the
Head of Howth, the promontory north of Dublin Bay, and the "park
where oranges have been laid" as Castle Knock in the Protestant
cemetery in Dublin's great Phoenix Park. Fionn can be associated
with both of these places, Howth because its settlement predates
that of Dublin and because it is mentioned in heroic narratives from
both the Ulster and the Fenian Cycles, and Phoenix Park because
its name is a false derivation from *fion uisce*, "white or clear water,"
which flows from several springs there. Consequently many critics
of the novel have assumed there must be an Irish popular tradition
that Fionn mac Cumhaill, a sleeping warrior, lies buried beneath
Dublin, stretching from the Head of Howth to Phoenix Park. If we
accept this it would seem that Joyce was inviting us to think the
sleeping Fionn was a counterpart of the sleeping Tim Finnegan and
the 628 pages of the text of the *Wake* is his dream, detritus from
the experience of the mythical hero who may have given his name
to Vienna, who defends his country from invaders, who commanded
the Fianna, and who suffered abuse and humiliation later in his
cycle. It seems therefore fitting that, as Richard Ellmann reports,
Joyce should have informed a friend that he conceived of his book
as the dream of old Fionn, lying in death beside the river Liffey and
watching the history of Ireland and world—past and future—flow
through his mind like the flotsam on the river of life (743, 1959,
557).
   If one were to read only the first few pages of the book, where
references to Fionn abound, and read only superficially through the

rest of the text, noting the nonce Joycean associations of Fionn mac Cumhaill with the resurgent nation of Finland and with Huckleberry Finn, the impulse to accept Joyce's word that the narrative is Fionn's dream would be easy. Such an assertion is already accepted in handbooks to the *Wake* and would be attractive as the crescendo conclusion of the present study.

But a close reading of the text will not support that thesis. As the language of the previous two paragraphs must signal, my reading, augmented by many critics, both of traditional Fenian literature in Irish and English and also of *Finnegans Wake*, does not support Joyce's spoken assurance that the book is all just Fionn's dream. This is not to say that Joyce lied to us. He told other people, especially non-Irishmen, that the book was "about" other things. Adaline Glasheen says that Joyce may not have absolutely lied, but he "equivocated like crazy." And part of the equivocation can be seen in the use of Fenian materials we have just reviewed.

To begin with, there is no suggestion in Fenian tradition that Fionn should be associated with Dublin or that his body should lie under the city, or in any way alongside the Liffey. The ancient Irish did not build coastal cities and instead resided inland; the Rock of Cashel and Armagh, the Seat of Patrick, represents the oldest continuous Irish settlement. Many supposed castles and settlements in Irish mythology, such as Tara or Bruig na Bóinne, "The Bend of the Boyne," i.e., New Grange, are in fact great tombs left from pre-Celtic civilizations. Dublin was, as Joyce acknowledges in the *Wake*, originally a Danish city, like Wicklow, Waterford, Cork, and Galway, etc. For this reason there is no mention of Dublin or any other modern city in Fenian manuscript tradition. Modern oral tradition, of course, could incorporate any place or anything from the modern world, as in Yeats's story of Fionn's falling over a haycock on his way to the magistrate. But major collections of Fenian lore, manuscript and oral, Irish and English, are silent about Fionn's associations with Dublin. Similarly, collections of Dublin lore, such as J. M. Flood's *Dublin in Irish Legend* (503, 1919), are silent on Fionn's associations with the city. Fionn is indeed associated with the Head or Hill of Howth, as are many other traditional figures, because it is an easily distinguishable land form whose presence has been noted from earliest times. Fionn has also been associated with hundreds of other locations, most of them land forms, caves, hills, rivers, large rocks, etc., and also some of the larger dolmens surviving, virtually indestructibly, from pre-Celtic times. Joyce, as we have noted, accepted Zimmer's discredited theory of the Norse origin of the Fenian narratives, and once he had he could associate Fionn with Dublin.

Returning to the great bulk of Fenian literature, in English as well as Irish, we find that the most of it, the endless adventures of the hunter-warrior-poet, the battles against the Lochlanners in the ballads, the *Céadach* or "helper" tales, the *bruidhein* or "enchanted dwelling" tales, all, except for the story of the Pursuit of Diarmaid and Gráinne, have very little to contribute to the outline of the action in the *Wake*, which is primarily a family drama. Most of the action of the *Wake* is urban or, as Chapelizod is outside Dublin, suburban. All-encompassing as the imagery of the *Wake* is, there is no discernible strain of nature imagery comparable to that found in many Old Irish manuscripts and parodied by Flann O'Brien in *At Swim-Two-birds.* There is, in short, nothing in the literary record of Fionn suggesting he could have had the experience to allow him alone to dream the dream of the *Wake*.

Concurrently, an examination of the differing texts of the *Wake* shows that there is no evidence to support Fionn mac Cumhaill as the dreamer, or, for that matter, the narrator, or the protagonist of the novel, if those roles can be separated. Joyce began work on the *Wake* very shortly after the publication of *Ulysses* in 1922. According to the letter he sent to Harriet Shaw Weaver, the actual draft history, then called "Work in Progress," began March 10, 1923, with a two-page version of the Roderick O'Connor sketch that presently appears, much transformed, on pages 380–82 of the final text (752, 1957, 202). For the next six months, as David Hayman outlines, Joyce composed and revised six brief sketches, all of which are parodies of medieval literary modes: "Roderick O'Connor," "Tristan and Isolde," "Saint Kevin," "St. Patrick and the Druid," "Here Comes Everybody," and, finally, "Mamalujo" (750, 1963, 6). From this point the chronology of the differing drafts, the first publications, and the compilation of the "ur-notebook," usually titled *Scribbledehobble*, is the matter of some critical dispute. What is clear, however, is that Joyce manifested no notable interest in Fionn mac Cumhaill or in Fenian tradition. From the 9,000 pages of holograph, typescripts, and revised proof, David Hayman has extracted a 239-page "First Draft," most of which was composed during the 1920s, although Joyce continued composing and revising until shortly before the final *Finnegans Wake* was published in 1939. In examining this "First Draft," we find the linking between Tim Finnegan the hod-carrier and Fionn mac Cumhaill is still in place on the second page, "Hohoho Mister Finn you're going to be Mister Finn again" (750, 1963, 47). Likewise, Fionn's body is still buried under Dublin, stretching from Howth to Phoenix Park. But thereafter Fenian allusions are considerably diminished. The examination of each requires considerable study as Joyce uses elusive permutations of names in one place and the actual name in another, but even with these qualifications it appears that Fionn and the various Fenian characters appear about half as frequently in the rough draft as in the final text. The argument of Rose and O'Hanlon, cited above (769, 1980), that Joyce added most of the Fenian references in the last weeks of composition, seems entirely plausible. Finally, Joyce signaled the delayed attention he gave to Fenian materials when he changed his interim title, "Work in Progress," to "Finnegans Wake" just shortly before publication. Fionn is not the spine of the monomyth, only one of its most important faces.

If the case for *Finnegans Wake* being "about" Fionn mac Cumhaill will not hold up critically, there is no agreed-upon nominee to turn to, no consensus candidate, no critical orthodoxy.

In the absence of an answer there has been contention. The breadth and depth of *Finnegans Wake* commentary is too extensive to review here, especially in light of the more modest goal of determining Fionn's place in it. Put more simply, the dreamer of the dream in *Finnegans Wake* is either no one or someone. "No one" does not mean no person but rather no specific person, and "someone" does mean a specific person, imaginary or real.

As with so many questions in *Finnegans Wake*, Joyce's own comments are often less than useful. The author is reported to have told one visitor that "Time and the river and the mountain are the real heroes of my book" (743, 1959, 565). In a frequently quoted interview given to Danish journalist Ole Vinding in 1936 he said, "There are in a way no characters. It's like a dream. The style is also changing, and unrealistic, like the dream world. If one had to name a character, it would be just an old man. But his own connection with reality is doubtful" (743, 1959, 709).

Fionn, of course, so often an older man in twentieth-century literature, would fit this description, but so would an indefinite number of other figures. Michael Begnal has argued that the dream-narrator stands apart from the action of the *Wake*, helping us maintain our distance from it, in the manner of the Stage Manager in Pirandello's *Six Characters in Search of an Author* or Prospero in *The Tempest*, except that the dreamer learns more and changes more than any of the figures in the action (730, 1969; 731, 1971; 732, 1975). Robert Bierman suggested that the idea for the dreamer might have come from the traditional Irish game in which a player is left alone with a blanket over his head and is asked to pretend he is asleep, dreaming; later he must speak of the dream to the other players (734, 1959). And if the dreamer is anyone, perhaps he is everyone. J. S. Atherton names the dreamer as the "universal mind" (725, 1967).

The most influential book currently on the identity of the dreamer is Roland McHugh's *The Sigla of "Finnegans Wake"* (761, 1976). In it McHugh, an etymologist who has given over much of his life to explicating the *Wake*, says the dreamer is the sign (or siglum) ᗰ that Joyce describes on page 119 and itemizes on page 299, footnote 4. The sign, siglum or character of ᗰ looks most like a capital letter E put on its side. Although the identity of the most important siglum is fluid, it can be distinguished from the other sigla who represent the different characters of "family."

Of all the nameable persons who might be the dreamer, two are significant, one fictional, the other historical. Anthony Burgess thought it might be a Mr. Porter, pub-keeper in Chapelizod, a western suburb of Dublin (737, 1966). Whatever the value of the assertion, Mr. Porter certainly is a character in the *Wake*. And his name provides many attractive puns: Chapelizod is a western "portal" of Dublin; his pub sells porter, the popular Irish dark brew; and he must carry up kegs of the stuff, as a porter, from the cellar. But most informed *Wake* commentators have rejected the Mr. Porter thesis although it lingers in the literature, perhaps because of the prominence its author has in the world of letters at large.

The historical personage whose life may have served in the making of *Finnegans Wake* is the English journalist William T. Stead (1849–1912). Nearly forgotten today, Stead (pronounced "sted") was an assistant editor of the *Pall Mall Gazette* who exposed vice in London, befriended prostitutes and other denizens of the street, was wrongly accused of an indecent assault, and was drowned on the *Titanic*. Stead is the discovery of Grace Eckley (742, 1985), whose work on him is still unfolding. Joyce certainly knew of Stead and makes a number of unambiguous references to him as well as the persistent pun "bedstead." There are also hundreds of links between Stead and Fionn, notably this exhortation three pages from the end, "Steadyon Cooloolus!" (625.21–22).

Whatever the identity of the personality beyond the text, the most usual protagonist of the *Wake* is HCE, or Humphrey Chimpton Earwicker, who was perceived even by the first baffled reviewers in 1939. His initials appear more than 1,000 times in the text, most often as some variant of Humphrey Chimpton Earwicker, but also to Howth Castle and Environs, Haveth Childers Everywhere, Here Comes Everybody, and more than 900 unique combinations. HCE has a wife usually known as ALP, Anna Livia Plurabelle, and two twin sons, Shaun and Shem, and a daughter, Issy. HCE is middle-aged, a Protestant, and apparently of Scandinavian parentage. Although outwardly a native-born Irish citizen, HCE feels himself regarded as an unwelcome foreigner in Chapelizod. In addition, HCE suffers other anxieties. He feels a guilt so intense that reference is made to it (23.16) before he can associate himself with it (p. 29). This is the mysterious Phoenix Park episode, the memory of which invites HCE's excuses, alibis, and apologies. Puns give us a hint of an explanation: "Phoenix Park" may have been for the resurrecting bird in classical mythology through an erroneous etymology, but, in addition, it can be made to sound like *felix culpa*, "the fortunate fall," after the phrase used in Christian apologetics for Original Sin. The first mention of the guilt is, "O foenix culprit" (23.16). HCE's evasiveness suggests some sexual misbehavior, not so likely infidelity (the admission of which might flatter masculine vanity), but rather something of the order of exposure or public masturbation. It may have been voyeurism, a weakness HCE shares with Leopold Bloom, but that seems an unlikely vice to engender such shame. It may also be some fulfillment of the incestuous hunger HCE feels for his daughter.

HCE's two sons, Shem and Shaun, cause their father quite another anxiety. The two are opposite numbers on almost every question, with Shem often taking the position Joyce himself took in family arguments and Shaun owing more to Stanislaus Joyce, at least as James Joyce conceived him. Shem, often called "the Penman," writes, and Shaun "the Post" delivers what is written, usually in a garbled and debased form. Shem is a Joycean artist who can breathe life into the detritus of experience but cannot come to terms with life; Shaun is a popularizer, a demagogue, and a journalist who finds his mission in the marketplace, a man of action who lacks the creative spark. Separate, they illustrate the principles Giordano Bruno of Nola preached about opposites. Together, they are united in the powers of HCE. In the family dreams Shaun criticizes his father and also apes him, often reducing his authority to clichés, while Shem favors the creative, flowing powers of his mother, ALP. Shaun is the potential ally of his father; Shem is the adversary.

As HCE can stand for Here Comes Everybody, an infinite number of figures may be found to be parallel with him. Because he is a Protestant, he can identify himself with many specific Biblical figures. If he is Adam then Shaun is Abel, Shem is Cain, Issy is Eve the temptress, and ALP is Mother Eve. If HCE is Noah, Shem and Shaun represent his numerous sons, including Shem and Sham, Issy becomes either the rainbow or strong drink, and ALP merges with Mrs. Noah, the ark, and the moon. In her ingenious chart, "Who is Who When Everybody is Somebody Else," Adaline Glasheen outlines more than sixty identifications for HCE, including Masterbuilder Solness from Ibsen's play, the Norse invaders of Ireland, Zeus, Adonis, and Deucalion from classical mythology, Buddha, Mohammad, God the Father, Shakespeare, Hamlet's father, King Lear, Richard III, and Falstaff, Joyce himself, his father, Gabriel Conroy, Simon Dedalus, and Leopold Bloom, Lord Wellington and Gladstone, an unnamed Russian general from the Crimean War, more than a dozen figures from Irish tradition, plus some others not readily categorized (747, 1977).

Joyce allows a play between Fionn's name and HCE's, and in at least one place he unites them: "that the ear of Fionn Erwicker aforetime was the trademark of a broadcaster with wicker local jargon for an ace's patent (Hear! Calls! Everywhair!)" (108.21–23). Joyce also links Fionn with Leopold Bloom, "bloomancowls" (456.16), and with Percy French's Phil the Fluter, "Flinn the Flinter" (240.23). Fionn also seems to evoke Daniel O'Connell, the orator and parliamentary leader, who will rise from his grave when summoned and who is, nevertheless, an old cannibal who will devour his own nation, like the old sow feasts on her litter (311.17–19). Joyce seems to recognize that Fionn could easily be confused with other figures from Irish tradition, as for example, Lugh Lámhfada of the Mythological Cycle, "Mr. Lhugewhite" (350.10), or with Brian Boru in the tall tale about the origin of Lough Neagh (310.30–36).

To obscure matters further, Joyce introduced references to Saint Finnloga, "Fynlogue" (327.3), the father of Saint Brendan; Finnuala from the story of the "Children of Lir" (289.28, etc.); Fintan MacBochra, the only Irishman to survive the Flood (25.9), who may be confused with the nineteenth-century Irish nationalist, Fintan Lalor; King Finnerty of Tara (41.25); Saint Finian of Clonard (372.29), not to mention Father Finn, the Jesuit author of boys' books (440.10), Huckleberry Finn (410.36, etc.), Finn's Hotel in Dublin where Nora worked before she left with Joyce (330.24, etc.), and Adam Findlater, a nineteenth-century Dublin grocer and philanthropist. A share of Fionn mac Cumhaill may perhaps be found in all of these. Additionally, Joyce can draw on the mythological analogues and counterparts reviewed in chapter 2 of this study, King Arthur, King Mark, Theseus, etc.

Once Fionn is fitted in place he harmonizes quite well with the structure of the book. Any number of Fionn's surrogate sons in the Fianna could fill the role of Shem and Shaun. Oisín, for example, is a writer like Shem, and his longstanding feud with Fionn, whom he may confuse with Saint Patrick, prompts Joyce to name him "Rageous Ossean" (139.21–22), which gave David Krause the title for his thesis on the role of the Ossianic tradition in Irish culture. Goll mac Morna is often considered a member of the Fianna, despite his allegiance to another family; he is at once a conventional adversary for Fionn and a type for him in several of the *Duanaire Finn* narratives. He seems more like Shaun. Throughout most Fenian narratives Fionn is not portrayed as a terribly aggressive lover, and thus the only traditional counterpart for Issy is Gráinne, with Diarmaid, the hunter and hunted, serving as Shem. HCE's mysterious guilt may be linked with Fionn's unhealthy lust for Gráinne or some forgotten act which caused popular storytellers to find him a comic and absurd figure.

Where does this leave us on the question of Fionn's role in *Finnegans Wake?* If the many references to Fionn mac Cumhaill can be harmonized and fitted into the general frame of narrative for HCE, can distinctions be made between them? The answer to this is not terribly difficult after more than five decades of textual explication of the *Wake.* Nowhere in the context of the work does Joyce try to expand the dramatic role of a traditional figure by making him the vehicle of an immediate emotion or idea, as, for example, Flann O'Brien does with Finn in *At Swim-Two-Birds* or Lady Gregory does with Fionn and the fugitive lovers in her *Grania.* Most of the thousands of allusions in *Finnegans Wake* can be interpreted, if at all, in a received context. Most of the Fenian allusions in the *Wake* could be glossed, as Rose and O'Hanlon point out, in Cross and Slover's *Ancient Irish Tales,* with some saved for an appendix of the best-known popular Fenian traditions. Joyce seems to have ignored many of the English-language adaptations of Fenian material, with the important exceptions of Macpherson's *Ossian,* which he cites frequently, and of Alice Milligan's *Last Feast* (133.26). Instead, Joyce, like a literary Dr. Frankenstein, takes the material for his creature HCE from the remains of uncountable human, literary, and mythical experiences. From these he forges one, to use a word Joyce coins in the text, "monomyth" (581.24). This achievement was perceived by the myth scholar and Joycean explicator, Joseph Campbell, who used it as the *donnée* in his influential study, *The Hero with a Thousand Faces* (817, 1949). The title offers a useful figure of speech: Fionn mac Cumhaill is one of the thousand faces in the monomyth.

THE TEXT OF FENIAN ALLUSION, TWO MAJOR EXAMPLES

  Almost thirty years ago Henry Beechhold demonstrated that Joyce makes extensive use of early Irish history and mythology in *Finnegans Wake,* including all the major cycles of Old Irish literature, and different epochs of Irish history, particularly early religious history, Druidical to early Christian. Although Beechhold missed a number of Fenian allusions we now recognize, he was still able to show that Joyce made mention of several of the best-known episodes in the biography of Fionn: the death of Fionn's father, Cumhal, at Cnucha, his childhood care from Bodmall and Luachra, his winning of knowledge from the magical salmon, his residence at the Hill of Allen, his antagonism toward Oisín, the pursuit of Diarmaid and Gráinne, the decline of the Fianna, and the defeat of the hero at Gabhra, with the promise that he cannot die (726, 1956; 727, 1958). Tracing this material in the text we find, somewhat disconcertingly, that it is scattered at random from end to end, generally without any thematic relationship to its context. As has been mentioned, Fionn is identified with Tim Finnegan and with the city of Dublin early in the text (pages 3, 5, and 6), and he is also cited with apparent significance in the third from the last line of the book, "Finn, again!" (628.14), but between these two points there does not seem to be any specific continuity in the order of the references, either in terms of the biography of Fionn as reconstructed in chapter 1, or, for that matter, in any ordering of it, thematic or chronological. But no random arrangement is without any pattern at all; to strive for perfect randomness is to chase after a logical contradiction, a structure of patternlessness. Thus, when assembled, the Fenians references can be seen to occur most frequently in two sections in which the examples are largely of the same type.

The two sections are the first part of Chapter 6 of Book I, the long riddle which runs from page 126 to 139, whose answer is "Finn MacCool" (139.14), and the second comes in the later pages of the long Chapter 3 of Book II, especially pages 373–78. The earlier section is dominated by heroic references, with some suggestions of farce, and the second is heavy with references to the Diarmaid and Gráinne story, a few of which are comically inappropriate. An examination of the *First Draft of Finnegans Wake* shows that Joyce conceived of them differently. Initially Joyce gave only a paragraph to what is now the thirteen-page riddle, but the answer was still "Finn MacCool" (754, 1963, 93). The Fenian allusions of the second passage, however, have no antecedents in the *First Draft* whatsoever.

The first example comes in the section Campbell and Robinson called, "Riddles—the Personages of the Manifesto" (731, 1961, 107), known more often today as the "Questions Chapter." The chapter is structured as a radio quiz program in which Shem asks the questions and Shaun provides the answers. The riddle whose answer is Fionn/Finn is the first of twelve in the chapter, the others having to do with matters unrelated to Irish heroic tradition. Most of the other riddles are quite short, although the eleventh, wherein Shem asks Shaun if he would help in saving his soul, runs twenty pages. Still, thirteen pages is terribly long to sustain a riddle, an extravagance which may parody the verbosity of some of the Old Irish texts.

The riddle begins clearly enough with the number one:

> 1. What secondtonone myther rector and maximost bridgemaker was the first to rise taller through his beanstale than the bluegun buaboababbaun or the giganteous Wellingtonia Sequoia; went nudiboots with trouter into a liffeyette when she was barely in her tricklies . . . (126.10–14).

Fionn is, of course, a mythic leader, "myther rector," and he is credited in oral tradition with building the Giant's Causeway. In oral tradition, also, he is a giant, "taller through his beanstale." *Bean* is Modern Irish for "wife," and the best-known tale of Fionn's wife is the comic "Knockmany." It appears to be alluded to in the neologism, "buaboababbaun," from the Irish *buadh*, "victory," *babán*, "baby," and *bán* (pronounced "bawn") "white." The Liffey begins, "barely in her tricklies," in the Bog of Allen where Fionn, a frequent fisherman, might try to catch trout barefoot ("went nudiboots").

The next twenty-three lines do not yield any obvious Fenian allusions, although there are a number of words of Irish origin, such as the name for the land form, "esker" (126.15), which might be associated with the landroving hunter, or the Irish placename "boyne" (126.22), one of the locations for the catching of the salmon of prophecy.

On the following page Fionn is described as: "escapemaster-in-chief from all sorts of houdingplaces; if he outharrods against barkers, to the scoolbred he acts whitely" (127.10–13). Many of Fionn's adventures depict him escaping from an enchanted house or other magical traps, as in the tales categorized as *bruidhean*. "Scoolbred," punning on the English "school" and the Irish *suibhal* (pronounced "shul"), "walking" or "traveling," suggests that however coarse Fionn's stories may have appeared to the cultivated, they were attractive to popular tastes.

The remaining passages come at irregular intervals: "and though he's mildewstaned he's mouldystoned; he is quercuss in the forest but plane member for Megalopolis; mountunmighty, faunonfleetfoot" (128.2–4). Most of Fionn's stories have a rural setting, and when he appears in the Old Irish counterpart to a city (Tara, for example), he is put at some disadvantage. Similarly, his stories seem deflated and unheroic in the modern city, as Flann O'Brien pointed out in *At Swim-Two-Birds*. "Mildewstaned" may be a Wagnerian allusion from the phrase for Isolde in Tristan, *"mild und leise,"* and certainly the revival of interest in Old Irish traditions in the generation of Standish James O'Grady had a Wagnerian flavor; but Fionn is also remembered in hundreds of ordinary locales in Ireland and Gaelic Scotland, particularly those with dolmens, cromlechs (e.g. "Crom-lechheight" [132.22]), and large stones. Fionn did not use horses, thus the Fianna prized fleetness of foot, which sometimes led him into trouble, "faunonfleetfoot," from the Irish *fán*, "straying."

"Boasts him to the thick-in-thews the oldest creater in Aryania and looks down on the Suiss family Collesons . . ." (129.33–335). "Collesons" looks like "Cool's son," or MacCool, although it is difficult to see why Cool's sons should be Swiss. "Thick-in-thews" puns with the Irish *tuigeann tú? "Do you understand"?"* and *tiugh,* "thick." As Flann O'Brien observed, Fionn was a giant but not mentally robust. As a mythological hero, based perhaps on a god, he could be the oldest creature in Indo-European (Aryan) tradition,

as well as in Éireann. "Thews" is also an archaic English word for
muscles, fitting for an old strong man.

". . . first of the fenians, roi des faineants; his Tiara of scones
was held unfillable till one Liam Fail felled him in Westmunster
. . ." (151.9–11). Despite the forthright "first of the fenians," this
passage may not refer directly to Fionn. Laziness, *fainéant*, is not
one of the libels affixed to the comic Fionn, even when the Fenians
were portrayed as parasites. "Tiara of scones" may be another reference to "Knockmany," tiara as crown and Tara as palace, except
that Fionn *could* fill it. "Liam Fail" puns on William and "Innisfail,"
a conventional name for Ireland, which may allude to William of
Orange whose followers crushed heroic, Fenian-like resistance in
West Munster for Westminster.

". . . when the streamy morvenlight calls up the sunbeam"
(131.28). "Morven," from the Scottish Gaelic *Mór-Bheanna*, was Macpherson's name for Fingal's kingdom in the *Poems of Ossian*, and
"streamy" is one of Macpherson's characteristic modifers. This clearly
is Fenian. But it is difficult to see how this calls up solar theories
of the cycle; the young Fionn may have been a solar hero, but Rhys
thought that Diarmaid had solar powers when competing with the
older hero for Gráinne.

". . . grossed after meals, weights a town in himself; Banba
prayed for his conversion, Beurla missed that grand old voice; a
Colossus among cabbages, the Melarancitrone of fruits; larger than
life, doughtier than death. . . . (132.25–29) . . . and as for the
salmon he was coming up in him all life long" (132.35–36). Most
of the references to food in this passage are difficult to explain,
except for the salmon of prophecy. Gluttony was not a conventional
libel for the comic Fionn. "Banba," a poetic name for Ireland, might
well pray for his conversion—especially a guilty Ireland uneasy about
the anti-clericalism of the Ossianic tradition, but why should Beurla,
from *Béarla*, Irish for the English language, miss his grand old voice?
Fionn, son of Cumhal, is frequently called a colossus in the *Wake*
(625.21–22), and it is fitting that he should be among the cabbages,
metonymy for the Irish peasantry. Similarly, the heroic Fionn is
conventionally "larger than life" and "doughtier than death."

". . . the employment he gave to geemen; sponsor to a squad
of piercers, ally to a host of rawlies; against lightning, esplosion,
fire, earthquake, flood, whirlwind, burglary, third party, loss . . ."
(133.10–13). The historical fianna were a kind of militia who often
performed duties which would be assigned to police in a modern

state; thus they are "G-men," in the now-archaic American slang. Additionally, the men who dominated the government of the new Irish Free State during the years Joyce was writing the *Wake* were the *Fianna Fáil*; these fianna are also G-men, government men. Fionn's Fianna, that of Leinster, were frequently called upon in the old narratives to provide an insurance for the high king at Tara. And in that they used bow and arrow they were "piercers."

". . . passed for baabaa blacksheep till he grew white woo woo woolly; was drummatoysed by MacMilligan's daughter and put to music by one shoebard . . ." (133.25–27). "MacMilligan's daughter," as mentioned earlier, is Alice Milligan, whose short one-act play, *Last Feast of the Fianna*, almost a toy-drama, was one of the very first plays of the Irish Literary Theatre, drumming up interest in the literary revival. "White" is, of course, a translation of Fionn's name, but how he grew white after being a black sheep is not clear; perhaps he was a black sheep, an outcast, because the Fenian cycle lacks the refinement of the Ulster cycle, which was more to the taste of W. B. Yeats. "Shoebard" is apparently Franz Schubert who, like several of his contemporaries, Mendelssohn, Jean LeSueur, and Étienne Mèhul, employed Ossianic motifs from Macpherson; see for example his lieder, *Ossians Lied nach dem Falle Nathos* (1815).

". . . his borth proved accidental shows his death its grave mistake; brought us giant ivy from the land of younkers and bewitthered Apostolopolos with the gale of his gall . . ." (134.20–22). As considered in our chapter 2, Fionn, like many mythological and legendary heroes, is given an unusual birth. Similarly, his death may be only figurative as he is a "sleeping warrior." Much of the middle of this passage remains a puzzle, but "gale" and "gall" are the conventional Irish-language names for natives, Gaels, and foreigners, Galls. The County Dublin place name "Fingal" is the "place of the fair-haired foreigners."

". . . the king was in his cornerwall melking mark so murry, the queen was steep in armbour feeling ain and furry . . ." (134.36 to 135.2). The general allusion here is to King Mark in Cornwall, about to be made a cuckold; the inclusion of this reference in the riddle about Fionn mac Cumhaill is a means of showing the consonance of the Mark-Tristan-Iseult triangle with the Fionn-Diarmaid-Gráinne triangle.

". . . annacrwatter . . . (135.6) . . . brow of a hazelwood, pool in the dark, changes blowicks into bullocks and a well or Artesia into a bird of Arabia . . ." (135.13–15). In other circumstances than these, water implies ALP, but "annacrwatter" may be fenn water, from the Irish *eanach* for "marsh" or "fenn," as in the Bog (or fenn) of Allen, associated with Fionn, from which the waters of the Liffey flow. Brendan O Hehir thinks the "brow of hazelwood" refers to the former Hazelwood Street, now Thomas Street, in Dublin (765, 1967, 85), as "dark" and "pool" certainly refer to *Dubh-linn*, the dark pool of Dublin. Whatever the reference of "blowicks" and "well of Artesia," "bird of Arabia" certainly refers to Phoenix Park, named for the clear, white water, *fionn uisce,* suggesting Fionn.

"... his headwood it's ideal if his feet are bally clay; he crashed in the hollow of the park, trees down, as he soared in the vaguum of the phoenix, stones up ..." (135.33–35). Here is another passage linking Fionn with Dublin, *Baile Átha Cliath* (pronounced "Ballyclee" in Hiberno-English). The medieval "Battle of Cnucha" describes Fionn's father Cumhal being killed a few miles west of modern Dublin at what is now Castleknock; and, of course, Joyce would have the son rise, like the phoenix, in Phoenix Park.

"... made up to Miss MacCormack Ni Lacarthy who made off with Darly Dermond, swank and swarthy; once garnet now dammat cuts groany; you might find him at the Florence but watch our for him in Wynn's Hotel ..." (137.2–5). Gráinne, as the daughter of Cormac mac Airt, could be called "MacCormack" in the Anglicized spelling of the name. "Ni" is the more correct and traditional feminine form; but Gráinne is not related to Carthaig, eponym of the Mc-Carthys, which is another demonstration of Kelleher's thesis about Joyce's superficial knowledge of the Irish past. "Darly Dermond" is, of course, Diarmaid, as is "dammat," a name the cuckold Fionn might want to apply to him. Saying that "dammat cuts groany" is apparently a way of characterizing Gráinne by her ecstatic cries in sexual intercourse. Brendan O Hehir traces the root of "Florence," used here as the name of a hotel, to *Finghin,* "fair-birth," a traditional name among the McCarthys, who anglicized it as "Florence" (765, 1967, 87). "Wynn's" is named for the Welsh family name which translates as "white," linking it to the Finn's Hotel where Nora Barnacle worked before she knew Joyce. Whether Joyce knew enough to link the Welsh Gwyn ap Nudd with Fionn seems a moot question.

"... a footprinse on the Megacene, hetman unwhorsed by Searingsand ..." (137.14–15). Henry Beechhold asserts that the "footprinse" must be Fionn with no hint of a suggestion why, perhaps because he usually walked or ran rather than ride a horse (727, 1958, 3). The "hetman" referred to here is probably Hetman Michael,

a character of James Branch Cabell's *Jurgen*, linked with Fionn elsewhere in the text, "Hetman MacCumhal" (243.14).

". . . his troubles may be over but his doubles have still to
come" (138.2–3). This may simply be another restatement of the
"sleeping warriors" myth, of which Fionn, King Arthur, Barbarossa,
and approximately thirty other heroes are examples.

". . . lustest ath he listeth the cleah whithpeh of a themise; is
a prince of the fingalian in a hiberniad of hoolies; has a hodge to
wherry him and a frenchy to curry him and a brabanson . . ."
(138.10–12). How all of this relates to Fionn is not clear; "ath" and
"cleah" are hidden references to *Baile Átha Cliath*, Dublin, certainly.
And Fionn is the "prince of the fingalian in hiberniad," epic literature
of Ireland, because Joyce believed him to be, at least in part, of
Norse origin, i.e., not only "Fingal" because of the form of his name
in Macpherson but also because he is, Joyce and Zimmer assert,
Fionn Gall, the "fair stranger." But Fionn has no special association
with hoolies, characteristically Irish fracases; and neither does he
have a "frenchy" to curry him, although a "brabanson," from the
Irish *breágh*, "fine, handsome," and *bean*, "woman," could refer to
Gráinne.

". . . was born with a nuasilver tongue in his moth and went
round the coast of Iron with his left hand to the scene; (138.20–21)
. . . for whom it is easier to found to see in Ebblannah . . ."
(138.22–23). Fionn's genealogy is traced back to Nuadu of the Silver
Hand, and Fionn has a silver tongue because, unlike Lugh or Cúch-
alainn, he composed poetry. Our reading has not uncovered a tradition in which he sails around Ireland, "Iron," on his left hand,
i.e., counterclockwise. Fionn rarely enters any kind of boat, and when
he does it is usually to engage the Lochlanners. Nevertheless, if he
had sailed around Ireland in this manner instead of on the right
hand, or sunwise, then he would have invited ill-fortune upon
himself. "Ebblannan," as O Hehir glosses, comes from *eanach*, "marsh"
or "fenn," and *leanbh*, "child," linking Fionn again with ALP (749,
1967, p. 88); *Eblana* was the ancient geographer Ptolemy's (2nd
century A.D.) name for what is now Dublin.

". . . loses weight in the moon night but girds girder by the
sundawn . . ." (138.35–36). This seems another indication that Joyce
still adhered to the discredited solar theory of myth proposed by
Max Müller in 1854.

". . .who could see at one blick a saumon taken with a lance,
hunter pursuing a doe, a swallowship in full sail, a whityrobe lifting

a host; faced flappery like old King Cnut and turned his back like Cincinnatus; is a farfar and a morefar and a hoar father . . ." (139.2–6). Most of these references depict Fionn with magical associations, beginning with his Salmon of Prophecy. As a hunter Fionn pursued many does, one of whom became the mother of Oisín, whose name means "fawn." Oisín resisted baptism by Saint Patrick, who, as a priest, could have worn a white robe to raise a host. Neither Fionn, Oisín, nor Patrick can easily be identified with the familiar King Cnut, who ordered the tide to recede, but Fionn and the Fenians, militiamen, could be identified with Cincinnatus, the citizen soldier. With his magical thumb giving him the power of prophecy as well as the power to heal, Fionn can be seen as a "farfar," from the Irish *fear-feasa*, "wizard." And he is certainly Oisín's "hoar," old and white father.

". . . is Timb to the pearly morn and Tomb to the morning night; and an he had the best bunbaked bricks in bould Babylon for his pitching plays he's be lost for the want of his wan wubblin wall?" (139.10–13). These are the last lines of the riddle, and they may be the most troublesome we have considered. "Pearly" in Irish, is, again, *fionn*, as is "wan" in the last line. The bricks of Babylon in the study of epic and heroic literature suggest Gilgamesh, whose epic survived on clay tablets; Gilgamesh does not appear to be mentioned in the *Wake*, although he is, Joseph Campbell would argue, one of the thousand faces of the hero, along with Fionn. O Hehir glosses "wubblin wall" as a translation of *falla fionntrach*, a "wall liable to collapse" (765, 1967, 88), which does provide an intriguing pun to end the riddle. The suggestion is that Fionn is unmistakably here, but the remainder of these lines are a hard crux.

An examination of the other passage of Fenian allusion, toward the end of chapter 3 of Book II, is so dense and confused as not to lend itself to the kind of explication just conducted. Here the majority of the references are to the Diarmaid and Gráinne story, although they do not come in any kind of order. If we were to examine them line by line from the text of the *Wake* we would find ourselves jumping back and forth in the original narrative. As pointed out above, Joyce gives no anticipation of this passage in the *First Draft of Finnegans Wake*. The whole of Chapter 3, Book II, is quite long, seventy-three pages, and fewer than five contain the bulk of the Fenian allusions. The chapter is entitled "Taverny in Feast" by Campbell and Robinson (738, 1961, 196), but is usually called the "Scene in the Pub" in contemporary *Wake* criticism. Most of the action of the chapter is taken up with the retelling of two stories, of Kersse the Tailor and the Norwegian Captain and also of the more celebrated "Buckley and the shooting of the Russian general," a tale Joyce once discussed with Samuel Beckett. Late in the chapter, where most of the allusions are recorded, pages 373–80, HCE is alone in the pub and hears a case against him reviewed on the radio during a broadcast of epical funeral games.

Although the whole of the narrative is not recapitulated in this passage, there are sufficiently large chunks of it to communicate to HCE that his Fenian mask is besmudged in the tale. As is fitting with the broadcast of the games, Fionn is encouraged to win the prize, Gráinne, or he will be left alone: "Finnish Make Goal! First you were Nomad, next you were Namar," from the Irish namá, "alone" (374.21–22). Word of Fionn's vulnerability is abroad and a potential rival can use some of Fionn's absurdity to defeat him as a lover: "He [perhaps Diarmaid] knows his Finsbury Follies backwoods so you batter so to your regent refutation" (374.28–30). Fionn recognizes that it is one thing to be unlucky in love, but a far more painful thing to be found a cuckold:

> Then old Hunphydunphyville'll be blasted to bumboards by the youthful herald who would once you were. He'd be our chosen one in the matter of Brittas more than anarthur. But we'll wake and see (375.5–8).
>
> So yelp your guilt and kitz the buck. You'll have loss of fame from Wimmegame's fake. Forwards! (375.16–17).

Fionn is not the only male who has to fear from "Wimmegame's fake"; Arthur too, "anarthur," is a cuckold, his wife having betrayed him for a younger lover, "the youthful herald who would once you were." Still, there is some time for the lubricious contemplation of what a marriage to Gráinne could bring: "you on her, hosy jigses, that'll be some nonstop marrimont" (375.26–27). But even in this reverie, Fionn's words contain the hint of his betrayal, "Fummuccumul with a graneen aveiled" (375.29); changing "Mac" to "muc" turns Fionn into a pig, cf. Irish muc. The apparent diminutive of Gráinne, "Graneen," contains a sharpening of the etymological root of her name, "spearpoint." "Aveiled" contains the Irish pun ai-thmhéala (pronounced "avele"), "regret" or "contrition." And the hero's shame will be the topic of popular discussion: "Mumblesome

[Mendelssohn's] Wadding Murch cranking up to the hornemooniuum" (377.14–15); the honeymoon will be punctured by the cuckold horn.

No matter how great the hero's fears, he cannot forget the beauty of the betrothed. She is "The wonder of the woman of the world, moya!" although the interjection "moya!" implies some irony: *mar bh'eadh,* "as if it were so." She is nubile: "Merryvirgin forbed" (376.25–26). And she comes from a good family. She is "Ineen MacCormick MacCoort MacCoon O'Puckins MacKundred" (376.1–2). As O Hehir points out, this is a parody of an Irish genealogy. As the daughter of Cormac mac Airt, Gráinne is Miss ("Ineen," Irish *inghean*) MacCormick. As Cormac is the son of Art, she can claim the name of MacCoort, and so on back to MacKundred, from *mac an Druaidh,* "son of the druid," which puns in English with the suggestion of infinity, hundred. But observers are not impressed with her manners, which appear somewhat countryfied and crude: "You cannot make a limousine lady out of a hillman minx. Listun till you hear the Mudquirt accent" (376.3–4). But the anticipation of Gráinne's lust is enough to excite any man: "The eitch is in her blood, arrah! For a frecklesome fresh-cheeky sweetworded lupsqueezer. And he shows how he'll pick him the lock of her fancy. Poghue! Pughue; Poghue!" (376.19–21). "Poghue" is obviously from *póg,* "kiss," one of the most familiar Irish loan words in English, under the usual transliteration "pogue."

If the "eitch is in her blood," Gráinne must also appeal to other men. Following an episode in Lady Gregory's *Gods and Fighting Men* in which Diarmaid performs tricks on a tun of wine as a demonstration of his manliness (25, 1970, 280), Joyce has him appear as a kind of sideshow performer: "Morialty and Kniferope Walker and Rowley the Barrel" (376.30–31); "Morialty" is from *Muircheartach,* "navigator." When Fionn becomes unwary from too much drink the lovers will have their chance: "Then old hunphydunphyville'll be blasted to the bumboards" (375.5–6); "How our myterbilder his fullen aslip. And who will wager but he'll Shonny Bhoy be . . ." (377.25–26). Fionn's dog (and niece!) Bran can be quieted with an apt perquisite: ". . . buy bran bisquits and you'll never say dog" (376.29).

The lovers yearn for the open places beyond Tara: "Blanruckard for ever!" (376.32), evidently named for Clann Riocaird, the first place Diarmaid and Gráinne stopped in their flight. If they did not know freedom of soul before, it is theirs now: "But of they never eat soullfriede they're acting it now" (376.36), punning with the

German *fried*, "freedom." Fionn and his Fianna hear the call to search all the bogs and fenns of Ireland: "Fenn, the Fenn, the kinn of all Fenns!" (376.33) and they pursue. Nine henchmen of Fionn named Barbh lose their lives trying to dislodge Diarmaid from a quickentree: "Three climbs three quickenthrees in the garb of nine" (377.11–12). Joyce does not follow the narrative beyond the cuckolding of Fionn, perhaps because the death of Diarmaid is irrelevant to HCE's anxieties of the moment, or perhaps because the metamorphosis of Fionn into pig, "Fummuccumul" (375.29), anticipates Diarmaid's end, gored by a boar. The question to be asked of this episode appeared seventy pages earlier in the plainest of English, "What morals, if any, can be drawn from Diarmuid and Grania?" (306.27–28). And the morals, "if any," appear to be demonstrated further when HCE is obliged in the next episode to listen to the cuckolding of King Mark by Tristan and Iseult (383–89).

These few pages contain, in addition, a number of Fenian references that appear to have nothing to do with the Diarmaid and Gráinne story. For example, there seems to be a veiled allusion to Cnucha, Castleknock, in the line: "And the real Hymernians strenging strong at knocker knocker"(376.12). There is a clear but apparently inappropriate reference to Fionn's nurses in childhood, Bodhmall and Liath Luachra, whose name means "Grey of Frost": "Badbols and the Grey One" (376.27). Similarly, the cuckolding of Fionn seems an odd time to remember his gaining the power of prophecy and poetry, snatched from the druid Finneigas or Finn Eces: "The finnecies of poetry wed music" (377.16–17). The line before that is also a puzzle: "Drawg us out *Ivy Eve in the Hall of Alum!*" (377.16).

At the same time, the final pages of Chapter 3 of Book II do not exhaust Joyce's interest in the Diarmaid and Gráinne story; allusions are scattered throughout the *Wake*. Joyce also appears to have taken some note of previous uses of the story in English. For example, he must be alluding to George Moore's anfractuous plan for writing his and Yeats's *Diarmuid and Grania*, noted briefly in our previous chapter. Moore was to write the play in French and have Lady Gregory translate into English; Taidgh O'Donoghue would translate it into Irish, whereupon Lady Gregory would retranslate it back into English with Yeats providing polish for the final text. In a pseudo-scholarly footnote (281.#2), Joyce deals with the matter thus: "Translout that gaswind into turfish, Teague, that's a good bog and you, Thady, poliss it off, there's a nateswipe, on to your blottom pulper."

Joyce's censure of Moore is apparent in "—lout" and "gaswind"; "turfish" is clearly Irish; and "Teague" is the common transliteration for Taidgh, as well as a conventional Protestant epithet for Catholics. "Thady" is a puzzle for Yeats, however, unless it is an allusion to the familiar Irish ballad, "The Bold Thady Quill," the quill being an appropriate instrument for a refined poet who adds polish to the words of a coarser writer.

POSSIBLE MEANINGS
OF THE FENIAN MATRIX IN *FINNEGANS WAKE*

No work of literature is so demanding of critical modesty as is *Finnegans Wake*. Only a vain and foolhardy critic pretends to have the final answer or an ultimate explication of the *Wake*. One handbook, *Joyce-Again's Wake*, by Bernard Benstock, devotes the first chapter to "What We Still Don't Know About *Finnegans Wake*" (733, 1965, 3–41). As in the natural sciences, today's new findings can invalidate yesterday's widely held hypotheses. With these qualifications, it is more useful to draw guidelines from the implications of our findings rather than try to push them to conclusions they may not support. The findings make no pretense at being final. There are as many as 190 more Fenian allusions scattered through the text, most of them having no apparent relationship to the context in which they appear. These are, of course, not the only obscurities in the book. There are probably enough cruxes in *Finnegans Wake* to employ all the explicators in academia from now until the exhaustion of ink and paper.

Some of our judgments about the use of Fenian materials in the *Wake* have already been stated, especially those relating to the appropriateness of using this cycle instead of others from Irish literature. Fionn's great popularity and the inversion of his reputation in popular tradition make him a more suitable figure in *Finnegans Wake* than Lugh or Cúchulainn could have been. Fionn's cuckolding, perhaps because it runs parallel to that of Leopold Bloom, King Arthur, Shakespeare's King Claudius, and Agamemnon, allows him to contribute to one of Joyce's most enduring themes. And the myth of his "sleeping" and eventual re-awakening, an attribute Fionn shares with the number of European heroes, is cognate with the premise of the *Wake*. To this should be added the insights of M. J. Sidnell, suggesting that the circular structure of the *Wake* is anticipated in Yeats's "Wanderings of Oisín" (773, 1971, 52–53). The premise of that poem, that the aged Oisín has just returned from a life of pleasure and ease with Niamh in Tír na nÓg and will now relate his adventures in sequence, reaching the present at the conclusion, was not an innovation in Yeats but rather conventional in Fenian tradition. Oisín always speaks of Fionn as a character outside time. And as he was never fixed in an epic, Fionn retains a mythic apartness from the time of chronologers, making him an apt figure to appear in *Finnegans Wake*.

Then again, there are hundreds of apt figures who also appear in the *Wake*. Adaline Glasheen has taken their census three times and requires nearly 300 pages to list them. The abundant references to Fionn and other Fenian characters simply do not justify the assertion that Fionn dreams the dream. No one chapter or lengthy section of the narrative is devoted to Fionn nor is one set in a Fenian locale. In the many Fenian allusions found in the text there are none in which the archetype of Fionn is expanded, or in which he is given action not finding an antecedent from traditional literature, Irish or English. In the two sections of most frequent Fenian references, reviewed earlier in this chapter, the traditional narratives alluded to are subsidiary to the main action focusing on HCE. The most notable exceptions come at the very beginning of the text where the story of Fionn's burial under Dublin is related and also the very last page of the book where Fionn is called to awake, "Finn, again!" (628.14). The subsequent three lines, however, do not appear to be addressed to Fionn, and they lead to the famous "last" sentence of the book which links the last page with the first: "A way a lone a last a loved a long the [628.15–16] riverrun, past Eve and Adam's, brings us by a commodius vicus of recirculation back to Howth Castle and Environ" (1.1–3). If this sentence is addressed to the waking Fionn then it also links him with HCE.

We may not be able to find a role for Fionn in the *Wake* other than being a type for HCE because none may exist. In a little-noted letter to J. S. Atherton, Harriet Shaw Weaver, Joyce's patron and confidant, provides a guideline (724, 1960, 17): ". . . [the] ascription of the whole thing to a dream of HCE seems to me nonsensical . . . My view is that Mr. Joyce did not intend the book to be looked upon as the dream of any one character, but that he regarded the dream form with its shiftings and changes and chances as a convenient device, allowing the freest scope to introduce any material he wished—and suited to a night-piece."

The teachings of modern psychology tend to encourage the assertion that the dreamer has no specific identity. As Rolfe Spear has noted, Freud told us that one man's dreams are all men's dreams (774, 1970, 13). The identify of the dreamer would therefore shift continuously, much as the identity of the mythic hero can reshape itself continuously. A speech Flann O'Brien wrote for Finn in *At Swim-Two-Birds*, cited in our chapter 4, explains:

> I am an Ulsterman, a Connachtman, a Greek, said Finn,
> I am Cuchulain, I am Patrick.
> I am Carbery-Cathhead, I am Goll.
> I am my own father and my own son.
> I am every hero from the crack of time.

In *Finnegans Wake* Joyce makes Fionn mac Cumhaill an Irish incarnation of the monomyth.

Notes

CHAPTER 1

1. Citations may be identified in the numbered bibliography that begins on page 197. The date is for the edition cited, which may not always be of the first publication.

2. The most pertinent passages from Brown's work are in vol. 18 (1920–21), 201–28, 661–73. Cf. Sheila McHugh, *"Sir Percyvelle": Its Irish Connections* (Ann Arbor: Edwards Brothers, 1946). This subject is treated at greater length in chapter 2, where Fionn is considered as a parallel to other European heroes, including Arthurian figures.

3. Hanmer's *Chronicle* was published in 1633. Wilson M. Hudson, who has commented on the *Chronicle* in "Ossian in English Before Macpherson," *Studies in English* [Texas] 19 (1950): 125, thinks that the episode is new with Hanmer and is not based on a lost Irish original.

4. Thomas Flannery provided the only scholarly edition in 1895 (Dublin: M. H. Gill), but the poem has been translated several times, the first as early as 1863. Curiously, Coimín's quite traditional composition (c. 1750) was just prior to Macpherson's *Ossian* (1760–63).

5. The *Agallamh* has been translated several times; the most celebrated of these seems to be that of S. H. O'Grady in *Silva Gadelica* II (London: Williams and Norgate, 1892), 101–264. The best modern Irish edition is by Nessa Ni Shéaghdha, 3 vols. (Dublin: Oifig an tSoláthair, 1942–45).

CHAPTER 2

1. This episode was reported to me by Ms. Philippa Robinson in a letter dated April 10, 1974. The folk recited was Gráinne bean Uí Somhnaill of Rann-na-Feirste (in English: Ranafest), a hamlet between Crolly and Anagaire, County Donegal.

CHAPTER 3

1. My own translation of the early Scots is, ". . . was accustomed to have from Fingal his company, in right good order."

2. *The Poems of Ossian Translated by James Macpherson*, edited by William Sharp (Edinburgh: Patrick Geddes, 1896), 32. All quotations from Macpherson are to this edition.

CHAPTER 4

1. *At-Swim-Two-Birds* (New York: Viking Compass Books, 1967), 95. All quotations are from this text.

2. The use of "man" for "drink" in Dublin parlance implies something like, "The only friend you'll ever have." Cf. Alf MacLochlainn, "A Jug of Punch," *Hibernia* 34, no. 20 (October 23, 1970): 23.

3. Other versions include the anonymous "Pursuit of Diarmuid and Gráinne," *The Gael* [New York] 22, no. 10 (October 1903): 332–33. Donald A. MacKenzie, "Diarmaid and Gráinne," *The Celtic Review* 6 (1909–10): 348–56. Cathal O'Byrne, "Gráinne, After the Death of Diarmid." In *The Dublin Book of Irish Verse*, edited by John Cook (Dublin: Hodges, Figgis, 1924), 685–86.

4. Originally published in 1917 (Dublin: Maunsel), the text used here is from Clarke's *Collected Poems* (New York: Macmillan, 1936), 268.

5. *Grianán:* sun-lit house

6. *Beltaine* 2 (February 1900): 4.

7. *Dublin Magazine,* n.s. 26 (April–June 1951): 1–41. The play has been re-published twice since then, in the *Variorum Edition of the Plays of W. B. Yeats,* edited by R. K. & C. Alspach (New York: Macmillan, 1966), 1172–1222, the edition used for all quotations here. A more recent edition comes with an excellent introduction by Anthony Farrow (Chicago: DePaul University, 1974).

8. First published in *Irish Folk-History Plays, First Series: The Tragedies* (New York: Putnam, 1912), reprinted in *Collected Plays,* II, *The Tragedies and the Tragic Comedies,* edited by Ann Saddlemyer (Garrard's Cross: Colin Smythe; New York: Oxford, 1970), 11–46, from which all quotations here are taken.

9. "Little Gidding," Part IV, *The Complete Poems and Plays of T. S. Eliot, 1919–1950* (New York: Harcourt, Brace, 1952), 144–45.

10. "The Tower," *Variorum Edition of the Poems of W. B. Yeats,* edited by P. Allt and R. K. Alspach (New York: Macmillan, 1957), 409.

CHAPTER 5

1. (New York: Viking, 1939), p. 5, lines 9–10. As the pagination of *Finnegans Wake* is identical in British and American editions, hardcover and paperback, the annotation conventions of *Wake* scholarship suggest 5.9–10.

Bibliography

CONTENTS

PRIMARY SOURCES: ENGLISH

Original Sources Composed in English

1. Anderson, John Redwood. *The Pursuit of Diarmuid and Graunia.* London: Oxford University Press, 1950.

2. Anonymous. "A Banter Between Finn MacCool and Brian Boru," in "A Day at the Seven Churches at Glendalough." *The Christian Examiner and Church of Ireland Magazine* 9, no. 51 (September 1829): 187–89.

3. Anon. *The Druid, or Vision of Fingal; A Choral Masque.* London, 1815.

4. Anon. *Fingal, Fine-Eirin; A Poem . . . , with Notes, Intended to Delineate the Manners and State of Society of Ancient Ireland.* London, 1813.

5. Anon. "The Pursuit of Diarmuid and Grainne." *The Gael* [New York] 22, no. 10 (October 1903): 332–33.

6. Anon. ["Q"] "A Legend of Fin-Mac-Cool." *Dublin Penny Journal* 1, no. 41 (April 6, 1833): 327–28.

7. Argyll, ninth duke of. John G. E. H. D. S. Campbell. *Diarmid; An Opera.* In *Passages From the Past.* London: Hutchinson; New York: Dodd, Mead, 1908. Pp. 652–72.

8. Beckett, Samuel. "Fingal." In *More Pricks Than Kicks.* London: Chatto and Windus, 1934; rpt., New York: Grove Press, 1970. Pp. 23–35. Cf. the argument of Mary Power (1981), #434.

9. Campbell, Archibald (Lord). "The Feinne." *The Highland Monthly* 1 (1899–1900), 445.

Carberry, Ethna. *See* MacManus, Anna, #52.

10. Carleton, William. "A Legend of Knockmany." In *Tales and Sketches, Illustrating the Character, Usages, Traditions, Sports and Pastimes of the Irish Peasantry.* Dublin: J. Duffy, 1845. Pp. 97–112; rpt. *Irish Fairy and*

Folk Tales, edited by W. B. Yeats. New York: Modern Library, n.d. Pp. 285–99.

11. Chalmers, Patrick R. "Fingalian; A Story of the Deer Forest." In *Best Sporting Stories,* compiled by J. W. Day. London: Faber, 1943. Pp. 41–65.

12. Clark, John. *Morduth; The Works of the Caledonian Bards, translated from the Galic* [sic]. Edinburgh: T. Cadell, 1778.

13. Clarke, Austin. *The Bright Temptation.* London: Allen and Unwin; New York: Morrow, 1932; rpt. Dublin: Dolmen Press, 1965.

14. ———. "Loss of Strength." In *Later Poems.* Dublin: Dolmen Press, 1961. Pp. 61–68.

15. ———. *The Vengeance of Fionn.* Dublin: Maunsel, 1917, 1918; rpt. in *Collected Poems.* New York: Macmillan, 1936. Pp. 259–308.

16. Colum, Padraic. *A Boy in Eirinn.* New York: E. P. Dutton, 1913.

17. ———. "Reminiscence" and "In the Carolina Woods." In *Collected Poems.* New York: Macmillan, 1932. Pp. 4–15, 144.

18. ———. "How the Harp Came to Tara," and other stories. In *The Frenzied Prince: Being Heroic Stories of Ancient Ireland.* Philadelphia: McKay, 1943. Pp. 76–106, 123–52.

19. De Paola, Tomie. *Fin M'Coul: The Giant of Knockmany Hill.* New York: Holiday House, 1981.

20. DeVere, Aubrey. *The Legends of St. Patrick, Oiseen the Bard and St. Patrick, Antar, and Zara.* In *Legends of Ireland's Heroic Age. DeVere's Poetical Works,* vol. II. London: Kegan Paul, Trench, 1884.

21. Eberly, Susan Schoon. "The Finding of Oisin. A Celtic Wonder Myth Retold. . . ." *Cricket: The Magazine for Children* 8, no. 1 (September 1980): 52–60.

22. Ferguson, Samuel (Sir). "The Death of Dermid." In *Lays of the Western Gael and other Poems.* London: Bell and Daldy, 1865. Pp. 153–60.

23. Figgis, Darrell. *The Return of the Hero.* London: Chapman and Dodd, 1923; rpt., New York: Charles Boni, 1930.

24. Green, Nancy. *The Bigger Giant, An Irish Legend.* Chicago: Follett, 1963; rpt., London: Faber, 1967; New York: Scholastic Book Services, n.d.

25. Gregory, Isabella Augusta Persse (Lady). *Gods and Fighting Men; The Story of the Tuatha De Danaan and the Fianna of Ireland . . .* New York: Scribner's, 1904; rpt., Garrard's Cross: Colin Smythe; New York: Oxford University Press, 1970.

26. ———. *Grania, Irish Folk-History Plays, First Series: The Tragedies.* New York: G. P. Putnam, 1912; rpt., *Collected Plays,* vol. II, edited by Ann Saddlemyer. Garrard's Cross: Colin Smythe; New York: Oxford University Press, 1970. Pp. 11–46.

27. ———. "The Legend of Diarmuid and Grania." *Samhain,* no. 1 (October 1901), 16–19.

28. Gwynn, Stephen. "Lay of Ossian and Patrick." *Blackwood's Edinburgh Magazine* 173 (January 1903): 34–39. Republished as *A Lay of Ossian and Patrick, with Other Irish Verses.* Dublin: Hodges Figgis, 1903.

29. ———. "Ossian's Vision of Hell." *The Gael* [New York] 22, no. 1 (January 1903): 24–25.

30. Healy, Cahir. "How Finn MacCool Became Knowledgeable: An Irish Folktale." *The Gael* [New York] 20, no. 2 (February 1901): 56.

31. Higgins, Frederick Robert. "Eithne" and "The Return of Niamh." In *Island Blood*. London: Macmillan, 1925. Pp. 12, 48.

32. ———. "An Old Air," "Offerings," and "A Plea." In *The Dark Breed*. London: Macmillan, 1927. Pp. 34–35, 47, 64–65.

33. Higginson, Thomas Wentworth. "Usheen in the Island of Youth." In *Tales of the Enchanted Islands of the Atlantic*. New York: Macmillan, 1898. Pp. 25–31.

34. Hinkson, Katherine Tynan. "The Pursuit of Diarmuid and Grainne." In *Shamrocks*. London: Kegan Paul, Trench, 1887. Pp. 1–54.

35. ———. "Waiting." In *Louise De La Valliere*. London: Kegan, Paul, Trench, 1886. Pp. 65–71.

36. Hogan, Frank. *Finn MacKool*. Unpublished drama, premiered New York: Theatre de Lys, September 29, 1975.

37. Hopper (Chesson), Nora. "Boholaun and I; A Vision of Diarmuid." In *Ballads in Prose*. London: John Lane; Dublin: Roberts, 1894. Pp. 83–87.

38. Hughes, Harold F. *Legendary Heroes of Ireland*. San Francisco: Harr Wagner, 1922.

39. Joyce, James. *Finnegans Wake*. New York: Viking, 1939.

40. Ledwidge, Francis. "A Dream Dance." In *The Complete Poems of Francis Ledwidge*. London: Jenkins, 1919. P. 229.

41. Lover, Samuel. "King O'Toole and Saint Kevin." In *Legends and Stories of Ireland*. London, 1831; rpt. London: Ward, Lock, Bowden, n.d. Pp. 1–12. Republished again in *Irish Literature*, edited by Justin McCarthy, et al. Philadelphia: J. D. Morris, 1904. Vol. 5, 2046–54.

42. Lynch, May. "Finn MacCool: Drama." *Plays: The Drama Magazine For Young People* 26 (March 1967): 55–59.

43. MacCall, Patrick Joseph. *Fenian Nights Entertainments; Being a Series of Ossianic Legends Told at a Wexford Fireside*. Shamrock Library, II. Dublin: T. G. O'Donoghue, 1897. From which is extracted "Fionn MacCumhaill and the Princess." In *Irish Literature*, edited by Justin McCarthy, et al. Philadelphia: J. D. Morris, 1904. Vol. 6, 2117–22; rpt. in *Humours of Irish Life*, edited by Charles L. Graves. London: T. F. Unwin; New York: F. A. Stokes, 1915.

44. McCallum, Hugh and John. *An Original Collection of the Poems of Ossian, Orran, Ulin, and Other Bards Who Flourished in the Same Age*. Montrose: James Watt, 1816.

45. MacColl, Evan. "A Word with the Fenian Brotherhood (Suggested by the Assassination of Thomas D'Arcy McGee, in 1868)." In *The English Poetical Works of Evan MacColl*. Toronto: Hunter, Rose; Edinburgh: MacLachlan and Stewart, 1883. Pp. 288–89.

46. McCormley, Margaret Casey. "Finn MacCool and the Salmon of Knowledge." *An Gael* [New York] 1, no. 4 (Fall 1983): 30–32.

47. McGee, Thomas D'Arcy. "The Celts." In *Oxford Book of Irish Verse, XVIIth Century—XXth Century*, edited by Donagh MacDonagh and Lennox Robinson. London: Clarendon Press, 1958. Pp. 91–92.

48. MacGregor, Patrick. *The Genuine Remains of Ossian, Literally Translated; With a Preliminary Dissertation*. London: Smith, Elder; Edinburgh: W. Tait, 1841.

49. MacKenzie, Donald A. "Diarmaid and Gráinne." *The Celtic Review* 6 (1909–10): 348–356.

50. ———. "The Fians of Knockfarrell." *The Celtic Review* 6 (1909–10): 18–30.

51. ———. *Finn and His Warrior Band; or, Tales of Old Alban*. London: Blackie, 1910, 1911.

52. MacManus, Anna [Ethna Carberry, pseud.]. *In the Celtic Past*. New York: Funk and Wagnalls, 1904.

53. Macpherson, James. *The Poems of Ossian, the Son of Fingal*. London: W. Strahan and T. Becket, 1765; rpt. Edinburgh: Patrick Geddes, 1896.

54. Mangan, James Clarence. "The Churl in the Grey Coat." *Irish Penny Journal*, no. 17 (October 24, 1840); rpt. in *The Prose of James Clarence Mangan*, edited by D. J. O'Donoghue. Dublin: O'Donoghue, M. H. Gill; London: A. H. Bullen, 1904. Pp. 144–59.

55. ———. "A Lament for the Fianna." In *Poetry of Irish History*, edited by S. J. Brown and M. J. Brown. New York: F. A. Stokes, 1927. Pp. 19–21.

56. Marryat, Frederick. *Peter Simple*. London: R. Bentley, 1834.

57. Masefield, John. *The Story of Ossian* [phonodisc]. London: Argo; New Rochelle, c. 1957.

58. Miller, Olive B. "Finn MacCool, The Greatest of Civil Engineers: A Tale of the Grand Canyon of Arizona as Told by Irish Work Gangs and Civil Engineers." In *Heroes, Outlaws, and Funny Fellows*. New York: Doubleday, 1939. Pp. 283–97.

59. Milligan, Alice. *The Last Feast of the Fianna. A Dramatic Legend*. London: David Nutt, 1900; rpt. with Edward Martyn's *Maeve*, edited by W. J. Feeney. DePaul University Irish Drama Series, II. Chicago: DePaul University, 1967. Pp. 47–60.

Moore, George. *Diarmuid and Grania*. See Yeats, William Butler, #80.

60. Moore, Thomas. "Dear Harp of My Country" and "The Wine-Cup is Circling." In *Thomas Moore's Complete Poetical Works*, edited by N. H. Dole. New York: T. Y. Crowell, 1895. Pp. 197–98, 218.

61. O'Brien, Flann [pseud. of Brian O'Nolan]. *At Swim-Two-Birds*. London: Longman's, Green, 1939; rpt., New York: Viking, 1951.

62. O'Byrne, Cathal. "Grainne, After the Death of Diarmid." In *The Dublin Book of Irish Verse: 1728–1909*, edited by John Cooke. Dublin: Hodges Figgis, 1924. Pp. 685–86.

63. O'Grady, Standish James. *Finn and His Companions . . .* London: T. Fisher Unwin, 1892; rpt. Dublin: Talbot Press; London: Unwin, 1921.

64. ————. *The Masque of Finn*. Dublin: Sealy, Bryers and Walker, 1907; rpt. with *Finn and His Companions*. Dublin: Talbot; London: Unwin, 1921.

65. O'Keefe, C. M. "St. Patrick and Ossian." *The Celtic Monthly, An Illustrated Irish-American Magazine* 3 (March 1880): 291.

66. O'Nolan, Ciarán. "The Return of Finn." *Comhthrom Féinne* [Dublin] 11, no. 1 (April 1935) [not seen].

67. Otway, Caesar. "Letter IV from Donegal." In *Sketches in Ireland, . . .* Dublin: W. Curry, 1827. Pp. 129–200. A portion of this was republished as "Legend of Fin M'Coul." *Dublin Penny Journal* 1, no. 14 (September 29, 1832): 110–111; another portion, titled "Salmon of Finn MacCool" appears in *Great Angling Stories*, edited by John M. Dickie. London: Chambers, 1947. Pp. 198–200.

68. Potter, Maureen. "The Giant's Wife." *Folk Tales and Legends from Great Britain*. London: BBC Radio Enterprises; New York: CMS Records, 1972. Phonodisc.

69. Rolleston, Thomas William. *The High Deeds of Finn MacCool and Other Bardic Romances of Ancient Ireland*. London: G. G. Harrap, 1934; rpt., New York: Lemma, 1972.

70. Russell, Violet. *Heroes of the Dawn*. Dublin: Maunsel, 1913.

71. Saul, George Brandon. "The Trial by Fable." *Poet Lore* 50 (Summer 1944): 175–80; rpt., somewhat revised, in *Hound and Unicorn: Collected Verse—Lyrical, Narrative, and Dramatic*. Philadelphia: Walton Press, 1969. Pp. 101–07.

72. Smith, John. *Sean Dana; le Oisian, Orran, Ulann. Ancient Poems of Ossian, Orran, Ulann, etc., collected in the Western Highlands and Isles; Being the Originals of the translations Some time Ago Published in Gaelic Antiquities*. Edinburgh: C. Elliot, 1787.

73. Stephens, James. *The Demi-Gods*. London: Macmillan, 1914.

74. ————. *Irish Fairy Tales*. London: Macmillan, 1920, 1923.

75. ————. "Oisín and Niamh." *Sinn Féin* 26 (February 26, 1910): 2.

76. Sutcliff, Rosemary. *The High Deeds of Finn MacCool*. London: John Lane; New York: E. P. Dutton, 1967.

Tynan, Katherine. *See* Hinkson, Katherine Tynan, #34, #35.

77. Varian, John. *Oisín the Hero*. Dublin: Sealy, Bryers and Walker, c. 1910. Bound with Suseen Varian's *Cuchulainn: A Cycle of Plays*.

78. Watters, Eugene Rutherford. *The Weekend of Dermot and Grace*. Dublin: Allen Figgis, c. 1963.

79. Whistler, Laurence. "Fingal's Cave." MS. in the Lamont Library, Harvard University, c. 1963.

80. Yeats, William Butler and George Moore. "Diarmuid and Grania." *Dublin Magazine*, n.s. 26 (April–June 1951): 1–41. *See also* "A Critical Edition of Diarmuid and Grania," edited by Ray Small. Unpublished dissertation, University of Texas (1958). "Diarmuid and Grania." In *Variorum Edition of the Plays of W. B. Yeats*, edited by R. K. and C. C. Alspach. New York: Macmillan, 1966. Pp. 1169–1222. Also *Diarmuid and Grania*,

edited by Anthony Farrow. DePaul University Irish Drama Series, X. Chicago: DePaul University, 1974.

81. Yeats, William Butler. "The Wanderings of Oisin." In *The Celtic Twilight*. London, 1889; rpt., New York: New American Library Signet Books, 1962. See also *The Variorum Edition of the Poems of W. B. Yeats*, edited by P. Allt and R. K. Alspach. New York: Macmillan, 1957. Pp. 1–63.

82. Young, Ella. *The Tangle-Coated Horse and Other Tales. Episodes From the Fionn Saga*. New York: Longman's, 1929.

English and Latin Works ante 1760 Making Reference to Fionn

83. *The Book of Howth. Calendar of the Carew Manuscripts*, edited by J. S. Brewer and W. Bullen, vol. V. London: Longman's Green, Reader and Dyer, 1871. Pp. 1–120.

84. Barbour, John. *The Bruce*, edited by W. W. Skeat. Scottish Texts Society, vols. 16–17. Edinburgh and London: W. Blackwood, 1894.

85. Boece [Boethius], Hector. *The Mar Lodge translation of the History of Scotland* [Latin, 1526; in English, 1541], edited by George Watson. Scottish Texts Society, 3rd Series, 17. Edinburgh: W. Blackwood, 1943, 1946.

86. Camden, William. *Camden's Britannia*, newly translated into English with large additions and improvements, . . . London: E. Gibson, 1695.

87. Campion, Edmund. *History of Ireland* [1571]. In James Ware's *Ancient Irish Histories* [1809]. See #101.

88. Cox, Richard (Sir). *Hibernia Anglicana, or the History of Ireland from the Conquest thereof by the English, to This Present Time*, . . . London, 1689.

89. Douglas, Gavin. *Palice of Honour* [1522], edited by J. Ballantyne. Edinburgh: Ballantyne Club, 1827; rpt. New York: AMS Press, 1971. See also *Selections From Gavin Douglas*, edited by David F. Coldwell. Oxford: Clarendon Press, 1964.

90. *Poetical Works of Gavin Douglas*, edited by John Small. 2 vols. Edinburgh: W. Patterson, 1874.

91. Dunbar, William. "The Droichis Part of the Play, or the Manere of the Crying of Ane Playe" [c. 1500]. In *Poems*, edited by James Kinsley. Oxford: Clarendon Press, 1958.

92. Farewell, James. *The Irish Hudibras, or Fingalian Prince, Taken from the Sixth Book of Virgil's Aeneid, and Adapted to Present Times*. London, 1689.

93. Hanmer, Meredith. *Chronicle of Ireland* [1633]. In James Ware's *Ancient Irish Histories* [1809]. See #101.

94. Leslie, John. *The History of Scotland*, [etc.], translated by J. Dalrymple [1596], edited by E. G. Cody. Scottish Texts Society, vols. 5, 14, 19, 34. Edinburgh: W. Blackwood, 1888–95.

95. Lyndsay, David (Sir). *The Poetical Works of Sir David Lyndsay of the Mount, Lyon King of Arms*, edited by David Laing. 2 vols. Edinburgh: W. Patterson, 1871.

96. MacCurtain, Hugh. *Brief Discourse in Vindication of the Antiquity of Ireland.* Dublin, 1717.

97. Martin, Martin. *Description of the Western Islands of Scotland* [1703]. Republished, Glasgow: T. D. Morison, 1884.

98. O'Flaherty, Roderick. *Ogygia; or, A Chronological Account of Irish Events Collected From Very Ancient Documents . . .* Latin edition, London, 1685. Translated into English by James Hely. 2 vols. Dublin, 1793.

99. Stanihurst, Richard. *Description of Ireland.* London, 1578. Republished as a part of Raphael Holinshed's *Chronicles,* IV. London: J. Johnson, 1808.

100. Walsh, Peter. *A Prospect of the State of Ireland from the year of the World 1756 to the Year of Christ 1652.* London, 1682.

101. Ware, James, comp. *Ancient Irish Histories. The Works of Spenser, Campion* [#87], *Hanmer* [#93], *and Marlebvrrovh.* 2 vols. Dublin: Hibernia Press, 1809; rpt. New York: DaCapo Press, 1971.

*Anthologies and Collections of
Miscellaneous Fenian Poems and Stories in English*

Many of these works include popular revisions of scholarly translations along with some reprints from original works in English as listed above.

102. Colum, Padraic. *An Anthology of Irish Verse; The Poetry of Ireland Times.* Black and Gold Library. New York: Liveright, 1948. Pp. 112–17.

103. Cooke, John, ed. *The Dublin Book of Irish Verse, 1728–1909.* Dublin: Hodges Figgis; London: Milford; Oxford: Oxford University Press, 1924. Pp. 449–50, 685–86.

104. Galvin, Patrick, ed. *Irish Stories and Tales.* New York: Pocket Library, 1957. [Not seen].

105. Fuller, Eunice. *The Book of Friendly Giants.* New York: Century, 1914. Pp. 87–105.

106. Garnier, Charles-Marie. *Legends of Ireland,* translated by Leslie Vyse. Cleveland: World Publishing, 1969. Pp. 99–157.

107. Graves, Alfred Percival, comp. *Irish Fairy Book.* London: T. Fisher Unwin; New York: Stokes, 1909. Pp. 293–305.

108. ———, comp. *Irish Songs and Ballads,* 3rd ed. London: D. Bogue, 1882. Pp. 145–46.

109. ———. *Songs of Old Ireland.* London: Boosey, 1882. Pp. 5–7, 16.

110. Hoagland, Kathleen, comp. *1000 Years of Irish Poetry.* New York: Devin-Adair, 1947.

111. Jackson, Kenneth Hurlstone, ed. *A Celtic Miscellany; Translations From The Celtic Literature.* London: Routledge and Kegan Paul; Cambridge: Harvard University Press, 1951. Republished Harmondsworth: Penguin Books, 1971.

112. Jacobs, Joseph, ed. *Celtic Folk and Fairy Tales.* London: David Nutt, 1892; rpt., New York: Dover Books, 1968. Pp. 156–68.

113. ——————, ed. *More Celtic Folk and Fairy Tales*. New York: G. P. Putnam's, 1895; rpt., New York: Dover, 1968. Pp. 194–203.

114. Jones, Mary Eirwin, ed. *Folktales of Ireland*. Oxford: Pen-in-Hand; New York: Medill McBride, 1949. Pp. 165–73.

115. Joynt, Maud, ed. *Golden Legends of the Gael*. Dublin: Talbot Press, c. 1920. Pp. 121–23.

116. McGarry, Mary, ed. *Great Folktales of Old Ireland*. New York: Bell, 1972. Pp. 69–95.

117. MacKenzie, Robert Shelton. *Bits of Blarney*. New York: Redfield, 1854; republished, New York: Alden, 1884. Pp. 48–69.

118. Müller-Lisowski, Käte. *Irische Volksmärchen*. Die Märchen der Weltliteratur. Jena: E. Diederichs, 1923. Pp. 38–50.

119. Neeson, Eoin. *The Second Book of Irish Myths and Legends*. Cork: Mercier Press, 1966. Pp. 52–109.

120. O'Byrne, W. Lorcan. *A Land of Heroes*. London: Blackie, 1899. Pp. 185–92.

121. O'Clery, Helen, ed. *The Ireland Reader*. New York: Franklin Watts, 1963. Pp. 61–69.

122. O'Faoláin, Eileen. *The Children of the Salmon and Other Irish Folktales*. Boston: Atlantic, Little-Brown, 1965. Pp. 274–86.

123. ——————. *Irish Sagas and Folktales*. New York: Henry Z. Walck, 1954. Pp. 125–74.

124. O'Faoláin, Seán, ed. and tr. *The Silver Branch: An Anthology of Old Irish Poetry*. New York: Viking Press; London: Cape, 1938; rpt., Freeport, N.Y.: Books for Libraries, 1968. Pp. 77–78, 88–93.

125. O'Sheridan, Mary Grant. *Gaelic Folktales. A Supplementary Reader*, rev. ed. Chicago: W. F. Roberts, 1911. Pp. 154–241.

126. Picard, Barbara Leonie. *Celtic Tales: Legends of Tall Warriors and Old Enchantments*. London: Edmund Ward, 1964; New York: Criterion Books, 1965. Pp. 70–126.

127. Pilkington, Francis Meredith. *Shamrock and Spear: Tales and Legends From Ireland*. London: Bodley Head, 1966. Pp. 142–59.

128. Preston, Dorothea. *Echoes of Erin: Told and Illustrated for Children*. Dublin: Talbot Press, c. 1920.

129. Protter, Eric and Nancy. *Celtic Folk and Fairy Tales*. New York: Duell, Sloan and Pearce, 1966. Pp. 94–97, 178–88.

130. Rhys, Grace Little. *A Celtic Anthology*. New York: T. Y. Crowell, 1927. Pp. 42–46.

131. Sharp, Elizabeth, comp. *Lyra Celtica: An Anthology of Representative Celtic Poetry*. Edinburgh: Patrick Geddes, 1896.

132. Wilson, Barbara Ker. "Tales from the Episode of the Fians." In *Scottish Folk-Tales and Legends*. Oxford: Oxford University Press, 1954. Pp. 175–207.

133. Yeats, William Butler, comp. *Irish Fairy and Folk Tales*. London, 1888; republished New York: Modern Library, c. 1935. Pp. 285–99.

PRIMARY SOURCES: IRISH

The Manuscript Tradition

Most of the texts are from the learned or manuscript tradition in Irish literature, but because some stories were collected from oral sources at an early date it is frequently difficult to distinguish.

Collections of Manuscript Narratives, with and without Translation

134. Brooke, Charlotte. *Reliques of Irish Poetry*. Dublin: G. Bonham, 1789.
135. Chauviré, Roger, ed. and tr. *Contes ossianiques*. Paris: Presses universitaires de France, 1949.
136. Cross, Tom Peete and Clark Harris Slover. *Ancient Irish Tales*. New York: Holt, 1936; London: Harrap, 1937; rpt. New York: Barnes and Noble, 1969.

Daly, John, *also* John O'Daly; *see* Ossianic Society, *Transactions of*, #144.

137. Dillon, Myles, ed. *Irish Sagas*. Dublin: Stationery Office, 1959; Cork: Mercier Press, 1968.
138. Dottin, Georges, ed. and tr. *L'epopée irelandaise: introduction, traduction, et notes*. Paris: La Renaissance du livre, n.d.
139. Hull, Eleanor. "Ossianic Poetry." In *The Poem Book of the Gael*. London: Chatto and Windus, 1913. Pp. 81–101.
140. Joyce, Patrick Weston. *Old Celtic Romances*. London: Kegan Paul, 1879. Republished Dublin: Talbot Press, 1961. Pagination, 1961 ed., 123–268.
141. Meyer, Kuno, ed. and tr. *Fianaigecht: Being a Collection of Hitherto Inedited Irish Poems and Tales Relating to Finn and His Fiana, With An English Translation*. Royal Irish Academy. Todd Lecture Series, 16. Dublin: Hodges Figgis; London: Williams and Norgate, 1910.
     Meyer deals with six narratives, some of which have Irish titles, and some English; the six are: I. *Reicne Fothaid Canainne*, 1–21. II. "The Quarrel Between Finn and Oisin," 22–27. III. *Ailill Aulom, Mac Con, and Find ua Baiscne*, 28–41. IV. *Erard mac Coisse cecinit*, 42–45. V. "The Finn Episode from Gilla in Chomded húa Cormaic's Poem 'A Rí ríchid, réidig dam,' " 46–51. VI. The Chase of Síd na mBan Finn and the Death of Finn," 52–100.
142. O'Connor, Frank. *Kings, Lords, and Commons*. London: Macmillan, 1961. Pp. 28–29.

O'Daly, John, *also* John Daly; *see* Ossianic Society, *Transactions*, #144.

143. O'Grady, Standish Hayes. *Silva Gadelica: A Collection of Tales in Irish With Extracts Illustrating Persons and Places. Edited from MSS*. London: Williams and Norgate, 1892. The first volume gives Irish texts for the narratives, and the second gives English translations. Seven narratives provide Fenian materials; here are their numbers (for both volumes) and English titles, with pagination for the second volume: XI. "The Enumeration of Finn's People," 99–100. XII. "The Colloquy [of the

Ancients]," 101–264. XVII. "The Pursuit of *Gilla decair*," 292–310. XIX. "The Carle in the Drab Coat," 324–31. XXI. "The Enchanted Cave of Keshcorran," 343–46. XXVI. "The Little Brawl at Almhain," 378–85. XXVIII. "The Boromean Tribute," 401–23.

See also Ossianic Society, Transactions, #144.

O'Kearney, Nicholas; *see also Ossianic Society, Transactions, #144*.

144. *Ossianic Society, Transactions of.* Vol. I. *Cath Gabhra. The Battle of Gabhra: Garristown in the County of Dublin* . . . , translated by Nicholas O'-Kearney (1853). Vol. II. *Feis Tighe Chonain Chinn-Sleibhe; or the Festivities of the House of Conan of Ceann-Sleibhe, in the County of Clare* . . . , translated by Nicholas O'Kearney (1855). Vol. III. *Toruigheacht Dhiarmada agus Ghrainne. The Pursuit After Diarmuid and Grainne* . . . , translated by Standish Hayes O'Grady (1856). Vol. IV. *Laoithe Fiannuigheachta; or Fenian Poems*, translated by John Daly (also "O'Daly") (1859). Vol. V. *Imtheacht na Tromdhaimhe. The Proceedings of the Great Bardic Instititution* . . . , translated by Owen Connellan (1860). Vol. VI. *Laoithe Fiannuigheachta; or Fenian Poems*, second series, translated by John Daly (or "O'Daly") (1861).

145. Stokes, Whitley and Ernst Windisch, eds. and trs. *Irische Texts, mit Übersetzungen und Wörterbuch*. Leipzig: S. Hirzel. Vol. I (1880), "Drei Gedichte aus der Finnsage," 146–64. Vol. I, pt. 1 (1900), *Acallamh* [sic] *na Senórach* ["The Colloquy of the Elders"], 1–438.

Major Texts of Narratives from Manuscript Tradition

For further information about the dating of these texts as well as problems in editing them, see R. I. Best, *Bibliography of Irish Philology and Printed Literature*. Dublin: Browne and Nolan, 1913. Pp. 100–104. *Bibliography of Irish Philology and Manuscript Literature*. Dublin: Dublin Institute for Advanced Studies, 1942. Pp. 80–83.

146. *Agallamh* [or *Acallamh*] *na Senórach*. "The Colloquy of the Elders."

Murphy, Gerard. "Acallamh na Senórach," *Irish Sagas*, edited by Myles Dillon. Cork: Mercier Press, 1966. Pp. 119–30.

Ní Shéaghdha Nessa. *Agallamh na Senórach*. Dublin: Oifig an tSolathair, 1942–45. 3 vols.

O'Grady, Standish Hayes. *See O'Grady, Silva Gadelica, #143*.

O'Sheridan, Mary Grant. *Lays and Ranns from the Folklore of the Gael*. Chicago: Privately Printed, c. 1922.

Stokes, Whitley. *See Stokes, Irishe Texte, #145*.

147. *Agallamh na Senórach Bec*. "The Little Colloquy of the Elders."

Hyde, Douglas. "An Agallamh Bheag." *Lia Fáil* 1 (1924): 79–107.

Hyde, Douglas. "The Cooking of the Great Queen." *Celtic Review* 10 (1916): 335–50.

Pennington, W. "The Little Colloquy." *Philological Quarterly* 9 (1930): 97–110.

148. *Aithed Finn.* "The Elopement of Finn."

   Meyer, Kuno. "Finn and Gráinne." *Zeitschrift für celtische Philologie* 1 (1897): 458–61.

149. *Bóramha.* "The Boromian Tribute."

   O'Grady, Standish James. *See* O'Grady, *Silva Gadelica,* #143.

   Stokes, Whitley. "The Boroma." *Revue Celtique* 13 (1892–93): 294–308.

150. *Bruidhean Atha.* "The Hostel at the Ford."

   Hull, Vernam E. "The Tales About Find; Original Texts Probably Composed About the Middle of the Eighth Century." *Speculum* 16 (July 1941): 322–33.

   Meyer, Kuno. "The Tales About Finn." *Revue Celtique* 14 (1893–94): 241–49.

151. *Bruidhen Beg na hAlmaine.* "The Little Brawl at Almhain."

   Ó Gallchobhair, T. "Bruighean Dhean na hAmhaine." In *Gadardhe na Geamhordhche.* Dublin, 1915. Pp. 1–13.

   Ní Shéaghdha, Nessa. "Bruidhean Bheag na hAlmhain." In *Trí Bruidhne.* Dublin, 1941.

   O'Grady, Standish Hayes. "Bruighean Bheag na h-Almhaine." *Iris-leabhar Muighe Nuadhad* 1, no. 1 (1907): 41–44.

   O'Grady, Standish Hayes. *See also* O'Grady, *Silva Gadelica,* #143.

152. *Bruidhean Caorthainn* [or *Bruighean Caorthuinn* in Scottish Gaelic]. "The Hostel or Fairy Palace of the Quicken Trees."

   Campbell, John Francis. "The Story of the Rowan Tree Dwelling." In *Leabhar na Feinne.* London: Spottiswoode, 1872. Pp. 86–88. [Ballad version].

   Joyce, Patrick Weston. *See* Joyce, *Old Celtic Romances,* #140.

   Mac Róigh, Fearghus. "Bruidhean Chaorthainn." In *Fearghus Mac Roig do chuir i. n-eagar.* Dublin, 1911. Pp. 14–64. [Folk version collected in Donegal].

   Pearse, Padraic H. "Bruidhean Chaorthainn." In *Sgéal Fiannaidheachta.* Dublin, 1908. Pp. 8–62.

153. *Bruidhean Chéise Chorainn.* "The Enchanted Cave of Keshcorran."

   Ní Shéaghdha, Nessa. "Bruidhean Chéise Coruinn." *Trí Bruidhne.* Dublin, 1941.

   Ó Gallchobhair, T. "Bruidhean Cheise Corainn." In *Gadaidhe Géar na Geamhoidhche.* Dublin, 1915. Pp. 69–79.

   O'Grady, Standish Hayes. *See* O'Grady, *Silva Gadelica,* #143.

154. *Cath Fionntrága.* "The Battle of Ventry, or, The White Strand."

   Anon. *Cath Finntrága.* The Battle of Ventry Harbor; which took place in the fourth century, and continued without intermission for 366 days. Boston, 1856.

   Meyer, Kuno. *Cath Finntrága, or the Battle of Ventry.* Oxford: Oxford University Press, 1885.

Ó Rahilly, Cecile. *Cath Finntrágha.* Edited from MS. Rawlinson B 487. Medieval and Modern Irish Series, 20. Dublin: Dublin Institute for Advanced Studies, 1962.

155. *Cath Gabhra.* "The Battle of Gabhra, or Gowra."

d'Arbois de Jubainville, Henry. *Mort du roi Cairpré et d'Oscar fils d'Ossian, à la bataille de Gabair.* Louvain: Muséon, 1884.

O'Kearney, Nicholas. *See Ossianic Society, Transactions,* vol. 1, #144.

156. *Eachtra an Amadáin Mhóir.* "The Adventures of the Big Fool."

Campbell, John Francis. *Popular Tales of the West Highlands.* London: A. Gardner, 1893. III, 160–93. [Highland folk version].

Curtin, Jeremiah. *Hero Tales of Ireland.* London: Macmillan; Boston: Little, Brown, 1894. Pp. 140–62. [Folk version].

Daly, John. *See Ossianic Society, Transactions,* vol. 4, #144.

Hyde, Douglas. *Lía Fáil* 1, no. 2 (1927): 191–227.

Kennedy, Patrick. *Bardic Stories of Ireland.* Dublin: McGlashan and Gill, 1871. Pp. 151–55.

Muehlhausen, L. "Neue Beiträge zum Perceval-Thema." *Zeitschrift für celtische Philologie* 27 (1927): 1–30.

157. *Eachtra Bhodaig an Chóta Lachtna.* "Adventure of the Churl in the Drab Coat."

Daly, John. "Eachdra agus imtheachta bhodaig an chota lachtna." *The Nation* [Dublin], n.s. 10 (1858): 171, 186, 203, 219.

O'Grady, Standish Hayes. *See O'Grady, Silva Gadelica,* #143.

Pearse, Padraic H. *Bodach an chóta lachtna.* Dublin: Royal Irish Academy, 1906.

158. *Fotha Catha Cnucha.* "The Cause of the Battle of Cnucha, or Castle-knock."

Hennessy, William H. "The Battle of Cnucha." *Revue Celtique* 2 (1873): 86–93.

Ponsinet, L. "Le droit celtique dans le pièce intitulée: Causes de la bataille de Cnucha." *Nouvelle Revue de Droit Français et étranger* 10 (1886): 475–81.

Windisch, Ernst. *Kurzgefasste irische Grammatik.* Leipzig, 1879.

159. *Imram Brain.* "The Voyage of the Bran, Son of Febal . . ."

Hull, Vernam E. "An Incomplete Version of the *Imram Brain* and Four Stories Concerning Mongan." *Zeitschrift für celtische Philologie* 18 (1929–30): 409–20.

Meyer, Kuno. *Immram Brain. The Voyage of the Bran, Son of Febal, To the Land of the Living . . .* London: David Nutt. 2 vols. 1897.

160. *Macgnímartha Finn.* "The Youthful Exploits of Finn."

Comyn, David. *Mac-ghníomhartha-Finn; The Youthful Exploits of Fionn . . .* Dublin: M. H. Gill, 1881. Revised, 1896.

Meyer, Kuno. "Macgniamartha Find." *Revue Celtic* 5 (1881–83): 195–204, 508.

Meyer, Kuno. "Boyish Exploits of Finn." *Ériu* 1 (1904): 180–90. [Translation of the above].

O'Donovan, John. "The Boyish Exploits of Finn MacCumhaill." In *Ossianic Society, Transactions of,* IV, edited by John Daly.

161. *Tochmarc Ailbe.* "Finn's Conversation with Alibe."

Stokes, Whitley. "Fionn's Conversation with Ailbhe." In J. F. Campbell, *Leabhar na Feinne.* London: Spottiswood, 1872. P. 151.

Thurneysen, Rudolf. "Tochmarc Ailbe, Das Werben um Ailbe." *Zeitschrift für celtische Philologie* 18 (1919–21): 251–82.

162. *Tóruigheacht Dhiarmada agus Ghráinne.* "The Pursuit of Diarmuid and Gráinne."

Breatnach, R. A. "Tóraigheacht Dhiarmada agus Ghráinne." In *Irish Sagas,* edited by Myles Dillon. Cork: Mercier Press, 1966. Pp. 135–47.

Meyer, Kuno. "Uath Beinne Etair. 'The Hiding of the Hill of Howth,' an episode of the Pursuit of Diarmuid and Gráinne." *Revue Celtique* 11 (1890): 125–34.

Neeson, Eoin. "Diarmaid and Graine." In *The Second Book of Irish Myths and Legends.* Cork: Mercier Press, 1968. Pp. 52–109.

Ní Shéaghdha, Nessa. *Tóruigheacht Dhiarmada agus Ghráinne: The Pursuit of Diarmaid and Grainne.* Irish Texts Society, 47. Dublin: Educational Company of Ireland, 1967.

O'Duffy, Richard J., ed. *The Pursuit of Diarmuid and Gráinne.* Irish Text and English Translation [by S. H. O'Grady]. Published for the Society for the Preservation of the Irish Language. Dublin: M. H. Gill, 1884.

O'Grady, Standish Hayes. *See* O'Grady, *Silva Gadelica,* #143; *Ossianic Society, Transactions,* #144.

Tucait Fagbála in fessa do Finn. See under *Bruidhean Atha,* translations by Hull and Meyer, #150.

Individual Narratives from Manuscript Tradition

Because the titles for many of these vary from Irish, English, Latin, French, and German recensions, they are listed here by editor or translator.

163. Connellan, Owen, tr. "The Hospitality of Cuanna's House." In *Irish Literature,* edited by Justin McCarthy, *et al.* Philadelphia: J. D. Morris, 1904. II, 629–32.

164. Gwynn, E. J., tr. "The Burning of Finn's House." *Ériu* 1 (1904): 13–37.

165. ———, tr. "Finn and the Man in the Tree." *Ériu* 11 (1932): 152–53.

166. [Hardy, P. Dixon?] "Legend of Fin M'Cool." *Dublin Penny Journal* 3, no. 123 (November 8, 1834): 147.

167. Hull, Vernam E., tr. "The Death of Fothath Conanne." *Zeitschrift für celtische Philologie* 20 (1936): 400–404.

168. ———, tr. "How Finn made Peace between Sodelb and Glangressach." *Zeitschrift für celtische Philologie* 18 (1930): 422–23.

169. Lloyd, J. H. and O. J. Bergin, Gertrude Schoepperle, eds. & trs. "The Death of Diarmaid." *Revue Celtique* 33 (1912): 157–79.

170. ———, eds. & trs. "The Reproach of Diarmaid." *Revue Celtique* 33 (1912): 41–57.

171. Meyer, Kuno, tr. "Bérla na Filed. Mitteilungen aus irischen Handschriften." *Zeitschrift für celtische Philologie* 8 (1910–12), 560–61.

172. ———, tr. "Cailte Cecinit." *Ériu* 1 (1904): 72–73.

173. ———, tr. "Finn and the Man in the Tree." *Revue Celtique* 25 (1904): 344–49.

174. ———, tr. "Mitteilungen aus irischen Handscriften." *Zeitschrift für celtische Philologie* 12 (1918): 374–75.

175. ———, tr. "Nachlass. Erläuterungen und Besserungen zu irischen Texten. 4 Finn und die Gespenster." *Zeitschrift für celtische Philologie* 13 (1920): 194.

176. Murphy, Gerard, tr. "Finn's Poem on May-Day." *Ériu* 17 (1955): 86–89.

177. Ní Mhuirghease, Máire, ed. "Bruighean Eochaidh Bhig Dheirg." In *Trí Bruidhne*. Dublin: privately published, 1941.

178. O'Curry, Eugene, tr. "Prophecy ascribed to Finn Mac Cumhaill." In *Lectures on the Manuscript Materials of Ancient Irish History*. Dublin: James Duffy, 1861. Pp. 622–23.

179. Stern, Ludwig, tr. "Finnsruth." *Zeitschrift für celtische Philologie* 1 (1897): 471–73.

180. ———. "Eine ossianische Ballade aus dem XII Jahrhundert." In *Festschrift Whitley Stokes . . . gewidnet*. Leipzig, 1900. Pp. 7–19.

181. ———, tr. "Le manuscrit irlandais de Leide." *Revue Celtique* 12 (1892): 12–22.

182. Stokes, Whitley, tr. "The Prose Tales in the Rennes Dindshenchas, No. 49, *Cenn Cuirrig*." *Revue Celtique* 15 (1894): 443–44.

183. ———, tr. "The Story of Find and Lomna from Cormac's Glossary." In *Three Irish Glossaries*. London, 1862. Pp. 34–35.

184. Thurneysen, Rudolf, tr. "Tuirill Bicrenn und seine Kinder." *Zeitschrift für celtische Philologie* 12 (1918): 244–45.

Irish Annals, Chronicles, Codices, and Histories
Which Include Mention of Fionn

Because the titles of these works vary from one source to another, they are standardized here in English.

185. *Ancient Laws of Ireland*. Edited by the Commissioners for Publishing the Ancient Laws and Institutes of Ireland. Dublin: Alexander Thom, 1865. III, 533.

186. *Annals of Clonmacnoise*. Translated by Conall MacGeoghegan in 1627, edited by Dennis Murphy. Dublin: Royal Society of Antiquaries of Ireland, 1896.

187. *Annals of Innisfallen.* Reproduced in Facsimile from the Original Manuscript (Rawlinson B 503) in the Bodleian Library, with a Descriptive
Introduction by R. I. Best and Eoin MacNeill. Dublin: Royal Irish
Academy; Browne and Nolan; London: Williams and Norgate, 1933.
6 vols.
188. *Annals of the Four Masters,* 2nd ed., edited by John O'Donovan. Dublin:
Hodges, Smith, and Co., 1856. 7 vols.
189. *Book of Aicill. See Ancient Laws of Ireland,* #185.
190. *Book of Armagh. Liber Ardmachanus,* edited by John Gwynn. Dublin,
1913.
191. *Book of the Dun Cow. Lebor na hUidre,* edited by Richard Irvine Best
and Osborn Bergin. Dublin: Royal Irish Society, 1929.
192. *Book of Leinster. Lebor Laignech,* edited by Richard Irvine Best, Osborn
Bergin, and M. A. O'Brien. Dublin: Dublin Institute for Advanced
Studies, 1954.
193. *Clonmacnoise Codex. Rawlinson B 502; A Collection of Pieces in Prose and
Verse in the Irish Language Compiled During the Eleventh and Twelfth
Centuries . . . ,* edited by Kuno Meyer. Oxford: Clarendon Press, 1909.
194. *Cormac's Glossary. Sanas Chormaic* [Compiled by Cormac, King of Cashel,
836–908 A.D.], edited by John O'Donovan, with notes and indices by
Whitley Stokes. Dublin: Irish Archaeological and Celtic Society, 1868.
Foras Feasa ar Éirinn. See Keating, Geoffrey, #195.
195. Keating, Geoffrey [Irish: Séathrun Céitinn]. *Foras Feasa ar Éirinn* [lit.
"The Story of the Foundations of Ireland]. Vol. I, edited by David
Comyn. Irish Texts Society, 4. London: David Nutt, 1902. Vols. II, III,
IV, edited by Patrick S. Dinneen. Irish Texts Society, 8, 9, 15. London:
David Nutt, 1908, 1914. [Although the Irish Texts Society edition
supersedes all others, we include earlier translations for reference.]
196. Keating, Jeoffry [sic]. *The General History of Ireland,* translated by Derm-
o'd O'Connor. London, 1723.
197. Keating, Geoffrey. *The General History of Ireland . . . ,* translated by
Dermo'd O'Connor. Dublin: James Duffy, 1841.
198. *Metrical Dindshenchas . . . ,* edited and translated by Edward Gwynn.
Royal Irish Academy, Todd Lecture Series. Dublin: Royal Irish Academy, 1903–35. 5 vols.
199. *Lives of the Irish Saints. Vitae Sanctorum Hiberniae,* edited and translated
by Charles Plummer. Oxford: Clarendon Press, 1910, 1922. 2 vols.
Rawlinson B 502. See Clonmacnoise Codex, #193.
Rawlinson B 503. See Annals of Innisfallen, #187.
Sanas Chormaic. See Cormac's Glossary, #194.
200. *Tripartite Life of Patrick with Other Documents relating to that Saint,*
edited and translated by Whitley Stokes. London: Her Majesty's Stationery Office, 1887.

Irish-Language Redactions and Retellings of Traditional Materials

Included here are original works in Irish which make use of Fenian
motifs, such as Micheál Coimín's mid-eighteenth century *Laoi Oisín ar thír*

na n-Óg and Micheál MacLiammóir's 1935 play, *Diarmuid agus Gráinne* as well as Irish anthologies and texts of Fenian narratives and poems. Most of these items are in Irish without English translation.

201. Anon. *Bardachd na Feinne.* N.p, n.d.

202. Anon. *Fian-Laothe .i. tiomargadh Laoitheadh bFiannaigheachta as dá Thir mhóra tre-Fhóid .i. ahÉirinn is hAlbain. Seogamh Laoide do thiomairg.* Dublin: Clódhanna teo., ar n-a chur amach do Chonnradh na Gaedhilge, 1916.

203. Anon. *Filiocht Fiannaiochta. Nua-eagrán.* Cork: Comhlucht Oideachais na hÉireann, 1954.

204. Anon. *Teach imtheacht an Ghiolla Dheacair, & tóruigheacht Chonáin & a chuidheachtan* . . . Dublin: Connradh na Gaedhilge, 1905.

205. Breathnach, Michael. *Pros na Fiannaidheachta.* Dublin: Cómhlucht Oideachais na hÉireann, c. 1932.

206. Coimín, Micheál. *Laoi Oisín ar thír na n-Óg. The Lay of Oisín in the Land of Youth,* edited and translated by Tomás O Flannghaile. Dublin: M. H. Gill, 1907.

207. ———. "The Lay of Oisín and the Land of Youth," translated by Bryan O'Looney. In *Ossianic Society, Transactions of,* IV (1861), edited by John Daly. Pp. 227–80.

208. ———. "Ossian in Tir na n-Og." In *Blanaid and Other Irish Historical and Legendary Poems from the Gaelic,* translated by Timothy Daniel Sullivan. Dublin: Eason, 1891. Pp. 115–42.

Coimín, Micheál. *See also* O'Briain, Padraig, #215.

209. Joynt, Maud. *Feis Tighe Chonáin.* Medieval and Modern Irish Series, No. 7. Dublin: Stationery Office, 1936.

210. MacLiammóir, Micheál. *Diarmuid agus Gráinne. Dráma tri ngíomh.* Dublin: Oifig Diolta Foillseacháin Rialtais, 1935.

211. MacLeod, Mary. *Gaelic Songs of Mary MacLeod,* edited by James Carmichael Watson. Scottish Gaelic Texts, vol. 9. Edinburgh: Oliver and Boyd, 1934. *See especially* "A Period Devoted to Telling Fian Tales," 283 ff.

212. MacNeill, Eoin and Seaghán Ó Cadhla. *Eachtra Finn mic Cumhaill le seachrán na sál gCam.* Dublin: Connradh na Gaedhilge, 1906.

213. MacPiarais, Pádraic. *Bruidhean Chaorthainn. Sgéal Fiannaigeachta.* Dublin: Connradh na Gaedhilge, 1912.

214. Ní Shéaghdha, Nessa. *Tóruigheacht Dhiarmada agus Ghráinne.* Dublin: Brun agus O Nualláin Teóranta, 1944.

215. O'Briain, Padraig. *Blaiththleasg de mhilseánaibh Gaedhilge.* Dublin, 1893. This includes two works by Micheál Coimín, "Eachtra Thoirdhealbhaigh mhic Strairn," and "Eachtra Chloine Thoroilbh mhac Strairn."

216. Ó Cadhlaigh, Cormac. *An Fhiannuidheacht.* Dublin: Oifig an tSolathair, 1938.

217. Ó Cionnfhaola, Micheál. *Fionn agus Chuideachta.* Dublin: Comhlucht Oideachair na hÉireann, 1923.

218. Ó Domhnaill, Niall. *Seanchas na Feinne.* Dublin: Oifig an tSolathair, 1942–43. 3 vols.

219. Ó Donnchadha, Tadhg. *Filidheacht Fiannaigheachta.* Dublin: Cómhlucht Oideachais na hÉireann, c. 1933.

220. Ó Gallchobhair, T. *Padraic ua Cuain and Tadhg Mac Giolla Fhionnáin* . . . Dublin, 1915.

221. O'Kelly, Seán [John]. *Eachtra an Amadáin Mhóir.* Dublin: M. H. Mac Ghuill, 1925.

222. O'Kelly, John Joseph. *Leabhar na Leoitheadh; A Collection of Ossianic Poems,* 2nd. ed. Dublin: M. H. Gill, 1913.

223. O'Néill, Séamus. *Buaidh an Ultaigh.* Dublin: Oifig an tSolathair, 1941.

224. Ó Siochfhradha, Pádriag. *Cath Fionntrágha* . . . Dublin: Connradh na Gaedhilge, 1911.

225. ———. *Laoithe na Féinne* . . . Dublin: Clólucht an Talbóidigh, 1941.

Fenian Narratives Collected from Oral Tradition

This list makes no pretense at being complete, in part because folklore is of lesser concern in the overall discussion. Readers seeking to know more about the relation of oral tradition to manuscript tradition should consult Alan Bruford, #329, and Gerard Murphy, #403. Additional Fenian narratives from oral tradition may be found in such unindexed journals as *Lía Fáil,* *Béaloideas,* and *Tocher* as well as the regional cultural and archaeological journals published in counties Cork, Kilkenny, and Louth.

226. Andrews, Elizabeth. *Ulster Folklore.* London, 1913; republished, New York: E. P. Dutton, 1919.

227. Anon. ("D"). "Poem of the Chase." *Irish Penny Journal* 1, no. 12 (September 19, 1840): 93–94.

228. Anon. ("D"). "The Chase, A Poem Translated from the Irish." *Irish Penny Journal* 1, no. 13 (October 3, 1840): 114–16.

229. Anon. ("L, J. M."). *Fionn ann an Tigh à Bhlàir-Bhuidhe gun Chomas Suidhe no eirigh.* Glasgow: MacLaren, 1920.

230. Anon. ("T, C. J."). *Folklore and Legends of Ireland.* Folklore and Legends of the World, vol. 4. London: Gibbings, 1889. Pp. 34–38, 47–51, 133–40.

231. Anon. ("W., E."). "Legend of Ossheen, the Son of Finn." *Dublin Penny Journal* 4 (January 9, 1836): 218–19.

232. Anster, John. "Rath of Badamar, or, The Enchantment." *Dublin University Magazine* 39 (March/April 1852): 325–28, 513–17. Cf. Whitley Stokes, "Find and the Phantoms," below (#310).

233. Argyll, ninth duke of. John G. E. H. D. S. Campbell. *Adventures in Legend, Being the Last Historic Legends of the Western Highlands.* Westminster: A. Constable, 1898. Pp. 19–44.

234. Cameron, Alexander. "Ossianic Ballads." *Scottish Review* 8 (1886): 334–67.

235. ————, ed. "Poems of Ossian, Collected by John M'Donald in the Western Perishes of Strathnaver, Ross, and Inverness-shire, in September and October, 1805." *Transactions of the Gaelic Society of Inverness* 13 (1886–87): 269–300.

236. ————, ed. *Reliquiae Celticae*. 2 vols. Inverness: Northern Chronicle Office, 1894. Vol. 1 is titled, "Ossianica," and includes:

Dean of Lismore's Book, 1–106; cf. collection by Thomas MacLauchlan below (#287).

Poems Illustrative of the Dean's Book, 110–18.

Edinburgh MS. XLVIII, 119–50.

Edinburgh MS. LXII, 151–66.

The Campbell Collection, 167–246.

MacFarlane's Ossianic Collection, 247–94.

The MacLagan MS., 295–370.

The Sage Collection, 371–92.

The Sage-Pope Collection, 393–99.

Sir George MacKenzie's Collection, 400–426.

The MacNicol Collection, 425–26.

Vol. 2 also includes some Fenian materials:

Fernaig MS., 1–137.

Book of Clanranald, 138–309.

Turner MS., 420.

237. Campbell, Archibald (Lord), ed. *Waifs and Strays in Celtic Tradition.* Argyllshire Series. London: David Nutt, 1889–1891. Vol. 1. *Craignish Tales*, ed. James MacDougall, 1889. Vol. 2. *Folk and Hero Tales*, ed. Duncan MacInnes, 1890. Includes Alfred T. Nutt's essay, "Development of the Fenian or Ossianic Saga," 399–430. Vol. 3. *Folk and Hero Tales*, edited by James MacDougall, 1891. Vol. 4. *The Fians; or Stories, Poems, and Traditions of Fionn and His Warrior Band*, edited by John Gregorson Campbell, 1891.

238. Campbell, Hector. "Ceudach Mac Righ nan Collach." In *Luirgeann Eachainn Nill, Folktales from Cape Breton*, compiled and translated by Margaret MacDonell and John Shaw. Stornoway: Acair, 1981. Pp. 53–68.

239. Campbell, J. J., ed. *Legends of Ireland*. London: Batsford, 1955. Pp. 156–210.

240. Campbell, John [*sometimes* Ian] Francis. "Fionn's Enchantment; A Popular Tale of the Highlands of Scotland." *Revue Celtique* 1 (1870–72): 193–202.

241. ————. *Leabhar na Feinne, Heroic Gaelic Ballads*. 1 vol. [only issued]. London: Spottiswoode, 1872. The whole of the 224 pages of this quarto volume are devoted to Fenian poetry taken from twenty-nine collections, MS. and published, here arranged according to theme and type.

Many of the MS. collection are also published in Alexander Cameron's *Reliquiae Celticae,* noted above (#236).

242. ———. *Popular Tales of the West-Highlands, Orally Collected.* 4 vols. Paisley: Gardner, 1861; republished, London: A. Gardner, 1890–1893; reprinted, Hildesheim, Germany: G. Olms Verlag, 1971. II, 116–120. III, 46–440. The final volume is devoted to criticism of Fenian literature.

243. Campbell, John Gregorson. *The Fians. See* Lord Archibald Campbell's *Waifs and Strays in Celtic Tradition,* #237.

244. ———. "Fionn's Ransom." *Transactions of the Gaelic Society of Inverness* 15 (1888–89): 46–62.

245. ———, ed. "West Highland Tale: How Finn Went to the Kingdom of the Big Men." *Scottish Celtic Review,* no. 3 (November 1882): 184–90.

246. Campbell, John Lorne, trans. *Stories From South Uist, Told by Angus MacLellan.* London: Routledge and Kegan Paul, 1961. Pp. 3–31.

247. Casey, Thomas. *Sgealta Thomais ui Chathasaith: Mayo Stories Told by Thomas Casey,* edited and translated by Douglas Hyde. Irish Texts Society, vol. 36. Dublin: Educational Company of Ireland, 1939. Pp. 201–22.

248. Cody, Patrick. "Folk-Lore, No. II." *Journal of the Kilkenny Archaeological Society* [later, *Royal Society of Antiquaries*] 2 (1852): 97–102.

249. Colum, Padraic, ed. *A Treasury of Irish Folklore.* New York: Crown Publisher, 1954. Pp. 87–123.

250. Curtin, Jeremiah. *Hero Tales of Ireland.* London: Macmillan; Boston: Little-Brown, 1894. Pp. 140–62.

251. ———. *Irish Folk Tales.* Dublin: Talbot Press, 1944, 1956. Pp. 124–33. Republished, Dublin: Folklore Society of Ireland, 1967.

252. ———. *Myths and Folktales of Ireland.* Boston and London: Little-Brown, 1890, 1911; rpt., Detroit: Singing Tree, 1968. Pp. 204–303.

253. Drummond, William Hamilton. *Ancient Irish Minstrelsy.* Dublin: Hodges and Smith, 1852.

254. Dunne, John. "The Fenian Traditions of Sliabh-na-m-ban." *Journal of the Kilkenny Archaeological Society* [later, *Royal Society of Antiquaries*] 1, pt. 3 (1851): 333–62.

255. Evans, Egerton, ed. "Fionn mac Cumhail and the Scottish Giants." *Ulster Folklife* 21 (1975): 85–89.

256. Flood, Joseph Mary. *Ireland: Its Myths and Legends.* Dublin, 1916; rpt., Port Washington: Kennikat, 1970. Pp. 84–99, 123–36.

257. Fournier, E. E. "The Treasure of the Fianna." *The Celtic Review* 1 (1904–1905): 261–63.

258. Gregory, Isabella Augusta Persse (Lady). *The Kiltartan History Book.* Dublin: Maunsel, 1909; republished, London: T. F. Unwin, 1926; rpt., Garrard's Cross: Colin Smythe, 1971.

259. ———. *The Kiltartan Poetry Book.* New York and London: G. P. Putnam's, 1919; reprinted, Garrard's Cross: Colin Smythe, 1971.

260. ———. *The Kiltartan Wonder Book.* Dublin: Maunsel, 1919; rpt., Garrard's Cross, 1971.

261. Grierson, Elizabeth. *The Book of Celtic Stories.* London: A. & C. Black, 1908. Also published as *Children's Book of Celtic Stories.* New York: Macmillan, 1908. Pp. 246–85, 306–24.

262. Hill, Thomas Ford. "Ancient Erse Poems, collected among the Scottish Highlands." *Gentleman's Magazine* 52 (1782): 33–36, 140–44, 398–400, 590–92, 662–65; cf. letter from T. F. Hill, 570–71. Republished as "Fragments of Erse Poetry." *Gentleman's Magazine Library* 4, English Traditional Lore . . . London: Elliot Stock, 1885. Pp. 138–73. T. H. Ford reprinted a second time as "Ancient Erse Poems, collected among the Scottish Highlands." *The Gael, an Gaodhal* [New York] 6 (1887). T. H. Ford collection is also collated in J. F. Campbell. *Leabhar na Feinne.* London: Spottiswoode, 1872.

263. Hyde, Douglas. *An Sgeuluidhe Gaodhalach.* London: David Nutt, n.d. "An Sgeuluidhe Gaodhalach; Contes Irelandais," translated by Georges Dottin. *Annales de Bretagne,* 12 (1896–1897), 239–265. *Contes Irelandais,* tr. Georges Dottin. Rennes: Philon et Hervé, 1901. *Beside the Fire,* tr. Douglas Hyde. London: David Nutt, 1910.

264. ———. "Báirne Mór." *Béaloideas* 3 (1931): 187–95.

265. Hyde, Douglas and T. Ó Caomhánaigh. "Cuireadh Mhaoil uí Mhannáin ar Fhionn mac Cumhaill agus Fianaibh Éirionn." *Lia Fáil* 3 (1930): 87–114.

266. Hyde, Douglas. *Legends of Saints and Sinners.* Every Irishman's Library. Dublin: Talbot Press; New York: F. A. Stokes, 1915. P. 110.

267. ———. "Oscur au Fléau, legende ossianiques." *Revue Celtique* 18 (1892–93): 417–25.

Hyde, Douglas. *See also* Thomas Casey, *Sgéalta Thomáis Uí Chathasaith,* #247.

268. Jackson, Kenneth Hurlstone. "Cailleach an Strutt Ruaidh; The Hag of the Red Stream." *Scottish Studies* 6 (1962): 85–93, 184–93.

269. Kelleher, A. and Gertrude Schoepperle. "Finn dans le Pays des Geants, et l'Anneau de Sliabh na Fideoige." *Revue Celtique* 32 (1911): 184–93.

270. Kennedy, Duncan. His MS collated by J. F. Campbell. *Leabhar na Feinne.* London: Spottiswoode, 1872.

271. Kennedy, Patrick. *Bardic Stories of Ireland.* Dublin: M'Glashan and Gill, 1871. Pp. 115–55.

272. ———. *Legendary Fictions of the Irish Celts.* London: Macmillan, 1866; rpt., Detroit: Singing Tree, 1968. Pp. 203–43.

273. Kennedy-Fraser, Marjorie and Kenneth MacLeod. "An Ossianic Lay: Aillte." In *Sea Tangle: Some More Songs of the Hebrides.* London: Boosey, 1913. Pp. 13–15.

274. Killinger, Karl von. *Sagen und Märchen aus Irland.* Stuttgart: F. O. Gotta'fcher Verlag, 1848. III, 33–70.

275. Killip, Margaret. *The Folklore of the Isle of Man.* London: B. T. Batsford; Totowa: Rowman & Littlefield, 1976.

276. Krappe, Alexander H. "La poursuite du Gilla Dacker et les Dioscures celtiques." *Revue Celtique* 44 (1932): 96–108, 216.

277. Leahy, William. "The Blackbird of the Grove of Carna," and "The Tale of Talc." *Transactions of the Gaelic Society of Dublin* 1 (1808): 196–98, 205–11.

278. Lynch, J. F. "Caherconlish." *Cork Historical and Archaeological Society Journal* 2 (1896): 385–92. Cf. commentary in same journal by James Grene Barry, 451–52.

279. McAnally, D. R. "The Henpecked Giant." In *Irish Wonders: Popular Tales as Told By the People.* New York: Ward and Lock, 1888; rpt., New York: Weathervane Books, 1977. Pp. 151–69.

280. MacDonald, T. D. "The Fingalians." In *Gaelic Proverbs and Proverbial Sayings.* Stirling: Eneas MacKay, 1926. Pp. 133–39.

281. MacDougall, James. *See* Archibald Campbell. *Waifs and Strays in Celtic Tradition,* vols. 1 and 3 (#237).

     MacFarlane's Ossianic Collection. *See* Alexander Cameron. *Reliquiae Celticae,* #236.

282. MacFarlane, Malcolm, ed. *Lamh-sgrìobhainn Mhic Rath. A Handful of Lays,* compiled by Duncan MacRae (fl. 1688–93). Dundee: C. S. MacLeoid, 1923. This collection was first published in Alexander Cameron's *Reliquiae Celticae* under the title "Fernaig MS."

     MacInnes, Duncan. *See* Archibald Campbell. *Waifs and Strays of Celtic Tradition,* vol. 2 (#237).

283. Macintyre, Neil [reciter]. "Rìgh na Gréige." In *Sgialachdan a Albainn Nuaidh,* edited by C. I. N. MacLeod. Glasgow: Gairm, 1969. Pp. 94–101. Translated and republished as "The King of Greece." In *Stories From Nova Scotia,* edited and translated by C. I. N. MacLeod. Antigonish, Nova Scotia: Formac, 1974. Pp. 77–85.

284. MacKay, Duncan A. "Manus." In *Bàrdachd á Albainn Nuaidh,* edited by C. I. N. MacLeod. Glasgow: Gairm, 1970. Pp. 14–16.

285. MacKechnie, John, ed. *Scottish West Highland Folk Tales. The Dewar Manuscripts,* vol. 1. Glasgow: MacLellan, 1964. Pp. 154–60.

286. MacKenzie, Donald. "The Princes of Land-Under-Waves." In *Wonder Tales From Scottish Myth and Legend.* Glasgow and Bombay: Blackie and Son, 1917. Pp. 57–75.

     MacKenzie, George, Sir. *See* Alexander Cameron. *Reliquiae Celticae,* #236.

     MacLagan MS. *See* Alexander Cameron. *Reliquiae Celticae,* #236.

287. MacLauchlan, Thomas, ed. & tr. *The Dean of Lismore's Book,* introduction by W. F. Skene. Edinburgh: Edmonston and Douglas, 1862. Republished in Alexander Cameron. *Reliquiae Celticae.* I, 2–109. See also Neil Ross, ed. *Heroic Poetry from the Book of the Dean of Lismore.*

     MacLellan, Angus. *See* John Lorne Campbell. *Stories from South Uist,* #246.

     MacLeod, Calum I. N. *See* Neil Macintyre, #283, and Duncan MacKay, #284.

288. Macleod, Kenneth. "Oisean an deigh na Feinne. ['Ossian After the Feinne']." *Celtic Review* 1 (1904): 172–74.

289. MacNeil, Joe Neil. "Beinn is Gleann is Àite-Suidhe Samhraidh." In *Cape Breton Storyteller*, transcribed, translated, and edited by John Shaw. Unpublished Dissertation, Harvard University, 1983. Contains 16 Fenian narratives.

290. ————. "Joe Neil MacNeil Tells a Fenian Tale: Fear a Chòta Liathghlais, The Man in the Light Grey Coat," translated by John Shaw. *Cape Breton's Magazine* 22 (June 1979): 30–36.

291. MacNeill, Eóin [*also* John]. *Duanaire Finn I: The Book of the Lays of Finn.* Irish Texts Society, No. 7. London: David Nutt, 1908. Volumes II and III are edited by Gerard Murphy, *see* #297 and #298.

292. MacNicoll, Donald. His ballad MS. collated in J. F. Campbell. *Leabhar na Feinne.* London: Spottiswoode, 1872.

MacRae, Duncan. *See* Malcolm MacFarlane. *A Handful of Lays,* #282.

293. Montgomery, Henry R., ed. *Specimens of the Early Native Poetry of Ireland, in English Metrical Translations.* Dublin: J. McGlashan, 1846; republished, Dublin: Hodges Figgis; London: Simpkin, Marshal, 1892. Pp. (1846) 59–80, 127–66.

294. Moore, Arthur William. *The Folk-lore of the Isle of Man.* Douglas: Brownson: London: David Nutt, 1891. Pp. 10–12.

295. Morris, Henry. "An Déigh a Chuaidh Fionn i dtreis." *Béaloideas* 1 (1928): 405–10.

296. Morris, [Henry?]. *Told at the Feis; Stories of Ancient Ireland.* Dublin: Educational Company of Ireland, c. 1927. Pp. 74–105.

297. Murphy, Gerard. *Duanaire Finn II.* Irish Texts Society, No. 28. London: Simpkin, Marshall, 1933.

298. ————. *Duanaire Finn III.* Irish Texts Society. No. 43. Dublin: Educational Company of Ireland, 1953.

299. Ó Baoill, Micí Sheáin Neill. "An Óige is an Saol Mor agus an Bás." In *Maith Thú, a Mhicí.* Dungannon: Clo Oirghialla, 1973. Pp. 1–6.

300. O'Flanagan, Theophilus. "The Marks of Finn MacComhal's Greyhound." *Transactions of the Gaelic Society of Dublin* 1 (1808): 215–23.

301. O Súilleabháin, Seán. *Folktales of Ireland.* Chicago: University of Chicago Press, 1966. Pp. 38–73.

302. Pattison, Thomas. *Selections from the Gaelic Bards.* Glasgow: A. Sinclair, 1866. Pp. 141–203.

303. Pope, Alexander [of Reay, Caithness]. A MS of Ossianic verse attributed to him is collated in J. F. Campbell. *Leabhar na Feinne.* London: Spottiswoode, 1872.

304. Robinson, Fred N. "A Variant of the Gaelic 'Ballad of the Mantle.'" *Modern Philology* 1 (1903–1904): 145–57.

305. Ross, Neill, ed. *Heroic Poetry from the Book of the Dean of Lismore.* Scottish Gaelic Texts Society, No. 3. Edinburgh: Oliver and Boyd, 1939. Materials taken from Thomas McLauchan, ed. *The Dean of Lismore's Book.* Edinburgh: Edmonston and Douglas, 1862.

Sage MS. and Sage-Pope MS. *See* Alexander Cameron. *Reliquiae Celticae,* #236.

306. Simpson, John Hawkins. *Poems of Oisín, Bard of Erin*. Dublin: M'Glashan and Gill; London: Bosworth and Harrison, 1857.

307. Smith, Alexander. *A Summer in Skye*. Boston: Ticknor and Fields; London: Strahan, 1866. Republished, Edinburgh: N. R. Mitchell, 1880; New York: J. W. Lovell, 1885. Pp. (1866) 159–69, 213–31, 559–70. A portion of this was republished as "In Fingalian Days." In *Mine Eyes to the Hills*, edited by P. R. Chalmers. London: A. & C. Black, 1931. P. 143.

308. Stern, Ludwig Christian. "Ossianische Gedichte aus Caithness." *Zeitschrift für celtische Philologie* 5 (1905): 551–65.

309. Stewart, Charles. "Abstract of Ossian's Covalla." *The Celtic Monthly; A Magazine for Highlanders* 2 (1894): 97–98, 120–21, 181.

310. Stokes, Whitley. "Find and the Phantoms." *Revue Celtique* 7 (1886): 289–307. Cf. John Anster. "Rath of Badamar," above (#232).

311. Stone, Jerome. "Ossianic Ballads by Jerome Stone," edited by Don MacKinnon. *Transactions of the Gaelic Society of Inverness* 14 (1888): 314–69.

312. Swire, Otta Flora. *The Highlands and their Legends*. Edinburgh: Oliver and Boyd, 1963.

313. ———. *The Inner Hebrides and their Legends*. London: Collins, 1964.

314. ———. *The Outer Hebrides and their Legends*. Edinburgh: Oliver and Boyd, 1966.

315. ———. *Skye; the Island and Its Legends*. New York: Oxford University Press, 1952.

316. Thomas, Edward. *Celtic Stories*. Oxford: Clarendon Press, 1918. Pp. 61–81.

Turner Ms. *See* Cameron, Alexander. *Reliquiae Celticae*, #236.

317. Watson, William J. "The Death of Diarmad." *Celtic Review* 10 (1914–16), 350–57.

SECONDARY SOURCES

Studies of Fenian Literature

318. Anon. "Ancient Irish Minstrelsy. The Fenian Poems." *Duffy's Hibernian Magazine* 3, no. 17 (November 1861): 197–204.

319. Anon. "Ossian and Ossianic Literature." *The Gael* [New York] 19, no. 5 (May 1900): 151–52.

320. Anon. "Ossianic Literature." *The Gael* 19, no. 6 (June 1900): 170.

321. Anon. "Ossianic and Other Early Legends." *The Gael* 22, no. 7 (July 1903): 217–18.

322. Anon. "Transactions of the Ossianic Society." *Living Age* 55 (December 19, 1857): 740–43.

323. d'Arbois de Jubainville, Henry. *Le cycle mythological irlandais et la mythologie celtique.* Paris: E. Thorin, 1884. [Not seen] Eight pages of the translation of this are important. *See Irish Mythological Cycle and Celtic Mythology,* translated by Richard I. Best. Dublin: Hodges Figgis; London: Simpkin, Marshall, 1903; rpt., New York: Lemma, 1970. Pp. 191–97.

324. ———. *L'epopée celtique en Irlande.* Cours de Litterature Celtique, vol. 5. Paris: E. Thorin, 1892. Pp. 379–92.

325. Breatnach, R. A. "The Pursuit of Diarmuid and Gráinne." *Studies* 47 (1958): 90–97.

326. Brøgger, Neils Chr. "Finn og Fenniene." In *Heltr og Halvguder hog Kelterne.* Oslo: Ernst G. Mortenen Forlag, 1961. Pp. 103–10.

327. Bromwich, Rachel. "A Note on Breton Lays." *Medium AEvium* 26 (1957): 36–38.

328. Brueyre, Loys. "Les héros d'Ossian, dans Macpherson et dans les traditions populaires." *Revue des traditions populaires* 2 (1887): 385–96, 444–55.

329. Bruford, Alan. "The Fenian Cycle: Pursuits, *Bruidhne* and Battles, and Anomalies." In *Gaelic Folktales and Medieval Romances.* Dublin: Folklore of Ireland Society, 1969. Pp. 106–33.

330. Campbell, Duncan. "The Imperial Idea in Early British History." *Transactions of the Gaelic Society of Inverness* 14 (1888): 276–97.

331. Candon, Thomas Henry. "The Legend of Diarmuid and Grania, Its History and Treatment by Modern Writers." Unpublished dissertation, Boston University, 1954.

332. Carney, James. "Father and 'Son' Figures in Irish Mythology." *The Irish Press* 19 (December 1962): 16.

333. Chadwick, Nora Kershaw. "Imbas Forosnai." *Scottish Gaelic Studies* 4, pt. 2 (1935): 97–135.

334. Christiansen, Reidar Thoralf. *The Vikings and the Viking Wars in Irish and Gaelic Tradition.* Skrifter utgitt av det Norske Videnskaps-Akademi, vol. 1. Oslo: I Kommisjon Hos Jacob Dybwad, 1931.

335. Connellan, Owen. "On the Fians of Erin and the Poems of Oisín." *Transactions of the Ossianic Society* 5 (1860): 205–27.

336. Cox, Edward Godfrey. "Mediaeval Irish Ideal of a Saint and a Gentleman." *South Atlantic Quarterly* 11 (October 1912): 311–17.

337. Craigie, W. A. "The Legend of the Fiann in the Highland Bards." In *The Old Highlands* [Being Papers Read Before the Gaelic Society of Glasgow, 1895-1906], edited by Neil Munro. *Transactions of the Gaelic Society of Glasgow,* vol. 3. Glasgow: Archibald Sinclair, 1908. Pp. 131–68.

338. ———. "The Ossianic Ballads." *Scottish Review* 34 (1899): 260–90.

339. ———. "Three Tales of the Fiann." *Scottish Review* 24 (October 1894): 270–97.

340. Cross, Tom Peete. "A Note on 'Sohrab and Rustum' in Ireland." *Journal of Celtic Studies* 1 (November 1950): 176–82.

341. ――――. "The Ossianic Cycle." In *Harper and Bard: The Beauties of Irish Literature.* Chicago: Thomas S. Blackwell, 1931. Pp. 101–28.

342. ――――. "Review of Kuno Meyer's *Miscellanea Hibernica.*" *Modern Philology* 16 (1918–19): 218–22.

343. Crowe, J. O'Beirne. "Religious Beliefs of the Pagan Irish." *Journal of the Royal Historical and Archaeological Association of Ireland,* 3rd ser., 1 (1868–69), 307–34.

344. Curtis, Edmund. "Age and Origin of the Fenian Tales." *Ivernian Society Journal* 1 (1909): 159–68.

345. deBlacam, Aodh. "Fenian Cycle." In *A First Book of Irish Literature.* Dublin: Talbot Press; Educational Company of Ireland, 1934. Pp. 60–67.

346. deBlacam, Aodh. "Fenian Cycle." In *Gaelic Literature Surveyed.* Dublin and Cork: Talbot Press, 1929. Pp. 57–86.

347. Dennis, L. J. "Fin [sic] MacCoul's Pebble (at Carlingford, Co. Down)." *Folk-Lore* 16 (1905): 186.

348. Dillon, Myles. "The Fenian Cycle." In *Early Irish Literature.* Chicago: University of Chicago Press, 1948. Pp. 32–50.

349. Edmonston-Scott, W. J. "The Traditional Genesis of the Fenian Saga." *Scottish Review* 38 (1915): 205–30, 350–81.

350. Fitzgerald, David. "Early Celtic History and Mythology." *Revue Celtique* 6 (1884): 193–259.

351. FitzGerald, Walter (Lord). "Notes on the Feena-Erin, Finn Mac Coole, and the Latter's Principal Abode: The Hill of Allen in the County Kildare." *County Louth Archaeological Journal* 1, no. 4 (October 1907): 5–22.

352. Ford, Patrick. "Finn and Ritual Knowledge in Ancient Irish Literature." Address given at the Modern Language Association meeting, Chicago, December 28, 1977.

353. Gantz, Kenneth F. "Charlotte Brooke's 'Reliques of Irish Poetry,' and the Ossianic Controversy." *Studies in English* [University of Texas] 9 (1940): 137–56.

354. Grant, K. W. "Fionn and the Fingalians." In *Myth Tradition and Story from Western Argyll.* Oban: The Oban Times Press, 1925. Pp. 20–24.

355. Gregory, Isabella Augusta Persse (Lady). "The Living Legends of the Fianna." *Monthly Review* 18, no. 2 (1904): 74–92.

356. van Hamel, Anton Gerard. "Aspects of Celtic Mythology." *Proceedings of the British Academy* 20 (1934): 207–48. Republished as a monograph. London: Humphrey Milford, 1935.

357. Heffernan, Carol T. "Combat at the Fountain: The Early Irish *Pursuit of the Gilla Decair* and the Old French *Yvain.*" *Éire-Ireland* 17, no. 4 (Winter 1982): 41–57.

358. Henderson, George. "The Fionn Saga." *Celtic Review* 1 (1904): 193–207, 352–66; 2 (1905): 1–19, 135–53, 255–72, 351–59; 3 (1906): 56–61.

359. Hudson, Wilson M. "Ossian in English Before Macpherson: Hanmer's *Chronicle of Ireland,* 1633." *Studies in English* [University of Texas] 19 (1950): 118–28.

360. Hull, Eleanor. *A Textbook of Irish Literature*, 2nd ed. Dublin: M. H. Gill, 1908. II, 1–77.
361. Hull, Vernam E. "Quarrel Between Finn and Oisín." *Modern Language Notes* 57 (June 1942): 434–36.
362. ———. "A Rhetoric in 'Finn and the Man in the Tree.'" *Zeitschrift für celtische Philologie* 30 (1967): 17–20.
363. Hyde, Douglas. "The Fenian Cycle . . ." In *The Story of Early Gaelic Literature*. London: T. Fisher Unwin; New York: P. J. Kennedy, 1903. Pp. 82–106, 121–35.
364. ———. "The Fenian Cycle," and "The Ossianic Cycle." In *A Literary History of Ireland*. London: T. Fisher Unwin, 1899; rpt., New York: Barnes and Noble, 1967. Pp. 363–87, 498–513.
365. ———. "The Reeve's Manuscript of the *Acallamh na Senórach*." *Revue Celtique* 38 (1921): 289–95.
366. Ibarra, Eileen Sullivan. "The Comic Character of Fin M'Coul, The Hibernian Hercules, in Carleton's 'A Legend of Knockmany.'" *Folklore* 82 (Autumn 1971): 212–15.
367. ———. "Folktales in Carleton's 'The Three Tasks.'" *Tennessee Folklore Society Bulletin* 38, no. 3 (September 1970): 66–71.
368. Jackson, Kenneth Hurlstone. "Elegy and Fenian Poetry." In *Studies in Early Celtic Nature Poetry*. New York: Macmillan, 1935. Pp. 110–26.
369. Jellingshaus, Herman F. *Ossians Lebensanschauung*. Tübingen: Mohr, 1904.
370. Kelleher, John. "Ossian and the Irish." Paper delivered before the American Committee for Irish Studies, Ann Arbor, Michigan, May 3, 1973.
371. [Kennedy, Patrick]. "Fictions of Our Forefathers: Fion MacCumhail and His Warriors." *Irish Quarterly Review* 9, no. 35 (October 1859): 649–728. Rpt. as a monograph. Dublin: McGlashan and Gill, 1860.
372. Krappe, Alexander Haggerty. "Diarmuid and Gráinne." *Folk-lore* 47 (1936): 347–61.
373. Krause, David. "The Hidden Oisín." *Studia Hibernica* 6 (1966): 7–24; rpt. in *The Profane Book of Irish Comedy*. Ithaca: Cornell University Press, 1982.
374. ———. "Rageous Ossean: Patron-Hero of Synge and O'Casey." *Modern Drama* 4 (December 1961): 268–91.
375. Leach, MacEdward. "Celtic Tales from Cape Breton." In *Studies in Folklore in Honor of Distinguished Service Professor Stith Thompson*, edited by Richmond W. Edson. Indiana University Press Folklore Studies, no. 9. Bloomington: Indiana University Press, 1957. Pp. 40–54.
376. Lloyd, J. H. "Diarmuid and Gráinne as a Folktale." *Gadelica* 1 (1912): 83–100.
377. Lynch, P. J. "Legends of Saint Patrick and Ossian." *The Gael* [New York] 9, no. 3 (March 1900): 82–84.
378. MacBain, Alexander. "Heroic and Ossianic Literature." *Transactions of the Gaelic Society of Inverness* 12 (1886): 180–211.

379. ———. "Who Were the Feinn? Did Fingal or Ossian Sing?" *Transactions of the Gaelic Society of Glasgow* 2 (1894): 67–106.

380. MacCana, Proinsias. "Fionn Cycle." In *Celtic Mythology*. London: Paul Hamlyn, 1970. Pp. 106–15.

381. MacCulloch, John Arnott. "Fionn and the Feinn." In *Celtic Mythology. The Mythology of All Races*, vol. 3. Boston: Marshall Jones, 1918; rpt., New York: Cooper Square, 1964, Pp. 160–83.

382. ———. "The Fionn Saga." In *Religion of the Ancient Celts*. Edinburgh: T. and T. Clark, 1911. Pp. 142–57.

383. MacDonald, Archibald. "Ossian and Saint Patrick." *An Deo-Greine* [Glasgow] 2, no. 4 (January 1907): 58–60.

384. McGurk, J. J. N. "Finn and the Fenians—Fact or Fairy Tale?" *Contemporary Review* 215 (July 1969): 30–33.

385. McHugh, Sheila Joyce. *'Sir Perceyvelle': Its Irish Connections*. Ann Arbor: Edwards Brothers, 1946.

386. MacKenzie, W. C. "The Fingalian Legends: Their Source and Historical Value." *Gentlemen's Magazine*, n.s. 65 (1900): 168–79.

387. MacKillop, James. "Finn MacCool: The Hero and the Anti-Hero." In *Views of the Irish Peasantry, 1800–1916*, edited by D. J. Casey and R. E. Rhodes. Hamden, Conn.: Archon Books, 1977. Pp. 86–106.

388. MacLean, Magnus. "The Féinn Cycle." In *The Encyclopedia of Religion and Ethics*, edited by James Hastings. Edinburgh: T. and T. Clark; New York: Scribner's, 1912. V, 823–27.

389. ———. "Ossianic Cycle." In *The Literature of the Celts, Its History and Romance*. London: Blackie and Son, 1902. Pp. 174–97.

390. MacManus, Seumas. "Fionn and the Fian." In *The Story of the Irish Race*. New York, 1921; rpt. New York: Devin Adair, 1944. Pp. 64–73.

391. MacNeill, Eoin. "Military Service in Medieval Ireland." *Journal of the Cork Historical and Archaeological Society* 46 (1941): 6–15.

392. MacNeill, Nigel. "The Finian Ballads." In *The Literature of the Highlanders*. London: Lamley, 1892. Second edition, with additional chapter by John MacMaster Campbell. Stirling: Eneas MacKay, 1929. Pp. (1929) 156–86.

393. MacRitchie, David. *Fians, Fairies, and Picts*. London: Kegan Paul, and Trench, 1893.

394. ———. "The Finn-Men of Britain." *Archaeological Review* 4 (1889): 1–26, 107–29.

395. Marr, Tracy. "The Earliest Finn Literature (7th–11th Century)." Unpublished Seminar Paper. Antigonish, Nova Scotia, 1983. 32 pages.

396. Meyer, Kuno. "The Death of Finn MacCumaill." *Zeitschrift für celtische Philologie* 1 (1897): 462–65.

397. ———. "Find mac Umaill." *Revue Celtique* 32 (1911): 391–95.

398. ———. "Nordisch-Irisches." *Akademie der Wissenschaft Sitzungsberichte der Preussischen* [Berlin] (1918): 1030–1047.

399. ———. "The Ossianic Cycle." *The Academy* 39, no. 985 (March 21, 1891): 283–84.

400. ———. "The Pedigree of Finn MacCumaill." *The Academy* 27, no. 668 (February 21, 1884): 135.

401. Mezger, Fritz. "Finn MacCumaill und Fingal bis zum 17. jahrhundert." *American Journal of Philology* 49 (October 1928): 361–67.

402. Murphy, Gerard. "Finn's Poem on May-Day." *Ériu* 17 (1955): 86–99.

403. ———. "Folklore as a Help to the Understanding of the Irish Fionn Cycle." *Folk-Liv; acta ethnologica Europaea* [Stockholm] (1938): 211–16.

404. ———. "Introduction." In *Duanaire Finn III*. Irish Texts Society, No. 43. Dublin: Educational Company of Ireland, 1953. Pp. x–cxxii.

405. ———. *The Ossianic Lore and Romantic Tales of Medieval Ireland*. Dublin: Colm Ó Lochlainn, 1955, 1961.

406. ———. "The Pursuit of Diarmuid Ó Duibhne." *Éigse* 7 (1953–55): 79.

407. Nagy, Joseph Falaky. "Demne Mael." *Celtica* 14 (1981): 8–14.

408. ———. "Intervention and Disruption in the Myths of Finn and Sigurd." *Ériu* 31 (1980): 123–31.

409. Nuner, Robert SuShane. "The Verbal System of the Agallamh na Senórach." Unpublished dissertation, Harvard University, 1958.

410. Nutt, Alfred T. "Aryan Explusion and Return Formula Among the Celts." *Folk-lore Record* 4 (1881): 1–44.

411. ———. "Correspondence, The Finn-Men of Britain" [a response to David MacRitchie]. *Archaeological Review* 4, no. 3 (October 1889): 232.

412. ———. "Development of the Fenian or Ossianic Saga." In *Waifs and Strays in Celtic Tradition*. Vol. 3 (1890). Pp. 399–430. London: David Nutt, 1891.

413. ———. "Introduction." In *Waifs and Strays in Celtic Tradition*. Vol. 4 (1891). ix–xxxviii. Pp. 281–89. London: David Nutt, 1891.

414. ———. "A New Theory of the Ossianic Saga." *The Academy* 39, no. 980 (February 14, 1891): 161–63.

415. ———. *Ossian and the Ossianic Literature*. Popular Studies in Mythology, Romance, and Folklore, No. 3. London: David Nutt, 1899, 1910.

416. O'Carroll, John James. "Celtic in the Intermediate Programme: The Ossianic Tales." *Irish Ecclesiastical Record* 11 (December 1880): 19–25, 78–83, 204–10, 333–40.

417. ———. "The Ossianic Poems." *The Gaelic Journal* 1 (1882–83): 7–11, 39–41, 69–74, 109–114, 162–65, 178–81, 202–205, 226, 251–55, 277–80, 311–14; 2 (1884): 2–3, 71–73, 118–22.

418. Ó Dubhthaigh, Bearárd. "Agallamh Oisín agus Phádraig: Lá Dhúinne an Sliabh Fuaid." *Éigse* 9 (1958–61): 34–52.

419. O'Faoláin, Seán. "Ossian—The Sow's Ear of Celtic Literature." *Modern Scot* [Edinburgh] 6 (1935): 44–51.

420. ———. "The Spurious Fenian Tale." *Folklore* 41 (June 30, 1930): 154–68.

421. O'Grady, Standish James. "Finn and the Fianna." In *History of Ireland: Critical and Philosophical*. Dublin: Ponsonby, 1881. Pp. 318–59.

422. ———. "The Fianna Eireen," and "The Burden of Oiseen." In *History of Ireland: Heroic Period.* Dublin: Ponsonby, 1878. Pp. 31–38.

423. O'Grady, Standish Hayes. *Remarks on the Oxford Edition of the Battle of Ventry.* London, 1887.

424. O'Growney, Eugene. "Fenian Gaeldom," pt. iv of "Scotland in Irish Gaelic Literature." *Transactions of the Gaelic Society of Glasgow* 2 (1891–95): 255–61.

425. O'Kearney. Nicholas. "Introduction." "In The Battle of Gabhra." *Transactions of the Ossianic Society* 1 (1853): 9–67.

426. ———. "Introduction." "In The Festivities at the House of Conan of Ceann-Sleibhe." *Transactions of the Ossianic Society* 2 (1855): 15–116.

427. O'Laverty, James. "Adonis and Diarmuid O'Duibhne." *Ulster Journal of Archaeology* 7 (1859): 340–42.

428. Oliver, Thomas Edward. "Some Analogues of 'Maistre Pierre Pathelin.' " *Journal of American Folklore* 22 (1909): 395–430.

429. O'Mullane, Michael J. *Finn MacCoole: His Life and Times.* Dublin: Catholic Truth Society of Ireland, c. 1920.

430. O'Nolan, Kevin. "Homer and Irish Heroic Narrative." *Classical Quarterly* 63, n.s. 19 (1969): 1–19.

431. O'Rahilly, Thomas Francis. "Finn and the *Fianna*," and "The Wisdom of Finn." In *Early Irish History and Mythology.* Dublin: Dublin Institute for Advanced Studies, 1946. Pp. 271–81, 318–40.

432. Ó Súilleabhain, Seán. "The Finn Cycle." In *A Handbook of Irish Folklore.* London: Jenkins; Hatboro, Pa.: Folklore Associates, 1963. Pp. 588–97.

533. Powell, Thomas. "Finn and Gwynn." *The Academy* [London] 27 (1884): 64, 189.

434. Power, Mary. "Samuel Beckett's 'Fingal' and the Irish Tradition." *Journal of Modern Literature* 9 (1981–82): 151–56. Cf. #8.

435. Rafroidi, Patrick. "The Uses of Irish Myth in the Nineteenth Century." *Studies* 62 (Fall-Winter 1973): 251–61).

436. Ramnoux, Cleménce. "The Finn Cycle; The Atmosphere and Symbols of a Legend," translated by Maria Jolas. In *A James Joyce Yearbook.* Paris: Transition Workshop, 1949. Pp. 130–58. Reprinted from *Psyché, Revue internationale de Psychoanalyse et des Sciences de l'Homme* 8 (June 1947).

437. Reinhard, John R. and Vernam E. Hull. "Bran and Sceolang." *Speculum* 11 (January 1936): 42–58.

438. Rolleston, Thomas William. "Tales of the Ossianic Cycle." In *Myths and Legends of the Celtic Race.* London: George Harrap; New York: T. Y. Crowell, 1911; New York: Farrar and Reinhart, 1934, 1949. Pp. 252–308.

439. Rollins, Ronald. "Finn Again: O'Casey Resurrects Celtic Heroes in *Red Roses for Me.*" *Irish University Review* 10 (1980): 52–58.

440. Ronsley, Joseph. "Lady Gregory's *Grania.*" *Canadian Journal for Irish Studies* 3, no. 2 (June 1977): 41–58.

441. Russell, George. "The Legends of Ancient Eire." *Irish Theosophist* 3 (April 15, 1895): 119–22.

442. Russell, T. O. "Where was the Dun of Finn MacCumhaill?" *Zeitschrift für celtische Philologie* 4 (1903): 339–44.

443. Schodet, Mirell. "The Theme of 'Diarmuid and Grania' on the Modern Stage." Unpublished thesis, University of Lille, 1972.

444. Scott, Robert Douglas. *The Thumb of Knowledge in Legends of Finn, Sigurd, and Taliesin.* New York: Publications of the Institute for French Studies, 1930.

445. Sigerson, George. "Fionn Period," and "Ossian: Age of Lamentations." In *Bards of the Gael and Gall,* 2nd ed. London: T. Fisher Unwin, 1907, 1925.

446. Sjoestedt-Jonval, Marie-Louise. "The Heroes Outside the Tribe." In *Gods and Heroes of the Celts,* tr. Miles Dillon. London: Methuen, 1949. Pp. 81–91. Original published in Paris: Presses Universitaires, 1940.

447. Squire, Charles. "Finn and the Fenians." In *The Mythology of the British Islands; An Introduction to Celtic Myth, Legend and Poetry, and Romance.* London: Blackie; New York: Scribner's, 1905. Pp. 201–26. Also issued, with same pagination, under another title: *Celtic Myth and Legend, Poetry, and Romance.* London: The Greshem Publishing Co., n.d.

448. Stern, Ludwig Christian. "Finn's Ruth." *Zeitschrift für celtische Philologie* 1 (1897): 471–73.

449. ———. "Die gälische Ballade vom Mantel in MacGregors Liederbuche." *Zeitschrift für celtische Philologie* 1 (1897): 294–326.

450. Stewart, Charles. "Date of Fingal and Ossian." *The Celtic Monthly. A Magazine for Highlanders* 1 (August 1893): 171–72.

451. Stokes, Whitley. "The Colloquy of the Two Sages." *Revue Celtique* 26 (1905): 3–7.

452. ———. "On the Deaths of Some Irish Heroes." *Revue Celtique* 23 (1902): 303–48.

453. Thomson, Derick S. "Bogus Gaelic Literature, c. 1750–1820." *Transactions of the Gaelic Society of Glasgow, 1955–1956* 5 (1958): 172–89.

454. ———. "Indexes of the Ossianic Ballads in the McLagan MSS." *Scottish Gaelic Studies* 7, no. 2 (December 1958): 177–224.

455. Weisweiler, Josef. "Derdriu und Gráinne," *Paideuma* [Frankfurt] 2 (1941–1943): 197–223. Reprinted in *Sonderdruck aus Paideuma,* Bd. II, heft 4/5. Leipzig, 1942.

456. ———. "Vorindogermanische Schichten der irischen Heldensage." *Zeitschrift für celtische Philologie* 24 (1953–54): 10–55, 165–97. Reissued as a monograph. Tübingen: M. Niemeyer, 1953.

457. Windisch, Ernst. "L'ancienne légends irlandais et les póesies ossianiques." *Revue Celtique* 5 (1881): 70–93. The article was later abridged and translated as "Ancient Irish Legendary Literature and Ossianic Poetry," translated by T. O'Neill Russell, *The Irish Echo* [Boston] 4, no. 1 (April 1893): 4–16.

458. ———. "Fotha Catha Cnucha in So." In *Kurzgefasste irische Grammatik mit Lessestücken*. Leipzig: S. Hirzel, 1879, Pp. 121–23.

459. Wood, Juliette. "The Folklore Background of the Gwion Bach Section of *Hanes Taliesin*." *Bulletin of the Board of Celtic Studies* 29, no. 4 (May 1982): 621–34. [Compares Taliesin with Fionn.]

460. Yeats, William Butler. "Finn and His Cycle." Pt. 2 of "Thoughts on Lady Gregory's Translations." In *Cutting of an Agate*. New York: Macmillan, 1912. Pp. 1–35.

461. Zimmer, Heinrich. "Keltische Beiträge, usw." *Zeitschift für Deutsches Alterthum und Deutsche Literatur* [Berlin] 35 (1891): 1–173.

General Studies of Celtic Literature and Culture and General Studies of Traditional Culture

462. Alspach, Russell K. *Irish Poetry from the English Invasion to 1798*. Philadelphia: University of Pennsylvania Press, 1943. Second edition, 1960.

463. ———. "Use by Yeats and Other Irish Writers of the Folklore of Patrick Kennedy." *Journal of American Folklore* 59 (October 1946): 404–12.

464. d'Arbois de Jubainville, Henry. *La civilisation des celtes et celle de l'epopee homerique*. Cour de Littérature Celtique, vol. 6. Paris: A. Fontemoing, 1899.

465. ———. *Essai d'un catalogue de la littérature epique de l'Irelande, précédé d'une etude sur les manuscrits en langue irlandais conserves dans les îles Britannique et sur le continent*. Paris: E. Thorin, 1883.

466. Arnold, Matthew. *The Study of Celtic Literature*. London: Smith, Elder, 1867. Reprinted many times.

467. Best, Richard Irvine. *Bibliography of Irish Philology and Printed Literature*. Dublin: H. M. Stationery Office; Browne and Nolan, 1913.

468. ———. *Bibliography of Irish Philology and Manuscript Literature*. Dublin: Dublin Institute for Advanced Studies, 1942.

469. Blackie, John Stuart. *Language and Literature of the Scottish Highlands*. Edinburgh: Edmonston and Douglas, 1876.

470. Bromwich, Rachel. "Celtic Inheritance of Medieval Literature." *Modern Language Quarterly* 26 (March 1965): 203–27.

471. ———. *Matthew Arnold and Celtic Literature*. Oxford: Clarendon Press, 1965.

472. Brown, Stephen James. *Ireland in Fiction: A Guide to Irish Novels, Tales, Romances, and Folk Lore*. Dublin: Maunsel, 1916, 1919; rpt., New York: Benjamin Blom, 1968.

473. Bryant, Sophie. *Celtic Ireland*. London: Kegan Paul, 1899.

474. Carney, James, comp. *Early Irish Literature*. Cork: Mercier Press; New York: Barnes and Noble, 1966. A binding together of three earlier monographs: Eleanor Knott, *Irish Classical Poetry*, and Gerard Murphy, *Ossianic Lore* and *Saga and Myth in Ancient Ireland*.

475. Carney, James. *Studies in Irish Literature and History.* Dublin: Dublin Institute for Advanced Studies, 1955.

476. Cassidy, James F. *The Women of the Gael.* Boston: Stratford, 1922.

477. Chadwick, Hector Munro and Nora Kershaw Chadwick. *The Growth of Literature.* 3 vols. Cambridge: Cambridge University Press; New York: Macmillan, 1932–1940.

478. Christiansen, Reidar Thoralf. *Studies in Irish and Scandinavian Folktales.* Copenhagen: Rosenkilde and Bagger, 1959.

479. Clarke, Austin. "Gaelic Ireland Rediscovered: The Early Period." In *Irish Poets in English,* edited by Seán Lucy. Cork: Mercier Press, 1973. Pp. 30–43.

480. Colum, Padraic. "Irish Poetry." *The Bookman* 54 (October 1921): 109–115.

481. ———. *The Road Round Ireland.* New York: Macmillan, 1926.

482. Cross, Tom Peete. *Motif Index of Early Irish Literature.* Indiana University Folklore Series, vol. 7. Bloomington: Indiana University Press, 1952.

483. ———. "Notes on the Chastity-Testing Horn and Mantle." *Modern Philology* 10 (1912–13): 289–99.

484. Cousins, James Henry. *The Wisdom of the West, an Introduction to the Interpretive Study of Irish Mythology.* London: Theosophical Publishing Co., 1912.

485. Cunliffe, Barry. *The Celtic World.* New York: McGraw-Hill, 1979.

486. Dalton, G. F. "The Ritual Killing of Irish Kings." *Folklore* 81 (1970): 1–22.

487. deBlacam, Aodh. "The Heroic Note in Irish Literature." *The Nation* 115 (September 27, 1922): 303–304.

488. Deering, Arthur. *Sir Samuel Ferguson, Poet and Antiquarian.* Philadelphia: University of Pennsylvania Press, 1931.

489. Delargy, J. H. "The Gaelic Story-Teller. With Some Notes on Gaelic Folk-Tales." *Proceedings of the British Academy* 31 (1945): 177–221.

490. Diechkoff, Cyril H. "Mythological Beings in Gaelic Folklore." *Transactions of the Gaelic Society of Inverness* 29 (1914–19): 235–58.

491. Dillon, Myles. "The Archaism of Irish Tradition." *Proceedings of the British Academy* 35 (1947): 245–64. Republished as a monograph, London: D. Cumberlege, 1948.

492. ———. *Early Irish Society.* Dublin: Colm Ó Lochlainn, 1954.

493. Dillon, Myles, ed. *Irish Sagas.* Cork: Mercier Press, 1968.

494. Dillon, Myles and Nora Kershaw Chadwick. *The Celtic Realms.* London: Weidenfield and Nicholson; New York: New American Library, 1967.

495. Dooley, Ann. "The Heroic Word: The Reading of Early Irish Sages." In *The Celtic Consciousness,* edited by R. O'Driscoll. Toronto: McClelland and Stewart, 1981. Pp. 155–59.

496. Dowling, Patrick J. *The Hedge Schools of Ireland.* London: Longman's 1935.

497. Dumézil, Georges. *Le troisième souverain; essai sur le dieu indo-iranian Aryaman et sur a formation de l'histoire mythique de l'irlande.* Paris: G. P. Maisonneuve, 1949. See also # 822, 823, 824, 825.

498. Dunn, Charles W. "Ireland and the Twelfth-Century Renaissance." *University of Toronto Quarterly* 24 (October 1954): 70–86.

499. Evans-Wentz, Walter Yeeling. *The Fairy-Faith in the Celtic Countries.* London, 1911; rpt., New Hyde Park: University Books, 1966.

500. Ferguson, Mary (Lady). *The Story of the Irish Before the Conquest,* 3rd. ed. Dublin: Sealy, Bryers, and Walker, 1903.

501. Fitzgerald, David. "De quelques légendes celtiques." *Revue des traditions populaires* 4 (1889): 80–87, 217–24.

502. Fitzgerald, Walter. *The Historical Geography of Early Ireland.* London: G. Philip, 1925.

503. Flood, Joseph Mary. *Dublin in Irish Legend.* Dublin: Talbot Press, 1919.

504. Flower, Robin. *The Irish Tradition.* Oxford: Clarendon Press, 1947.

505. Forster, J. Margaret. "Folklore of County Monaghan, Ireland, Twenty Years Later." *California Folklore Quarterly* 2 (October 1943): 309–14.

506. Gassowski, Jersy. *Mithologia Celtow.* Warsawa: Wydaw-A Artystyczne i Folmowe, 1978.

507. Gruffydd, William John. *Math vab Mathonwy.* Cardiff: University of Wales Press, 1928. *See especially* pages 119–27.

508. Gwynn, Stephen Lucius. *Irish Books and Irish People.* London: T. F. Unwin; Dublin: Talbot Press, 1919; New York: Stokes, 1920.

509. Gwynn, Stephen Lucius. *Irish Literature and Drama in the English Language.* New York: Thomas Nelson, 1936.

510. ———. *To-Day and To-Morrow in Ireland.* Dublin: Hodges Figgis, 1903.

511. van Hamel, Anton. "Aspects of Celtic Mythology." *Proceedings of the British Academy* 20 (1934): 207–48.

512. Henderson, George. *The Norse Influence on Celtic Scotland.* Glasgow: James MacLehose, 1910. *See especially* pp. 275–79.

513. ———. *The Survival of Belief Among the Celts.* Glasgow: James MacLehose, 1911.

514. Henry, Françoise. *Irish Art in the Early Christian Period to A.D. 800.* London: Methuen; Ithaca; Cornell University Press, 1965.

515. ———. *La sculpture irlandaise pendent les douze premiers siècles de l'ere chrêtienne.* Paris: Leroux, 1933.

516. Hubert, Henri. *The Greatness and Decline of the Celts.* New York: Alfred A. Knopf, 1934.

517. ———. *The Rise of the Celts.* New York: Alfred A. Knopf, 1934.

518. Hull, Eleanor. *Folklore of the British Isles.* London: Methuen, 1928.

519. ———. *Pagan Ireland.* Epochs in Irish History. Dublin: M. H. Gill: London: David Nutt, 1904.

520. Jacobsthal, Paul. *Early Celtic Art.* London: Oxford University Press, 1944.

521. Joyce, Patrick Weston. *Ireland.* History of All Nations, edited by Henry Cabot Lodge, vol. 12. Philadelphia: John D. Morris, 1906.

522. ———. *A Social History of Ancient Ireland . . .* 2 vols. Dublin: M. H. Gill; London: Longman's, 1903; rpt., New York: Benjamin Blom, 1968.

523. ———. *The Story of Ancient Irish Civilisation.* Dublin: M. H. Gill; London: Longman's, 1907.

524. Kavanagh, Peter. *Irish Mythology: A Dictionary.* 3 vols. New York: Peter Kavanagh Hand Press, 1959.

525. Kelleher, John V. "Early Irish History and Pseudo-History." *Studia Hibernica* 3 (1963): 113–27.

526. ———. "Irish Humor." Address given at the Annual Convention of the American Committee for Irish Studies, Stonehill College, Easton, Massachusetts, April 25, 1975.

527. ———. "Matthew Arnold and the Celtic Revival." In *Perspectives in Criticism,* edited by Harry Levin. Cambridge: Harvard University Press, 1950. Pp. 197–221. Reprinted as a monograph by the American Committee for Irish Studies. Chicago: University of Chicago Press, 1971.

528. Kennelly, T. Brendan. "Modern Irish Poets and the Irish Epic." Unpublished Dissertation, Trinity College, Dublin, 1967.

529. Kenney, James F. *Sources for the Early History of Ireland. An Introduction and Guide.* Vol. I, *Ecclesiastical* [only issued]. New York: Columbia University Press, 1929.

530. Knott, Eleanor, ed. *The Bardic Poems of Tadhg Dall O Huiginn.* Irish Texts Society, vol. 23. London: Simkin and Marshall, 1926.

531. Knott, Eleanor. *Irish Classical Poetry, Commonly Called Bardic.* Dublin: Colm O lochlainn, 1957. Reprinted with two works by Gerard Murphy in *Early Irish Literature,* compiled by James Carney.

532. Krappe, Alexander Haggerty. *Balor with the Evil Eye; Studies in Celtic and French Literature.* New York: Institut des Études Françaises, Columbia University, 1927.

533. Lindsay, Jack. *Our Celtic Heritage.* London: Weidenfeld and Nicolson, 1962.

534. Little, Tinison. "On Early Irish Celtic Poetry." *Contemporary Review* 205 (April 1964): 204–207.

535. MacBain, Alexander. *Celtic Mythology and Religion.* New York: E. P. Dutton, 1917.

536. MacCall, Seamas. *And So Began the Irish Nation.* Dublin and Cork: Talbot Press, 1931.

537. MacCana, Proinsias. "Mythology in Early Irish Literature." In *The Celtic Consciousness,* edited by R. O'Driscoll. Toronto: McClelland and Stewart, 1982. Pp. 143–54.

538. MacCurtin, Hugh. *A Brief Discourse in Vindication of the Antiquity of Ireland.* Dublin, 1717.

539. MacDonagh, Thomas. *Literature in Ireland.* Dublin: Talbot Press; New York: F. A. Stokes, 1916; rpt., Port Washington: Kennikat, 1970.

540. MacKenzie, Donald A. *Scottish Folk Lore and Folk Life.* London: Blackie, 1935.

541. MacInnes, John. "The Oral Tradition in Scottish Gaelic Poetry." In *Proceedings of the Third International Congress of Celtic Studies,* edited

by W. H. F. Nicolaisen. Edinburgh: University of Edinburgh Press, 1968. Pp. 29–44.

542. Mackenzie, John. *The Beauties of Gaelic Poetry. Sar-Obair nam Bard Gaelach,* . . . Edinburgh: J. Grant, 1907.

543. MacLean, Magnus. *The Literature of the Highlands.* London, Glasgow, and Dublin: Blackie, 1904.

544. MacNeill, Eóin. *Celtic Ireland.* Dublin: M. Lester; London: L. Parsons, 1921.

545. MacNeill, John [Eóin] and A. C. Carney. *Celtic and Teutonic Religions.* London: Catholic Truth Society, 1935.

546. MacNeill [Sweeney], Márie. *The Festival of the Lughnasa.* New York: Oxford University Press, 1962.

547. ———. "Irish Folklore as a Source for Research." *Journal of the Folklore Institute* 2 (1965): 350–54.

548. MacRitchie, David. *The Savages of Gaelic Tradition.* Inverness: Northern Counties Newspaper and Print, 1920.

549. Malet, Hugh. "Gods of the Gaels." *History Today* 20 (March 1970): 174–82.

550. Marcus, Phillip L. *Standish James O'Grady.* Lewisburg, Pa.: Bucknell University Press, 1971.

551. ———. *Yeats and the Beginning of the Irish Renaissance.* Ithaca: Cornell University Press, 1970.

552. Markale, Jean. *Women of the Celts,* translated by A. Mygind, P. Hauch, and P. Henry. London: Gordon Cremonesi, 1975.

553. Martin, Martin. *Description of the Western Islands of Scotland.* 1703; rpt., Glasgow: T. D. Morrison, 1884.

554. Mercier, Vivian. *The Irish Comic Tradition.* London: Oxford University Press, 1962.

555. Merry, Eleanor Charlotte. *The Flaming Door: A Preliminary Study of the Mission of the Celtic Folk-Soul.* London: The Occult Book Society, 1937.

556. Meyer, Kuno. *Death Tales of the Ulster Heroes.* Todd Lecture Series, vol. 14. Dublin: Hodges Figgis, 1906.

557. Moore, Thomas. *History of Ireland.* 4 vols. Paris: Baudry and European Library, 1835–46.

558. Morris, Lloyd R. *The Celtic Dawn: A Survey of the Renaissance in Ireland, 1889–1916.* New York: Macmillan, 1917.

559. Murphy, Gerard. "Bards and Filidh." *Éigse* 2, no. 2 (Winter 1940): 200–207.

560. ———. *Early Irish Metrics.* Dublin: Royal Irish Academy and Hodges Figgis, 1961.

561. ———. "The Origin of Irish Nature Poetry." *Studies* 20 (1931): 87–102.

562. ———. *Saga and Myth in Ancient Ireland.* Dublin: Colm ó Lochlainn, 1955. Reprinted in James Carney's *Ancient Irish Literature,* with Murphy's *Ossianic Lore* and Eleanor Knott's *Irish Classical Poetry.*

563. Neilson, William. *An Introduction to the Irish Language.* Dublin, 1808; republished, Achill: The Mission Press, 1845.

564. Neunkirchen, Hans. *The Celtic Element in English Literature.* Leipzig: Velhagen Klafting, 1932.

565. Nutt, Alfred T. "Celtic Myth and Saga." *Folk-lore* 1 (1890): 234; 3 (1892): 387; 4 (1893): 365.

566. ———. "Critical Study of Irish Literature, Indispensable for the History of the Irish Race." *National Literary Society of Dublin Magazine*, nvm. (November 1902); reprinted as a monograph, New York: Burt Franklin, 1971.

567. ———. "An Essay Upon the Irish Vision of the Happy Otherworld and the Celtic Doctrine of Rebirth." In *Immram Brain. The Voyage of the Gran, Son of Febal, To the Land of the Living.* 2 vols. London: David Nutt, 1895–97. I, 101–331; II, 1–305.

568. O'Connor, Frank. *A Short History of Irish Literature. A Backward Look.* London: Macmillan; New York: G. P. Putnam's, 1967.

569. O'Conor [sic], Norreys Jephson. *Changing Ireland: Literary Backgrounds of the Irish Free State, 1889-1922.* Cambridge: Harvard University Press, 1924.

570. Ó Cuív, Brian. "Literary Creation and Irish Historical Tradition." *Proceedings of the British Academy* 49 (1963): 233–62.

571. O'Curry, Eugene. *Lectures on the Manuscript Materials on Ancient Irish History.* Dublin: James Duffy, 1861; republished, Dublin: W. V. Hinch and P. Traynor, 1878; 1861 edition rpt., New York: Burt Franklin, 1973.

572. ———. *On the Manners and Customs of the Ancient Irish.* 3 vols. Dublin and London: Williams and Norgate; New York: Scribner's, 1873.

573. O'Donoghue, David J. *The Poets of Ireland: A Biographical Dictionary of Irish Writers of English Verse.* Dublin: Hodges Figgis, 1912; rpt., Detroit: Gale Research, 1968.

574. O'Grady, Standish James. *Early Bardic Literature, Ireland.* London: Low, Searle; Dublin: Ponsonby, 1879; rpt., New York: Lemma, 1970.

575. ———. *Selected Essays and Passages.* Dublin: Talbot Press; London: T. F. Unwin, 1918.

576. O'Halloran, Sylvester. *The Complete History of Ireland, From the Earliest Times: Being Compiled From a Connected Continuation by Approved Standard Writers . . .* 2 vols. New York and London: R. Martin, c. 1845.

577. ———. *A General History of Ireland from the Earlest Account to the Close of the 12th Century . . .* 2 vols. London: Printed for the Author, 1778.

578. ———. *The History of Ireland, From the Invasion by Henry the Second, to the Present Times . . .* London and New York: Virtue and Company, 1845.

579. ———. *An Introduction to the Study of the History and Antiquity of Ireland . . .* London: J. Murray, 1772.

580. O'Keeffe, James G., ed. *Buile Shuibhne Geilt. The Frenzy of Suibhne.* Texts Society, vol. 12. London: David Nutt, 1913.

581. Ó Lochlainn, Colm. "Literary Forgeries in Irish." *Éigse* 2, Pt. 2 (1940): 123–36.

582. O'Rahilly, Cecile. *Ireland and Wales, Their Historical and Literary Relations.* London: Longman's, Green, 1924.

583. Ó Ríordáin, Sean P. *Antiquites of the Irish Countryside.* London: Methuen, 1953.

584. Ó Súilleabhain, Seán and Reidar Thoralf Christiansen. *The Types of the Irish Folktale.* Helsinki: Suomalainen tiedekatemia, 1963.

585. Pinchin, Edith F. *The Bridge of the Gods in Gaelic Mythology.* London: Theosophical Press, 1934.

586. Pinkerton, John. *Inquiry into the History of Scotland, Preceding the Reign of Malcolm III, or the Year 1056,* rev. ed. 2 vols. Edinburgh: Bell and Bradfute, 1814.

587. Powell, T. G. E. *The Celts.* London: Thames and Hudson; New York: Praeger, 1958.

588. Power, Patrick C. *The Story of Anglo-Irish Poetry, 1800–1922.* Cork: Mercier Books, 1967.

589. Quiggin, Edmund Crosby. "Prolegomena to the Study of the Later Irish Bards, 1200–1500." *Proceedings of the British Academy* 5 (1911–12): 89–143. Reprinted as a monograph, New York: Haskell House, 1967.

590. Rees, Alwyn and Brinley Rees. *Celtic Heritage.* London: Thames and Hudson, 1961.

591. Reinhard, John Revell. *The Survival of Geis in Medieval Romance.* Halle: Niemeyer, 1933.

591. Renan, Ernest. *The Poetry of the Celtic Races and Other Studies,* translated by William G. Hutchinson. London: Walter Scott, 1896; rpt., Port Washington: Kennikat, 1970.

592. Rhys, John. *Celtic Folklore, Welsh and Manx.* Oxford: Clarendon Press, 1901.

593. ————. *Lectures on the Origin and Growth of Religion as Illustrated by Celtic Heathendom.* The Hibbert Lectures, 1886. London: Williams and Norgate, 1887; 3rd. ed., 1898.

594. Ridgeway, William, Sir. "Ireland and the Heroic Age." In *Early Age of Greece,* II. Cambridge: Cambridge University Press, 1931. Pp. 504–714.

595. Roosevelt, Theodore. "Ancient Irish Sagas." In *History as Literature, and Other Essays.* New York: Scribner's, 1913. Pp. 275–300.

"San-Marte." *See* G. A. Schultz, # 598.

596. Saul, George Brandon. *The Shadow of the Three Queens: A Handbook Introduction to Traditional Irish Literature and Its Backgrounds.* Harrisburg: Stackpole, 1953. Revised and retitled, *Traditional Irish Literature and Its Backgrounds.* Lewisburg, Pa.: Bucknell University Press, 1970.

597. Schofield, William Henry. *Mythical Bards and the Life of William Wallace.* Studies in Comparative Literature, No. 5. Cambridge: Harvard University Press, 1920.

598. Schultz, Geheimrath Albert ["San-Marte"]. *Beiträge zur breton. und celtisch-germ. Heldensage.* Quedlinburg, 1847.

599. Skelton, Robin and David R. Clark, eds. *The Irish Renaissance: A Gathering of Essays, Memoirs, Letters and Dramatic Poetry from the Massachusetts Review.* Dublin: Dolmen Press, 1965.

600. Skene, William Forbes. *Celtic Scotland; History of Ancient Alban.* 3 vols. Edinburgh: Douglas, 1886.

601. Slover, Clark Harris. "Early Literary Channels Between Britain and Ireland." *University of Texas Studies in English* 6 (1926): 5–52.

602. Smith, Robert J. "Irish Mythology," and "Festivals and Calendar Customs." In *Irish History and Culture*, edited by Harold Orel. Lawrence: University of Kansas Press, 1976. Pp. 1–24, 129–46.

603. Snyder, Edward Douglas. *The Celtic Revival in English Literature, 1760–1800.* Cambridge: Harvard University Press, 1923; rpt., Gloucester: Peter Smith, 1965.

604. Spaan, David B. "The Otherworld in Early Irish Literature." Unpublished Dissertation, University of Michigan, 1970.

605. Squire, Charles. *The Mythology of Ancient Britain and Ireland.* Religions Ancient and Modern. Chicago: Open Court, 1906; London: Constable, 1909.

606. Stanford, W. B. *Ireland and Classical Tradition.* Totowa, New Jersey: Rowman and Littlefield, 1976.

607. Stokes, Whitley, ed. "The Annals of Tigernach." *Revue Celtique* 16 (1895): 374–419; 17 (1896): 6–33; 18 (1897): 9–59, 150–97, 267–303.

608. Stokes, Whitley. "On Irish Metric." *Revue Celtique* 6 (1883–85): 298–308.

Sweeney, Máire MacNeill. *See* Máire MacNeill, #546, #547.

609. Taylor, Estella Ruth. *The Modern Irish Writers; Cross Current of Criticism.* Lawrence: University of Kansas Press, 1954.

610. Thompson, William Irwin. *The Imagination of the Insurrection, Dublin, Easter, 1916: A Study of an Ideological Movement.* New York: Oxford University Press, 1967.

611. Thomson, Derick, S. "Scottish Gaelic Folk-Poetry *ante* 1650." *Scottish Gaelic Studies* 8, Pt. 1 (December 1955): 1–17.

612. Thrall, William Flint. "Historical Setting of the Legend of Snedgus and MacRiafla." *Studies in Philology* 22 (1925): 347–82.

613. Thurneysen, Rudolf. *Die irische helden- und königsage bis zum Siebzehnten Jahrhundert.* Halle: M. Niemeyer, 1921.

614. ———. *Sagen aus dem alten Irland.* Berlin: Wiegandt und Grieben, 1901.

615. Vallancey, Charles. *Vindication of the Ancient History of Ireland . . .* Dublin: L. White, 1786.

616. Vendryes, Joseph. "L'unité en trois personnes chez les Celts." *Comptes Rendu l'academie des Inscriptions et Belles-Lettres*, nvm (1935): 324–41.

617. deVries, Jan. *Heroic Song and Heroic Legend.* Oxford: Oxford University Press, 1963.

618. ———. *Keltische Religion.* Stuttgart: W. Kohlhammer Verlag, 1961. *See also La religion des celtes,* translated by L. Jospin. Paris: Payot, 1963.

619. Walczyk, Nancy. "An Irish Story-Teller on the American Plains; or, Finn MacCool Meets Natty Bumpo." Address before the American Committee for Irish Studies. Columbus, Ohio, May 21, 1983.

620. Walczyk, Nancy Madden. "Eóin Ua Cathail: Exile in *Tír na n-Óg.*" Unpublished Dissertation, University of Wisconsin, Milwaukee, 1983.

621. Walker, Joseph C. *Historical Memoirs of the Irish Bards.* Dublin, 1786; rpt., New York: Garland Press, 1971.

622. Walsh, Robert. *Fingal and Its Churches . . .* Dublin: McGee, 1888.

623. Weisweiler, Josaf. "Keltische Frauentypen." *Paideuma* [Frankfort] 2 (1941–43): 1–19.

624. Wilde, William Robert Wills, Sir. *Irish Popular Superstitions: Readings in Popular Literature.* Dublin: McGlashan; London: W. S. Orr, 1852.

625. Williams, J. F. Caerwyn. "The Court Poet in Medieval Ireland." *Proceedings of the British Academy* 58 (1971): 85–135.

626. Wood-Martin, William. *Traces of the Elder Faiths of Ireland; A Folklore Sketch; A Handbook of Irish Pre-Christian Traditions.* 2 vols. London and New York: Longman's, Green, 1902.

627. Zimmer, Heinrich. *Auf welchem wege kamen die Goidelen vom Kontinent nach Ireland.* Berlin: Verlag der Königlichen Akademie der Wissenschaften, 1912.

628. Zimmer, Heinrich and Kuno Meyer. *Die romanischen Literaturen und Sprachen, mit Einschluss des Keltischen.* Berlin und Leipzig: B. G. Teubner, 1909.

Studies of English Use of Fenian Tradition

Arthuriana

629. Brown, Arthur C. L. "The Grail and the English 'Sir Perceval.' " *Modern Philology* 16 (1918–19): 533–63; 17 (1919–20): 361–83; 18 (1920–21): 201–28, 661–73; 22 (1924–25): 79–96, 113–32. Issued in one volume as *Origin of the Grail Legend.* [New York?], 1935, rpt., New York: Russell and Russell, 1966.

630. Bliss, A. J. "Celtic Myth and Arthurian Romance." *Medium AEvum* 30 (1961): 19–25.

631. Glennie, John Stuart. *Arthurian Localities; Their Historical Origin, Chief Country, and Fenian Relations; with a Map of Arthurian Scotland.* Edinburgh: Hertford, 1869. This volume is a collection of appendices from the *Early English Texts Society,* vols. 10, 21, 36, and 112.

632. Loomis, Roger Sherman. *Arthurian Tradition and Chrétien de Troyes.* New York: Columbia University Press, 1949.

633. ———. *Celtic Myth and Arthurian Romance.* New York: Columbia University Press, 1927.

634. ———. "More Celtic Elements in Gawain and the Green Knight." *Journal of English and Germanic Philology* 42 (April 1943): 149–84.
635. McHugh, Sheila Joyce. *"Sir Perceyvelle": Its Irish Connections.* Ann Arbor: Edwards Brothers, 1946. See also the review by Gerard Murphy, *Studies* 37 (1948): 368–71.
636. Marx, Jean. *La legende arthurienne et la Graal.* Paris: Presses universitaires de France, 1952.
637. Mülhausen, Ludwig. "Neue Beiträge zum Perceval-Thema." *Zeitschrift für celtische Philologie* 17 (1928): 1–31.
638. Nitze, William Albert. *Arthurian Romance and Modern Poetry and Music.* Chicago: University of Chicago Press, 1940.
639. ———. *Perceval and the Holy Grail; An Essay on the Romance of Chrétian de Troyes.* University of California Publications in Modern Philology, No. 28. Berkeley: University of California Press, 1949.
640. Pace, R. B. "Sir Perceval and the Boyish Exploits of Finn." *PMLA,* n.s. 25, no. 4 (December 1917): 598–604.
641. Schoepperle, Gertrude. *Tristan and Isolt: A Study of the Sources of the Romance.* 2 vols. London: David Nutt, 1913.
642. Zimmer, Heinrich. "Keltische Beiträge." *Zeitschrift für Deutsches Alterthum und Deutsche Literatur* 35 (1891): 1–173.

James Macpherson

A complete bibliography of Macpherson and the Ossianic controversy would more than fill this volume. Several items on the limited checklist will lead the reader to sources of more information. See especially the work of George F. Black, #646 and John J. Dunn's supplement. Paul VanTieghem produced bibliographies of the Ossianic tradition in French literature, #690, and in eighteenth-century pre-Romanticism, #691. Rudolf Tombo collected materials on Ossian in German literature, #687, as did V. I. Maslov for Russian literature, #670.

643. Anon. "Celtic Studies and the Scotch." *Saturday Review* [London] 72 (1891): 277.
644. von Baudissin, Klaus. "Ossian in der bildenen Kunst." *Westermanns Monatschefte* 136 (1924): 273–77.
645. Betteridge, H. T. "Ossianic Poems in Herder's Volkslieder." *Modern Language Review* 30 (1935): 334–38.
646. Black, George F. "Macpherson's Ossian and the Ossianic Controversy." *Bulletin of the New York Public Library* 30 (1926): 413–15, 424–39, 508–24. Reprinted as a monograph, New York: New York Public Library, 1926, 1927. *See also,* John J. Dunn, "Macpherson's Ossian and the Ossianic Controversy: A Supplemental Bibliography." *Bulletin of the New York Public Library* 75 (1971): 465–73.
647. Black, George F. "President Jefferson and Macpherson's Ossian." *Transactions of the Gaelic Society of Inverness* 33 (1925–27): 355–61.

648. Boswell, James. *Life of Johnson.* Oxford Standard Edition, edited by R. W. Chapman. London: Oxford University Press, 1904, 1953.

649. ———. *Journal of a Tour to the Hebrides with Samuel Johnson* is published with Johnson's *Journey to the Western Islands of Scotland,* see below (#662).

650. Burke, T. Travers. *Fingal, An Epic Poem Versified from the 'Genuine Remains of Ossian.'* [London?]: Cowie, Jolland, 1844.

651. Bysveen, Josef. *Epic Tradition and Innovation in James Macpherson's 'Fingal.'* Atlantic Highlands: Humanities Press, 1983.

652. Campbell, John Francis. "Ossian." In *Popular Tales of the West Highlands, Orally Collected.* London: A. Gardner, 1891, IV, 1–236.

653. Carpenter, F. I. "The Vogue of Ossian in America; A Study in Taste." *American Literature* 2 (1931): 405–17.

654. Chinard, G. "Jefferson and Ossian." *Modern Language Notes* 38 (1923): 201–205.

655. Dunn, John Joseph. "The Role of Macperson's Ossian in the Development of British Romanticism." Unpublished dissertation, Duke University, 1966.

Dunn, John Joseph. *See* Black, George F., #646.

656. Fitzgerald, Robert P. "The Style of Ossian." *Studies in Romanticism* 6 (1966): 22–23.

657. Flower, Robin. *Byron and Ossian.* Byron Foundation Lecture, No. 10. Nottingham: Nottingham University Press, 1928.

658. Fridén, Georg. *James Fenimore Cooper and Ossian.* Essays and Studies on American Language and Literature. Uppsala: Lundequistska Bokh, 1949.

659. Grierson, H. J. C. "Blake and Macpherson." *Times Literary Supplement* (April 7, 1945): 163.

660. Hayne, Barrie. "*Ossian,* Scott and Cooper's Indians." *Journal of American Studies* 3 (1969): 73–87.

661. Hench, Atcheson L. "Jefferson and Ossian." *Modern Language Notes* 43 (1928): 5–37.

662. Johnson, Samuel. *Journey to the Western Islands of Scotland.* Bound with James Boswell. *Journal of a Tour to the Hebrides with Samuel Johnson, L. L. D.* Oxford Standard Edition, edited by R. W. Chapman. London: Oxford University Press, 1924, 1930.

663. Koestler, Arthur. *The Act of Creation.* New York: Macmillan, 1964. Especially, pp. 401–402.

664. Leisy, E. E. "Thoreau and Ossian." *New England Quarterly* 18 (1945): 96–98.

665. MacBain, Alexander. "Macpherson's *Ossian.*" *Celtic Magazine* 12 (1887): 145–54, 193–201, 240–54.

666. Macintosh, Donald T. "James Macpherson and the Book of the Dean of Lismore." *Scottish Gaelic Studies* 6, Pt. 1 (September 1947): 9–20.

667. MacKenzie, Henry, comp. *Report of the Committee of the Highland Society of Scotland . . .* Edinburgh: Constable; London: Longman's, 1805.

668. Macpherson, James. *Dàna Oisein Mhic Fhinn, air an cur amach airson maith coitcheannta muinntir na Gaeltachd* [The Gaelic translation of Ossian]. Edinburgh: Clobhuailte le Tearlach Stiubhart, 1818.

669. Manning, Susan. "Ossian, Scott, and Nineteenth-Century Scottish Literary Nationalism." *Studies in Scottish Literature* [Columbia, South Carolina] 17 (1982): 39–54.

670. Maslov, Vasily Ivanovich. *Ossian in Russia (Bibliography).* Leningrad, 1928.

671. Moore, John Robert. "Wordsworth's Unacknowledged Debt to Macpherson's Ossian." *PMLA* 40 (1925): 362–78.

672. Okun, Henry. "Ossian in Painting." *Warburg and Courtauld Institute Journal* 30 (1967): 327–56.

673. Peers, E. Alison. "Influence of Ossian in Spain." *Philological Quarterly* 4 (1925): 121–38.

674. Ross, Neil. "Introduction" [discusses Macpherson's use of traditional materials]. In *Heroic Poetry from the Book of the Dean of Lismore,* Scottish Gaelic Texts Society, No. 3. Edinburgh: Oliver and Boyd, 1939. Pp. xiii–xxviii.

675. Saintsbury, George. *History of English Prosody.* 3 vols. New York: Macmillan, 1906–10. IV, 44.

676. ———. *Peace of the Augustans; A Survey of Eighteenth Century Literature as a Place of Refreshment.* London: Bell, 1916; republished, Oxford: Oxford University Press, 1946.

677. Saunders, Thomas Bailey. *The Life and Letters of James Macpherson . . .* London: Swan, Sonnenschein; New York: Macmillan, 1894; rpt., New York: Greenwood Press, 1971.

678. Seamon, A. T. "James Macpherson and Standish O'Grady." Unpublished dissertation, National University of Ireland, University College, Dublin, 1979; *DAI* 43, no. 3 (Autumn 1982): #2974C.

679. Smart, John S. *James Macpherson, An Episode in Literature.* London: David Nutt, 1905.

680. Stern, Ludwig Christian. "Die Ossianischen Heldenlieder." *Zeitschrift für vergleichende Litteraturgeschichte,* N.F. 8 (1895): 51–86, 143–74. "Ossianic Heroic Poetry," translated by J. L. Robertson. *Transactions of the Gaelic Society of Inverness* 22 (1900): 257–325.

681. Stewart, Larry L. "Ossian in the Polished Age: The Critical Reception of James Macpherson's *Ossian.*" Unpublished dissertation, Case-Western Reserve University, 1972.

682. ———. "Ossian, Burke, and the 'Joy of Grief.' " *English Language Notes* 15 (1977): 29–32.

683. Thomson, Derick S. "Bogus Gaelic Literature, c. 1750–c. 1820." *Transactions of the Gaelic Society of Glasgow, 1956–1957* 5 (1958): 172–88.

684. ———. *The Gaelic Sources of Macpherson's Ossian.* Aberdeen: Aberdeen University Press, 1952.

685. ———. " 'Ossian' Macpherson and the Gaelic World of the Eighteenth Century." *Aberdeen University Review* 40 (1963): 7–20.

686. Thoreau, Henry David. "Homer, Ossian, Chaucer." *The Dial: A Magazine for Literature, Philosophy, and Religion* 4 (1844): 290–305.

687. Tombo, Rudolf. "Ossian in Germany. A Bibliography, General Survey." *Germanic Studies* 1, no. 2 (1901): 1–157. Republished as a monograph, *Ossian in Germany: Bibliography, General Survey, Ossian's Influence on Klopstock and the Bards*. New York, 1901.

688. Tyson, Gerald. " 'Feast of Shells:' The Context of James Macpherson's Ossianic Poetry." Unpublished Dissertation, Brandeis University, 1969.

689. VanTieghem, Paul. *Ossian en France . . .* Paris: F. Rieder, 1917.

690. ———. "Ossian et l'Ossianisme." In *Le préromenticisme, études d'histoire littérature européenne.* 2 vols. Paris: F. Rieder, 1924–30. I, 197–288.

691. ———. *Ossian et l'Ossianisme dans la litterature europeenne au XVIIIᵉ siècle.* Neophilologiese Bibliotheek, No. 4. Groningen, DenHaag: F. B. Wolters, 1920.

Flann O'Brien

A fuller checklist of O'Brien's writings has been compiled by Timothy O'Keeffe, #713, pp. 122–34. See also W. David Powell's checklist of O'Brien, #716, pp. 104–12.

692. Anon. "Eire's Columnist." *Time* 42 (August 23, 1943): 88–89.

693. Anon. "Obituary, Brian Nolan." *New York Times* (April 2, 1966): 2.

694. Anon. "A Whacking Read." *Newsweek* 67 (May 23, 1966): 121–22.

695. ApRoberts, Ruth. "*At Swim-Two-Birds* and the Novel as Self-Evident Sham." *Éire-Ireland* 6 (Summer 1971): 76–97.

696. Benstock, Bernard. "A Flann for All Seasons." *Irish Renaissance Annual* 3 (1983): 15–29.

697. ———. "Three Faces of Brian Nolan." *Éire-Ireland* 3 (Autumn 1968): 51–65.

698. Carens, James F. *Flann O'Brien.* Columbia Essays on Modern Writers. New York: Columbia University Press, 1975.

699. Clissmann, Anne T. *Parody and Fantasy in the English Novels of Flann O'Brien.* Dublin: Gill and Macmillan, 1975.

700. Clissmann, Anne T., and David Powell, eds. "A Flann O'Brien-Myles na Gopaleen Number." *The Journal of Irish Literature* 3, no. 1 (January 1974). Includes much previously unpublished material, plus a study by Miles Orvell, cited below, and a checklist of unpublished materials by David Powell.

701. Coulter, Philip R. "The Artist and the Critic: Flann O'Brien's Novels *At Swim-Two-Birds* and *The Third Policeman.*" Unpublished Master's Thesis, McGill University, 1971.

702. Dobbs, Margaret E. "A Poem Ascribed to Flann MacLonáin." *Ériu* 17 (1955): 16–34.

703. Dornier, Marie-Antoinette. "*At Swim-Two-Birds:* Flann O'Brien." Unpublished Master's Thesis, Université de Strasbourg, 1969.

704. Florey, Mary B. "Sleep, Democracy, Limbo, and the Plight of the Artist in *At Swim-Two-Birds.*" Unpublished Master's Essay, Syracuse University, 1970.

705. Hilton, Timothy. "Ireland's Great Cyclist." *New Statesman* 74 (December 8, 1967): 815–16.

706. Hughes, Catharine R. "Discovering Flann O'Brien." *America* 120 (May 3, 1969): 523–25.

707. Janik, Del Ivan. "Flann O'Brien: The Novelist as Critic." *Éire-Ireland* 4, no. 4 (1969): 64–72.

708. Kennedy, Sighle. " 'The Devil and Holy Water,' Samuel Beckett's *Murphy* and Flann O'Brien's *At Swim-Two-Birds.*" In *Modern Irish Literature: Essays in Honor of William York Tindall*. Library of Irish Studies, vol. 1. New Rochelle: Iona College Press, 1972. Pp. 251–60.

709. Klein, Ernst-Ulrich. *Die frühen Romane Flann O'Briens: "At Swim Two-Birds" und "The Third Policeman"; ein Beitrag zur Geschichte des englischen Romans*. Münster: Münster University Press, 1971.

710. Lee, L. L. "The Dublin Cowboys of Flann O'Brien." *Western American Literature* 4 (1969): 219–25.

711. Mellamphy, Ninian. "Aestho-Autogamy and the Anarchy of Imagination: Flann O'Brien's Theory of Fiction in *At Swim-Two-Birds.*" *Canadian Journal of Irish Studies* 4 (1978): 8–25.

712. O'Keeffe, James George, ed. *Buile Shuibhne Geilt. The Frenzy of Suibhne.* Irish Texts Society, vol. 12. London: David Nutt, 1913.

713. O'Keeffe, Timothy, comp. *Myles: Portraits of Brian O'Nolan (Flann O'-Brien/Myles na Gopaleen).* London: Martin Brian and O'Keeffe, 1973. Includes four biographical essays: Kevin O'Nolan, "The First Furlongs," 13–31; Niall Sheridan, "Brian, Flann, and Myles," 32–53; John Garvin, "Sweetscented Manuscripts," 54–61; Jack White, "Myles, Flann, and Brian," 62–76; a critical study by J. C. C. Mays, "Brian O'Nolan: Literalist of the Imagination," 77–119; a poetic tribute by John Montague, "Sweetness," 120–21; the bibliography compiled by Timothy O'Keeffe, 122–34; as well as a previously unpublished translation from the Irish by Brian O'Nolan, 9.

714. Orvell, Miles. "Entirely Fictitious: The Fiction of Flann O'Brien." *Journal of Irish Literature* 3, no. 1 (January 1974): 93–103.

715. Orvell, Miles and [William] David Powell. "Myles na Gopaleen: Mystic, Horse-Doctor, Hackney-Journalist and Ideological Catalyst." *Éire-Ireland* 10, no. 2 (Summer 1975): 44–72.

716. Powell, [William] David. "An Annotated Bibliography of Myles an Gopeleen's [Flann O'Brien's] 'Cruiskeen Lawn' Commentaries on James Joyce." *James Joyce Quarterly* 9 (1971): 50–62.

717. ———. "A Checklist of Brian O'Nolan." Journal of *Irish Literature* 3, no. 1 (January 1974): 104–12.

718. Powell, William David. "The English Writings of Flann O'Brien." Unpublished Dissertation, University of Southern Illinois, 1970.

719. Pritchett, Victor Sawdon. "Death of Finn." *New Statesman* 60 (August 20, 1960): 250–51.

720. Sheridan, Neill. "Brian, Flann, and Myles." *Irish Times* (April 2, 1966); rpt., *Myles: Portraits of Brian O'Nolan* . . . , compiled by Timothy O'Keeffe. London: Martin Brian and O'Keeffe, 1973. Pp. 32–53.

721. Thomas, Dylan. "Recent Fiction." *New English Weekly* 15, no. 5 (May 18, 1939): 78–80.

722. Tube, Henry. "It Goes Without Synge." *Spectator*, nvm (September 13, 1968): 360–61.

723. Wain, John. "To Write for My Own Race: The Fiction of Flann O'Brien." *Encounter* 29 (January 1967): 71–72, 74–85. Revised and expanded, *A House for the Truth*. London: Macmillan; New York: Viking, 1973, 67–104.

James Joyce

This highly selective checklist lists only some materials dealing with *Finnegans Wake*. Readers can find more on *Finnegans Wake* or any of Joyce's work in Robert H. Deming, *A Bibliography of James Joyce Studies*, 2nd ed. Boston: G. & K. Hall, 1977. In addition, there are the well-known updates in *PMLA*, *The James Joyce Quarterly*, etc.

724. Atherton, James S. *The Books at the Wake: A Study of Literary Allusions in James Joyce's Finnegans Wake*. London: Faber and Faber; New York: Viking, 1960.

725. ———. "The Identity of the Sleeper." *A Wake Newslitter* 4 (1967): 83–85.

726. Beechhold, Henry F. "Early Irish History and Mythology in *Finnegans Wake*." Unpublished Dissertation, Pennsylvania State University, 1956.

727. ———. "Finn MacCool in *Finnegans Wake*." *James Joyce Review* 2 (June 1958): 3–12.

728. ———. "Joyce's *Finnegans Wake*." *Explicator* 19 (January 1961): 27.

729. ———. "Joyce's Otherworld." *Éire-Ireland* 7, no. 1 (Spring 1972): 103–15.

730. Begnal, Michael H. "The Narrator of *Finnegans Wake*." *Éire-Ireland* 4, no. 3 (Autumn 1969): 38–49.

731. ———. "Who Speaks When I Dream? Who Dreams When I Speak?; A Narrational Approach to *Finnegans Wake*." In *Litters From Aloft: Papers Delivered at the Second Canadian James Joyce Seminar*, edited by Ronald Bates and Harry J. Pollock. University of Tulsa Monograph Series, No. 13, 1971. Pp. 74–90.

732. ———, with Grace Eckley. *Narrator and Character in Finnegans Wake*. Lewisburg: Bucknell University Press, 1975.

733. Benstock, Bernard. *Joyce-Again's Wake: An Analysis of Finnegans Wake*. Seattle: University of Washington Press, 1965.

734. Bierman, Robert. "Dreamer and the Dream of *Finnegans Wake*." *Renascence* 11 (1959): 197–200.

735. Boldereff, Frances Motz. *Reading Finnegans Wake*. Woodward, Pa.: Classic Non-Fiction Library, 1959.

736. Burgess, Anthony. *Joysprick: An Introduction to the Language of James Joyce*. London: Andre Deutsch; New York: Macmillan, 1973.

737. ———. "What It's All About." In *A Shorter Finnegans Wake*. London: Faber and Faber, 1966. Pp. 7–24.

738. Campbell, Joseph and Henry Morton Robinson. *A Skeleton Key to Finnegans Wake*. New York: Harcourt, 1944; rpt., Viking Compass Books, 1961.

739. Chase, Richard V. "Finnegans Wake: An Anthropological Study." *American Scholar* 13 (1944): 418–26.

740. Connolly, Thomas E., ed. *Scribbledehobble, The Ur-Workbook for Finnegans Wake*. Evanston: Northwestern University Press, 1961.

741. Deming, Robert H. *A Bibliography of James Joyce Studies*. Lawrence: University of Kansas Libraries, 1964.

742. Eckley, Grace. *Children's Lore in Finnegans Wake*. Syracuse: Syracuse University Press, 1985.

Eckley, Grace. *See also* Begnal, Michael H., #732.

743. Ellmann, Richard. *James Joyce*. New York: Oxford University Press, 1959.

744. Erdman, Jean. "Coach with Six Insides; Dramatization of *Finnegans Wake* by James Joyce." *Commonweal* 86 (June 23, 1967): 394.

745. Gheerbrant, Bernard. *James Joyce, sa vie, son oeuvre, son royonnement*. Paris: LaHune, 1949.

746. Gillet, Louis. *Claybook for James Joyce*, translated by Georges Markow-Totevy. London and New York: Abelard Schuman, 1958.

747. Glasheen, Adaline. *A Third Census of Finnegans Wake: An Index of the Characters and Their Roles*. Berkeley: University of California Press, 1977.

748. Hart, Clive. *A Concordance to Finnegans Wake*. Minneapolis: University of Minnesota Press, 1963.

749. ———. *Structure and Motif in Finnegans Wake*. Evanston: Northwestern University, 1962.

750. Hayman, David, ed. *A First-Draft Version of Finnegans Wake*. Austin: University of Texas Press, 1963.

751. ———. "From *Finnegans Wake*: A Sentence in Progress." *PMLA* 73 (March 1958): 136–54.

752. Joyce, James. *Letters*. Vol. I, edited by Stuard Gilbert, 1957. Vols. II and III, edited by Richard Ellmann, 1966. New York: Viking Press.

753. Joyce, Stanislaus. *My Brother's Keeper*, edited by Richard Ellmann. New York: Viking Press, 1958.

754. Kelleher, John V. "Identifying the Printed Sources for *Finnegans Wake*." *Irish University Review* 1, no. 2 (Spring 1971), 161–77.

755. Kopper, Edward A., Jr. "Saint Patrick and Finnegans Wake." *A Wake Newslitter* 4, no. 5 (October 1967): 85–93.

756. Magalaner, Marvin. "The Myth of Man: Joyce's *Finnegans Wake*." *University of Kansas City Review* 16 (1950): 265–77; rpt. in *Myth and*

Literature, edited by John B. Vickery. Lincoln: University of Nebraska Press, 1965. Pp. 201–12.

757. Marcus, Phillip L. *"Finnegans Wake:* The Fenian Materials in Perspective." Unpublished MS. Ithaca, New York, c. 1973.

758. McAleer, Edward C. "James Joyce and Dr. Kuno Meyer." *Notes and Queries* (February 1959): 49–50.

759. McHugh, Roland. *Annotations to Finnegans Wake.* Baltimore: Johns Hopkins, 1980.

760. ———. *The Finnegans Wake Experience.* Berkeley: University of California Press, 1981.

761. ———. *The Sigla of Finnegans Wake.* London: E. Arnold; Austin: University of Texas Press, 1976.

762. Mercier, Vivian. "James Joyce and an Irish Tradition." In *Society and Self in the Novel,* edited by Mark Schorer. New York: Columbia University Press, 1956. Pp. 78–116.

763. ———. "Parody: James Joyce and an Irish Tradition." *Studies* 45 (Summer 1956): 194–218.

764. Mink, Louis O. *A Finnegans Wake Gazetteer.* Bloomington: Indiana University Press, 1978.

765. O Hehir, Brendan. *A Gaelic Lexicon for Finnegans Wake, and Glossary for Joyce's Other Works.* Berkeley: University of California Press, 1967.

766. Ramnoux, "The Finn Cycle; The Atmosphere and Symbols of a Legend," translated by Maria Jolas. In *A James Joyce Yearbook.* Paris: Transition Workshop, 1949. Pp. 130–58. Original in French, *Psyché, Revue internationale de psychoanalyse et des Sciences de l'Homme* 8 (June 1947).

767. Rogers, Howard Emerson. "Irish Myth and the Plot of *Ulysses.*" *ELH* 15 (December 1948): 306–27.

768. Rose, Danis and John O'Hanlon, "Finn MacCool and the Final Weeks of Work in Progress." *A Wake Newslitter* 17, no. 5 (October 1980): 69–87.

769. Senn, Fritz and Michael Begnal, eds. *Conceptual Guide to Finnegans Wake.* University Park: Pennsylvania State University Press, 1974.

771. Senn, Fritz. "Ossianic Echoes." *A Wake Newslitter,* n.s. 3 (1966): 25–36.

772. ———. "Reverberations." *James Joyce Quarterly* 3 (1966): 222.

773. Sidnell, M. J. "A Daintical Pair of Accomplasses: Joyce and Yeats." In *Litters from Aloft: Papers Delivered at the Second Canadian James Joyce Seminar,* edited by Ronald Bates and Harry J. Pollock. University of Tulsa Monographs, No. 13, 1971. Pp. 50–73.

774. Spear, Rolfe. "The Argument of *Finnegans Wake.*" Unpublished Dissertation, Syracuse University, 1970.

775. Staples, Hugh B. "Some Notes on the One Hundred and Eleven Epithets of HCE." *A Wake Newslitter* 1 (December 1964): 3–6.

776. Stern, Frederick C. "Pyrrhus, Fenians, and Bloom." *James Joyce Quarterly* 5 (1968): 211–28.

777. Swinson, Ward. "Macpherson in *Finnegans Wake.*" *A Wake Newslitter* 9 (1972): 89–95.

778. Thornton, Weldon. *Allusions in Ulysses: An Annotated List.* Chapel Hill: University of North Carolina Press, 1961, 1968.

779. Tindall, William York. *A Reader's Guide to Finnegans Wake.* New York: Farrar, Straus, and Giroux, 1969.

780. Thuente, Mary Helen. "Irish Geography and History in *Finnegans Wake.*" Address given at the Modern Language Association meeting. New York, December 29, 1978.

781. Troy, William. "Notes on *Finnegans Wake.*" In William Troy. *Selected Essays*, edited by Stanley Edgar Hyman. New Brunswick: Rutgers University Press, 1967. Pp. 94–109.

782. Worthington, Mabel P. and Matthew J. C. Hodgart. *Songs in the Works of James Joyce.* New York: Columbia University Press, 1959.

783. Zimmer, Heinrich. "Keltische Beiträge." *Zeitschrift für Deutsches Alterthum und Deutsche Literatur* 35 (1891): 1–173.

William Butler Yeats

Although the works of Yeats discussed here are far from his most significant, they have invited much commentary. Readers seeking more information about them should consult K. P. S. Jochum, *W. B. Yeats: A Classified Bibliography* . . . Urbana: University of Illinois Press, 1978. Annual updates of Yeats scholarship may be found in *PMLA* and elsewhere.

784. Alspach, Russell K. "Some Sources of Yeats' 'Wanderings of Oisín.'" *PMLA* 58 (1943): 849–66.

785. Bjersby, Birgit. *The Interpretation of the Cuchulain Legend in the Works of W. B. Yeats.* Uppsala: University of Uppsala Press; Cambridge: Harvard University Press, 1950.

786. Clancy, C. J. "Yeats' Oisin." *Eire* 19 [Gainesville, Florida] 1 (August 1977): 17–24.

787. Cosman, Madeleine Pelner. "Mannered Passion: W. B. Yeats and the Ossianic Myths." *Western Humanities Review* 14 (1960): 163–77.

788. Diskin, Patrick. "Some Sources for Yeats' 'The Black Tower.'" *Notes and Queries* 7 (1961): 107–108.

789. Farrow, Anthony. "Introduction." In *Diarmuid and Grania*, by George Moore and William Butler Yeats. Irish Drama Series, vol. 10. Chicago: DePaul University, 1973. Pp. 1–15.

790. Hoare, Dorothy MacKenzie. *The Works of Morris and Yeats in Relation to Early Saga Literature.* Cambridge: Cambridge University Press, 1937.

791. Holloway, Joseph. *Joseph Holloway's Abbey Theatre: A Selection from His Unpublished Journal: Impressions of a Dublin Playgoer*, edited by Robert Hogan and Michael J. O'Neill. Cardondale: University of Southern Illinois Press, 1967.

792. Kelleher, John V. "Yeats' Use of Irish Materials." *Tri-Quarterly* 4 (1965): 115–25.

793. Masefield, John. "Finn and the Chessmen." In *Some Memories of W. B. Yeats.* New York: Macmillan, 1940.

794. Sidnell, M. J. "A Daintical Pair of Accomplasses: Joyce and Yeats." In *Litters From Aloft: Papers Delivered at the Second Canadian James Joyce Seminar*, edited by Ronald Bates and Harry J. Pollock. University of Tulsa Monographs, No. 13, 1971. Pp. 50–73.

795. Telfer, Giles W. L. "Yeats' Ideas of the Gael." In *The Dolmen Press Yeats Centenary Papers, 1965*, edited by Liam Miller. Dublin: Dolmen Press; Chester Springs: DuFour Editions, 1969. Pp. 85–108.

796. Thuente, Mary Helen. *W. B. Yeats and Irish Folklore*. New York: Barnes and Noble, 1981.

797. Yeats, Michael. "W. B. Yeats and Irish Folksong." *Southern Folklore Quarterly* 30 (1966): 153–78.

Austin Clarke

Although Clarke's "Vengeance of Fionn," #15, receives only brief discussion here, it has been one of the author's most widely read words. To see this poem in relation with the author's other works, see the bibliographies of M. J. MacManus, #804, Liam Miller, #806, Gerard Lyne, #801, pp. 137–55; and Thomas Dillon Redshaw, #807.

798. Campbell, Joseph. "The New Epic." *New Ireland* 5, no. 17 (March 2, 1918): 273–75.

799. Garratt, Robert F. "The Poetry of Austin Clarke." Unpublished Dissertation, University of Oregon, 1973.

800. Gibbons, Patrick J. "The Vengeance of Fionn: an appreciation." *Irish Monthly* 46, no. 546 (December 1918): 706–10.

801. Harmon, Maurice, ed. "Austin Clarke Special Issue." *Irish University Review* 4, no. 1 (Spring 1974). Of the eleven articles in the issue, these were of immediate relevance to our study: Brendan Kennelly, "Austin Clarke and the Epic Poem," 26–41; Robert Welsh, "Austin Clarke and Gaelic Poetic Tradition," 41–50; and Gerard Lyne, "Austin Clarke: A Bibliography," 137–55.

802. Lane, Temple. "Austin Clarke." *Books Abroad* 36 (1962): 270–72.

803. McGrory, Kathleen. "Medieval Aspects of Modern Irish Writing: Austin Clarke." In *Modern Irish Literature: Essays in Honor of William York Tindall*, edited by R. J. Porter and J. D. Brophy. Library of Irish Studies, vol. 1. New Rochelle: Iona College Press, 1972. Pp. 289–99.

804. MacManus, M. J. "Bibliographies of Irish Writers: No. 8. Austin Clarke." *Dublin Magazine* 10, no. 2 (April–June 1935): 41–43.

805. Martin, Augustine. "The Rediscovery of Austin Clarke." *Studies* 54 (1965): 408–34.

806. Miller, Liam. "The Books of Austin Clarke; a Checklist." In *A Tribute to Austin Clarke on His Seventieth Birthday . . .* , edited by Liam Miller and John Montague. Dublin: Dolmen Press, 1966. Pp. 23–27.

807. Redshaw, Thomas Dillon. "Appréciation. His Work, A Memorial: Austin Clarke (1896–1974)." *Éire-Ireland* 9, no. 2 (Summer 1974): 107–11; bibliography, 111–15.

808. Rosenthal, M. L. "Contemporary Irish Poetry . . . Austin Clarke . . ." In *The New Poets; American and British Poetry Since World War II.* London: Oxford University Press, 1967. Pp. 263–74.

809. Saul, George Brandon. "The Poetry of Austin Clarke." In *The Celtic Cross: Studies in Irish Culture and Literature,* edited by Ray. B. Browne, W. J. Roscelli, and Richard Loftus. Lafayette: Purdue University Press, 1964. Pp. 26–36.

810. Schirmer, Gregory. " 'A Mad Discordancy': Austin Clarke's Early Narrative Poems." *Éire-Ireland* 16, no. 2 (Summer 1981): 16–28.

Backgrounds in Mythology and Folklore

811. Aarne, Anttii Amatus. *The Types of the Folktale, A Classification and Bibliography,* translated by Stith Thompson. Helsinki: Suomalainen Tiedeakatemia, 1928.

812. Bernard, Mary. *The Mythmakers.* Athens: Ohio University Press, 1967.

813. Boatwright, Mody C. "On the Nature of Myth." *Southwest Review* 39 (1954): 131–36.

814. Briggs, Katharine. *An Encyclopedia of Fairies.* New York: Pantheon, 1976.

815. Brown, Norman O. *Hermes the Thief: The Evolution of a Myth.* Madison: University of Wisconsin Press, 1947.

816. Burke, Kenneth. "Myth, Poetry, and Philosophy." *Journal of American Folklore* 73 (1960): 283–306.

817. Campbell, Joseph. *The Hero with a Thousand Faces.* New York: Pantheon Books, 1949; rpt., Cleveland: Meridien Books, 1956.

818. Cohen, Percy. "Theories of Myth." *Man,* n.s. 4 (1969): 337–53.

819. Cook, Albert. *Myth and Language.* Bloomington: Indiana University Press, 1980.

820. Dorson, Richard M. "Theories of Myth and the Folklorist." *Daedalus* 88 (1959): 232–54.

821. Douglas, Mary. *Natural Symbols: Explorations in Cosmology.* New York: Pantheon Books, 1970.

822. Dumézil, Georges. *The Destiny of the King.* Chicago: University of Chicago Press, 1973.

823. ———. *The Destiny of the Warrior.* Chicago: University of Chicago Press, 1970.

824. ———. *Légendes sur les Nartes, suives de cinq notes mythologiques.* Bibliotheques de l'Institut Francais de Leningrad, vol. II. Paris: Institut d'Etudes Slaves, 1930.

825. ———. *The Stakes of the Warrior.* Berkeley: University of California Press, 1983. *See also* #497.

826. Eliade, Mircea. *Myth and Realty,* translated by Willard Trask. New York: Harper and Row, 1963.

827. Else, Gerald F. *Origins and Early Form of Greek Tragedy.* Martin Classical Lectures, vol. 20. Cambridge: Harvard University Press, 1967.

828. Fordham, Frieda. *An Introduction to Jung's Psychology*, 3rd ed. Harmondsworth: Pelican, 1966.
829. Frazer, James G. *The Golden Bough, A Study in Magic and Religion*, 3rd ed. 13 vols. New York: Macmillan, 1955.
830. Fromm, Erich. *The Forgotten Language: An Introduction to the Understanding of Dreams, Fairy Tales, and Myths*. New York: Rinehart, 1951.
831. Frye, Northrop. *Fables of Identity*. New York: Harcourt Harbinger Books, 1963.
832. Galinsky, G. Karl. *The Herakles Theme: The Adaptations of the Hero in Literature from Homer to the Twentieth Century*. Oxford: Oxford University Press, 1972.
833. Girard, René. *To Double Business Bound: Essays on Literature, Mimesis, and Anthropology*. Baltimore: Johns Hopkins University Press, 1978.
834. Graves, Robert. *The Greek Myths*, 2 vols. Baltimore: Penguin Books, 1955.
835. ———. *The White Goddess: An Historical Grammar of Poetic Myth*, rev. ed. New York: Farrar, Straus and Giroux, 1966.
836. Grotjahn, Martin. *Beyond Laughter: A Psychoanalytic Approach to Humor.* New York: McGraw-Hill, 1957.
837. von Hahn, J. G. *Sagawissenschaftliche Studien*. Jena, 1876.
838. Hardin, Richard F. " 'Ritual' in Recent Criticism: The Elusive Sense of Community." *PMLA* 98, no. 5 (October 1983): 846–62.
839. Hocart, Arthur Maurice. *Kingship*. London: Oxford University Press, 1927.
840. Jacobs, Melville, ed. *The Anthropologist Looks at Myth*. Austin: University of Texas Press, 1966.
841. Jung, C. G. *Essays on a Science of Mythology*. New York: Harper and Row, 1963.
842. ———, ed. *Man and His Symbols*. New York: Dell Laurel Edition, 1964.
843. Jung, C. G. *Psyche and Symbol*, edited by V. S. de Laszlo. New York: Doubleday Anchor Books, 1958.
844. Kirk, G. S. *Myth: Its Meaning and Functions in Ancient and Other Cultures*. Berkeley: University of California Press, 1970.
845. Kolker, Robert P. "Toward a Definition of Myth in Literature." *Thoth* 5 (1964): 3–21.
846. Kluckhohn, Clyde. "Myth and Ritual: A General Theory." *Harvard Theological Review* 35 (1942): 45–79.
847. Leach, Edmund, ed. *The Structural Study of Myth and Totemism*. London: Tavistock Publications, 1967.
848. LeComte, Edward S. *Endymion in England: The Literary History of a Greek Myth*. New York: King's Crown Press, 1944.
849. Lévi-Strauss, Claude. *Myth and Meaning*. New York: Schocken Books, 1978.
850. ———. *The Raw and the Cooked*. New York: Harper and Row, 1969.

851. Littleton, C. Scott. *The New Comparative Mythology: An Anthropological Assessment of the Theories of Georges Dumezil*, rev. ed. Berkeley: University of California Press, 1973.

852. McCune, Marjorie, ed. *The Binding of Proteus: Perspectives on Myth and the Literary Process*. Lewisburg: Bucknell University Press, 1980.

853. Middleton, John, ed. *Myth and Cosmos: Readings in Mythology and Symbolism*. New York: Natural History Press, 1967.

854. Nutt, Alfred. "Aryan Expulsion and Return formula Among the Celts." *Folk-lore Record* 4 (1881): 1–44.

855. Panofsky, Dora and Erwin. *Pandora's Box: the Changing Aspects of a Mythical Symbol*, 2nd ed. New York: Pantheon Books for the Bollingen Foundation, 1963.

856. Patai, Raphael. *Myth and Modern Man*. Englewood Cliffs: Prentice Hall, 1972.

857. Propp, Vladimir. *Morphology of the Folktale*, 2nd ed. Austin: University of Texas Press, 1968.

858. Radin, Paul. *The Trickster: A Study in American Indian Mythology*. London: Routledge and Kegan Paul, 1955.

859. Raglan, Fitzroy Richard Somerset (Lord). *The Hero: A Study in Tradition, Myth, and Drama*. London: Methuen, 1936; rpt., New York: Vintage Books, 1956.

860. Raine, Kathleen. *On the Mythological*, with a Selected Bibliography of Myth in Literature by James A. S. McPeek. A CEA Chapbook, published as a supplement to the *CEA Critic*. 32, no. 1 (October 1969).

861. Rank, Otto. *Myth of the Birth of the Hero*, translated by Robbins and Jelliffe. New York: R. Brunner, 1952.

862. Ruthven, K. K. *Myth*. The Critical Idiom, no. 31. London: Methuen, 1976.

863. Sebeok, Thomas, ed. *Myth: A Symposium*. Bloomington: Indiana University Press, 1965.

864. Thompson, Stith. *The Folktale*. New York: Henry Holt; rpt., Berkeley: University of California Press, 1977.

865. Trousson, Raymond. *Le Thème de Prométhée dans la Littérature Européene*, 2 vols. Geneva, 1964.

866. Turner, Victor. *Drama, Fields, and Metaphors: Symbolic Action in Human Society*. Ithaca: Cornell University Press, 1974.

867. Turville-Petre, E. O. G. *Myth and Religion of the North: The Religions of Ancient Scandinavia*. London: Weidenfield and Nicholson; New York: Holt, Rinehart, and Winston, 1964.

868. Vickery, John B., ed. *Myth and Literature: Contemporary Theory and Practice*. Lincoln: University of Nebraska Press, 1966.

869. Weisinger, Herbert. *The Agony and the Triumph: Papers on the Use and Abuse of Myth*. East Lansing: Michigan State University Press, 1964.

870. Wikander, Stig. *Der Arische Männerbund: Studien zur Indo-Iranischen Sprachand Religiongeschichte*. Lund: Ohlsson, 1938.

Index

Hamlet, 178; *see also* Shakespeare, William
Hanmer, Meredith, *Chronicle of Ireland*, 32, 75, 77, 112
Hard Gilly. *See Tóraidheacht an Ghiolla Dheacair*
Hard Life, The. See O'Brien, Flann
Harrison, Jane Ellen, 41
Hayman, David, 165, 174
Head of Howth. *See* Howth
Hebrides, 73, 74, 97, 130, 143, 145
"Hebrides Overture." *See* Mendelssohn, Felix
Hecate, 123
Hedda Gabler, 157
Henderson, George, 44, 51, 52
Hennessy, W. M., 40
Henry, Françoise, 15, 19
Hephaestus, 146
Heracles, 7, 8, 9, 14, 47, 48, 55, 56, 58, 67, 124
Herder, Johann Gottfried, 4
Heroes of the Dawn. See Russell, Violet
Hesiod, 4, 37
Hetman, Michael. *See* Cabell, James Branch
Heyne, Gottlob, 4
Higginson, Thomas Wentworth, 115, 200
High cross. *See* Celtic Cross
High king. *See* Ardríg
Hill of Allen. *See* Allen, Hill of
Hinkson, Katharine Tynan, 148, 200
Hiroshima, 159
Hogan, Frank, 118
Holinshed's Chronicles, 73, 76–77, 79, 170
Holland, Philemon, 77
Holloway, Joseph, 156
Holy Roman Empire, 24
Home, John, 81, 88, 94
Homer, 1, 81, 82, 94
Hopper (Chesson), Nora, 148–49, 200
"Hostel of the Quicken Trees." *See Bruidhean Chaorthainn*
Howth, 76, 123, 172, 173, 175; *see also Book of Howth*
Howth Castle, 177
Huckleberry Finn. *See* Finn, Huckleberry, 173
Hudson, Wilson M., 195

Hughes, Harold F., 18, 114
Hull, Eleanor, 42, 51
Hull, Vernam, 49–50
Hume, David, 81
Hurley, 20
Hyde, Douglas, 17, 19, 111, 138, 167
Hyginus, 37

Ibsen, Henrik, 178
Iceland, 65
Iliad, 124
Illan, 30
Imbas forosnai, 7, 50
Imram Brain, The Voyage of Bran, 8, 209
"In Praise of May," 21
Indians. *See* North American Indians
Indo-European tradition, 182
Inverness-shire, Scotland, 72
Irish Fairy Tales. See Stephens, James
Irish language, xiv, 154, 166–67, 169, 181–91
Irish potato famine. *See* Famine
Irish Renaissance, 105–17, 138
Irish Republican Brotherhood, 11; *see also* Fenians (political history)
Irish Times, The, 134
Ironbones, 27
Iseult. *See* Tristan and Iseult
Ishtar, 146
Italy, 22, 105, 164
Ivernians, 42

Jacobites, xii, 72
Jacobsthal, Paul, 164
Jason, 56
Jeffers, Robinson, 34
Jefferson, Thomas, 81, 95, 238
Jesuits, 179
Jesus. *See* Christ
Johnson, Samuel, 1, 71, 74, 79, 85
Joyce, James, xii, 9, 24, 77, 125, 127, 135, 136, 151, 163, 242–45; attitudes toward Ireland, 166–70; "Dead, The," 166 (*see also* Conroy, Gabriel); *Dubliners*, 170; *Exiles*, 169; *Finnegans*

Longes mac nUisnig. See Deirdre
Lönnrott, Elias, 88
Loomis, Roger Sherman, 61
Los Lurgann (Speedy Foot), 57
Lothar, 123
Lough Lurgan, 57
Lough Neagh, 59, 178
Love spot. *See Ball seirce*
Lover, Samuel, 124, 132
Luachar. *See* Grey of Luachair
Luchta, 123
Lugh Lámhfada, 6, 38, 41, 46, 122, 124, 165, 178, 186, 191
Lydney Park, 7, 50
Lyndsay, David, 72–73
Lyons, France, 46

Mabinogion, 61
Mabou, Nova Scotia, xii
mac-. Patronymics beginning with the lowercase mac- are not surnames and are not alphabetized here; thus Fionn mac Cumhaill, not "Mr. mac Cumhaill"
MacBain, Alexander, 8, 39
Macbeth. See Shakespeare
MacCall, Patrick Joseph, 132
McCallum, Hugh and John, 23, 96–97
McCarthy family, 185
McCarthy, Sean, 118
MacColl, Evan, 107
MacCulloch, J. A., 51
MacCunn, Hamish, 149
MacCurtain, Hugh, 79
MacDonald, T. D., 69
McGee, Thomas D'Arcy, 106–107
Macgeoghan, Conall, 78
Macgníamhartha Finn (Boyhood Deeds of Finn), 21, 47, 61, 62–63, 108, 209–210
MacGregor, James and Duncan, 85
MacGregor, Patrick, 97
McHugh, Roland, 176
McHugh, Sheila, 62–63, 195
MacKenzie, Donald A., *Finn and His Warrior Band,* 18, 113, 196
MacKenzie, Henry, 86, 102
Maclagan, James, 87

MacLochlainn, Alf, 196
MacManus, Anna, 149, 201
MacManus, Seumas, 5
MacNeill, Eoin, 42–43, 55
MacNeill, Máire [Sweeney], 46
MacNeill, Nigel, 96
MacNicoll, Donald, 85
Macpherson, James, xiii, xiv, 1–3, 12, 24, 38, 70, 78, 79–94, 101, 112, 114, 115, 149, 162, 183, 184, 186, 237–40; "Cath-loda," 92; "Comala," 90; *Dana Oisean Mhic Fhinn,* 86; "Dar-thula", 83, 96; "Fingal: An Epic," 82, 86–87 (quoted); *Fragments of Ancient Poetry Collected in the Highlands of Scotland* (1760), 70, 79, 80, 81, 85, 88; *Poems of Ossian* (1763), xiii, xiv, 23, 24, 34, 70, 71, 74, 79–94, 95, 101, 102, 113, 119, 179–80, 183, 195; "Temora: An Epic," 82, 84, 85, 90, 91, 92
MacRitchie, David, 44
Mad Sweeney, 136, 139, 140, 141
Maeve. *See* Medb
Magh Life, 170
"Maistre Pierre Pathelin," 131
Malinowski, Bronislaw, 40, 41
Mamalujo (conception in Joyce's *Finnegans Wake*), 135, 174
Man, Isle of, 12, 59, 217; *see also* Manx language
Manannán mac Lir, 27
Mangan, James Clarence, 27, 103, 106
Manx language, xii; *see also* Man, Isle of
Marcus, Phillip, 110, 149
Marivaux, Pierre, de, 147
Mark, King, 59, 62–63, 165, 179, 184, 190
Markievicz, Countess [Constance Gore-Booth], 114
Marr, Tracy, 224
Marryat, Frederick, 130–31
Mars, 46, 146, 162; *see also* Ares
Martin, Martin, 85
Masefield, John, 3, 147, 149–50 (quoted)
Mayo, Co., Ireland, 58
Meath, Co., Ireland, 17
Medb (Maeve), 14, 133
Mèhul, Etienne, 184

Pound, Ezra, 151
Powel, Thomas, 60
Pritchett, V. S., 142
Prometheus, 9, 66
Prospero, 175–76
Protestantism, 128, 129, 138
Proust, Marcel, 137
Pryderi, 61
Psalter of Cashel, 21
Ptolemy, 123, 186
Pugin, Augustus, 105
Purcell, Patrick, 140
"Pursuit of Diarmaid and Gráinne." *See*
    Tóruigheacht Dhiarmada agus Ghráinne
"Pursuit of the Hard/Difficult Gilly/Ser-
    vant." *See Tóraidheacht an Ghiolla
    Dheacair*
Pwyll, Prince of Dyfed, 61, 62
Pyle, Howard, 114
Pyramus and Thisbe, 39

Q-Celts, 42, 43
"Quarrel Between Finn and Oisín," 126
Quicken trees, 144; *see also Bruidhean
    Chaorthainn*
Quiggin, E. C., 59

"Rageous Ossean." *See* Krause, David
Raglan, Fitzhugh, Lord, 55–57, 58, 67
Ranafest, Co., Donegal, 195
Rank, Otto, von, 55, 57
Red Branch Cycle. *See* Ulster Cycle
Rees, Alwyn and Brinley, 48
Reginsmál, 65
Reinhard, John, 49
Reliques of Irish Poetry. See Brooke, Char-
    lotte
*Report of the Highland Society of Scotland.
    See* MacKenzie, Henry
Revue Celtique, 17, 110, 111
Rhiannon, 61
Rhys, John, 40, 109, 115, 145, 158
Richard III. See Shakespeare, William
Rígfhénnid, 13, 57, 58, 108
Rinaldo, 89

Ringsend, Co., Dublin, 136
Ritual killing, 145
Robbe-Grillet, Alain, 134
Robertson, William, 51, 72
Robin Hood, 45, 56, 87, 114
Robinson, Henry Morton. *See* Campbell,
    Joseph, *Skeleton Key to Finnegans Wake*
Robinson, Lennox, 155, 156
Robinson, Philippa, 67, 195
Rock of Cashel, 173
Rock opera, 118
Roland, 45
Rolleston, T. W., 18, 113
Roman tradition, 146
Romulus, 56
Ros-Crana (also Roscrana), 90, 98–99
Rose, Danis, 168–69, 175, 179
Rosg catha, 53
Ross, Anne, 25
Ross and Cromarty, Co., Scotland, 72
Rowan trees. *See* Quicken trees
Ruaidhrí Ó Conchubhair, 10
Russell, George ("AE"), 18, 113
Russell, Violet, 18, 113
Ruthven, 81

Sabatini, Rafael, 107
Sadb, 58
Saddlemyer, Ann, 196
Salmon, 20, 60, 112, 180, 182, 186
Samhain, 13, 49
Satan, 52
Saunders, T. Bailey, 88
Scandinavia, 23, 24, 45, 65, 91, 130,
    164, 177, 178; *see also* Danes; Loch-
    lann; Norway
Sceolang, 49
Schoepperle, Gertrude, 63
Schubert, Franz, 82, 184
Schultz, Geheimrath Albert, 65, 234
Schweik, Good Soldier (character cre-
    ated by Jaroslav Hašek; also spelled
    Svejk), 132
Scotland, 12, 18, 31, 58, 71–75, 77, 143
Scott, Robert Douglas, 14

Scott, Walter, Sir, 19, 75, 81, 103; *The Antiquary*, 23, 75; *Waverley*, 23, 75, 81
Scottish Gaelic, xii, xiv, 65, 71
"Scribbeldehobble Notebook." *See* Joyce, James
Sean Dana. See Smith, John
Selene, 123
Selma, 84, 92
Sentimental Journey, 91
Setanta, 47
Shakespeare, William, 73, 178; *Hamlet*, 178; *King Lear*, 178; *Macbeth*, 30, 73; *Richard III*, 178; *Tempest, The*, 175–76; *see also* Claudius, King; Falstaff; Prospero
Shamanism, 50
Shanachie, 17, 124
Shannon River, 25, 136, 170
Shenstone, William, 81
Sheridan, Niall, 135, 138
Sidhe, 52, 109
Sidnell, M. J., 191–92
Siegfried, 39, 56, 105
Sigla of "Finnegans Wake," The. See McHugh, Roland
Sigurd, 14, 48, 56, 65, 165
Simpson, John Hawkins, *Poems of Oisín, Bard of Erin*, 103
Sinn Féin, 114
Sinsar of the Battles, 25
Sir Perceyvelle, 62–63
Sir Tristrem. See Thomas the Rhymer
Six Characters in Search of an Author. See Pirandello, Luigi
Sjoestedt, Marie–Louise, 5, 13, 27
Slavic languages, 164
Sleeping Warriors motif, 7, 32, 172, 184
Slieve Guillean, 58
Slievenamon, 23, 49
Sligo, Co., Ireland, 26, 144
Slover, C. H. *See* Cross, T. P.
Smart, John S., 88
Smith, John, Dr., 96
Smollett, Tobias, 85
Snámh Dá Én, 136, 140
Snorri, Sturluson, 88
Snyder, E. D., 94–95
Sohrab and Rustum, 83, 128

Solomon, 89
Sophocles, 37
Spaan, David, 32
Spain, 77
Spear, Rolfe, 193
Staffa Island, 97
Stanford, William B., 146
Stanihurst, Richard, 76
Starno, 90–91
Stead, William T., 176
Stephens, James (author): *Irish Fairy Tales*, 21, 113–14, 115, 202
Stephens, James (political leader), 106
Stern, Ludwig, 86
Stokes, Whitley, 112
Stone, Jerome, 81, 85, 95
Strathmashie, Laird of, 85
Strindberg, August, 16
Sutcliff, Rosemary, 18, 114, 117
Swaran, 90
Sweeney, Mad, 136, 139, 140, 141
Sweeney, Máire MacNeill. *See* MacNeill, Máire
Swift, Jonathan, xv, 105
Switzerland, 46, 182
Sydow, C. W., von, 26
Synge, John Millington, xv, 112, 142, 167

Táin Bó Cuailnge (The Cattle Raid of Cooley), xii, 11, 14, 16, 124, 139
Taliesin, 14, 48, 60
Tammuz, 146
Tangle-Coated Horse, The. See Young, Ella
Tara, 13, 29, 30, 41, 58, 76, 77, 84, 100, 101, 143, 149, 150, 173, 179, 184
Tarachow, Stanley, 127
Tasha of the White Arms, 58
Teinm laída, 7, 50
Television, xi, 124, 125
Temhair. *See* Tara
Temora. *See* Macpherson, James
Tempest, The. See Shakespeare, William
Tennyson, Alfred, Lord, 94, 138
Theatre de Lys, 118
Theseus, 4, 8, 56, 58, 67, 165
Thessaly, 27

FIONN MAC CUMHAILL

was composed in 10-point Malibu Autologic Trump Mediaeval by Williams Press, Inc.;
with display type in VGC Phototypositor Deepdene by Eastern Graphics;
printed sheet-fed offset on 50-pound, acid-free Glatfelter B-31 Natural,
Smyth sewn and bound over 88-point binder's boards in Holliston Roxite C,
also adhesive bound with paper covers by Braun-Brumfield, Inc.;
with dust jackets and paper covers printed in 2 colors by Vicks Lithograph & Printing Corporation;
and published by
SYRACUSE UNIVERSITY PRESS
SYRACUSE, NEW YORK 13210